Lecture Notes in Computer Science 12438

More information about this series at http://www.springer.com/series/7407

Bogdan Filipič · Edmondo Minisci ·
Massimiliano Vasile (Eds.)

Bioinspired Optimization Methods and Their Applications

9th International Conference, BIOMA 2020
Brussels, Belgium, November 19–20, 2020
Proceedings

 Springer

Editors
Bogdan Filipič 🆔
Jožef Stefan Institute
Ljubljana, Slovenia

Edmondo Minisci 🆔
University of Strathclyde
Glasgow, UK

Massimiliano Vasile 🆔
University of Strathclyde
Glasgow, UK

ISSN 0302-9743   ISSN 1611-3349   (electronic)
Lecture Notes in Computer Science
ISBN 978-3-030-63709-5   ISBN 978-3-030-63710-1   (eBook)
https://doi.org/10.1007/978-3-030-63710-1

LNCS Sublibrary: SL1 – Theoretical Computer Science and General Issues

This Springer imprint is published by the registered company Springer Nature Switzerland AG
The registered company address is: Gewerbestrasse 11, 6330 Cham, Switzerland

Preface

Welcome to the proceedings of the 9th International Conference on Bioinspired Optimization Methods and Their Applications (BIOMA 2020), held during November 19–20, 2020, Brussels, Belgium.

BIOMA was launched in 2004 as an international scientific forum for presenting new ideas in bioinspired optimization and reporting on the applications of this methodology. It is held biennially and known among the attendees for its collaborative atmosphere and networking opportunities. However, organizing the conference this year, we were faced with an unforeseen challenge, the COVID-19 pandemic. After considering the options of either postponing the meeting or adapting to the new reality, we decided for the latter and held the conference virtually, with online presentations. While from the scientific quality point of view it was carried out in its best tradition, the social dimension was certainly different as we had to rely on the distance conferencing technology. Nevertheless, it was a learning experience that both the organizers and attendees can build upon under the new circumstances.

The conference was held jointly with the international conference on Uncertainty Quantification and Optimization (UQOP), organized by the H2020 UTOPIAE network. While the two forums share optimization as a common topic, BIOMA specializes in bioinspired algorithms as a means for solving the optimization problems. As such, it benefited from the paper submissions contributed by the UTOPIAE members studying and applying these algorithms. The event received 68 submissions. These were evaluated by the members of the Program Committee in a single-blind peer-review procedure where each paper was evaluated by three reviewers. Based on the evaluation scores, 24 papers, contributed by 73 authors from 14 countries, were accepted for presentation at the conference and publication in the LNCS proceedings. They come in two categories: theoretical studies and methodology advancements on the one hand, and algorithm adjustments and their applications on the other.

The conference mission of building on the synergy between theoretical research and practical aspects of bioinspired optimization was also reflected in the two invited keynotes that complemented the program of regular paper presentations. Gabriela Ochoa from the University of Stirling, UK, talked about recent advances in local optima and search trajectory networks, and Enrique Alba from the University of Málaga, Spain, on bioinspired algorithms for smart cities. We are grateful to them for accepting our invitation to present some of the the most recent achievements in the field to our forum.

We want to thank all of you who made BIOMA 2020 possible: the authors for submitting the papers, the members of the Program Committee and additional reviewers for reviewing, the Organizing Committee members for preparing and running the conference under demanding conditions, as well as the invited speakers, paper presenters, and other attendees for making the virtual event lively and interactive. We are glad to see the community is adapting to new circumstances and staying connected.

October 2020

Bogdan Filipič
Edmondo Minisci
Massimiliano Vasile

Organization

General Chair

Massimiliano Vasile   University of Strathclyde, UK

Program Chairs

Bogdan Filipič   Jožef Stefan Institute, Slovenia
Edmondo Minisci   University of Strathclyde, UK

Organizing Committee

Margarita Antoniou   Jožef Stefan Institute, Slovenia
Gianluca Filippi   University of Strathclyde, UK
Cristian Greco   University of Strathclyde, UK
Christie Maddock   University of Strathclyde, UK
Thierry Magin   Von Karman Institute, Belgium
Gregor Papa   Jožef Stefan Institute, Slovenia
Alessandro Parente   Université Libre de Bruxelles, Belgium

Keynote Speakers

Enrique Alba   University of Málaga, Spain
Gabriela Ochoa   University of Stirling, UK

Program Committee

Mehmet Emin Aydin   University of the West of England, UK
Thomas Bartz-Beielstein   TH Köln, Germany
Maria J. Blesa   Universitat Politècnica de Catalunya, Spain
Christian Blum   Spanish National Research Council, Spain
Francisco Chicano   University of Málaga, Spain
Carlos Coello Coello   CINVESTAV-IPN, Mexico
Carlos Cotta   University of Málaga, Spain
Fabio D'Andreagiovanni   Sorbonne University, France
Bilel Derbel   University of Lille, France
Marco Dorigo   Université Libre de Bruxelles, Belgium
Erik Dovgan   Jožef Stefan Institute, Slovenia
Rolf Drechsler   University of Bremen, Germany
Tome Eftimov   Jožef Stefan Institute, Slovenia
Michael Emmerich   Leiden University, The Netherlands
Bogdan Filipič   Jožef Stefan Institute, Slovenia

Jan Gmys	University of Mons, Belgium
Wolfgang Konen	TH Köln, Germany
Peter Korošec	Jožef Stefan Institute, Slovenia
Barbara Koroušić Seljak	Jožef Stefan Institute, Slovenia
Arnaud Liefooghe	University of Lille, France
Shih-Hsi Liu	California State University, Fresno, USA
Katherine Malan	University of South Africa, South Africa
Nouredine Melab	University of Lille, France
Juan J. Merelo	University of Granada, Spain
Marjan Mernik	University of Maribor, Slovenia
Edmondo Minisci	University of Strathclyde, UK
Nalina Niranjan	Nitte Meenakshi Institute of Technology, India
Boris Naujoks	TH Köln, Germany
Nadia Nedjah	State University of Rio de Janeiro, Brazil
Gabriela Ochoa	University of Stirling, UK
Akira Oyama	Japan Aerospace Exploration Agency, Japan
Gregor Papa	Jožef Stefan Institute, Slovenia
Mario Pavone	University of Catania, Italy
Tapabrata Ray	University of New South Wales, Australian Defence Force Academy, Australia
Annalisa Riccardi	University of Strathclyde, UK
Frédéric Saubion	University of Angers, France
Patrick Siarry	Université Paris-Est, France
Jörg Stork	TH Köln, Germany
Thomas Stützle	Université Libre de Bruxelles, Belgium
El-Ghazali Talbi	University of Lille, France
Jim Tørresen	University of Oslo, Norway
Tea Tušar	Jožef Stefan Institute, Slovenia
Daniel Tuyttens	University of Mons, Belgium
Massimiliano Vasile	University of Strathclyde, UK
Sébastien Verel	Université du Littoral Côte d'Opale, France
Vida Vukašinović	Jožef Stefan Institute, Slovenia
Takeshi Yamada	NTT Communication Science Laboratories, Japan
Xin-She Yang	Middlesex University, UK
Martin Zaefferer	TH Köln, Germany
Aleš Zamuda	University of Maribor, Slovenia
Jernej Zupančič	Jožef Stefan Institute, Slovenia

Additional Reviewers

Lorenzo Angelo Ricciardi
Callum Wilson
Francesco Marchetti

Contents

Theory and Methods

Synthetic vs. Real-World Continuous Landscapes: A Local Optima Networks View

Marco A. Contreras-Cruz[1] [iD], Gabriela Ochoa[2]([✉]) [iD],
and Juan P. Ramirez-Paredes[1] [iD]

[1] Electronics Engineering Department, University of Guanajuato, Salamanca, Mexico
{ma.contrerascruz,jpi.ramirez}@ugto.mx
[2] Computing Science and Mathematics, University of Stirling, Stirling, UK
gabriela.ochoa@stir.ac.uk

Abstract. Local optima networks (LONs) are a useful tool to analyse and visualise the global structure of fitness landscapes. The main goal of our study is to use LONs to contrast the global structure of synthetic benchmark functions against those of real-world continuous optimisation problems of similar dimensions. We selected two real-world problems, namely, an engineering design problem and a machine learning problem. Our results indicate striking differences in the global structure of synthetic vs real-world problems. The real-world problems studied were easier to solve than the synthetic ones, and our analysis reveals why; they have easier to traverse global structures with fewer nodes and edges, no sub-optimal funnels, higher neutrality and multiple global optima with shorter trajectories towards them.

Keywords: Local optima networks · Funnel structures · Fitness landscapes · Real-world optimisation problems

1 Introduction

The structure of fitness landscapes is known to relate to the performance of optimisation algorithms. Several tools and metrics have been proposed to characterise fitness landscapes [12], however, few of them deal with the landscapes' global structure. Local optima networks (LONs) help to fill this gap, by providing information about the number, distribution, and connectivity patterns of local optima [14]. LONs were inspired by work in theoretical/computational chemistry, where the structure of energy landscapes (derived from the atomic interactions in clusters and molecules) is modelled as a graph [5]. The central idea of LONs is to compress the search space into a graph where nodes are local optima and edges are possible transitions between optima with a given search operator. Several topological network features can be extracted from LONs [14]; recent work have also studied the landscapes' funnel structure [15,16]. The notion of funnels comes from the study of energy landscapes; according to Doye et al.

© Springer Nature Switzerland AG 2020
B. Filipič et al. (Eds.): BIOMA 2020, LNCS 12438, pp. 3–16, 2020.
https://doi.org/10.1007/978-3-030-63710-1_1

[6] a funnel "is a region of configuration space that can be described in terms of a set of downhill pathways that converge on a single low-energy structure or a set of closely related low-energy structures." Funnels are important global structure features, a single global funnel will facilitate optimisation, but the presence of sub-optimal funnels will hinder it.

Network-based models of fitness landscapes have only recently been applied to continuous optimisation problems outside the realm of molecular energy minimisation, examples are [1,2,17]. Our work extends these results in order to contrast the global (funnel) structure of synthetic vs. real-world continuous optimisation problems, we also develop some aspects of the methodology. Our main contributions are to:

- Apply the LON model to real-world continuous optimisation problems (including engineering design and machine learning) and contrast their structure against the structure of synthetic benchmark functions.
- Contrast two initialisation methods, uniform and Latin hypercube, when sampling the fitness landscapes to extract the LON models.
- Explore the effect of increasing the problem dimension on the global (funnel) structure of the underlying landscapes.

2   Definitions

We start by formalising the notions of fitness landscapes and local optimum, before defining the local optima network models considered in our study. We use two models to discover the global structure of continuous optimisation problems: the Monotonic LON model, and the Compressed Monotonic LON model, introduced in [16].

Fitness Landscape. In the context of continuous optimisation, a fitness landscape is a triplet $(\mathbf{X}, N, f)$ where $\mathbf{X} \in \mathbb{R}^n$ is the set of all real-valued solutions of n dimensions, *i.e.*, the search space; N is a function that assigns to every solution $\mathbf{x} \in \mathbf{X}$ a set of neighbors $N(\mathbf{x})$; and $f : \mathbb{R}^n \to \mathbb{R}$ is the fitness function. A potential solution $\mathbf{x}$ is denoted as vector $\mathbf{x} = (x_1, x_2, \ldots, x_n)$, and the neighbourhood is based on hypercubes. Formally, the neighbourhood of a candidate solution $\mathbf{x}_k$ is defined as, $\mathbf{x}_j \in N(\mathbf{x}_k) \leftrightarrow |x_{ki} - x_{ji}| < s_i, i = \{1, \ldots, n\}$ where $\mathbf{s} = (s_1, s_2, \ldots, s_n)$ is a vector that represents the size of the neighbourhood in all dimensions.

Local Optimum. A solution $\mathbf{x}^* \in \mathbf{X}$ such that $\forall \mathbf{x} \in N(\mathbf{x}^*), f(\mathbf{x}^*) \leq f(\mathbf{x})$.

Monotonic LON Model. The monotonic LON is the directed graph $MLON = (L, ME)$ where the nodes L are local optima and the edges $ME \subset E$ are monotonic perturbation edges.

Monotonic Perturbation Edges. There is a monotonic perturbation edge from a local optimum l_1 to a local optimum l_2, if l_2 can be obtained from a random perturbation of l_1 followed by a local minimisation process, and $f(l_2) \leq f(l_1)$. The edge is called monotonic because the transition between two local optima is non-deteriorating. In this model, the edges are weighted with the number of times a transition between two local optima occurred.

Compressed Monotonic LON Model. This is a coarser model that compresses connected local optima at the same fitness into single nodes. The purpose is to facilitate modelling landscapes with neutrality.

Compressed Monotonic LON. It is the directed graph $CMLON = (CL, CE)$ where the nodes are compressed local optima CL, and the edges $CE \subset ME$ are aggregated from the monotonic edge set ME by summing up the edge weights.

Compressed Local Optimum. A compressed local optimum is a single node that represents a set of connected nodes in the MLON model with the same fitness value.

Monotonic Sequence. A monotonic sequence is a path of connected local optima where their fitness values are always decreasing. Every monotonic sequence has a natural end, which represent a funnel bottom, also called sink in graph theory.

Funnel. We can characterise funnels in the CMLON as all the monotonic sequences ending at the same compressed local optimum (funnel bottom or sink).

3   Methodology

Our methodology for sampling and constructing the networks is based on the *basin-hopping* (BH) algorithm, proposed in the context of computational chemistry [18]. BH is an iterative algorithm, where each iteration is composed of a random perturbation of a candidate solution, followed by a local minimisation process and an acceptance test. In this study, we adopted a variant of the BH algorithm called monotonic basin-hopping (MBH) proposed in [10] (see in Algorithm 1), where the acceptance criterion considers only improving solutions.

   To construct the network models a number of runs are conducted. Each run on a given problem instance produces a search trajectory, which is recorded as a set of nodes (local minima) and edges (consecutive transitions), and stored in the sets L, and ME, respectively. Note that different runs can in principle traverse the same nodes and edges, even if they start from different initialisation points. The MLON network is constructed in a post-processing stage where the trajectories generated by a fixed number of runs (100 in our implementation) are aggregated to contain only unique nodes and edges.

We compared two techniques to generate the initial candidate solutions ($\mathbf{x}_0$ in Algorithm 1) during the sampling process: uniform and Latin hypercube sampling. The uniform sampling generates initial solutions following a uniform distribution within the problem bounds, whereas the Latin hypercube sampling (LHS) technique partitions the search space into equally probable bins and positions the samples at each axis-aligned hyperplane.

Algorithm 1. Monotonic basin-hopping sampling.

Require: search space $\mathbf{X} \in \mathbb{R}^n$, fitness function $f(\mathbf{X})$, step size p
 1: Initial random solution $\mathbf{x}_0 \in \mathbf{X}$
 2: $\mathbf{x} \leftarrow \text{LocalMinimization}(\mathbf{x}_0)$
 3: $L \leftarrow \{\mathbf{x}\}$
 4: **repeat**
 5:    $\mathbf{x}' \leftarrow \text{Perturbation}(\mathbf{x}, p)$
 6:    $\mathbf{y} \leftarrow \text{LocalMinimization}(\mathbf{x}')$
 7:    **if** $f(\mathbf{y}) \leq f(\mathbf{x})$ **then**
 8:       $L \leftarrow L \cup \{\mathbf{y}\}$
 9:       $ME \leftarrow ME \cup (\mathbf{x}, \mathbf{y})$
10:       $\mathbf{x} \leftarrow \mathbf{y}$
11:    **end if**
12: **until** Stopping criterion is not reached
13: **return** L, ME

As the local minimiser we used the Limited-memory Broyden-Fletc.her-Goldfarb-Shanno algorithm (L-BFGS) [13], which is an extension of BFGS, a well-known quasi-Newton algorithm. L-BFGS is scalable to higher dimensions because it avoids storing a fully dense approximation of the Hessian matrix.

The step size p has to be appropriately selected for each problem. If p is too small, the candidate solution can be easily trapped in a low quality local optimum and unable to escape from its basin of attraction; whereas if p is too large, the candidate solution can move drastically to regions of worse quality, degenerating into random search and losing the progress attained, especially if the search has already reached relatively low fitness solutions. In order to select p, we followed the suggestion in [10], which indicates to vary p until roughly half of the steps attempted escape the starting basin of attraction. In continuous space, there is a precision issue to decide if two solutions correspond to the same local optimum. In this work, we used a position threshold ϵ that depends on the optimisation problem. Two solutions represent the same local optimum if the absolute difference between each of their components is less than ϵ.

Once the models are constructed, we can extract different metrics to bring insight into the search difficulty and the global structure of the studied landscapes. Table 1 describes the metrics used in this study. The network metrics were gathered from the CMLON model. Note that when there is little neutrality in the search space, the number of nodes in the CMLON model is close to the number of local optima in the underlying landscape, whereas when neutrality is high, the number of nodes in the CMLON is smaller than the number of underlying landscape optima. The ratio between the number of compressed optima over the total number of local optima is captured by the *neutral* metric described in Table 1.

Table 1. Performance and network metrics.

Performance metrics	
Success	Proportion of runs that reached the global minimum.
Deviation	Mean deviation from the global minimum.
Network metrics	
Nodes	Number of nodes in the CMLON (compressed local optima).
Funnels	Number of sinks (CMLON nodes without outgoing edges).
Neutral	Proportion of CMLON nodes to the number of local optima.
Strength	Normalized incoming strength of the globally optimal sinks.

4 Experimental Setup

4.1 Synthetic Functions

We consider three classical test functions, modified Ackley (Ackley 4), Griewank, and Schwefel 2.26, which are all differentiable, separable, scalable, and multimodal, but are known to differ in their global structures. Figure 1 shows 3D visualisations of the functions with two variables. The Ackley 4 function [7] has two global minima close to the origin, presents a single pronounced funnel toward both minima, and evaluates within the range $[-35, 35]$. The Griewank function has a single funnel structure, many local optima almost at the same fitness level than the single global optimum (located at the origin), and evaluates in the range $[-600, 600]$. The Schwefel 2.26 function has multiple funnels, a single global optimum located far from the origin, at $f(\mathbf{x}^*) = f(420.9687, \ldots, 420.9687)$, and evaluates in the range $[-500, 500]$. For each function, we considered 3 instances with $n = \{3, 5, 8\}$.

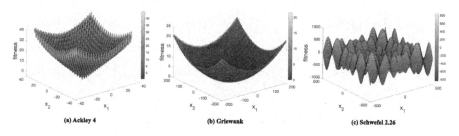

(a) Ackley 4   (b) Griewank   (c) Schwefel 2.26

Fig. 1. 3D visualization of the selected synthetic benchmark functions with two variables.

4.2   Real-World Functions

Engineering Design Problem. We selected the radar pulse modulation problem named "spread spectrum radar polly phase code design problem", as described and implemented in the CEC2011 "Competition on Testing Evolutionary Algorithms on Real-World Optimisation Problems" [4]. This problem can be scaled to n dimensions and belongs to the class of continuous min-max global optimisation problems. In both problems, the global optima are known. We selected 3 instances with $n = \{3, 5, 8\}$, to allow a closer comparison with the synthetic functions. In what follows, we call this the *Radar* function.

Machine Learning Problem. We used the sum of squares clustering problem from the "Machine Learning and Data Analysis" problem set [9]. The problem is to determine the position of k cluster centres in order to minimise the sum of squared distances between each data point (in a dataset) and its nearest cluster center. Let us denote $\mathcal{C} = \{\mathbf{c}_1, \mathbf{c}_2, \ldots, \mathbf{c}_k\}$ as the set of centers where $\mathbf{c}_j \in \mathbb{R}^q$; and $\mathcal{D} = \{\mathbf{d}_1, \mathbf{d}_2, \ldots, \mathbf{d}_m\}$ as the dataset, with $\mathbf{d}_i \in \mathbb{R}^q$. A candidate solution is represented as a vector $\mathbf{x} \in \mathbb{R}^{qk}$ that concatenates the centers coordinates. Several test instances can be generated, changing the value of k and the dataset. We selected the *Ruspini* dataset that contains 75 observations in a 2-dimensional space ($\mathbf{d}_i \in \mathbb{R}^2$). Since the observations are in a 2-dimensional space, and the problem representation concatenates the cluster centres, instances can only be generated with an even dimension. In order to closely compare with the other benchmark functions, we selected 3 instances with $n = \{4, 6, 8\}$ (corresponding respectively to $k = \{2, 3, 4\}$). In what follows, we call this the *Clustering* function.

4.3   Parameter Settings and Experiments

To extract the networks, 100 runs of the monotonic basin-hoping sampling algorithm (Algorithm 1) were conducted on each function with a stopping criterion based on a predefined number of cycles. The number of cycles was determined experimentally for each problem, by observing the convergence behavior of 30 runs. Table 2 summarises the parameters used for each function.

Table 2. Parameter settings for each function.

Function	Dimensions	Step size	Cycles	ϵ
Ackley 4	$3, 5, 8$	1.63	300	10^{-2}
Griewank	$3, 5, 8$	3.60	200	10^{-2}
Schwefel 2.26	$3, 5, 8$	151.00	4000	10^{-2}
Radar	$3, 5, 8$	1.27	100	10^{-1}
Clustering	$4, 6, 8$	48.64	100	1.0

All the experiments were conducted in an Intel Core i7 computer, with a processor running at 3.5 GHz and 16 GB of RAM. We used the basin-hopping implementation provided in the Python package Scipy [8]. For constructing models, computing the metrics and visualising the networks we used the igraph package [3] with the R statistical language. For visualising the networks, we used force-directed graph layout algorithms as provided in igraph.

5   Results

5.1   Synthetic Functions

Performance and Network Metrics. Figure 2 reports the performance and network metrics described in Table 1 for the synthetic functions with $n = \{3, 5, 8\}$. Results are shown for both initialisation methods, which are indicated using the subscript *uni* for the uniform initialisation and *lhs* for the hypercube sampling.

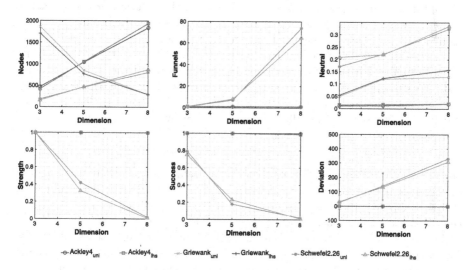

Fig. 2. Network and performance metrics on the synthetic functions. For each function, the subscripts *uni* and *lhs* denote uniform initialisation and hypercube sampling, respectively.

Let us first consider the performance metrics (Success and Deviation). The Ackley 4 and Griewank functions are easy to solve by the MBH algorithm, regardless of the initialisation method used. However, the MBH algorithm shows a reduction in the success rate in the Schwefel 2.26 function as the problem dimension increases. For $n = 3$, the uniform initialisation showed a higher success rate than the success rate of the LHS. However, with $n = 5$, it is the other way around, supporting that LHS might be beneficial for high dimension problems.

The problem becomes very hard to solve with $n = 8$, where MBH with both initialisation methods failed to find the global optimum in most runs. We can also verify the difficulty of the Schwefel 2.26 function, looking at how the deviation from the optimum increases with n.

With respect to the network metrics, the number of nodes in the CMLON model increases with the problem dimension for Ackley 4 and Schwefel 2.26. For the Griewank function, the trend is reversed, the number of nodes decreases when the problem dimension increases. These results are aligned with the earlier findings by Locatelli et al. [11], where the Griewank function was found to behave closer to its convex quadratic function as n increases. Theoretically, the number of local optima in the Griewank function increases exponentially with n due to its oscillatory non-convex part; however, local optimisers (such as L-BFGS) can only capture a lower number of optima because the convex quadratic function is more pronounced than the oscillatory non-convex component. The number of funnels indicates that Ackley 4 and Griewank feature a single funnel structure for all the studied problem dimensions; which helps to explain that these functions are not difficult to solve. For the Schwefel 2.26 function, as the dimension increases, some sub-optimal funnels appear, which helps to explain the deterioration in the MBH performance. The neutral metric represents the proportion of connected local optima with the same fitness value. In an analysis per function, we can observe that Schwefel 2.26 shows higher neutrality than the other functions. Finally, the strength metric measures the incoming weighted degree of the global optimum node. We can appreciate visually that this metric correlates well with the success rate. For Ackley 4 and Griewank, the strength is the highest possible value (1.0), and it does not seem to be affected by n. For Schwefel 2.26, an increase in n represents a reduction in strength.

Network Visualisation. Visualisation is a useful tool to get insight into the structure of networks. Figure 3 shows the CMLONs for the synthetic functions with $n = \{3, 5, 8\}$; the plots captions indicate the success rate for each instance. Due to space restrictions, we only show networks generated with uniform initialisation. However, both initialisation methods produced similar visual results. The graphs decorations highlight relevant features of the search dynamics; node sizes are proportional to their incoming strength, and edges to their weight, i.e. the number of times a transition between two nodes occurred in the sampling process. Pink nodes correspond to global funnels, and blue nodes to sub-optimal funnels. The global optima is highlighted with bright red, while the sub-optimal funnel bottoms with dark blue nodes. The Ackley 4 function shows a single funnel structure for all dimensions, with the number of nodes increasing with n. The Griewank function also shows a single funnel for all dimensions; however, the number of nodes decreases with n as discussed above, and also due to the higher neutrality observed in this function. For the Schwefel 2.26 function, sub-optimal funnels (blue nodes) start to emerge as n increases, which explains the success rate deteriorating with n.

To illustrate the advantage of modelling the search space with LONs, we used 3D visualisations of the networks to gain insight into the landscapes funnel structure. Figure 4 shows 3D networks of the synthetic functions with $n = 5$, where the fitness values are added as the third dimension to the 2D graph layouts. We can observe that Ackley 4 shows a deep funnel towards a single global optimum. Griewank also shows a single funnel, but with a flatter structure; we can see the several local optima are located almost at the same fitness level than the global optimum. Schwefel 2.26 shows multiple funnels, where the suboptimal funnel bottoms (dark blue nodes) are at different fitness levels. Contrasting the standard 3D visualisation, only possible for functions with $n = 2$ (Fig. 1), with the network visualisations for $n = 5$ (Fig. 4), we can observe that the overall shape of the functions global structure is maintained. The networks

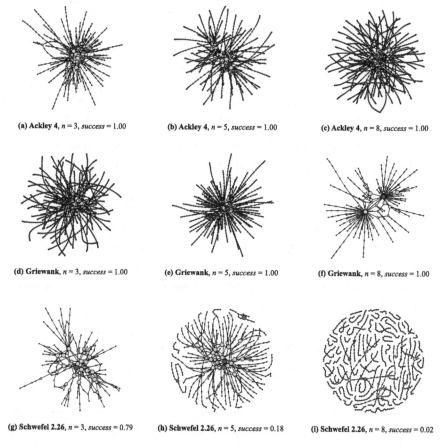

(a) Ackley 4, $n = 3$, *success* = 1.00   (b) Ackley 4, $n = 5$, *success* = 1.00   (c) Ackley 4, $n = 8$, *success* = 1.00

(d) Griewank, $n = 3$, *success* = 1.00   (e) Griewank, $n = 5$, *success* = 1.00   (f) Griewank, $n = 8$, *success* = 1.00

(g) Schwefel 2.26, $n = 3$, *success* = 0.79   (h) Schwefel 2.26, $n = 5$, *success* = 0.18   (i) Schwefel 2.26, $n = 8$, *success* = 0.02

Fig. 3. CMLON visualisations for the synthetic instances with $n = \{3, 5, 8\}$. Node sizes are proportional to their incoming strength. Pink nodes belong to the funnel containing the global optimum (red node), while blue nodes belong to sub-optimal funnels (bottoms coloured in a dark blue). (Color figure online)

visualisations, therefore, offer a novel way of visualising the structure of functions of higher dimensions.

5.2 Real-World Problems

Performance and Network Metrics. Figure 5 reports the performance and network metrics described in Table 1 for the real-world functions with $n = \{3, 5, 8\}$ for the radar function and $n = \{4, 6, 8\}$ for the clustering function.

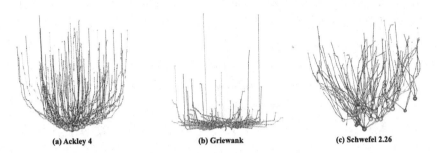

(a) Ackley 4   (b) Griewank   (c) Schwefel 2.26

Fig. 4. 3D visualisation of the CMLON networks for the three synthetic functions with $n = 5$. The fitness value represents the third dimension. Nodes sizes are proportional to their incoming strength. Pink nodes belong to the funnel containing the global optimum (red node), while blue nodes belong to sub-optimal funnels (bottoms coloured in a dark blue). (Color figure online)

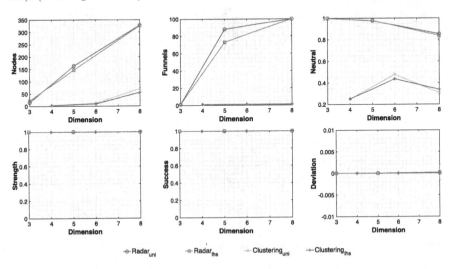

Fig. 5. Network and performance metrics on the real-world functions. For each function, the subscripts *uni* and *lhs* denote uniform initialization and hypercube sampling, respectively.

Results are shown for both initialisation methods, which are indicated using the subscript *uni* for the uniform initialisation and *lhs* for the hypercube sampling. The performance metrics (Success and Deviation) indicate that the real-world problems are easy to solve for all the dimensions and initialisation methods considered. The strength network metric (1.0 in all cases) clearly correlates with the performance metrics, supporting that the studied problems are easy to solve. Looking at the other network metrics, we can see that the number nodes increases with the dimension for both problems, and it is lower for the clustering problem. When contrasting with the synthetic functions (Fig. 2), we can see that the real-world problems produced much lower number of nodes. For the clustering function, a single global funnel is observed in all dimensions. The number of funnels increases with the dimension for the radar function, but all these funnels are global, there are no sub-optimal funnels in the studied real-world problems. This is consistent with the good performance of MBH in these problems. The differences between the two sampling methods are not marked for most metrics, with uniform sampling showing higher values for some of them. The neutral metric clearly indicates higher values for the real-world problems as compared with the synthetic functions (Fig. 2). Specially the radar function shows very high neutrality. Finally, another marked difference we found between the synthetic and real-world functions was the total number of different global optima. The synthetic functions revealed a very low number of global optima in all the studied dimensions (two for the Ackley 4 function, and one for the Griewank and Schwefel 2.26 functions) whereas the real-world functions produced a larger number of global optima. For example, for the uniform sampling, the number of global optima for the radar function was: 7014, 6477, and 1934, for $n = 3$, 5, and 8, respectively; whereas for the clustering function the number of global optima was 2, 6 and 24, for $n = 4$, 6, and 8, respectively.

Network Visualisation. Figure 6 shows the CMLONs for the real-world functions. For consistency with Fig. 3, the captions also indicate the success rate, which was 1.0 in all cases. We can observe that the networks for the real-world problems (Fig. 6) are much smaller (in terms of the number of nodes and edges) than the synthetic functions (Fig. 3); their overall structure is also different. The radar function with $n = 3$ has several thousands of global optima (7014 in our sampling process), however they are all connected and compressed into a single node in the CMLON model (red node in Fig. 6(a)). The CMLON in this case shows a single easy to traverse funnel structure, where one or two hops (edges) are sufficient to reach a global optimum. As n increases (Fig. 6(b) and (c)) the number of funnel sinks (nodes without outgoing edges) increases, but they are all global sinks (red nodes). Moreover, from none to three edges are sufficient to reach a global optimum (no edges means that the first optimum attained is a global optimum), whereas more steps are required to reach a global optimum for the easy to solve synthetic functions (Fig. 3(a)–(f)). The clustering function (Fig. 6(d)–(f)), shows small networks with a single global funnel and short paths

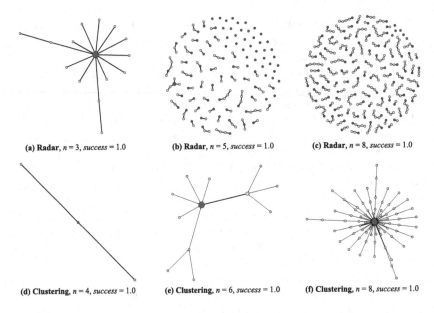

(a) **Radar**, $n = 3$, *success* = 1.0   (b) **Radar**, $n = 5$, *success* = 1.0   (c) **Radar**, $n = 8$, *success* = 1.0

(d) **Clustering**, $n = 4$, *success* = 1.0   (e) **Clustering**, $n = 6$, *success* = 1.0   (f) **Clustering**, $n = 8$, *success* = 1.0

Fig. 6. CMLON visualisations for the real-world problems with different dimensions.

lengths to attain the global optimum. The networks for this problem increase in size (number of nodes and edges) with increasing problem dimension.

6   Conclusions

We extracted and analysed basin-hoping network models from synthetic and real-world continuous optimisation problems, and explored the effect of alternative initialisation methods as well as the problem dimension. Our main goal was to analyse and contrast the global (funnel) structure of the studied landscapes. The number of funnels tend to increase with the problem dimension, however, only one of the studied synthetic functions, Schwefel 2.26, showed sub-optimal funnels. We found striking differences between the synthetic and the real-world functions. Surprisingly, the real-world functions were easier to solve than the synthetic functions and our network analysis and visualisation revealed why this is the case.

The real-world problems produced much smaller network models (in terms of nodes and edges) and optimal funnels with shallow depth; a few hops were sufficient to reach a global optimum. The real-world problems also have many global optima, as opposed to one or two as observed in the synthetic functions, and much higher levels of neutrality measured as the proportion of connected local optima at the same fitness level. These findings indicate that designing and improving algorithms according to their performance on synthetic functions may be misleading. Our approach offers a novel way of visualising and analysing the global structure of continuous functions with more than two variables. Future work will explore higher dimensions and additional real-world problems. The new set of metrics extracted from network models can also be used to guide parameter tuning and automatic algorithm selection in real-world engineering and machine learning optimisation problems.

Acknowledgment. Marco A. Contreras-Cruz thanks to the National Council of Science and Technology (CONACYT) for the scholarship with identification number 568675/302121. He also thanks to the Office of Research and Graduate Programs (DAIP) of the University of Guanajuato and the CONACYT, for the financial support during his research visit to the University of Stirling (from June to December 2019).

References

1. Adair, J., Ochoa, G., Malan, K.M.: Local optima networks for continuous fitness landscapes. In: Proceedings of the Genetic and Evolutionary Computation Conference Companion, pp. 1407–1414. ACM (2019)
2. Ballard, A.J., et al.: Energy landscapes for machine learning. Phys. Chem. Chem. Phys. **19**(20), 12585–12603 (2017)
3. Csardi, G., Nepusz, T.: The igraph software package for complex network research. Int. J. Complex Syst. **1965**, 1–9 (2006). http://igraph.org
4. Das, S., Suganthan, P.N.: Problem definitions and evaluation criteria for CEC 2011 competition on testing evolutionary algorithms on real world optimization problems, pp. 341–359. Jadavpur University, Nanyang Technological University, Kolkata (2010)
5. Doye, J.P.: Network topology of a potential energy landscape: a static scale-free network. Phys. Rev. Lett. **88**(23), 238701 (2002)
6. Doye, J.P., Miller, M.A., Wales, D.J.: The double-funnel energy landscape of the 38-atom Lennard-Jones cluster. J. Chem. Phys. **110**(14), 6896–6906 (1999)
7. Jamil, M., Yang, X.S.: A literature survey of benchmark functions for global optimization problems. arXiv preprint arXiv:1308.4008 (2013)
8. Jones, E., Oliphant, T., Peterson, P.: SciPy: open source scientific tools for Python (2001). http://www.scipy.org/
9. Kerschke, P., Gallagher, M., Preuss, M., Teytaud, O.: The machine learning and data analysis (MLDA) problem set, v1 (2019). https://www.wi.uni-muenster.de/sites/wi/files/users/kerschke/gecco2019/gecco2019_umlop_mlda.pdf
10. Leary, R.H.: Global optimization on funneling landscapes. J. Glob. Optim. **18**(4), 367–383 (2000)
11. Locatelli, M.: A note on the Griewank test function. J. Glob. Optim. **25**(2), 169–174 (2003)
12. Malan, K., Engelbrecht, A.P.: A survey of techniques for characterising fitness landscapes and some possible ways forward. Inform. Sci. **241**, 148–163 (2013)
13. Nocedal, J., Wright, S.: Numerical Optimization. Springer Science & Business Media, New York (2006)
14. Ochoa, G., Tomassini, M., Vérel, S., Darabos, C.: A study of NK landscapes, basins and local optima networks. In: Proceedings of the 10th Annual Conference on Genetic and Evolutionary Computation, pp. 555–562. ACM (2008)
15. Ochoa, G., Veerapen, N.: Mapping the global structure of TSP fitness landscapes. J. Heuristics **24**(3), 265–294 (2017). https://doi.org/10.1007/s10732-017-9334-0

16. Ochoa, G., Veerapen, N., Daolio, F., Tomassini, M.: Understanding phase transitions with local optima networks: number partitioning as a case study. In: Hu, B., López-Ibáñez, M. (eds.) EvoCOP 2017. LNCS, vol. 10197, pp. 233–248. Springer, Cham (2017). https://doi.org/10.1007/978-3-319-55453-2_16
17. Vinkó, T., Gelle, K.: Basin-hopping networks of continuous global optimization problems. Cent. Eur. J. Oper. Res. **25**(4), 985–1006 (2017)
18. Wales, D.J., Doye, J.P.: Global optimization by basin-hopping and the lowest energy structures of Lennard-Jones clusters containing up to 110 atoms. J. Phys. Chem. A **101**(28), 5111–5116 (1997)

Variable Response Duration Promotes Self-organization in Decentralized Swarms

Kaelan Engholdt[1], H. David Mathias[1(✉)], and Annie S. Wu[2]

[1] University of Wisconsin – La Crosse, La Crosse, WI 54601, USA
{engholdt8911,dmathias}@uwlax.edu
[2] University of Central Florida, Orlando, FL 32816, USA
aswu@cs.ucf.edu

Abstract. In self-organizing multi-agent systems, inter-agent variation is known to improve swarm performance significantly. Response duration, the amount of time that an agent spends on a task, has been proposed as a form of inter-agent variation that may be beneficial. In the biological literature, variability in agent response duration in natural swarms for desynchronizing agent actions has been discussed for some time. This form of variation, however, is not well understood in artificial swarms. In this work, we explore inter-agent variation in response duration as a desynchronization technique. We find that variation in response duration does desynchronize agent behaviors and does improve swarm performance on a two-dimensional tracking problem in which the swarm must push a tracker, staying as close as possible to a moving target. By preventing agents from reacting identically to task stimuli and keeping some agents on task longer, response duration helps smooth the swarm's path and allows it to better track the target into path features such as corners.

Keywords: Multi-agent system · Inter-agent variation · Response duration · Response threshold

1 Introduction

In this paper, we investigate variable response duration as a mechanism for promoting effective self-organization in a decentralized swarm. The decentralized and redundant structure of swarms make them potentially very robust and adaptable. These same qualities, however, also make the task of coordinating agents within a swarm a challenging problem. For a swarm to address any reasonably interesting problem, the agents in the swarm must be able to distribute themselves intelligently among multiple tasks, even in problems where task stimuli are globally sensed by all agents. Such coordinated responses can be difficult to achieve when all agents act independently. A significant body of work has studied how variation in *when* agents are triggered to act, i.e. variation in response

Supported by NSF Grant IIS1816777.

threshold, can desynchronize agent actions enough to generate effective division of labor [6,15,16,20,21,23,24]. Biological studies hypothesize that variation in *how long* agents work before they stop to re-assess their actions can also contribute to desynchronizing decentralized swarms of agents [22]. This work examines the effectiveness of variable response duration on swarm self-organization and its strengths and weaknesses relative to and in conjunction with variable response thresholds.

Effective self-organization of decentralized swarms requires desynchronization of the agents within a swarm to achieve diversity in agent actions. If agents make action decisions at different times, they are likely to encounter different stimuli and, thus, have the potential to act differently. A commonly used method of desynchronization is variation in response threshold. Giving each agent a different threshold for each task stimulus causes agents to be triggered at different times by a given stimulus. As a result, agents enter the workforce gradually rather than all at the same time and entry into the workforce may stop after task needs have been fully addressed by a subset of agents. Simply assigning agents randomly generated thresholds over a uniform distribution is sufficient to generate division of labor in a swarm [15,23]. Studies have examined both static distributions of thresholds [8,12,15,18,19,23,24] and dynamically evolved thresholds [2–7,9,10,13,14,19,21].

Weidenmuller's [22] study on honeybee thermoregulation points out that a different factor may also contribute to the desynchronization of agent actions in a decentralized swarm: variation in response duration. Response duration refers to the amount of time that an agent works on a task before stopping to re-assess its actions. Instead of all agents evaluating task demands and selecting an action in every unit of time, agents may work differing numbers of time units on a task before stopping to reconsider task demands. The varying durations cause agents to be desynchronized with respect to when they evaluate task stimuli, increasing the chance that they will sense different stimuli and react diversely.

Active adjustment of the amount of time agents spend on tasks is not new to swarm self-organization studies. Factors such as the amount of time that agents have been resting or active [1,17], agent success rate or productivity on task [25], and perceived relative task demands [11] have been used to affect when agents start and stop work on tasks. In all of these approaches, however, response durations are tied in part to external forces, e.g. the availability of jobs or density of jobs. As such, even though agents act independently, there exists the possibility that the external forces that are driving their response durations could inadvertently synchronize agents.

We are interested in response duration as an inherent characteristic of an agent and whether variation in agent response duration within a swarm can contribute to more effective self-organization. We study the performance of a decentralized swarm on a collective tracking problem. We first examine whether the desynchronizing effects of variable response duration is able to improve a swarm's ability to self-organize. We then explore the implications of varying the average expected response duration lengths of the agents. Finally we present interesting results combining two mechanisms for desynchronizing decentralized swarms: variable response durations combined with variable response thresholds. Our results indicate that variable response duration is a viable method for improving self-organization in swarms and suggest that the interaction of multiple forms of inter-agent variation may result in richer behavior than any single form alone.

2   Problem Description

In seminal work on inter-individual variation in bumblebees [22], Weidenmuller explores collective nest thermoregulation. In that problem, individual bees choose between two tasks, flapping their wings or shivering, to lower or raise the temperature in the hive, respectively. Thermoregulation is a one-dimensional problem in which the two tasks are in opposition. For the testbed in this work, we use a two-dimensional tracking problem in which the swarm attempts to move an object to track, as closely as possible, a target. The target's path is unknown to the agents comprising the swarm. Superficially very different from thermoregulation, this problem is quite similar though more complex.

A simulation is divided into a predetermined number of time steps. During each time step, the target moves a fixed distance in a direction determined by the underlying path. Random paths may change direction as often as every time step, creating frequently changing task demands, while periodic paths create periods of nearly constant task demands followed by brief periods of abrupt changes.

To track the target, each agent can undertake one of four tasks in each timestep: push_NORTH, push_SOUTH, push_EAST, or push_WEST. Task demands for the swarm are determined by movement of the target. Agents are aware of the demands in the form of the task stimuli, the distances between the target and tracker in each dimension. Let $\Delta x = \text{target}.x - \text{tracker}.x$ and $\Delta y = \text{target}.y - \text{tracker}.y$. Task stimuli are defined as: $\sigma_N = -\Delta y$, $\sigma_E = -\Delta x$, $\sigma_S = \Delta y$, and $\sigma_W = \Delta x$.

Whether an agent acts in a given time step is determined by the task stimuli and one or more forms of inter-agent variation described previously. Without inter-agent variation, agents respond in lockstep to stimuli, inhibiting the ability of the swarm to perform a variety of tasks.

Performance of a swarm is measured relative to the following two domain goals:

Domain Goal 1. *Minimize the average positional difference, per time step, between the target location and the tracker location.*

Domain Goal 2. *Minimize the difference between total distance traveled by target and the total distance traveled by the tracker.*

We note that neither criterion alone is sufficient to gauge the swarm's success. Consider using only Goal 1. The tracker could remain close to the target while alternately racing ahead or falling behind. This would result in a good average difference but a path length that is significantly greater than that traveled by the target. Alternately, using only Goal 2, the tracker could travel a path that is the same length as that of the tracker while straying quite far, taking a very different path.

Both the honeybee thermoregulation problem and the tracking problem are examples of decentralized task allocation problems. There are certainly more effective methods to achieve tracking and the focus of this work is not on that problem domain. Rather the tracking problem is used here because it is an example of a decentralized task allocation problem in which task demands and contributions are clearly defined and measured, dynamic variation in task demand over time can be systematically described, and overall performance can be accurately measured as well as visually assessed.

3   Experimental Details

To examine the effect of response duration, we vary the time period for which an agent performs a task. This is done via a parameter named `Prob_check`. This parameter represents the probability that in any time step an agent will undergo task selection. If an agent does not undergo task selection, it continues working on its current task. It is important to note that `Prob_check` is inversely proportional to response duration. That is, a high `Prob_check` value results in less time spent on a task (more frequent task selection) while low `Prob_check` values result in more time spent on a task (less frequent task selection). We perform experiments with `Prob_check` values in $[0.1, 1.0]$ in increments of 0.1.

We perform experiments using two target paths, circle and serpentine.

- circle: Target continuously revolves about a central point at a fixed distance, resulting in a circular path with radius r. This creates continuously changing task demands and requires the swarm to perform all tasks equally.
- serpentine: A periodic path that oscillates up and down, moving from west to east. The motion is defined by amplitude and period values. `Path_amplitude` dictates how far the target moves in the north and south directions. `Path_period` controls the distance between peaks in the waveform.

The bottom of Table 1 shows parameters that allow some variation in the circle and serpentine paths. These include seven radii for circle and four pairs of amplitudes and periods for serpentine. With these parameter values, we can affect the rate at which task demands change.

The top of Table 1 lists parameters that are fixed for all experiments. These include the number of agents in the swarm and the number of time steps in each simulation. Two other parameters require some explanation. When selecting a task, agents may choose `push_NORTH`, `push_SOUTH`, `push_EAST`, or `push_WEST`. Urgent task selection means that agents will select the task with the greatest task demand. In each time step, the target moves a fixed distance defined by `Target_step_len`. This value is fixed at 3 for these experiments. The maximum

Table 1. Parameters with values fixed across all experiments (top) and those with values that vary by experiment (bottom).

Parameter	Value
Population size	200
Time steps	500
Task selection	Urgent
Target_step_len	3
Step_ratio	1.5
Prob_check	$[0.1, 1.0]$ by 0.1
Radius (circle)	3, 5, 10, 15, 20, 25, 30
Path_amplitude (serpentine)	6, 9, 12, 15
Path_period (serpentine)	10, 20, 30, 40

distance the tracker can move is defined by the Target_step_len times the Step_ratio. With a Step_ratio of 1.0, all agents would have to push in the right direction in order for the tracker to keep up with the target. Higher Step_ratio values allow for some agents to remain idle or undertake a wrong task without severe consequences for the swarm.

Each experiment consists of 100 runs. We average data across all runs and calculate 95% confidence intervals. We measure swarm performance by two data, average positional difference between the target and tracker (Goal 1) and difference between target and tracker path lengths (Goal 2).

- Average Positional Difference: This is the mean over all time steps of the Euclidean distance between the target and the tracker positions. This measures the deviation between the target and tracker paths over the course of the run. The optimum value for this metric is zero.
- Path Length Difference: This is a measure of the difference between the total path lengths traveled by the tracker and the target. A negative value for this metric indicates that the tracker did not travel as far as the target, where as a positive value means the tracker traveled a longer path than did the target. The optimum value for this metric is zero.

4   Results

4.1   Can Variable Response Duration Improve Self-organization?

We begin by asking the general question: does the desynchronization of agents that results from variable response duration improve a swarm's ability to self-organize? Figure 1 shows two example instances of a tracker's attempt to follow a target along a circular path and a serpentine path. The left column shows the results for Prob_check = 1.0, which is uniform response duration. The right column shows the results for Prob_check = 0.4, where each agent has a 40%

chance of re-assessing its current action in each timestep and a 60% chance of ignoring current task demands and continuing with its current task. The top row shows a circular path. The bottom row shows a serpentine path.

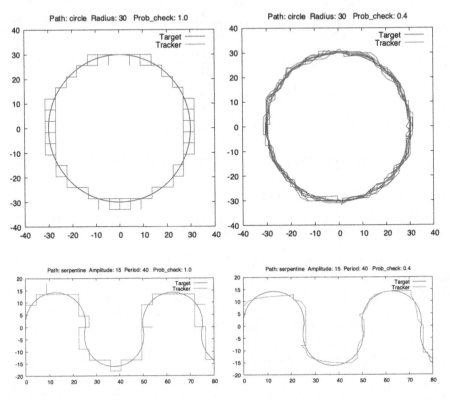

Fig. 1. Examples of tracker paths with `Prob_check` = 1.0 (left column) and `Prob_check` = 0.4 (right column) following target on a circular path (top row) and serpentine path (bottom row).

The plots in the left column show that, without any other mechanisms to diversify agent actions, all agents act identically in every timestep because they all perceive the same task demands in each timestep. As a result, the tracker only moves in the four cardinal directions and the path it traces as it follows the target is very blocky. The plots in the right column provide evidence that variable response duration can have a desynchronizing effect that diversifies agent actions. The `Prob_check` value less than 1.0 causes only a subset of agents to re-assess their actions in each timestep. Even though all of those agents may select the same task, the swarm as a whole has a diversity of agent actions in each timestep because of the agents that maintain their current task. As a result, the tracker is able to move in more than just the four basic directions and is able to follow the path of the target more closely and trace a smoother path. Thus, the desynchronization effect of variable response duration can produce diversity in agent actions that can improve self-organization.

4.2   Implications of Variable Response Duration

While variable response duration appears to desynchronize agent actions, it also causes the swarm to react less promptly to task demands as swarms in which all agents re-assess their actions in every timestep. As a result, the desynchronization benefits of variable response duration may come at a cost of lowered swarm responsiveness to changing task demands. That suggests that a problem with frequently changing task demands will be more difficult for smaller Prob_check values (longer durations) than larger Prob_check values (shorter durations). We explore this hypothesis by examining the full range of Prob_check values and how they respond to paths that require increasing levels of responsiveness.

For a given Prob_check value d, we can estimate the expected duration that agents will stay on a task before re-assessing its actions. Let τ be the number of time steps that an agent performs a task. For Prob_check value d, the expected value of τ is given by $E(\tau) = 1/d$. We then calculate the average number of time steps that agents act for each Prob_check value in an example run of the tracking simulation. Table 2 shows that the empirically observed durations from a sample tracking run closely match the expected $(E(\tau))$ value for all of the Prob_check values.

Table 2. Expected and observed number of time steps for an agent with a given Prob_check value to consider changing tasks.

Prob_check d	$E(\tau)$	Observed duration	Prob_check d	$E(\tau)$	Observed duration
0.1	10.00	10.150221	0.6	1.67	1.664558
0.2	5.00	5.003253	0.7	1.43	1.431783
0.3	3.33	3.335890	0.8	1.25	1.249157
0.4	2.50	2.500249	0.9	1.11	1.111148
0.5	2.00	1.998521	1.0	1.00	1.000000

Figure 2 shows the Path Length Difference and Average Positional Difference measures averaged over 100 simulation runs for Prob_check values from 0.1 to 1.0 on circle paths with radii ranging from 30 down to 3. The x-axes of each plot indicates Prob_check values. The y-axes of the left column of plots indicate Path Length Difference. The y-axes of the right column of plots indicate Average Positional Difference. Each row of plots gives the results for a circular target path with radii ranging from 30 down to 3. As a target path's radius decreases, required swarm responsiveness is expected to increase and we expect higher Prob_check values to be needed to maintain performance.

The left column of Fig. 2 shows the average Path Length Difference averaged over 100 runs with 95% confidence interval. Recall that the optimal Path Length Difference is zero; a positive value indicates that the tracker travels farther than the target; a negative value indicates that the tracker travels a shorter distance than the target. Looking at the top plot in the left column

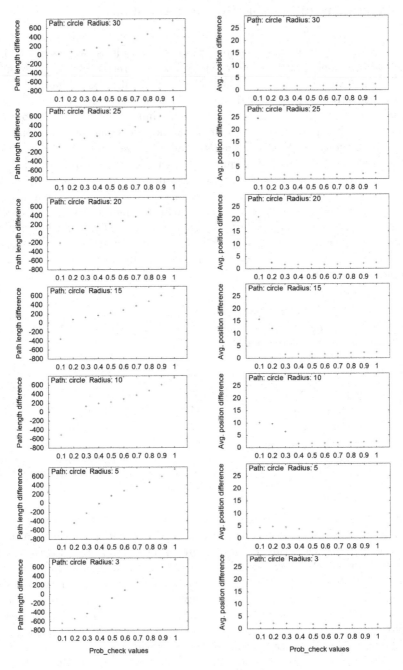

Fig. 2. Path Length Difference (left column) and Average Positional Difference (right column) measures averaged over 100 runs with 95% confidence intervals. Rows show results from circles with path radii from 30 to 3.

of Fig. reffig:comparespsdurations, we see that, on a circle of radius 30, tracker and target path lengths are most similar at the lowest Prob_check values. As Prob_check values increase, the tracker travels increasingly longer distances relative to the target. These extra distances are due to the overshooting that occurs when too many agents respond, as seen in the blocky movements of the left plot in Fig. 1. As we move down the rows in Fig. 2, the plots show data from smaller and smaller circles. As the circle radii shrink, the optimal Path Length Difference values are found at increasingly higher Prob_check values. At radius 10, optimal Prob_check is between 0.2 and 0.3; at radius 3, optimal Prob_check is between 0.5 and 0.6. Also as the circle radii shrink, lower Prob_check values start producing more and more negative Path Length Difference values due to swarm responsiveness being too low for the tracker to keep up with the target. Thus, as the target path (and task demands) change more quickly, higher Prob_check values are needed to achieve optimal performance because agents need to re-assess and adjust their actions more frequently to keep up with the target movement.

The right column of Fig. 2 shows the Average Positional Difference averaged over 100 runs with 95% confidence interval. The optimal Average Positional Difference is zero. The top right plot of Fig. 2 shows that all Prob_check values except for Prob_check = 0.1 achieve Average Positional Difference of approximately 2 or less. As we move down the rows in Fig. 2, Prob_check = 0.1 results improve but still lag behind higher Prob_check values. The change in the results for Prob_check = 0.2 and 0.3 as circle radius decreases is more interesting. At high circle radii, these values are relatively low. At radii of 15 and 10, the Average Positional Difference for Prob_check = 0.2 and 0.3, respectively, increase significantly. As radii continue to decrease, the results for both slowly drop back down to values around 2. Higher Prob_check values consistently achieve low Average Positional Difference values.

Examination of individual runs explains these observed results as follows. At high circle radii, the change in task demand is low from one time step to the next. As a result, even trackers with relatively low Prob_check values can follow the target path. As circle radii decrease, the change in task demand from one time step to the next increases. The increased change requires a more responsive swarm for the tracker to be able to keep up with the target. When the target task demand changes become too great for given Prob_check value to keep up, we see an increase in the Average Positional Difference. At this point, the tracker lags so far behind the target that significant corner-cutting occurs. Because the example runs presented are on a circular path, the corner cutting by the tracker leads it to travel in a circular path within the target's circular path. As the circle radii continue to decrease, the change in task demand becomes more frequent. Although the swarm has difficulty keeping up with the target, the decreasing radii results in lower Average Positional Difference because the tracker is constantly moving within the target path due to corner cutting. This behavior is not unique to the circular target path; similar degradation trends are observed in other path results.

4.3 Combining Response Duration and Response Thresholds

While the results above show that variation in response duration can benefit a swarm's ability to self-organize, they also suggest that the effectiveness of this mechanism may depend on a good pairing of `Prob_check` value with the dynamism of the path being tracked. In other words, optimal use of response duration is only possible with a priori knowledge of the problem to which a swarm is applied. Because a priori information is not always available, we explore other situations where variation in response duration may be generally beneficial.

Specifically, we find that combining variable response durations with variable response thresholds can provide added benefits. Variable response thresholds have been shown to be a successful method for desynchronization of decentralized agents. When agent resources are insufficient for addressing all problem demands, however, such systems will fall behind and task attendance may lag task demand. In the tracking problem such lags often manifest as corner cutting. Empirical studies show that the lowered responsiveness that emerges from longer response durations often results in a delayed reaction that resembles "inertia" in agent task choices. Figure 3 shows an example of a serpentine path with a swarm using variable response thresholds alone (left) and a swarm using variable response thresholds combined with variable response duration (right). While the path on the left cuts corners, in the path on the right, the delayed response generated by variable response duration pushes the tracker further into each turn and reduces the corner cutting effect. Thus, while both variable response thresholds and variable response durations may be used to desynchronize the actions of decentralized agents, they do so using different mechanisms and there appear to be potential advantages to combining multiple mechanisms.

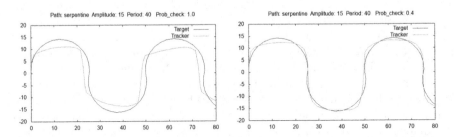

Fig. 3. Effects of combining variable response duration with variable response thresholds. Left: Variable response thresholds alone results in corner cutting. Right: When variable response thresholds is combined with variable response duration, the delayed reaction resulting from longer response durations mitigates corner cutting.

5   Conclusions

In this work, we examine the impact of variable response duration on the ability of a decentralized swarm to self-organize. We demonstrate that inter-agent variation in response duration serves to desynchronize agent actions, improving self-organization. A side effect of variable response duration is delayed response to changing task demands when compared to swarms in which all agents undergo task selection in every timestep. We can mitigate this effect with knowledge of the target path. Tracking of paths with more frequent changes in task demands benefits from higher `prob_check` values (more frequent task selection).

A priori knowledge of a problem is not always possible and we may not be able to choose effective `prob_check` values. Thus, we combine variation in response duration with variation in response thresholds. We show that these forms of inter-agent variation are complementary due to using different mechanisms for desynchronization. The delayed response due to response duration counters the tendency to cut corners caused by use of response thresholds alone. Thus, for the tracking problem, this combination appears to be beneficial.

One limitation of this work is that we consider only a single problem domain. In future work, we plan to use additional problems to test the utility of response duration. In addition, we will explore combinations of response duration with other forms of inter-agent variation to determine if similar synergies exist.

References

1. Agassounon, W., Martinoli, A.: Efficiency and robustness of threshold-based distributed allocation algorithms in multi-agent systems. In: Proceedings of the International Conference on Autonomous Agents and Multi-Agent Systems, pp. 1090–1097 (2002)
2. Campos, M., Bonabeau, E., Theraulaz, G., Deneubourg, J.: Dynamic scheduling and division of labor in social insects. Adapt. Behav. **8**, 83–96 (2000)
3. Castello, E., et al.: Adaptive foraging for simulated and real robotic swarms: the dynamical response threshold approach. Swarm Intell. **10**, 1–31 (2018)
4. Castello, E., Yamamoto, T., Nakamura, Y., Ishiguro, H.: Task allocation for a robotic swarm based on an adaptive response threshold model. In: Proceedings of the 13th IEEE International Conference on Control, Automation, and Systems, pp. 259–266 (2013)
5. Cicirello, V.A., Smith, S.F.: Distributed coordination of resources via wasp-like agents. In: Truszkowski, W., Hinchey, M., Rouff, C. (eds.) WRAC 2002. LNCS (LNAI), vol. 2564, pp. 71–80. Springer, Heidelberg (2003). https://doi.org/10.1007/978-3-540-45173-0_5
6. de Lope, J., Maravall, D., Quinonez, Y.: Response threshold models and stochastic learning automata for self-coordination of heterogeneous multi-task distribution in multi-robot systems. Rob. Auton. Syst. **61**, 714–720 (2013)
7. de Lope, J., Maravall, D., Quinonez, Y.: Self-organizing techniques to improve the decentralized multi-task distribution in multi-robot systems. Neurocomputing **163**, 47–55 (2015)
8. dos Santos, F., Bazzan, A.L.C.: An ant based algorithm for task allocation in large-scale and dynamic multiagent scenarios. In: Proceedings of the Genetic and Evolutionary Computation Conference, pp. 73–80 (2009)
9. Gautrais, J., Theraulaz, G., Deneubourg, J., Anderson, C.: Emergent polyethism as a consequence of increase colony size in insect societies. J. Theor. Biol. **215**, 363–373 (2002)

10. Goldingay, H., van Mourik, J.: The effect of load on agent-based algorithms for distributed task allocation. Inf. Sci. **222**, 66–80 (2013)
11. Jones, C., Mataric, M.J.: Adaptive division of labor in large-scale minimalist multi-robot systems. In: Proceedings of the IEEE/RSJ International Conference on Intelligent Robots and Systems, pp. 1969–1974 (2003)
12. Kanakia, A., Touri, B., Correll, N.: Modeling multi-robot task allocation with limited information as global game. Swarm Intell. **10**(2), 147–160 (2016). https://doi.org/10.1007/s11721-016-0123-4
13. Kazakova, V.A., Wu, A.S.: Specialization vs. re-specialization: effects of Hebbian learning in a dynamic environment. In: Proceedings of the 31st International Florida Artificial Intelligence Research Society Conference, pp. 354–359 (2018)
14. Kazakova, V.A., Wu, A.S., Sukthankar, G.R.: Respecializing swarms by forgetting reinforced thresholds. Swarm Intell. **14**(3), 171–204 (2020). https://doi.org/10.1007/s11721-020-00181-3
15. Krieger, M.J.B., Billeter, J.B.: The call of duty: self-organised task allocation in a population of up to twelve mobile robots. Rob. Auton. Syst. **30**, 65–84 (2000)
16. Lee, W., Kim, D.: History-based response threshold model for division of labor in multi-agent systems. Sensors **17**, 1232 (2017)
17. Liu, W., Winfield, A., Sa, J., Chen, J., Dou, L.: Towards energy optimisation: emergent task allocation in a swarm of foraging robots. Adapt. Behav. **15**, 289–305 (2007)
18. Meyer, B., Weidenmuller, A., Chen, R., Garcia, J.: Collective homeostatis and time-resolved models of self-organised task allocation. In: Proceedings of the 9th EIA International Conference on Bio-inspired Information and Communication Technologies, pp. 469–478 (2015)
19. Price, R., Tiňo, P.: Evaluation of adaptive nature inspired task allocation against alternate decentralised multiagent strategies. In: Yao, X., et al. (eds.) PPSN 2004. LNCS, vol. 3242, pp. 982–990. Springer, Heidelberg (2004). https://doi.org/10.1007/978-3-540-30217-9_99
20. Riggs, C., Wu, A.S.: Variation as an element in multi-agent control for target tracking. In: Proceedings of the IEEE/RSJ International Conference on Intelligent Robots and Systems, pp. 834–841 (2012)
21. Theraulaz, G., Bonabeau, E., Deneubourg, J.: Response threshold reinforcement and division of labour in insect societies. Proc. Roy. Soc. B **265**, 327–332 (1998)
22. Weidenmüller, A.: The control of nest climate in bumblebee (*Bombus terrestris*) colonies: interindividual variability and self reinforcement in fanning response. Behav. Ecol. **15**, 120–128 (2004)
23. Wu, A.S., Mathias, H.D., Giordano, J.P., Hevia, A.: Effects of response threshold distribution on dynamic division of labor in decentralized swarms. In: Proceedings of the 33rd International Florida Artificial Intelligence Research Society Conference (2020)
24. Wu, A.S., Riggs, C.: Inter-agent variation improves dynamic decentralized task allocation. In: Proceedings of the 31st International Florida Artificial Intelligence Research Society Conference, pp. 366–369 (2018)
25. Yasuda, T., Kage, K., Ohkura, K.: Response threshold-based task allocation in a reinforcement learning robotic swarm. In: Proceedings of the 7th IEEE International Workshop on Computational Intelligence and Applications, pp. 189–194 (2014)

Inflationary Differential Evolution for Constrained Multi-objective Optimisation Problems

Gianluca Filippi[(✉)] and Massimiliano Vasile

James Weir Building, 75 Montrose St, Glasgow G1 1XJ, Scotland
{g.filippi,massimiliano.vasile}@strath.ac.uk

Abstract. In this paper we review several parameter-based scalarisation approaches used within Multi-Objective Optimisation. We propose then a proof-of-concept for a new memetic algorithm designed to solve the Constrained Multi-Objective Optimisation Problem. The algorithm is finally tested on a benchmark with a series of difficulties.

Keywords: Constrained multi-objective optimisation · Scalarisation · Memetic algorithm

1 Introduction

Many real-word problems involve several competing objectives that have to be concurrently optimised. Most everyday decisions are based on intuition and common sense. However areas as engineering, physics, economics, etc. require more rigorous mathematical modelling and programming [14, 20, 25]. This paper deals with Multi-Objective Optimisation Problems (MOPs) and in particular with deterministic and continuous Constrained Multi-Objective Optimisation Problems (CMOPs) [22].

There are mainly three approaches for Multi-Objective Optimisation (MOO) [13, 22]. The *a posteriori* methods, based on the definition of a partial order, calculate a set of equally valuable solutions. The decision maker then, informed of this trade-off, chooses within the set. In the *a priori* methods the decision maker is required to specify additional preferences to define a total order between different options, for example by defining an utility function. The optimisation eventually finds a single minimal solution. The *interactive* methods finally require feedback and preferences from the user multiple time during the execution of the algorithm. We are here interested in the posterior approaches for which the whole set of possible solutions can be generated by two algorithmic methods: the direct multi-objective approach or the parameter-based scalarisation procedure. For the former, the interested reader can find useful information in [6, 8] while we dedicate this paper to the latter. By scalarisation we mean that the different objectives are aggregated and then a Single-Objective Optimisation Problem (SOP) is solved. By using different parameters of the aggregation function finally

B. Filipič et al. (Eds.): BIOMA 2020, LNCS 12438, pp. 29–42, 2020.
https://doi.org/10.1007/978-3-030-63710-1_3

the MOP is translated to a number of SOPs and the set of optimal solutions is reconstructed [17].

We propose the use of Evolutionary Computation (EC) for the solution of the scalarisation problem. This methodology has indeed become popular showing excellent performance. Many dialects of EC have been developed and in this paper we present an advancement of the memetic algorithm Multi–Population Adaptive Inflationary Differential Evolution Algorithm (MP-AIDEA) [10] where Weighted Chebyshev Scalarisation (WCS) is combined with Pascoletti-Serafini Scalarissation (PSS) together with a novel constraint handling approach.

A review of the possible approaches to Constrained Optimsation Problem (COP) in general is in [11] and to penalty functions in particular is in [23]. We propose here an indirect approach with an adaptive exterior penalty function for hard constraint handling.

The assessment of the quality of a MOO algorithm is a delicate matter. Useful indications on how to categorise difficulties in MOPs have been described in [7]. A benchmark based on these information has been defined in [26] while the complexity introduced by a constrained search space has been included in [9]. Taking inspiration from [5] we finally extend the test cases in [26] introducing constraint functions that disconnect the objective space.

The paper is structured as follows. Section 2 presents an overview of basic concepts about MOP and MOO. In particular, Sect. 2.1 presents the criteria used to order different solutions, Sect. 2.2 defines the optimisation problem that is analysed in the following of the paper and Sect. 2.3 presents the normalisation procedure. Section 3 reviews the most common and promising approaches for parameter-based scalarisation. Section 4 describes our approach. Section 5 presents the benchmark and the algorithm tuning. Section 6 gives the results. Section 7 finally concludes.

2   Basic Concepts

We start by giving some basic definitions from MOO that will be used in the following.

2.1   Ordering Criteria

Consider the two generic non empty sets $\mathbb{K} \subset \mathbb{R}^s$ and $\mathbb{S} \subset \mathbb{R}^s$, with $s \in \mathbb{N}$.

Definition 1 (Cone). *The set $\mathbb{K}$ is called a cone if $\mathbf{k} \in \mathbb{K}, \lambda \geq 0 \implies \lambda\mathbf{k} \in \mathbb{K}$. Pointedness of $\mathbb{K}$ means that $\mathbb{K} \cap -\mathbb{K} = \{0_{\mathbb{R}}\}$. The set $\mathbb{S}$ is said to be bounded below with respect to the cone $\mathbb{K}$ if there exist $\mathbf{s} \in \mathbb{R}^s$ such that $\mathbb{S} \subset \mathbf{s} + \mathbb{K}$.*

Definition 2 (Dominance). *A point $\mathbf{s} \in \mathbb{S}$ is said to be K-minimal for $\mathbb{S}$ if $(\mathbf{s} - \mathbb{K}) \cap \mathbb{S} = \{\mathbf{s}\}$. It is instead defined weakly K-minimal if $(\mathbf{s} - int(\mathbb{K})) \cap \mathbb{S} = \{\mathbf{s}\}$ where $int(\mathbb{K})$ is the interior of $\mathbb{K}$. It is finally defined properly K-minimal (in the sense of Benson [2]) if it is a minimal point for $\mathbb{S}$ and also $0_{\mathbb{R}}$ is a minimal* point of $cl(cone(\mathbb{S} + \mathbb{K} - \{\mathbf{s}\}))$ where $cl(\mathbb{S})$ is the closure of $\mathbb{S}$. The set of all the (weakly) K-minimal points is called the (weakly) efficient set $(\varepsilon_w(\mathbb{S}))$ $\varepsilon(\mathbb{S})$.

In the case $\mathbb{K} = \mathbb{R}^m_+$ the K-minimal points are also called Edgeworth-Pareto (EP)-minimal points and the K-dominance become the more famous Pareto dominance.

2.2 Problem Statement

The scalarisation approaches presented in the paper are applied to the following CMOP:

$$\begin{aligned} \text{minimise} \quad & \mathbf{f}(\mathbf{x}) = [f_1, f_2, ..., f_m]^T \\ \text{subject to} \quad & c_i(\mathbf{x}) \le 0, \quad i = 1, ..., n \\ & \mathbf{x} \in \mathbb{X} \end{aligned} \tag{1}$$

with $\mathbb{X} \subset \mathbb{R}^n$ the parameter space, $m, n \in \mathbb{N}$, $m \ge 2$ and $\mathbb{Y} = \{\mathbf{f}(\mathbf{x}) \text{ s.t. } \mathbf{x} \in \mathbb{X}, g_j(\mathbf{x}) \le 0, j = 1, ..., n\}$ the feasible objective space. We require that f_i and g_j are locally $\mathcal{C}^2$.

In the following we will assume that the closed convex pointed cone $\mathbb{K}$ introduces an anti-symmetric partial order $\le_K$ in the objective space $\mathbb{Y}$. The cone $\mathbb{K}$ is then used to define the efficient set in the objective space $\varepsilon(\mathbb{Y})$ and the corresponding efficient set in the parameter space $\varepsilon(\mathbb{X})$.

2.3 Normalisation

In case of prior knowledge about the reference points $\mathbf{z}^*$ (best) and $\mathbf{z}^{**}$ (worst), the objective functions $\mathbf{f}$ can be normalised in order to reduce the difference in the order of magnitude between the components f_i:

$$\bar{\mathbf{f}} = \frac{\mathbf{f} - \mathbf{z}^*}{\mathbf{z}^{**} - \mathbf{z}^*}. \tag{2}$$

$\mathbf{z}^*$ and $\mathbf{z}^{**}$ can be defined as reference solutions by the decision maker. However $\mathbf{z}^*$ usually corresponds to the ideal point $\mathbf{z}_{ideal}$ or to the utopian point $\mathbf{z}_{utopian}$ while $\mathbf{z}^{**}$ corresponds to the nadir point $\mathbf{z}_{nadir}$. A visualisation of $\mathbf{z}_{ideal}$, $\mathbf{z}_{utopian}$ and $\mathbf{z}_{nadir}$ is in Fig. 1 for a MOP with two objective functions f_1 and f_2. They are theoretic points that collapse the extreme behaviour of the different solutions in the Pareto front. $\mathbf{z}_{ideal}$ is the combination of the best solutions for the different objectives. $\mathbf{z}_{nadir}$ represents instead the worst possible combination of points. $\mathbf{z}_{utopian}$, is finally defined by means of an ϵ from $\mathbf{z}_{ideal}$. The points $\mathbf{z}_{ideal}$ and $\mathbf{z}_{nadir}$ will be used in the following of the paper while $\mathbf{z}_{utopian}$ has been here introduced for the sake of completeness.

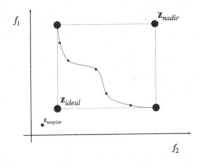

Fig. 1. Representation of utopian, ideal and nadir points for a generic bi-objective optimisation problem.

3   Review of Scalarisation Strategies

This section reviews the most important parameter-based scalarisation approaches: Epsilon-Constraint Scalarisation (ECS), Weighted-Sum Scalarisation (WSS), Benson Scalarisation (BS), WCS and PSS.

We consider a generic preference vector $\omega = [\omega_1, ..., \omega_m]^T$ for the objective functions $\mathbf{f} = [f_1, f_2, ..., f_m]^T$ and a generic reference point $a = \mathbf{z}^*$. ω and a can be either defined a priory by the decision maker or (as stated in Sect. 1 and used in Sect. 4) made varying in order to reconstruct the entire efficient set.

The scalarisation methods are compared in Table 1 as in [19] where the following criteria have been considered: the possibility to use different ordering cones, the necessity or not of boundedness and convexity conditions, the provability for obtaining properly efficient solutions, the use of reference and preference information and the introduction by the method of additional constraint functions.

Table 1. Characteristics of six scalarisation methods

Method	WSS	ECS	BC	WCS	PSS	CS
Ordering cone	any	$\mathbb{R}_+^m$	$\mathbb{R}_+^m$	$\mathbb{R}_+^m$	any	any
Boundedness from below	−	−	−	+	−	−
Convexity	+	−	−	−	−	−
Proof of properly efficient solutions	+	−	−	−	−	+
Preference weights	+	−	−	+	−	+
Reference points	−	−	−	−	+	+
Additional constraints or variables	−	+	+	+	+	−

3.1   Epsilon Constraint Scalarisation

The ECS was introduced by Haimes et al. in 1971 [18]. In this approach, one of the functions in $\mathbf{f}$ in Eq. (1) is maintained as the objective while the remaining functions are treated as inequality constraints

$$\min_{\mathbf{x} \in X} f_i$$
$$\text{s.t.} \quad f_k \leq \epsilon_k \quad k \in \{1, ..., m\} \setminus \{i\} \tag{3}$$
$$c_j \leq 0 \quad \forall j \in \{1, ..., n\}$$

The boundedness from below for the ECS is not an essential condition. However, the set of thresholds ϵ_k has to be decided carefully by the decision maker. A wrong selection, indeed, could bring to a not finite optimal solution or to an infeasible solution. The ECS can be applied only in the case when the ordering cone equals $\mathbb{R}^m_+$. The method does not require convexity condition on the problem under consideration. It generates weakly efficient solutions and does not provide conditions for generating properly efficient solutions. Decision maker's preferences, namely weights of objectives and reference points, are not taken into account. Finally, the problem size increases due to adding the constraints.

3.2   Weighted-Sum Scalarisation

The WSS was suggested by Gass and Saaty [16] in 1955 and it is probably the most commonly used scalarization technique for MOP. Here the Eq. (1) translates to:

$$\min_{\mathbf{x} \in X} \sum_{i=1}^{n} \omega_i f_i \tag{4}$$

As for the ECS the boundedness below is not required but in that case the weights ω have to be chosen carefully. Weakly and properly efficient solutions are guaranteed under the convexity condition. Weights of objectives are used but reference points are not considered. The method does not introduce additional constraints.

3.3   Benson's Scalarisation

The method was introduced in [1]. Here an initial guess $\mathbf{x}_0$ is given by the decision maker. The sum of the deviations l_i is maximised to find a new dominating point:

$$\max_{\mathbf{x} \in X} \sum_{i=1}^{n} l_i$$
$$\text{s.t.} \quad f_i(\mathbf{x}_0) - l_i - f_i(\mathbf{x}) = 0 \quad i = 1, ..., m$$
$$l \geq 0 \tag{5}$$
$$c_j \leq 0 \quad \forall j = 1, 2, ..., n$$

The BS requires the ordering cone $\mathbb{K}$ to equal $\mathbb{R}^m_+$. The boundedness below is not a requirement, however if the condition is not satisfied, more attention has to be put on the selection of x_0. There is no necessity for the problem to be convex. BS provides necessary and sufficient conditions to converge to efficient solutions, but not to properly efficient solutions. Preferences from the decision maker are not taken into account. Finally, besides functions c_j, additional constraints are considered.

3.4   Weighted Chebyshev Scalarisation

The idea of the WCS is first presented in [3]. The Eq. (1) translates to:

$$\begin{aligned}
&\min_{\mathbf{x}\in\mathbb{X}} \|\mathbf{f} - \mathbf{z}_{\text{ideal}}\|_{\infty}^{\omega} \\
&\text{s.t.} \quad c_j \leq 0 \quad \forall j = 1, 2, ..., n
\end{aligned} \tag{6}$$

where $\|\mathbf{f} - \mathbf{z}_{ideal}\|_{\infty}^{\omega}$ is the weighted Chebyshev distance $\max_i\{\omega_i(f_i - z_{ideal,i}\}$ between $\mathbf{f}(\mathbf{x}) \in \mathbb{Y}$ and the ideal point $\mathbf{z}_{\text{ideal}}$.

The linearisation is often considered:

$$\begin{aligned}
&\min_{\mathbf{x}\in\mathbb{X}, t\in\mathbb{R}} t \\
&\text{s.t.} \quad \omega_i(f_i - z_{\text{ideal},i}) \leq t, \forall i = 1, 2, ..., m \\
&\qquad\quad c_j \leq 0, \qquad\qquad\quad \forall j = 1, 2, ..., n
\end{aligned} \tag{7}$$

The WCS requires the cone $\mathbb{K}$ to be $\mathbb{R}_+^m$. The bondedness below is a necessary condition for the existence of $\mathbf{z}_{\text{ideal}}$. Instead the convexity assumption is not needed. The method assures generation of weakly efficient solutions and efficient solutions. However it is not guaranteed to generate properly efficient solutions. The preference vector $\boldsymbol{\omega}$ over the objective space is considered. The ideal point could be considered as a special case for the reference point. However the solutions are not guaranteed to be close to the reference point. In the linearised version, the size of the problem is increased by new constraints.

3.5   Pascoletti-Serafini Scalarisation

A first description of the PSS is given by Gerstewitz in [4]. As stated in [12], the PSS is a generalisation of ECS, WSS and WCS and it can be represented as:

$$\begin{aligned}
&\min_{\mathbf{x}\in\mathbb{X}} t \\
&\text{s.t.} \quad a + tr - f(x) \in \mathbb{K} \\
&\qquad\quad c_j \leq 0, \qquad\qquad \forall j = 1, 2, ..., n
\end{aligned} \tag{8}$$

Equation (8) can be interpreted as the process where the ordering cone $\mathbb{K}$ is moved in the direction $-r$ along the line $a + tr$ minimising the intersection $(a + tr - \mathbb{K}) \cap f(\mathbb{X})$ until it becomes the empty set.

An arbitrary ordering cone can be adopted. The boundedness below and the convexity are not required conditions. The method guarantees to get at least weakly efficient solutions but it does not provide conditions to generate properly efficient solutions. It does use reference points but not preference vectors. Finally it uses additional functional constraints.

3.6   Conic Scalarisation

The Conic Scalarisation (CS) method was first introduced by Gasimov in [15] where beside the preference weighted vector $\boldsymbol{\omega}$ and the reference point $\mathbf{a}$, the augmentation parameter $\boldsymbol{\alpha}$ is considered:

$$\min_{\mathbf{x} \in \mathbb{X}} \sum_i \omega_i (f_i - a_i) + \alpha \sum_i |\omega_i (f_i - a_i)|$$
$$s.t. \quad c_j \leq 0 \qquad\qquad \forall j = 1, 2, ..., n \tag{9}$$

As stated in [19], CS is a generalisation of WSS, BS and PSS. An arbitrary ordering cone can be used. The boundedness below is not an essential condition. No convexity is required. There are also conditions that guarantee to generate properly efficient minimal points. Preference and reference information is used. Finally, no additional constraints are required.

4   Memetic Strategy for the Constrained Scalarisation

We make the reasonable assumptions that the MOP is bounded below, which is usually satisfied for engineering problems, that no other cone than $\mathbb{R}^m_+$ is necessary and that we are interested in efficient solutions and not necessary in proper efficient solutions. For these reasons we have implemented in the memetic optimiser MP-AIDEA [10] a combination of WCS and PSS in order to solve CMOPs with the scalarisation approach.

4.1   Scalarisation Approach

We briefly describe here the extension of MP-AIDEA [10] highlighting the differences that have been introduced. The general structure of the algorithm is summarised in Algorithm 1. A set of N_{pop} different populations with n_{pop} elements each are first initialised: either a first guess is used or they are defined randomly. The optimisation process then hybridises the Differential Evolution (DE) step (line 3) where the N_{pop} populations are evolved and the local search (line 6) where their best candidate solutions are refined. The number of local refinements is adapted within MP-AIDEA allowing them to be run only if the converged solution in the DE is outside the basins of attraction of the previous recorded local minima which depend on the distances between previous best solutions of the DE and best solutions of the local search. More information about this point can be found in [10]. The DE is then locally and globally restarted (line 10) until the maximum number of evaluations $n_{\mathrm{feval,max}}$ (considering both DE and local search) of the objective function is achieved (termination condition in line 2). In particular, the number of local restarts n_{LR} for each population and the corresponding dimension of the bubble δ_{local} where the starting vector is initialised are both auto-adapted within the algorithm. The radius of the bubble for the global restart δ_{global} and the convergence threshold ρ of DE are instead defined by the user.

More details about the DE step are in Algorithm 2. The building blocks that make any Evolutionary Algorithm (EA) are: initialisation (line 2), variation (line 6), evaluation (lines 3 and 7), selection (line 8) and termination (line 4). In particular, the population at the first generation $(G = 1)$ is defined from Algorithm 1. Within the main loop (lines 4–10) all the agents at the current generation G are selected as parents and are subjected to the variation step for the definition of generation G+1. The two schemes DE/Rand/1/bin and DE/CurrentToBest/2/bin [24] have been implemented for the parent's variation. The best for each agent between the corresponding parent at generation G and offspring at generation G+1 is finally selected. The differences here introduced in the DE to solve the scalarisation problem affect only the evaluation of the fitness function of the candidate solutions. To translate the MOP presented in Eq. (1) to a single objective problem we propose, within the DE, to apply the WCS described in Sect. 3.4:

$$\min_{\mathbf{x} \in \mathbb{X}} \max_i \{\omega_i (f_i - z_{\text{ideal},i})\} \; \forall i = 1, 2, ..., m$$
$$\text{s.t.} \quad g_j \leq 0 \qquad\qquad \forall j = 1, 2, ..., n \tag{10}$$

when the problem is not normalised, and

$$\min_{\mathbf{x} \in \mathbb{X}} \max_i \{\omega_i \bar{f}_i\} \; \forall i = 1, 2, ..., m$$
$$\text{s.t.} \quad c_j \leq 0 \quad \forall j = 1, 2, ..., n \tag{11}$$

when it is normalised. During the local search, instead, the PSS described in Eq. (8) is implemented because a differentiable fitness function is required. The following constrained minimisation problem is then considered

$$\min_{\mathbf{x} \in \mathbb{X}, t \in \mathbb{R}} t$$
$$\text{s.t.} \quad \omega_i (f_i - z_i) \leq t, \forall i = 1, 2, ..., m \tag{12}$$
$$\quad c_j \leq 0, \qquad\qquad \forall j = 1, 2, ..., n$$

when the problem is not normalised and

$$\min_{\mathbf{x} \in \mathbb{X}, t \in \mathbb{R}} t$$
$$\text{s.t.} \quad \omega_i (\bar{f}_i - \bar{z}_i) \leq t, \forall i = 1, 2, ..., m \tag{13}$$
$$\quad c_j \leq 0, \qquad\qquad \forall j = 1, 2, ..., n$$

when it is normalised. In Eqs. (12) and (13) z_i $(\bar{z}_i)$ is the best candidate solution f_i $(\bar{f}_i)$ obtained in the previous DE. As stated in [12], Eqs. (12) and (13) could be considered as a reformulation (a linearisation) of the WCS where an additional variable is introduced and where the direction $r_i = 1/\omega_i$. However we consider here a different reference than the ideal point $\mathbf{z}_{\text{ideal}}$.

4.2   Constraint Handling

Within the DE step and with reference to [11,23] we propose the following indirect approach with an adaptive exterior penalty function for hard constraint

---

Algorithm 1. MP-AIDEA for the scalarisation problem

1: Initialisation
2: **while** $n_{\text{feval}} < n_{\text{feval,max}}$ **do**
3:    *Run the DE step* (Algorithm 2)
4:    **for** $p \in [1, 2, ..., N_{\text{pop}}]$ **do**
5:      **if** $\mathbf{x}_{p,\text{best}}$ not in the basin of attraction of previous solutions **then**
6:        *Run local search* (Eq. (12)) with $\mathbf{x}_{0,p} = \mathbf{x}_{\text{best},p}$, $t_{0,p} = 0$ and the reference
        vector $\mathbf{z}_p$: $\min_{\mathbf{x}\in\mathbb{X}, t\in\mathbb{R}} t$ s.t. $\omega_i(f_i(\mathbf{x}) - z_i) \leq t \wedge c_j(\mathbf{x}) \leq 0$, $\forall i = 1, 2, ..., m$, $\forall j = 1, 2, ..., n$
7:        update $\mathbf{x}_{p,\text{best}}$ from the local search.
8:      **end if**
9:    **end for**
10:   *Initialise* populations for local or global restart in the next DE step [10].
11: **end while**

Algorithm 2. DE step

1: **for** $p \in [1, 2, ..., N_{\text{pop}}]$ **do**
2:   *Initialise* (input) the genotype $\mathbf{x}_{p,q}^{(G)}$ for the p-population at generation $G = 1$
   where $q = 1, 2, ..., n_{\text{pop}}$
3:   *Evaluate* the phenotype of each candidate solution: $f_{s,p,q}^{(G)}$ (Algorithm 3)
4:   **while** the population is not contracted **do**
5:    *Select* parents: all generation G;
6:    *Variate* the parent's genotype: two strategies randomly alternated
    (DE/Rand/1/bin, DE/CurrentToBest/2/bin) define generation $G+1$;
7:    *Evaluate* new candidates $f_{s,p,q}^{(G+1)}$ (Algorithm 3):
8:    *Select* between parents and children with a greedy criterion
9:    update generation: $G = G+1$.
10:   **end while**
11:   $\mathbf{x}_{p,\text{best}} = \arg\min_i f_{s,p,q}^{(\text{end})}(\mathbf{x}_{p,q})$;
12:   $\mathbf{z}_p = \{f_1(\mathbf{x}_{p,\text{best}}), f_2(\mathbf{x}_{p,\text{best}}), ..., f_m(\mathbf{x}_{p,\text{best}})\}$.
13: **end for**

Algorithm 3. DE, Evaluation

1: **for** each q-agent in the population, with $q \in [1, 2, ..., n_{\text{pop}}]$ **do**
2:   $f_{s,p,q} = \max_i \{\omega_i(f_i(\mathbf{x}_{p,q}) - z_{\text{ideal},i})\}$, $i \in [1, 2, ..., m]$
3:   $c_{p,q} = \max_j \{c_j(\mathbf{x}_{p,q})\}$, $j \in [1, ..., n]$
4: **end for**
5: **for** each q-agent with $k \in [1, 2, ..., n_{\text{pop}}]$ **do**
6:   **if** $c_{p,q} > 0$ **then**
7:    $f_{s,p,q} = \max_i \{f_{s,p,q}\} + c_{p,q}$
8:   **end if**
9: **end for**

---

handling where hardness refers to the absolute satisfaction of the constraint. By 'indirect approach' we mean that the COP is translated to a Free Optimisation Problem (FOP): this type of constraint handling is done before the EA run. The following mapping is used:

$$f_s(\mathbf{x}_{p,q}) = \begin{cases} f_s(\mathbf{x}_{p,q}) & \text{if } \max_i c_i(\mathbf{x}_p) \leq 0 \\ \max_q\{f_s(\mathbf{x}_{p,q})\} + \max_j\{c_j(\mathbf{x}_{p,q})\} & \text{else} \end{cases} \tag{14}$$

where, for a generic population, f_s is the scalarised value of $\mathbf{f}$ for the given agent q in the population p, $\max_q\{f_s(\mathbf{x}_{p,q})\}$ is the maximum of f_s over the current population and $\max_j\{c_j(\mathbf{x}_{p,q})\}$ is the maximum constraint violation for the considered element q. Algorithm 3 summarises the fitness evaluation within the DE step including also the constraint handling.

For the local search (line 6 of Algorithm 1) instead the constraints in Eqs. (12) and (13) are directly handled within the nonlinear programming solver *fmincon* [21].

5   Testing Procedure

5.1   Benchmark

The test functions used in this paper have been selected from [26] where a benchmark for unconstrained MOPs is defined. A set of constraints $\mathbf{c}$ inspired by [5] has been further introduced to increase the complexity by disconnecting the feasible set $\mathbb{Y}$. A similar benchmark generation can be found in [9].

The general structure of each bi-objective optimisation problem is:

$$\begin{aligned} &\text{minimise}\, \mathcal{T} = [f_1, f_2]^T \\ &\text{where}\quad f_1 = f_1(x_1) \\ &\qquad\quad f_2 = g(x_2,...,x_m)h(f_1(x_1), g(x_2,...,x_m)) \\ &\text{s.t.}\quad c_i \leq 0,\ \ i = 1,...,n \\ &\qquad\quad \mathbf{x} \in \Omega \end{aligned} \tag{15}$$

where for all the test cases it is considered that $i \in \{1,2\}$ and the constraint functions are:

$$\begin{aligned} c_1 &: 1.69x_1^2 + 1.01(gh)^2 - 2.6x_1(gh) - 0.02 \geq 0 \\ c_2 &: (x_1 - 0.5)^2 + (gh - 0.5)^2 - 0.5 \leq 0. \end{aligned} \tag{16}$$

The objective functions $\mathcal{T}_{1,2,3}$ are presented in the following.

Test Case 1. $\mathcal{T}_1$ has a convex Pareto front

$$\begin{aligned} f_1(x_1) &= x_1 \\ g(x_2,...,x_m) &= 1 + 9/(m-1)\sum_{i=2}^{m} x_i \\ h(f_1, g) &= 1 - \sqrt{f_1/g} \end{aligned} \tag{17}$$

where $m = 30$ and $x_i \in [0,1]$. The Pareto optimal front is at $g(\mathbf{x}) = 1$.

Test Case 2. T_2 is the non-convex counterpart of T_1

$$f_1(x_1) = x_1$$
$$g(x_2, ..., x_m) = 1 + 9/(m-1) \sum_{i=2}^{m} x_i \qquad (18)$$
$$h(f_1, g) = 1 - (f_1/g)^2$$

where $m = 30$ and $x_i \in [0, 1]$. The Pareto optimal front is at $g(\mathbf{x}) = 1$.

Test Case 3. T_3 presents the discreteness: the Pareto front is divided in several non continuous convex parts:

$$f_1(x_1) = x_1$$
$$g(x_2, ..., x_m) = 1 + 9/(m-1) \sum_{i=2}^{m} x_i \qquad (19)$$
$$h(f_1, g) = 1 - \sqrt{f_1/g} - (f_1/g)\sin(10\pi f_1)$$

where $m = 10$ and $x_i \in [0, 1]$. The Pareto optimal front is at $g(\mathbf{x}) = 1$.

5.2 Tuning

This section presents the tuning procedure applied to the modified version of MP-AIDEA presented in Sect. 4.1 and its results. The maximum number of function evaluations for each test problem has been fixed to $n_{\text{feval,max}} = 5e4$. The combination of the following parameters instead have been tuned: the number of populations $N_{\text{pop}} \in \{2, 4\}$, the number of agents in each populations $n_{\text{pop}} \in \{30, 45\}$, the dimension of the bubble for the global restart $\delta_{\text{global}} \in \{0.15, 0.25\}$ and the convergence threshold $\rho \in \{0.05, 0.15\}$ for the DE step. The efficient set of each problem has been uniformly discretised using 10 trigonometric couple of weights $w_{f1} = \frac{\cos\theta}{\cos\theta + \sin\theta}$ and $w_{f2} = \frac{\sin\theta}{\cos\theta + \sin\theta}$ with $\theta \in [0, \frac{\pi}{2}]$. Each combination of parameter setting and weights have been repeated 10 times. The results have been compared with the analytical Pareto front of $T_{1,...,3}$ and finally the setting with the minimum average error has been selected. The tuning's results are presented in Table 2.

Table 2. MP-AIDEA tuning results

T	N_{pop}	n_{pop}	δ_{global}	ρ
1	2	45	0.25	0.05
2	2	45	0.25	0.05
3	4	45	0.25	0.05

6 Results

The efficient sets for $T_{1,2,3}$ are finally plotted in Fig. 2 for 10 equally spaced preferences weights $w_{f1} = \frac{\cos\theta}{\cos\theta + \sin\theta}$ and $w_{f2} = \frac{\sin\theta}{\cos\theta + \sin\theta}$ where $\theta \in [0, \frac{\pi}{2}]$. As it can be seen in the figures, the approach proposed in Sect. 4.1 is capable to find the efficient set for the MOP satisfying the constraint functions. In particular it has been noted that the implementation of the multi-population restart within MP-AIDEA is of fundamental importance for such problems, as this benchmark, that have a disconnected objective space.

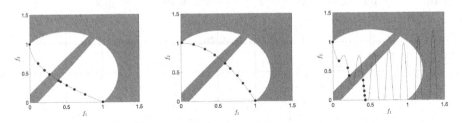

Fig. 2. Efficient sets for $\mathcal{T}_1$ (a), $\mathcal{T}_2$ (b) and $\mathcal{T}_3$ (c). The shaded area represents the unfeasible domain. The black line is the sub-domain containing the global efficient set. Red points are the solution of the proposed method.(Color figure online)

7   Conclusions

In this paper we have presented a review of the most important scalarisation methods for MOPs highlighting the corresponding advantages and disadvantages. We have proposed then a new memetic approach for the solution of CMOPs. A combination of WCS and PSS has been implemented in the memetic optimiser MP-AIDEA in order to translate the MOP to a corresponding set of SOPs. A novel adaptive exterior penalty function has been used for the constraint handling. The approach has been tested demonstrating its capability of finding efficient points. Future steps will regard further analysis of the performance of the proposed algorithm with both comparison between different scalarisation techniques and different optimisation solvers. Finally, besides the parameter-based scalarisation approach, also the direct multi-objective selection will be considered.

References

1. Benson, H.P.: Existence of efficient solutions for vector maximization problems. J. Optim. Theory Appl. **26**(4), 569–580 (1978). https://doi.org/10.1007/BF00933152
2. Benson, H.P.: An improved definition of proper efficiency for vector maximization with respect to cones. J. Math. Anal. Appl. **71**(1), 232–241 (1979). https://doi.org/10.1016/0022-247X(79)90226-9
3. Bowman V.J.: On the relationship of the Tchebycheff norm and the efficient frontier of multiple-criteria objectives. In: Thiriez, H., Zionts, S. (eds) Multiple Criteria Decision Making. Lecture Notes in Economics and Mathematical Systems (Operations Research), vol. 130, pp. 76–86. Springer, Heidelberg (1976). https://doi.org/10.1007/978-3-642-87563-2_5

4. Boţ, R.I., Grad, S.M., Wanka, G.: A general approach for studying duality in multiobjective optimization. Math. Methods Oper. Res. **65**(3), 417–444 (2007). https://doi.org/10.1007/s00186-006-0125-x

5. Burachik, R.S., Kaya, C.Y., Rizvi, M.M.: A new scalarization technique to approximate pareto fronts of problems with disconnected feasible sets. J. Optim. Theory Appl. **162**(2), 428–446 (2013). https://doi.org/10.1007/s10957-013-0346-0

6. Burke, E.K., Graham, K.: Search Methodologies: Introductory Tutorials in Optimization and Decision Support Techniques. Springer, Heidelberg (2014). https://doi.org/10.1007/978-1-4614-6940-7

7. Deb, K.: Multi-objective genetic algorithms: problem difficulties and construction of test problems. Evol. Comput. **7**(3), 205–230 (1998). https://doi.org/10.1162/evco.1999.7.3.205

8. Deb, K.: Multi-objective optimisation using evolutionary algorithms: an introduction. In: Wang, L., Ng, A., Deb ,K. (eds) Multi-objective Evolutionary Optimisation for Product Design and Manufacturing, pp. 1–24. Springer, London (2011). https://doi.org/10.1007/978-0-85729-652-8_1

9. Deb, K., Pratap, A., Meyarivan, T.: Constrained test problems for multi-objective evolutionary optimization. In: Zitzler, E., Thiele, L., Deb, K., Coello Coello, C.A., Corne, D. (eds) Evolutionary Multi-Criterion Optimization. EMO 2001. Lecture Notes in Computer Science, vol. 1993, pp. 284–298 (2001). https://doi.org/10.1007/3-540-44719-9_20

10. Di Carlo, M., Vasile, M., Minisci, E.: Adaptive multi-population inflationary differential evolution. Soft Comput. **24**(5), 3861–3891 (2019). https://doi.org/10.1007/s00500-019-04154-5

11. Eiben, A.E., Smith, J.E.: Introduction to Evolutionary Computing (Natural Computing Series). Springer, Heidelberg (2003). https://doi.org/10.1007/978-3-662-44974-8. www.springer.com/series/

12. Eichfelder, G.: Scalarizations for adaptively solving multi-objective optimization problems. Comput. Optim. Appl. **44**(2), 249–273 (2009). https://doi.org/10.1007/s10589-007-9155-4

13. Emmerich, M.T., Deutz, A.H.: A tutorial on multiobjective optimization: fundamentals and evolutionary methods. Nat. Comput. **17**(3), 585–609 (2018). https://doi.org/10.1007/s11047-018-9685-y

14. Epstein, J.M.: Why model? J. Artif. Soc. Soc. Simul. **11**(4), 12 (2008). http://jasss.soc.surrey.ac.uk/11/4/12.html

15. Gasimov, R.N.: Characterization of the Benson proper efficiency and scalarization in nonconvex vector optimization. In: Koksalan, M., Zionts, S. (eds) Multiple Criteria Decision Making in the New Millennium. Lecture Notes in Economics and Mathematical Systems, vol. 507, pp. 189–198. Springer, Heidelberg (2001). https://doi.org/10.1007/978-3-642-56680-6_17

16. Gass, S., Saaty, T.: The computational algorithm for the parametric objective function. Naval Res. Logist. Q. **2**(1–2), 39–45 (1955). https://doi.org/10.1002/nav.3800020106

17. Gunantara, N.: A review of multi-objective optimization: methods and its applications. Cogent Eng. **5**(1), 1–16 (2018). https://doi.org/10.1080/23311916.2018.1502242

18. Haimes, Y.Y., Lasdon, L.S., Wismer, D.A.: On a bicriterion formation of the problems of integrated system identification and system optimization. IEEE Trans. Syst. Man Cybern. **SMC−1**(3), 296–297 (1971). https://doi.org/10.1109/TSMC.1971.4308298

19. Kasimbeyli, R., Ozturk, Z.K., Kasimbeyli, N., Yalcin, G.D., Erdem, B.I.: Comparison of some scalarization methods in multiobjective optimization: comparison of scalarization methods. Bull. Malays. Math. Sci. Soc. **42**(5), 1875–1905 (2019). https://doi.org/10.1007/s40840-017-0579-4

20. Levins, R.: Strategies of abstraction. Biol. Philos. **21**(5), 741–755 (2006). https://doi.org/10.1007/s10539-006-9052-8

21. MATLAB: 9.7.0.1216025 (R2019b). The MathWorks Inc., Natick, Massachusetts (2018)

22. Miettinen, K.M.: Nonlinear Multiobjective Optimization. Kluwer Academic Publishers Group, Dordrecht (2012)

23. Smith, A.E., Coit, D.W.: Penalty functions. In: Baeck, T., Fogel, D., Michalewicz, Z. (eds.) Handbook of Evolutionary Computation, Chap. 5.2. Oxford University Press, Institute of Physics Publishing (1995). https://doi.org/10.1887/0750308958/b386c48

24. Storn, R., Price, K.: Differential evolution - a simple and efficient heuristic for global optimization over continuous spaces. J. Global Optim. **11**(4), 341–359 (1997). https://doi.org/10.1023/A:1008202821328

25. Wymore, A.W.: Model-Based Systems Engineering. CRC Press, Boca Raton (1993)

26. Zitzler, E., Deb, K., Thiele, L.: Comparison of multiobjective evolutionary algorithms: empirical results. Evol. Comput. **8**(2), 173–195 (2000). https://doi.org/10.1162/106365600568202

An Analysis of Phenotypic Diversity in Multi-solution Optimization

Alexander Hagg[1,2](✉)[iD], Mike Preuss[2][iD], Alexander Asteroth[1][iD], and Thomas Bäck[2][iD]

[1] Bonn-Rhein-Sieg University of Applied Sciences, Sankt Augustin, Germany
{alexander.hagg,alexander.asteroth}@h-brs.de
[2] Leiden Institute of Advanced Computer Science, Leiden University, Leiden, The Netherlands
{m.preuss,t.h.w.baeck}@liacs.leidenuniv.nl

Abstract. More and more, optimization methods are used to find diverse solution sets. We compare solution diversity in multi-objective optimization, multimodal optimization, and quality diversity in a simple domain. We show that multiobjective optimization does not always produce much diversity, multimodal optimization produces higher fitness solutions, and quality diversity is not sensitive to genetic neutrality and creates the most diverse set of solutions. An autoencoder is used to discover phenotypic features automatically, producing an even more diverse solution set with quality diversity. Finally, we make recommendations about when to use which approach.

Keywords: Evolutionary computation · Multimodal optimization · Multi-objective optimization · Quality diversity · Autoencoder

1 Introduction

With the advent of 3D printing and generative design, a new goal in optimization is emerging. Having the option of choosing from different solutions that are good enough to fulfill a task can be more effective than being guided by single-solution algorithms. The optimization field should aim to understand how to solve a problem in different ways.

Three major paradigms for multi-solution optimization exist. The major difference between multi-objective optimization (MOO), multimodal optimization (MMO) and quality diversity (QD) is the context in which solution diversity is maintained. In MOO the goal is to find the Pareto set, which represents the trade-offs between multiple criteria. MMO finds solutions that cover the search space as well as possible. QD finds combinations of phenotypic features to maximize the variation in solutions' expressed shape or behavior - a new focus in evolutionary optimization [17].

This work received funding from the German Federal Ministry of Education and Research (BMBF) (grant agreement no. 03FH012PX5).

B. Filipič et al. (Eds.): BIOMA 2020, LNCS 12438, pp. 43–55, 2020.
https://doi.org/10.1007/978-3-030-63710-1_4

We analyze the diversity of solution sets in the three paradigms and introduce a new niching method that allows comparing genetic and phenotypic diversity (Sect. 2). State of the art diversity metrics (Sect. 3) are used in a new problem domain (Sect. 4) to evaluate all paradigms (Sect. 5) after which we make recommendations when to use which approach (Sect. 6).

2   Diversity in Optimization

The intuitive understanding of diversity assumes that there are more ways to "do" or to "be" something and involves the concepts of *dissimilarity* and *distance*. Evidence can be found in the large number of approaches and metrics, and the lack of agreement in when to use which one. This section gives an overview over three paradigms that have arisen in the last decades.

Finding solutions that are diverse with respect to objective space has been a paradigm since the 1970s. Multi-objective optimization tries to discover the Pareto set of trade-off solutions with respect to two or more objectives. The method has no control over the diversity of genomes or their expression other than the expectation that trade-offs require different solutions. The most successful method is the Non-dominated Sorting Genetic Algorithm (NSGA-II) [5].

The first ideas to use genetic diversity in optimization were not used to find different solutions, but to deal with premature convergence to local optima. The concept of *niching* was integrated into evolutionary optimization by introducing sharing and crowding [6,8]. In the 1990s, multi-local or multimodal optimization came into focus. This paradigm has the explicit goal to find a diverse set of high quality locations in the search space, based on a single criterion. Various algorithms have been introduced, like basin hopping [26], topographical selection [23], nearest-better clustering [16] and restarted local search (RLS) [15].

The introduction of novelty search [11] led to studying the search for novel, non-optimal solutions. QD, reintroducing objectives [3,12], finds a diverse set of high quality optimizers by performing niching in phenotypic space. In applications for developing artificial creatures and robot controller morphologies [3,12], QD only allows solutions that belong the same phenotypic niche to compete. To this end it keeps track of an archive of niches. Solutions are added to the archive if their phenotype is novel enough or better than that of a similar solution.

This work does not aim at giving an exhaustive overview over all methods, for which we refer to some of the many survey papers [1,4,15,21,22,27]. We consciously choose not to talk about methods that combine ideas from the three paradigms, but rather compare the three paradigms in their "purest" form.

2.1   Niching with Voronoi Tessellation

To remove variations in the search dynamics when comparing different algorithms, we introduce a niching variant using ideas from Novelty Search with Local Competition (NSLC) [12] and CVT-Elites [25]. Voronoi-Elites (VE) accepts all new solutions until the maximum number of archive bins is surpassed (Algorithm 1). Then the pair of elites that are phenotypically closest to each other are compared, rejecting the worst-performing. An example archive is shown in Fig. 6 at step five). By locating selection pressure on the closest solutions, VE tries to equalize the distances between individuals. The generators of the Voronoi cells do not have to coincide with the centroids, like in CVT-Elites, and the boundaries of the archive are not fixed. VE can be used to compare archive spaces of different dimensionality. When the genetic parameters are used as archive dimensions, VE behaves like an MMO algorithm by performing niching in genetic space. When we use phenotypic descriptors, VE behaves like a QD algorithm.

Algorithm 1. Voronoi-Elites

   Initialize population
   for iter 1 to n **do**
      Select parents $\mathcal{P}$ randomly
      Mutate $\mathcal{P}$ using normal distribution to create offspring $\mathcal{O}$
      Evaluate performance and descriptors of $\mathcal{O}$
      Add $\mathcal{O}$ to archive $\mathcal{A}$
      while $|\mathcal{A}| > maxSize$ **do**
         Find pair in $\mathcal{A}$ with smallest distance
         Remove individual (in pair) with lowest fitness
      end while
   end for

2.2   Related Work

A number of survey and analysis articles have appeared in the last decade. In [1] a taxonomy for diversity in optimization was introduced. [28] investigates how genetically diverse solution sets in MOO are found and shows that quality indicators used in MOO can be applied to MMO. [24] compares two algorithms from MMO to two QD algorithms in a robotics task, showing that clearing's performance can be comparable to that of QD. Finally, [13] discusses 100 solution set quality indicators in MOO and [22] discusses diversity indicators for MOO.

3   Metrics

From the large number of diversity metrics available we only consider metrics that do not depend on precise domain knowledge, because no knowledge about actual local optima is available in real world applications. Three commonly used distance-based metrics are selected to evaluate the experiments in this work. The *Sum of Distances to Nearest Neighbor (SDNN)* measures the size of a solution set as well as the dispersion between members of that set. *Solow-Polasky Diversity (SPD)* measures the effective number of species by using pairwise distances between the species in the set [20]. If the solutions are similar with respect to each other, SPD tends to 1, otherwise to N. The sensitive parameter θ, which determines how fast a population tends to N with increasing distance, needs to be parameterized for every domain. It is set to 1 for genetic distances and to 100 for phenotypic distances in this work. *Pure Diversity (PD)* is used in high-dimensional many-objective optimization [21,27]. It does not have parameters, which makes it more robust, and depends on a dissimilarity measure ($L_{0,1}$-norm).

Publications in the field of QD have focus on a small number of metrics. The total fitness is used directly or through the *QD-score* [18], which calculates the total fitness of all filled niches in a phenotypic archive. To achieve this, the solutions from a non-QD algorithm are projected into a fixed phenotypic niching space. This score is domain-dependent and does not allow comparing QD algorithms that have different archiving methods. A comparison between archives created from different features introduces a bias towards one of the archives. The *collection size* indicates the proportion of the niching space that is covered by the collection, but again can only be used on a reference archive [4]. Archive-dependent metrics do not generalize well and introduce biases. We therefore only use distance-based diversity metrics. The high dimensionality of phenotypic spaces is taken into account by using appropriate distance norms.

4   Polygon Domain

We construct a domain of free form deformed, eight-sided polygons. The genome (Fig. 1a) consists of 16 parameters controlling the polar coordinate deviation of the polygon control points. The first eight genes determine the deviation of the radius of the polygon's control points, the second eight genes determine their angular deviation. Since the phenotypes can be expressed as binary bitmap images (Fig. 1b and c, resolution of 64×64 pixels) we use the Hamming distance in the diversity metrics to circumvent the problem of high dimensionality [7].

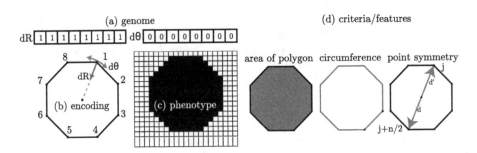

Fig. 1. Free form encoding of polygons. The genome (a) consists of 16 parameters that define axial and radial deformations (b). The phenotype is considered to be the pixel representation of the polygon (c). Shown is a 20×20 phenotype, although we use 64×64 pixels. Features/criteria are shown in (d).

Three aspects describing the polygons are defined that can be used either as criteria or as features (Fig. 1d): the area of the polygon A, its circumference l and point symmetry P through the center. The polygon is sampled at $n = 1000$ equidistant locations on the polygon circumference. The symmetry error E_s is calculated as the sum of distances of all $n/2$ opposing sampling locations. The symmetry metric is calculated as shown in Eq. 1.

$$f_P(x_i) = \frac{1}{1 + E_s(x_i)}, E_s(x_i) = \sum_{j=1}^{n/2} ||x_i^j, x_i^{j+n/2}|| \tag{1}$$

5   Evaluation

We ask which paradigm (objective space, search space or phenotype space) provides the highest phenotypic diversity of shapes. We compare VE, RLS and NSGA-II in multiple experiments. Throughout these experiments we fix the number of function evaluations and solutions and use five replicates per configuration. In NSGA-II the features are used as optimization criteria, maximizing A and minimizing l. The true Pareto set consists of circles with varying sizes. The number of generations is set to 1024 and mutation strength to 10% of the parameter range. The probability of crossover for NSGA-II is 90% and probability of mutation $\frac{1}{dof} = 0.0625\%$, with $dof = 16$ degrees of freedom. VE's archive size is varied throughout the experiments. The number of children and population size is set to the same value. RLS uses as many restarts as the size of the VE archive, the step size is set to $\rho = 0.065$ (after a small parameter sweep) and L-BFGS-B is used as a local search method (within the bounds of the domain). The initial solution set for VE and NSGA-II is created with a Sobol sequence - the initial RLS solution is in the center of the parameter range but RLS' space filling character assures a good search space coverage.

5.1   Genetic or Phenotypic Diversity

Biology has inspired evolutionary optimization to compose a solution of a genome, its encoding, and a phenotype, its expression. The phenotype often is a very high-dimensional object, for example a high-resolution 2D image, and can involve the interaction with the environment. Since the phenotypic space is usually too large, a low-dimensional representation, the genome, is used as search space. An expression function is constructed that turns a genome into its phenotype. Although the expression function should ideally be a bijective mapping, it often does not prevent multiple genomes to be mapped to the same phenotype. The phenomenon of such a surjective mapping is called genetic neutrality, which is not the same but akin to genetic neutrality in biology. In biology, a neutral mutation is understood to be a mutation that has no effect on the survivability of a life form. In evolutionary computation, genetic neutrality is referred to as genetic variants that have the same phenotype [9].

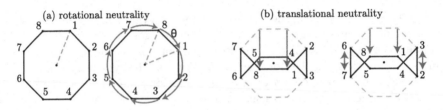

Fig. 2. Genetic neutrality. The same phenotype is expressed when rotating the control points by a $\frac{\pi}{8}$ angle (left) or by translating the control points as shown (right).

Fig. 2(a) shows an example polygon. If the angle θ equals 0°or 45°, phenotypically speaking, these shapes are the same. In this case, eight genomes all point to the same phenotype. Similarly, Fig. 2(b) shows how, through translations of the keypoints, a similar shape can appear based on different genomes. We postulate the first hypothesis: diversity maintenance in a neutral, surjective genetic space leads to lower phenotypic diversity than when using phenotypic niching.

While diversity is often thought about in terms of the distribution of points in the search space, we make a case to measure diversity in phenotypic space, which is independent of the encoding and does not suffer from the effects of genetic neutrality. Phenotypes may also include other factors that are not embodied within the solution's shape itself, but emerge through interaction with the environment. This is taken advantage of in several publications on neuroevolution [11,12]. In this work we only analyse the narrow interpretation of phenotypes, which does not include behavior.

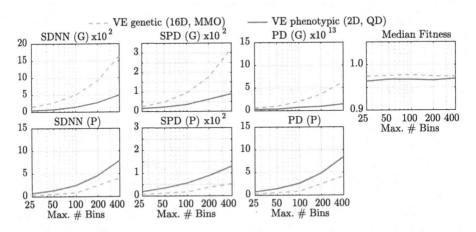

Fig. 3. Voronoi-Elites (VE) performed in 16D genetic and 2D phenotypic space. Top: genetic diversity (SDNN = Sum of Distances to Nearest Neighbor, SPD = Solow-Polasky Diversity, and PD = Pure Diversity) and median fitness, bottom: phenotypic diversity. The number of bins/solutions is increased (x-axis).

The Voronoi tessellation used in VE makes it easy to compare archives of different dimensionality by fixing the number of niches. We apply VE as an MMO algorithm, performing niching in 16-dimensional genetic space, and as a QD algorithm with a two-dimensional phenotypic space. The number of bins is increased to evaluate when differences between genetic and phenotypic VE appear (Fig. 3). At 25 solutions, the approaches produce about the same diversity, but genetic VE finds higher quality solutions. As the number of bins is increased, based on where niching is performed (genetic or phenotypic space), the diversity in that space becomes higher. Phenotypic VE beats genetic VE in terms of phenotypic diversity, which gives us evidence that the first hypothesis is valid. At the same time, the average fitness values of genetic VE are higher than that of phenotypic VE, although the difference gets lower towards 400 solutions.

Table 1. Parameter settings in order of increasing genetic neutrality.

Case	Axial min	Axial max	Radial min	Radial max	Neutrality
A	0	1	−0.05	0.05	−
B	0	1	−0.125	0.125	+
C	−0.25	1	−0.25	0.25	++
D	−0.5	1	−0.5	0.5	+++
E	−1	1	−1	1	++++

We compare phenotypic VE to NSGA-II and RLS. When we bound dr between 0 and 1 and $d\theta$ between $+/-0.125 \times \pi$, we can minimize genetic neutrality. Neutrality is increased by expanding those bounds (Table 1). In contrast to VE, the phenotypic diversity of RLS' solutions is expected to decrease as genetic neutrality increases. Since there is no mechanism to distinguish between similar shapes with different genomes, there is an increasing probability that RLS finds similar solutions. We expect that the solution set produced by RLS due to its space filling character is more diverse than using NSGA-II.

Finally, it can make more sense to treat objectives as features and, instead of searching for the Pareto set, allowing all combinations of features and increasing the diversity of the solution set. We expect NSGA-II to easily find the Pareto set, which consists of circles of various scales, maximizing the area while minimizing the length of the circumference, while QD should find a variety of shapes that can be any combination of large and small A and l. We postulate the second hypothesis: allowing all criteria combinations, instead of using a Pareto approach, leads to higher diversity, while still approximating the Pareto set.

The number of solutions is set to 400. A result similar to Fig. 3 appears for the standard algorithms in Fig. 4. Phenotypic diversity is highest for VE, especially after the genetic neutrality threshold is crossed (at B). Diversity of NSGA-II is lowest, as is expected for this setup. Although diversity of VE is higher than that of RLS, the latter's solutions are all maximally symmetric (see

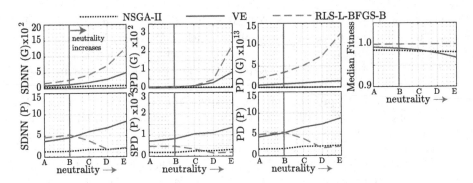

Fig. 4. Genetic (top) and phenotypic (bottom) diversity, and median fitness. Right of red marker: neutrality increases, using parameter bounds shown in Table 1.

fitness plots), making RLS much more appropriate when quality is more important than diversity. These results confirm the first part of the second hypothesis. The Pareto set can be calculated a priori, as we know that circular shapes maximize area while minimizing circumference. The members of the Pareto set adhere to the following genome: $(r_1, \ldots, r_8, \theta_1, \ldots, \theta_8)$, where r_i and θ_i have the same respective value. To create 100 shapes from the Pareto set we take ten equidistant values for r and θ and combine them.

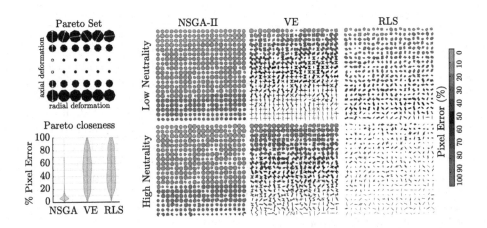

Fig. 5. The ground truth Pareto set is shown over the entire parameter range, with negative as well as positive values for the radial deformation. Bottom left: closeness to Pareto set, measured as pixel errors. The six figures on the right show example solution sets for low and high neutrality.

Part of the resulting Pareto set is shown in Fig. 5. The distance to the Pareto set is measured in phenotypic space, by measuring the smallest pixel error, the sum of pixel-wise differences, between a solution and the Pareto set. We see that the a number of solutions in VE and RLS are close to the Pareto set (Fig. 5 bottom left). Example results with low and high neutrality are shown on the right. Solutions that are close to the Pareto set are shown in the brightest green color. This is evidence for the second half of the second hypothesis. VE again seems to be more robust w.r.t. genetic neutrality, as it finds more solutions close to the Pareto set in high-neutrality domains (bottom row) than RLS.

5.2   Phenotypic Diversity Without Domain Knowledge

Up to this point we have used domain knowledge to construct a phenotypic niching space with VE. Intuitively, the area and circumference seem like good indicators for phenotypic differences. But this comparison between QD and MMO is not completely fair, as the latter does not get any domain information. On the other hand, the features used in QD might not be the most diversifying.

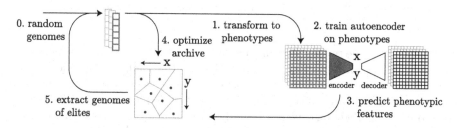

Fig. 6. AutoVE. Generating phenotypic features with an autoencoder. A random set of genomes is created (0), their phenotypes are calculated (1) and used as a training set for an autoencoder (2). The autoencoder can now be used to predict phenotypic features of new solutions (3), which is used to fill the archive (4), after which the elite solutions are extracted from the archive (5) and used to retrain the autoencoder.

We remove the domain knowledge from QD and construct a phenotypic niching space by using a well known dimensionality reduction technique to map the phenotypes to a latent space, as was done in [2,14]. To our best knowledge, this data driven phenotypic niching approach, which we name Auto-Voronoi-Elites (AutoVE), has never been applied to shape optimization. An initial set of genomes, drawn from a quasi-random, space-filling Sobol sequence [19] and expressed into their phenotypes, is used to train a convolutional autoencoder (cAE) (see Fig. 6). The bottleneck in the cAE is a compressed, latent space that assigns every phenotype to a coordinate tupel. The encoder predicts these coordinates of new shapes in the latent space, which are used as phenotypic features. QD searches phenotypes that expand and improve the cAE archive. The cAE is retrained with the new samples. The cAE consists of two convolutional layers in the encoder and four transposed convolutional layers in the decoder. We set the filter size to three pixels, the stride to two pixels, and the number of filters to eight. The cAE is trained using ADAM [10] with a learning rate of 0.001 and 350 training epochs and a mean square error loss function. Latent coordinates are normalized between 0 and 1. The number of generations (1024) is divided over two iterations for AutoVE and the number of latent dimensions is set to two (to compare with manual VE), five or ten.

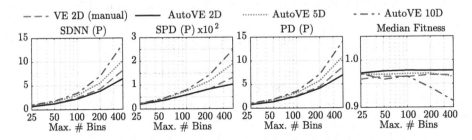

Fig. 7. Phenotypic diversity and fitness of manually crafted features (VE) compared to using an autoencoder (AutoVE) with 2, 5 or 10 latent dimensions.

Fig. 7 shows that the two-dimensional manual and autoencoded phenotypic space (AutoVE 2D) produce similar diversity, whereby the quality of solutions from AutoVE 2D is higher. The higher-dimensional latent spaces increase the solution set diversity at the cost of fitness. This is to be expected, as lower-fitness optima are protected in their own niches. Finally, the diversity of higher-dimensional AutoVE is around 50% higher than any of the other tested methods.

6   Conclusion

The main contributions of this work are as follows: a domain was introduced that allows comparing three different diversity paradigms; a case was made to measure diversity in phenotypic rather than genetic space; the hypothesis that QD is less sensitive to genetic neutrality than MMO was confirmed; the hypothesis that while the diversity of solutions sets of QD and RLS is higher than that of MOO, they also find some solutions close to the ground truth Pareto set, was confirmed; we showed that phenotypic diversity in QD is higher than MMO and MOO. Furthermore, we introduced VE, a simpler and self-expanding version of QD. We also used an autoencoder to discover phenotypic features in a shape optimization problem, showing that we do not need to manually predefine features to get a highly diverse solution set, allowing us to fairly compare QD to MOO and MMO. Using an autoencoder produces higher diversity than manually defined features, making AutoVE a strong choice for high diversity multi-solution optimization.

Since all paradigms have their strengths and weaknesses, we propose a guide for when to use which approach. MOO should be used when you want to optimize all the criteria and want to know the trade-off solutions between those criteria. MMO is appropriate when you have a non-neutral bijective encoding, when you have a single criterion you want to optimize for or if you want to perform a gradient-based, Quasi-Newton or (direct) evolutionary local search to refine local optima. We cannot easily do this in QD due to the effect of neutrality that allows a search to "jump out of" a phenotypic niche. QD should be used if you have some criteria where you are less determined about whether to optimize for them, for example during the first phase of a design process. Some representatives from the Pareto set will still be discovered. When you are interested in the largest diversity of solutions and are more willing to get some solutions with lower fitness than when using MMO, QD is the better alternative. One of the biggest strengths of QD is the possibility to understand relationships between features or even to discover features automatically.

Some research effort should be focused on hybridization. MOO and QD are connected, as the boundary of valid solutions in the phenotypic archive is close to the Pareto front, yet there is room for improvement. Connecting MMO and QD means to use a local search method in QD, which needs to overcome the genetic neutrality problem. We cannot search close to a solution in genetic space and expect newly created solutions to be close in phenotypic space.

We gave insights about different variations of diversity and when and where to apply them, depending on whether one is most interested in trade-offs between criteria, increasing diversity while maximizing fitness, or maximizing diversity while finding high-performing solutions in a manually defined or automatically extracted phenotypic space. It is often easy to manually define two or three phenotypic descriptors, but human imagination can run out of options quickly. Automatic discovery of phenotypic features is a more attractive option for increasing solution diversity. Real world multi-solution optimization and understanding solution diversity are important steps towards increasing the efficacy and efficiency at which engineers solve problems.

References

1. Basto-Fernandes, V., Yevseyeva, I., Emmerich, M.: A survey of diversity-oriented optimization. In: EVOLVE 2013-A Bridge between Probability, Set Oriented Numerics, and Evolutionary Computing, pp. 101–109 (2013)
2. Cully, A.: Autonomous skill discovery with quality-diversity and unsupervised descriptors. In: Proceedings of the Genetic and Evolutionary Computation Conference, pp. 81–89 (2019)
3. Cully, A., Clune, J., Tarapore, D., Mouret, J.B.: Robots that can adapt like animals. Nature **521**(7553), 503–507 (2015)
4. Cully, A., Demiris, Y.: Quality and diversity optimization: a unifying modular framework. IEEE Trans. Evol. Comput. **22**(2), 245–259 (2017)
5. Deb, K., Pratap, A., Agarwal, S., Meyarivan, T.: A fast and elitist multiobjective genetic algorithm: NSGA-II. IEEE Trans. Evol. Comput. **6**(2), 182–197 (2002)
6. DeJong, K.: Analysis of the Behavior of a Class of Genetic Adaptive Systems. Department of Computer and Communication Sciences, University of Michigan, Ann Arbor (1975)

7. Hamming, R.W.: Error detecting and error correcting codes. Bell Syst. Tech. J. **29**(2), 147–160 (1950)
8. Holland, J.H.: Adaptation in Natural and Artificial Systems. MIT Press, Cambridge (1975)
9. Hu, T., Payne, J.L., Banzhaf, W., Moore, J.H.: Robustness, evolvability, and accessibility in linear genetic programming. In: Silva, S., Foster, J.A., Nicolau, M., Machado, P., Giacobini, M. (eds.) Genetic Programming. EuroGP 2011. Lecture Notes in Computer Scienc, vol. 6621, pp. 13–24. Springer, Berlin, Heidelberg (2011). https://doi.org/10.1007/978-3-642-20407-4_2
10. Kingma, D.P., Ba, J.: Adam: a method for stochastic optimization. arXiv preprint arXiv:1412.6980 (2014)
11. Lehman, J., Stanley, K.O.: Abandoning objectives: evolution through the search for novelty alone. Evol. Comput. **19**(2), 189–223 (2011)
12. Lehman, J., Stanley, K.O.: Evolving a diversity of virtual creatures through novelty search and local competition. In: Proceedings of the 13th Annual Conference on Genetic and Evolutionary Computation, pp. 211–218 (2011)
13. Li, M., Yao, X.: Quality evaluation of solution sets in multiobjective optimisation: a survey. ACM Comput. Surv. (CSUR) **52**(2), 1–38 (2019)
14. Meyerson, E., Lehman, J., Miikkulainen, R.: Learning behavior characterizations for novelty search. In: GECCO 2016 - Proceedings of the 2016 Genetic and Evolutionary Computation Conference, pp. 149–156 (2016)
15. Pošík, P., Huyer, W.: Restarted local search algorithms for continuous black box optimization. Evol. Comput. **20**(4), 575–607 (2012)
16. Preuss, M.: Improved topological niching for real-valued global optimization. In: Di Chio, C., et al. (eds.) Applications of Evolutionary Computation. EvoApplications 2012. Lecture Notes in Computer Science, vol. 7248, pp. 386–395. Springer, Berlin, Heidelber (2012). https://doi.org/10.1007/978-3-642-29178-4_39
17. Pugh, J.K., Soros, L.B., Stanley, K.O.: Quality diversity: a new frontier for evolutionary computation. Front. Robot. AI **3**, 40 (2016)
18. Pugh, J.K., Soros, L.B., Szerlip, P.A., Stanley, K.O.: Confronting the challenge of quality diversity. In: Proceedings of the 2015 Annual Conference on Genetic and Evolutionary Computation, pp. 967–974 (2015)
19. Sobol', I.M.: On the distribution of points in a cube and the approximate evaluation of integrals. Zhurnal Vychislitel'noi Matematiki i Matematicheskoi Fiziki **7**(4), 784–802 (1967)
20. Solow, A.R., Polasky, S.: Measuring biological diversity. Environ. Ecol. Stat. **1**(2), 95–103 (1994)
21. Tian, Y., Cheng, R., Zhang, X., Jin, Y.: Platemo: a matlab platform for evolutionary multi-objective optimization. IEEE Comput. Intell. Mag. **12**(4), 73–87 (2017)
22. Tian, Y., Cheng, R., Zhang, X., Li, M., Jin, Y.: Diversity assessment of multiobjective evolutionary algorithms: performance metric and benchmark problems [research frontier]. IEEE Comput. Intell. Mag. **14**(3), 61–74 (2019)
23. Törn, A., Viitanen, S.: Topographical global optimization. In: Floudas, C.A., Pardalos, P.M. (eds.) Recent Advances in Global Optimization, pp. 384–398. Princeton University Press, New Jersey (1992)
24. Vassiliades, V., Chatzilygeroudis, K., Mouret, J.B.: Comparing multimodal optimization and illumination. In: Proceedings of the Genetic and Evolutionary Computation Conference Companion, pp. 97–98 (2017)
25. Vassiliades, V., Chatzilygeroudis, K., Mouret, J.B.: Using centroidal voronoi tessellations to scale up the multidimensional archive of phenotypic elites algorithm. IEEE Trans. Evol. Comput. **22**(4), 623–630 (2017)

26. Wales, D.J., Doye, J.P.: Global optimization by basin-hopping and the lowest energy structures of lennard-jones clusters containing up to 110 atoms. J. Phys. Chem. A **101**(28), 5111–5116 (1997)
27. Wang, H., Jin, Y., Yao, X.: Diversity assessment in many-objective optimization. IEEE Trans. Cybern. **47**(6), 1510–1522 (2016)
28. Wessing, S., Preuss, M.: On multiobjective selection for multimodal optimization. Comput. Optim. Appl. **63**(3), 875–902 (2015). https://doi.org/10.1007/s10589-015-9785-x

Parameter Evolution Self-Adaptive Strategy and Its Application for Cuckoo Search

Yifan He[1(✉)], Claus Aranha[2], and Tetsuya Sakurai[2]

[1] Graduate School of Systems and Information Engineering,
University of Tsukuba, Tsukuba, Japan
`he.yifan.xs@alumni.tsukuba.ac.jp`
[2] Faculty of Engineering, Information and Systems,
University of Tsukuba, Tsukuba, Japan
{`caranha,sakurai`}`@cs.tsukuba.ac.jp`

Abstract. Cuckoo Search (CS) is a simple yet efficient swarm intelligence algorithm based on Lévy Flight. However, its performance can depend heavily on the parameter settings. Though many studies have designed control strategies for scaling factor α, few have considered the adaption of the stability parameter β (of Lévy Flight). In this paper, we propose the Parameter Evolution Self-Adaptive strategy (PESA) to control β. PESA uses an evolutionary algorithm that runs in parallel to CS. We show that PESA can also be extended to control the parameters of other meta-heuristics, using Differential Evolution (DE) as a second example. We compare our strategy with the well-established self-adaptive strategy used in JADE, both in CS and DE, on classical benchmark functions. We discuss the increased flexibility of PESA and analyze the effect of changing the frequency of updating parameter values in CS.

Keywords: Self-adaption · Cuckoo search · Lévy Flight

1 Introduction

Cuckoo Search (CS) is a simple yet efficient meta-heuristic. The efficiency of CS derives mainly from the utilization of Lévy Flight (LF). LF is a type of random walk where the step length is drawn from a heavy-tailed distribution. Therefore, the parameters (i.e., scaling factor α and stability parameter β) of the step-length distribution can heavily influence CS performance. Although it has been suggested that a fixed value for the stability parameter ($\beta = 1.5$) could work on any problem, results from practical studies (for example, Kordestani's recent work [6]) shows that the optimal setting of β depends on the problem. Therefore, a (self-)adaptive strategy for controlling β is promising. However, while the (self-)adaptive strategies of other CS parameters such as α and p_a have been well-studied in the literature [8,11,16], the self-adaptive strategy for β has not been well discussed yet. Some studies have developed such a strategy

© Springer Nature Switzerland AG 2020
B. Filipič et al. (Eds.): BIOMA 2020, LNCS 12438, pp. 56–68, 2020.
https://doi.org/10.1007/978-3-030-63710-1_5

for a limited range, or a set of discrete candidate values [6,11]. However, to the best of our knowledge, there is no self-adaptive strategy in the CS literature to control β in its complete domain (i.e., (0, 2]).

Self-adaptive strategies for parameter control have been well studied in other Evolutionary Algorithms. For example, JADE [20] has been designed to adapt the two parameters of Differential Evolution (DE). In JADE, the algorithm continuously estimates the expectation value of good parameters based on successful parameters in the last generation. This algorithm has been shown to be effective and was further developed by other researchers in recent years [14]. However, the strategy in JADE cannot control β in CS without proper modification (as we found in our pre-experiment). So in this study, we propose a novel self-adaptive strategy that can control β in CS, as well as a variety of parameters in other meta-heuristics, called Parameter Evolution Self-Adaptive strategy (PESA).

PESA is an indicator-based strategy to control algorithm parameter values at an individual level. This strategy maintains two populations: a population of solutions and a population of algorithm parameters. PESA searches the parameter population using a secondary EA and a fitness function based on the progress of individuals in the solution population. PESA's structure makes it easy to apply it to several meta-heuristics and several types of parameters. This work is related to previous research on using EA to fine-tune control parameters. However, two key ideas of our method are the online evolution of parameters (selection and mutation of new parameters done at optimization time), and its general design that aims to work with several EAs.

In this work, we consider two implementations of PESA: First, we show an implementation to adaptively control the β parameter from CS in its full continuous interval (i.e., [0.1, 1.9]). Next, we consider an implementation to control the F and CR parameters from DE. We compare the PESA implementations for each search algorithm to JADE (and its corresponding modifications for use with the CS: JACS). On a set of 14 benchmark functions on 30 dimensions, PESA performs a better control of β when compared to JACS, while it has comparable results to JADE on the control of F and CR. This may indicate that the proposed strategy can be used with little modification for the control of parameters in a wide range of meta-heuristics. We also analyze the sensitivity of PESA to the frequency of control parameter updates.

2 Background

2.1 Cuckoo Search and Lévy Flight

CS was proposed by Yang in 2009 [18]. It has a simple structure, and many subsequent studies have shown it is an efficient meta-heuristic search. Its efficiency is derived from the powerful Lévy Flight operator (LF). Generally, LF is a random walk based on a stable distribution. Since a (non-Gaussian) stable distribution holds infinite variance, a large step of any arbitrary size can occur. This property helps CS escape from local optima during the optimization. The LF operator is formulated in Eq. (1), where $x^{(t)}$ is the position of search point

x at time t. $L(\alpha, \beta)$ is a step generated from a stable distribution with scaling factor α and stability parameter β.

$$x^{(t)} = x^{(t-1)} + L(\alpha, \beta) \tag{1}$$

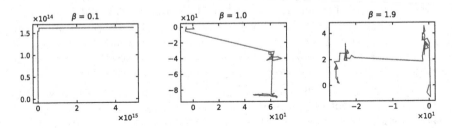

Fig. 1. 50-step Lévy Flights with different β and $\alpha = 1$ started from $(0,0)$. When $\beta = 0.1$, the search range is nearly infinite, which shows a possibility of using Lévy Flight to search an unbounded space.

Figure 1 illustrates 50 steps of three LFs with same $\alpha = 1$, same start point $(0,0)$, but different βs. The scale of search ranges are quite different. Generally, a stable distribution holds infinite variance for $1 \leq \beta < 2$, and its expectation value is diverged when $0 < \beta < 1$. When $\beta = 2$, it becomes a Gaussian distribution. These properties show that any large step can be found in LF when $\beta \neq 2$, and LF can lose its average position and go everywhere in the search space when $0 < \beta < 1$. Therefore, LF with a proper β can be used for searching an unbounded space [4].

2.2 Parameter Adaption Strategies in Cuckoo Search

Because of the importance of parameter tuning, self-adaptive strategies are frequently studied and applied in meta-heuristics literature. In the case of CS, the adaption of the scaling factor α is a well-studied problem. Several studies have proposed adaptive strategies that adjust α based on generations [16,21] and individual fitness [12]. Researchers have also applied adaptive CS to solve some application problems [15,17].

On the other hand, the adaptation of the stability parameter β has not been studied as much as α in the adaptive CS literature. Mlakar has proposed a hybrid self-adaptive CS [11]. However, in his study, β is limited to [1.2, 1.8]. Kordestani has utilized multiple β values and designed learning automation to switch between fixed values (0.75 and 1.90) based on probability [6]. Abedi has proposed a similar design, where the solution is explored with $\beta = 1.0, 1.5$ and 2.0 [1]. Lee has injected LF mutation into Evolutionary programming [7]. He has also developed an "adaptive" strategy, where four candidates are generated with fixed β (1.0, 1.3, 1.7, 2.0), and the best one is selected as offspring.

We find that most of the (self-)adaptive strategies in the CS literature are dealing with α and p_a. In a few existing studies for adaption of β, the candidate values are discrete [1,6,7] or a restricted range [11]. What is more, even in the case of deterministic parameter CS, performance with small β is seldom discussed.

2.3 Parameter Adaption in Other Meta-Heuristics

Since the (self)-adaption design of parameter β in CS has not been well discussed, we introduce self-adaptive adaption in another famous meta-heuristics named differential evolution (DE). Specifically, we introduce JADE [20]. Many variants of JADE and other (self-)adaptive design of DE can be found in the review work by Al-Dabbagh [2]. The full description of JADE can be referred to Zhang's study [20]. In JADE, each solution has an associated parameter value, and the selection of new parameters happens at the same time as the selection of new solutions. Parameters are obtained from a probability distribution, and the shape of this distribution is estimated during the optimization process.

Another idea for select parameter values of an EA is to use a secondary EA. The most well-known approach for this is the Meta-EAs [3,9]. Usually, a Meta-EA maintains multiple sub-populations of the primary EA, each with a corresponding parameter setting. The Meta-EA will analyze a full run of each sub-population, and therefore is computationally expensive.

A slightly different approach is to use a secondary EA that runs in parallel with the primary EA to guide parameter control in self-adaptive strategies. Posik has proposed a method to co-evolve the solutions and mutation steps in evolutionary strategy (ES) [13]. In this way, we can consider JADE as a parallel Estimation of Distribution Algorithm (EDA) guiding the DE's parameters. PLADE [19] has applied particle swarm optimization (PSO) to guide DE parameters. However, to our best knowledge, such a technique has not been applied to control the stability parameter in CS.

3   Proposed Method

3.1   Parameter Evolution Self-Adaptive Strategy

In this paper, we propose the Parameter Evolution Self-adaptive strategy (PESA), which is a generalization of JADE [20], PLADE [19], and Posik's study [13].

PESA uses two parallel populations of the same size: a *solution population* and a *parameter population*. Individual x_i in the solution population is the standard solution candidate for an EA, while p_i is the set of parameters that will be used to operate on x_i, and will be evaluated by a secondary, and possibly different, EA.

The fitness y_i of an individual x_i is calculated as usual, using the problem's fitness function f. On the other hand, the fitness indicator I_i of parameter candidate p_i is calculated by an indicator function g, which evaluates the search progress of the corresponding solution in the last n_{step} generations. This implies that the secondary EA evaluates, selects, and modifies the parameter population less frequently than the primary EA, this difference being controlled by the n_{step} parameter. An important characteristic to keep in mind is that this secondary EA does not consume extra fitness evaluations. The assessment of parameters is based on the solution information that has already been computed in the first EA. The outline of PESA is described in Algorithm 1.

Algorithm 1. Parameter Evolved Self-Adaptive Strategy (PESA)

1: **Input:** solution population $X = \{x_1, \cdots, x_N\}$, parameter population $P = \{p_1, \cdots, p_N\}$, fitness function f, indicator function g;
2: **while** termination criteria is not satisfied **do**
3:     increase generation counter t;
4:     evaluate solution fitness: $y_i^t = f(x_i^t)$
5:     calculate offspring solution x_i^{t+1} based on x_i^t and parameter p_i;
6:     **if** t is multiple of n_{step} **then**
7:         evaluate parameter fitness: $I_i = g(x_i^t, y_i^t, x_i^{t-1}, y_i^{t-1}, \cdots, x_i^{t-n_{step}}, y_i^{t-n_{step}})$
8:         calculate next parameter p_i' based on I_i and secondary EA;

As shown in Fig. 2, compared with Meta-EAs [3,9], each parameter setting in PESA corresponds with an individual rather than a sub-population of base-level EA. This further lead to two difference in the evolutionary process. First, a parameter is assessed by the search progress of only one individual. Second, in Meta-EAs, the fitness of a parameter is computed based on an independent run of one sub-population. However, in our PESA, individuals do not run independently; the search progress of one solution may be partially contributed by another individual. This shows that the fitness of a parameter in PESA should be well-designed.

Posik has proposed a co-evolutionary algorithm for real parameter optimization [13]. In that study, the two populations, a population of solutions and a population of mutation steps, are co-evolved. Compared to his study, our method co-evolves solutions with parameters rather than mutation steps. An essential difference between parameters and mutation steps is that a parameter can generate multiple types (size) of step sizes. Therefore, evolving parameters is generally more difficult. To deal with this problem, we introduce a multi-generation assessment, where each parameter is assessed for n_{step} generations.

It is not hard to note that JADE (without external archive) [20] is a special case of PESA. PESA determines that the quality of parameters is assessed by an indicator function, and then selected independently from the selection process of solutions. In JADE, there is no explicit indicator function, and the selection of parameters and solutions are both based on the fitness of the solution. This could be expressed in PESA as $I_i = \max(y_i^{t-1} - y_i^t, 0)$ as the indicator function.

3.2   Parameter Evolution Cuckoo Search

PESA is a general strategy for controlling parameters of an EA, which requires the definition of the indicator function and the secondary EA rules for generating new parameters.

In this paper, we introduce Parameter Evolution Cuckoo Search (PECS) as a specific implementation of PESA for cuckoo search. Since parameter α and β are highly correlated, we design self-adaption for stability parameter β but tune α for simplicity. In PECS, the solutions are evolved by CS (in Line 5 of Algorithm 1), and the parameters are evolved by another EA (Line 8 of the same algorithm).

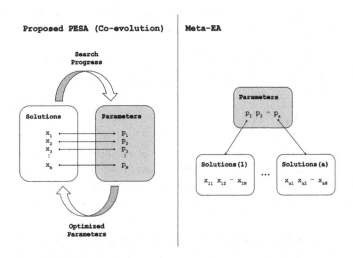

Fig. 2. Conceptual Difference between Parameter Evolved Self-Adaptive Strategy (PESA) and Meta-EA. Meta-EA evaluates a parameter set by running an entire subpopulation with that parameter, while PESA evaluates a parameter set based on a single corresponding individual.

The indicator function that expresses the fitness of a parameter set is computed cumulatively by the corresponding improvement over n_{step} generations of CS, as in Eq. (2). A new parameter set is generated following the crossover step described in Eq. (3) and the mutation step in Eq. (4), with probability p_c and p_m, respectively. In these equations, β_{select} is a stability parameter chosen by roulette selection, every time before the parameter reproduction step. The selection probability of β_i is equal to $I_i/\Sigma I_i$. σ is a random uniform value between 0 and 1. The selection between the new parameter set and the old one is based on the comparison of a pair of positions, before and after implementing LF (i.e., x_i and x_i'). This marks an important difference between the selection of solutions by CS and the selection of parameters by the secondary EA.

$$I_i+ = \max\{f(x_i) - f(x_i'), 0\} \tag{2}$$
$$\beta_i' = \beta_i + \sigma * (\beta_{select} - \beta_i), \ \sigma \in [0, 1] \tag{3}$$
$$\beta_i'' = \beta_i' + L(\theta, \lambda) \tag{4}$$

Implementation of Lévy Flight. To implement LF, we use Eqs. (1) and (5). The first case of the equation below is based on Gutowski's study [4], where a simulation method is constructed to generate only positive LF random numbers for $\beta \in (0, 2)$. We multiply $\{-1, 1\}$, which means the equal probability of 1 and -1, to achieve both positive and negative LF random numbers. The symbol $rand$ stands for a uniform random number in $[0, 1]$. The second case is implemented by Mantegna's algorithm [10]. This algorithm approximates a symmetrical stable distribution, however, for a limited range of $\beta \in [0.3, 1.99]$.

$$L(\alpha, \beta) = \begin{cases} \alpha \cdot \{-1, 1\} \cdot (rand^{-\frac{1}{\beta}} - 1), & 0.1 \le \beta < 0.3 \\ \alpha \cdot \frac{u}{|v|^{1/\beta}} & 0.3 \le \beta \le 1.9 \end{cases} \tag{5}$$

4   Experiments

We show our PESA can control the stability parameter β (with a tuned α) in CS, as well as F and CR in DE. In other words, we compare the performance of different adaptive strategies to solve the parameter space of CS and DE. The source code for all algorithms, extra figures and data are in our public website[1].

4.1   Comparison with Self-Adaptive Strategy in JADE

CS-based Algorithms. Totally, we have four algorithms to compare, namely PECS, JACS, Random Parameter CS (RPCS), and CS (Tuned).

– **PECS:** CS where β is controlled by the proposed PESA.
– **JACS:** CS where β is controlled by JASA. In our pre-experiments, we find that without a proper modification, JACS performs poorly on most of the problems. Thus, we implemented a modification to realize the quality of LF in terms of fitness improvement by applying weighted mean. This modification is similar to what proposed by Tanabe [14].
– **RPCS:** CS where β is randomly generated from $[0.1, 1.9]$ before mutation.
– **CS (Tuned):** CS where β is fine-tuned on each benchmark problem.

DE-based Algorithms. To test PESA's performance on controlling DE, we include PEDE (DE controlled by PESA). As comparison methods, we use JADE and Random Parameter DE (RPDE). The mutation method of all three methods is DE/current-to-pbest/1, and all three algorithms (PEDE, JADE, RPDE) are implemented without an external archive for simplicity.

---

[1] https://y1fanhe.github.io/research/bioma2020.

Experimental Settings for CS-based Algorithms. For a fair comparison, we tuned parameters of all CS-based algorithms based on the average evaluation cost and average fitness of 21 runs with maximum evaluations of 15,000 on Sphere and Rastrigin. We set the population size N as 20, which is a common value. We tuned α and β in pairs to get a proper α. Based on the results, we set α on all problems as 1e-07. We then tuned p_a to 0.1. For JACS, we tuned the scaling factor of Cauchy distribution $\gamma = 0.1$ and learning rate $c = 0.1$. We set the initial value of μ_β as 1.0 (average of 0.1 and 1.9). For PECS, we set θ and λ to 0.1 and 1.0, respectively. This setting is the same as LF by Cauchy distribution with a scaling factor of 0.1. We tuned p_c and p_m to 0.7 and 0.3, respectively. We set n_{step} as 5, and discuss the influence of this parameter in Sect. 4.2. For CS (Tuned), we run algorithm with $\beta = \{ 0.1, 0.2, ..., 1.9 \}$ and chose the best β to compare.

In our experiment, a total of 14 benchmark problems (30-dimension) are included. We have implemented them based on Jamil's review work on continuous benchmark problems [5]. They are F_1: Sphere, F_2: Sum Squares, F_3: Rosenbrock, F_4: Zakharov, F_5: Ackley, F_6: Alpine N.1, F_7: Periodic, F_8: Styblinski-Tank, F_9: Rastrigin, F_{10}: Griewank, F_{11}: Schwefel, F_{12}: Salomon, F_{13}: Xin-She Yang's N.2, and F_{14}: Xin-She Yang's N.4 function. F_1 - F_4 are unimodal problems and F_5 - F_{14} are multimodal problems.

The experiment is performed with 31 repetitions. Each algorithm will run with a maximum evaluation of 300,000. The termination criterion is when the fitness meets the tolerance (to the optimal fitness value). The tolerance for each problem is computed as follows. We first run CS with β from 0.1 to 1.9 for 300,000 evaluations for 31 repetition and use the distance from the best average fitness to the optimal fitness as tolerance. We record the success rate in 31 runs as well as the mean and standard deviation of the number of evaluation numbers in successful runs as results.

Experimental Settings for DE-based Algorithms. We use a population of 100 and a pbest rate of 0.05 for all methods. F and CR are controlled by a self-adaptive strategy within $[0, 1]$. For JADE, the parameters used for self-adaptive strategy is $\mu_F = \mu_{CR} = 0.5$, $\gamma = 0.1$, $c = 0.1$. These settings are the same as in Zhang's study [20]. We use the tuned parameters in the previous experiments for the parameters of the adaptive strategy in PEDE. The maximum evaluations are set to 300,000. We run JADE in the same procedure to set tolerance for DE-based algorithms.

Experimental Results. Tables 1 and 2 presents the results of six CS-based algorithm and three DE-based algorithms on F_1–F_{14}, respectively. We additionally performed the aggregated Friedman test and the aggregated Wilcoxon Signed-Rank test. The results have shown that the improvement of PECS over JACS and RPCS in terms of the number of evaluations is statistically significant (p-values 0.028 and 0.003, respectively), while there is no statistical difference between all four CS-based methods in terms of success rate (p-value = 0.155).

Table 1. Success rate (SR), mean and standard deviation of evaluation numbers for CS-based algorithms (The numbers after CS are the best values of β)

Fun	Method	SR	Mean	Std	Fun	Method	SR	Mean	Std
F_1	PECS	1.00	**5.47e + 04**	6.67e + 03	F_8	PECS	1.00	**7.23e + 04**	2.79e + 04
	JACS	1.00	9.03e + 04	2.92e + 03		JACS	1.00	1.00e + 05	1.09e + 04
	RPCS	1.00	7.07e + 04	3.89e + 03		RPCS	1.00	1.74e + 05	3.95e + 04
	CS (0.6)	0.68	2.63e + 05	2.44e + 04		CS (0.4)	0.65	2.62e + 05	2.11e + 04
F_2	PECS	1.00	**5.80e + 04**	5.70e + 03	F_9	PECS	**0.94**	1.73e + 05	4.89e + 04
	JACS	1.00	9.34e + 04	3.47e + 03		JACS	0.81	1.57e + 05	3.86e + 04
	RPCS	1.00	7.90e + 04	4.88e + 03		RPCS	0.16	2.66e + 05	2.86e + 04
	CS (0.5)	0.94	2.22e + 05	2.98e + 04		CS (0.4)	0.81	2.50e + 05	3.17e + 04
F_3	PECS	0.81	8.61e + 04	7.13e + 04	F_{10}	PECS	0.71	4.37e + 04	3.92e + 04
	JACS	0.61	8.76e + 04	5.67e + 04		JACS	**0.81**	5.62e + 04	1.59e + 04
	RPCS	0.52	1.24e + 05	6.37e + 04		RPCS	0.26	1.27e + 05	7.47e + 04
	CS (0.4)	**0.87**	7.41e + 04	5.34e + 04		CS (0.2)	0.77	3.01e + 04	4.49e + 03
F_4	PECS	0.00	-	-	F_{11}	PECS	0.71	2.29e + 05	4.40e + 04
	JACS	0.00	-	-		JACS	0.39	2.29e + 05	3.11e + 04
	RPCS	0.00	-	-		RPCS	0.00	-	-
	CS (0.3)	**0.77**	2.71e + 05	1.86e + 04		CS (0.2)	**0.94**	2.30e + 05	3.01e + 04
F_5	PECS	1.00	**6.15e + 04**	5.96e + 03	F_{12}	PECS	0.00	-	-
	JACS	1.00	1.03e + 05	4.57e + 03		JACS	0.00	-	-
	RPCS	1.00	1.14e + 05	1.19e + 04		RPCS	0.00	-	-
	CS (0.5)	0.68	2.73e + 05	1.48e + 04		CS (0.2)	**0.61**	1.31e + 05	5.45e + 04
F_6	PECS	1.00	3.91e + 04	2.68e + 04	F_{13}	PECS	1.00	1.76e + 05	3.31e + 04
	JACS	1.00	**2.89e + 04**	2.13e + 04		JACS	1.00	2.16e + 05	3.44e + 04
	RPCS	0.97	2.79e + 04	1.64e + 04		RPCS	0.00	-	-
	CS (0.3)	0.74	1.38e + 05	6.16e + 04		CS (0.3)	1.00	**5.87e + 04**	1.37e + 04
F_7	PECS	1.00	**1.54e + 04**	2.45e + 03	F_{14}	PECS	1.00	**2.61e + 04**	2.52e + 03
	JACS	1.00	1.75e + 04	1.74e + 03		JACS	1.00	4.08e + 04	2.67e + 03
	RPCS	1.00	1.60e + 04	1.90e + 03		RPCS	1.00	4.83e + 04	3.54e + 03
	CS (0.6)	1.00	5.83e + 04	1.14e + 04		CS (0.5)	1.00	1.31e + 05	1.88e + 04

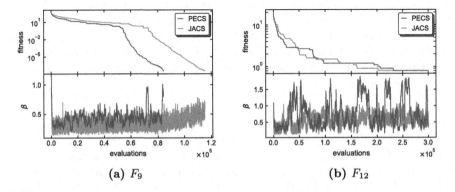

(a) F_9 (b) F_{12}

Fig. 3. Mean of β and fitness in best run on F_9 and F_{12} for adaptive CS

JADE is better than PEDE in terms of success rate, however, without statistical significance (p-value = 0.058). All DE-based algorithms perform in the same tier in terms of the number of evaluations (p-value = 0.054). These results show that PESA can work better than JASA on controlling CS and perform a comparable result with JASA on controlling DE. This may indicate that our PESA can work in a more general case compared to JASA.

Table 2. Success rate (SR), mean and standard deviation of evaluation numbers for DE-based algorithms

Fun	Method	SR	Mean	Std	Fun	Method	SR	Mean	Std
F_1	PEDE	1.00	3.43e + 04	2.24e + 03	F_8	PEDE	0.48	6.38e + 04	7.40e + 03
	JADE	1.00	**3.33e + 04**	1.20e + 03		JADE	**0.90**	8.96e + 04	6.10e + 03
	RPDE	1.00	3.70e + 04	7.28e + 02		RPDE	0.35	6.79e + 04	1.03e + 04
F_2	PEDE	1.00	3.94e + 04	2.13e + 03	F_9	PEDE	1.00	**1.52e + 05**	5.24e + 03
	JADE	1.00	**3.78e + 04**	1.33e + 03		JADE	1.00	1.77e + 05	3.20e + 03
	RPDE	1.00	4.21e + 04	7.51e + 02		RPDE	0.00	-	-
F_3	PEDE	0.03	2.75e + 05	0.00e + 00	F_{10}	PEDE	0.74	5.38e + 04	6.56e + 03
	JADE	**0.55**	1.99e + 05	7.28e + 03		JADE	**1.00**	5.57e + 04	1.62e + 04
	RPDE	0.00	-	-		RPDE	0.87	5.66e + 04	4.76e + 03
F_4	PEDE	**1.00**	9.92e + 04	5.69e + 03	F_{11}	PEDE	**0.32**	2.10e + 05	4.58e + 04
	JADE	0.94	1.05e + 05	1.20e + 04		JADE	0.16	2.49e + 05	4.18e + 04
	RPDE	1.00	1.66e + 05	4.42e + 03		RPDE	0.00	-	-
F_5	PEDE	1.00	**5.76e + 04**	1.98e + 03	F_{12}	PEDE	0.00	-	-
	JADE	1.00	6.47e + 04	2.64e + 03		JADE	**0.16**	6.87e + 04	1.08e + 04
	RPDE	1.00	7.34e + 04	1.08e + 03		RPDE	0.03	1.41e + 05	0.00e + 00
F_6	PEDE	1.00	**2.38e + 04**	1.20e + 04	F_{13}	PEDE	0.65	1.86e + 05	4.65e + 04
	JADE	1.00	3.80e + 04	1.16e + 03		JADE	**0.71**	1.29e + 05	2.76e + 04
	RPDE	1.00	5.94e + 04	3.36e + 03		RPDE	0.00	-	-
F_7	PEDE	1.00	9.86e + 04	8.02e + 03	F_{14}	PEDE	0.10	2.42e + 05	2.43e + 04
	JADE	1.00	**9.79e + 04**	6.03e + 03		JADE	**1.00**	2.67e + 05	1.31e + 04
	RPDE	0.00	-	-		RPDE	0.97	1.24e + 05	4.55e + 04

Discussion. It is interesting to see how β evolves with different strategies. As an example, the evolutionary process best fitness and mean of β in the best runs of PECS and JACS on F_9 and F_{12} are plotted in Fig. 3. On F_9, we can find that both methods decrease β at first to perform a global search, and increase to perform precious local search later. What is more, our PECS increases β much earlier than JACS, and thus holds a better convergence speed. On F_{12}: Salomon function, the evolutionary process of β in PECS is periodic. The ring-shaped local optima occur periodically on the domain. This may indicate that the search process of parameters is too greedy, and the parameters are evolved to large β at an early phase. On this problem, the performance of all self-adaptive CS is worse than a fine-tuned CS with $\beta=0.2$. This also shows the nature of self-adaptive EAs; the strategy can only reward the short-term benefits.

4.2 Comparison on Using Different n_{step}

In our PECS, a parameter is assessed with n_{step} generations. The setting of n_{step} can influence performance. A small n_{step} leads to an inaccurate assessment on the performance of parameters, while with a large n_{step}, parameters have less chance to be updated. Also, the solution may move far away from the current position after a large generation. Figure 4 presents the evolutionary process of β by $n_{step}=\{$ 1, 5, 10, 50 $\}$ on F_9. It is not hard to find that on all the three problems, small n_{step} leads to a rapid change in β. On F_9, when $n_{step}=1$, the fitness keeps a high value for a large number of evaluations, which indicates that the algorithm cannot escape from the local optimal. However, when $n_{step}=50$, the convergence speed is slower than $n_{step}=5$ and 10. A similar observation can be found in most of the testing problems. Therefore, $n_{step}=5$ or 10 should be a good choice for this parameter.

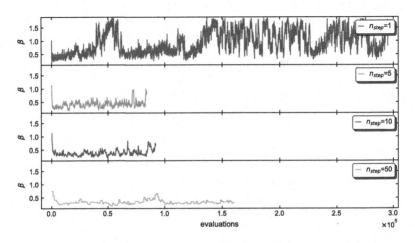

Fig. 4. Mean of β in best run of PECS on F_9 with different n_{step}

5 Conclusions

In this study, we proposed a novel self-adaptive strategy (PESA) to control the stability parameter of LF in CS from a wide range ($[0.1, 1.9]$). The proposed self-adaptive strategy is a co-evolution between solutions and parameters. We also showed that the proposed PESA is a generalization of many literature methods, such as JADE [20]. In the experiments, we showed that for both CS and DE, the proposed PESA could perform better or at least comparable results, compared with the strategy in JADE (JASA).

In the future, we will assess our methods on CEC benchmarks and compared them with other state-of-the-art algorithms. We will apply our strategy to more EAs to test its flexibility. We will extend our method to control multiple parameters simultaneously. Also, it is essential to discover a new metric to guide the search for parameters. What is more, it is also interesting to adapt our method to a multi-objective evolutionary algorithm.

References

1. Abedi Firouzjaee, H., Kordestani, J.K., Meybodi, M.R.: Cuckoo search with composite flight operator for numerical optimization problems and its application in tunnelling. Eng. Optim. **49**(4), 597–616 (2017)
2. Al-Dabbagh, R.D., Neri, F., Idris, N., Baba, M.S.: Algorithmic design issues in adaptive differential evolution schemes: review and taxonomy. Swarm Evol. Comput. **43**, 284–311 (2018)
3. Grefenstette, J.J.: Optimization of control parameters for genetic algorithms. IEEE Trans. Syst. Man Cybern. **16**(1), 122–128 (1986)
4. Gutowski, M.: Lévy flights as an underlying mechanism for global optimization algorithms. preprint arXiv:math-ph/0106003 (2001)
5. Jamil, M., Yang, X.S.: A literature survey of benchmark functions for global optimisation problems. Int. J. Math. Model. Numer. Optim. **4**(2), 150–194 (2013)
6. Kordestani, J.K., Firouzjaee, H.A., Reza Meybodi, M.: An adaptive bi-flight cuckoo search with variable nests for continuous dynamic optimization problems. Appl. Intell. **48**(1), 97–117 (2017). https://doi.org/10.1007/s10489-017-0963-7
7. Lee, C.Y., Yao, X.: Evolutionary programming using mutations based on the lévy probability distribution. IEEE Trans. Evol. Comput. **8**(1), 1–13 (2004)
8. Li, X., Yin, M.: Modified cuckoo search algorithm with self adaptive parameter method. Inf. Sci. **298**, 80–97 (2015)
9. Luke, S., Talukder, A.K.A.: Is the meta-EA a viable optimization method? In: Proceedings of the 15th Annual Conference on Genetic and Evolutionary Computation, pp. 1533–1540 (2013)
10. Mantegna, R.N., Stanley, H.E.: Stochastic process with ultraslow convergence to a gaussian: the truncated lévy flight. Phys. Rev. Lett. **73**(22), 2946 (1994)
11. Mlakar, U., Fister Jr., I., Fister, I.: Hybrid self-adaptive cuckoo search for global optimization. Swarm Evol. Comput. **29**, 47–72 (2016)
12. Ong, P.: Adaptive cuckoo search algorithm for unconstrained optimization. Sci. World J. **2014**, 943403 (2014)
13. Posik, P.: Real-parameter optimization using the mutation step . In: Co-Evolution2005 IEEE Congress on Evolutionary Computation, vol. 1, pp. 872–879. IEEE (2005)
14. Tanabe, R., Fukunaga, A.: Success-history based parameter adaptation for differential evolution. In: 2013 IEEE Congress on Evolutionary Computation, pp. 71–78. IEEE (2013)
15. Valian, E., Tavakoli, S., Mohanna, S., Haghi, A.: Improved cuckoo search for reliability optimization problems. Comput. Ind. Eng. **64**(1), 459–468 (2013)
16. Walton, S., Hassan, O., Morgan, K., Brown, M.: Modified cuckoo search: a new gradient free optimisation algorithm. Chaos, Solitons Fract. **44**(9), 710–718 (2011)
17. Wang, J., Zhou, B.: A hybrid adaptive cuckoo search optimization algorithm for the problem of chaotic systems parameter estimation. Neural Comput. Appl. **27**(6), 1511–1517 (2015). https://doi.org/10.1007/s00521-015-1949-1
18. Yang, X.S., Deb, S.: Cuckoo search via lévy flights. In: 2009 World Congress on Nature & Biologically Inspired Computing (NaBIC), pp. 210–214. IEEE (2009)

19. Zhan, Z.H., Zhang, J.: Self-adaptive differential evolution based on PSO learning strategy. In: Proceedings of the 12th Annual Conference on Genetic and Evolutionary Computation, pp. 39–46 (2010)
20. Zhang, J., Sanderson, A.C.: JADE: adaptive differential evolution with optional external archive. IEEE Trans. Evol. Comput. **13**(5), 945–958 (2009)
21. Zhang, Y., Wang, L., Wu, Q.: Modified adaptive cuckoo search (MACS) algorithm and formal description for global optimisation. Int. J. Comput. Appl. Technol. **44**(2), 73 (2012)

Refining the CC-RDG3 Algorithm with Increasing Population Scheme and Persistent Covariance Matrix

Dani Irawan[1]([✉])[ID], Margarita Antoniou[2][ID], Boris Naujoks[1], and Gregor Papa[2][ID]

[1] Institute for Data Science Engineering and Analytics, TH Köln, Gummersbach, Germany
{dani.irawan,boris.naujoks}@th-koeln.de
[2] Jožef Stefan Institute, Ljubljana, Slovenia
{margarita.antoniou,gregor.papa}@ijs.si

Abstract. The cooperative coevolution framework has been used extensively to solve large scale global optimization problems. Recently, the framework is used in CC-RDG3 where it uses recursive differential grouping and covariance matrix adaptation evolution strategies (CMA-ES). It was shown that the algorithm performs well on the CEC2013-LSGO benchmark functions. In this study, some modifications to the CC-RDG3 algorithm are proposed to improve performance. The modifications should be applied differently depending on the modality of the problem at hand.

Keywords: Cooperative coevolution · Large scale optimization · Evolutionary algorithms

1 Introduction

The cooperative coevolution (CC) framework [15] is a popular framework for solving large scale global optimization (LSGO) problems. The framework uses a divide-and-conquer concept where the large scale problem is decomposed into smaller problems with fewer variables, that are further optimized. However, the decomposition step in using the CC framework is still a challenge despite the various decomposition methods that have been proposed before.

One of the most popular decomposition schemes is the differential grouping (DG) [13,14] and its family, such as the extended DG (XDG) [19], and the recursive DG (RDG) and RDG3 [17,18], which decomposes the problem based on variable interaction. The variable interactions are detected based on the second-order differentials. The rationale behind these schemes is that tightly-interacting variables should be in the same group while interactions among distinct subcomponents should be weak [4]. Some algorithms indeed rely on separability between the subproblems and their performance may deteriorate if the decomposition produces bad grouping [16].

© Springer Nature Switzerland AG 2020
B. Filipič et al. (Eds.): BIOMA 2020, LNCS 12438, pp. 69–83, 2020.
https://doi.org/10.1007/978-3-030-63710-1_6

Once the problem is decomposed, the optimal values of the subproblems should be found by an optimizer. Many evolutionary algorithms (EAs) have been used as optimizers in the context of the CC framework for LSGO. The Covariance Matrix Adaptation Evolution Strategy (CMA-ES) algorithm proposed in [8], is an evolution strategy that relies on the adaptation of the full covariance matrix of a normal search distribution. This algorithm performs well on unimodal functions, but its performance deteriorates in multimodal functions. To tackle this problem, Auger et al. [1] suggested a CMA-ES with an increasing population (IPOP-CMA-ES), where the algorithm adopts a restart strategy with successively increasing the population size giving promising results.

The CMA-ES has been used together with RDG3 within the CC framework and named as the CC-RDG3 algorithm. In this work, we refine the CC-RDG3 algorithm that uses a standard CMA-ES optimizer, by using IPOP-CMA-ES. Furthermore, instead of a complete restart of the CMA-ES in every cycle, we use a persistent covariance matrix instead.

Another important aspect after the decomposition and during the optimization is the budget allocation. The simplest method in this context is, after the problem is decomposed, to use a round-robin method to assign the computational time equally to each subproblem, ignoring the different effects that each subproblem can have to the general problem. The contribution based budget allocation CC (CBCC) [12] and CC with a sensitivity analysis-based budget assignment method (SACC) [10] investigate the influence of each subcomponent and allocate accordingly the number of iterations for the optimization. In this study, the SACC method is also tested.

The combinations of the various modifications are tested on numerous test-functions from standard LSGO benchmark suites and compared with the base CC-RDG3 algorithm. The results of each combination vary and depend hugely on the characteristics of the test problem, especially on the modality.

The remainder of this paper is organized as follows. Section 2 contains a short description of the CC framework and the RDG3 decomposition method used. Section 3 explains the proposed refinement of the CC-RDG3 algorithm. Section 4 presents the numerical experiments and the benchmark used, the obtained results along with their comparison and analysis. Lastly, Sect. 5 concludes this paper and shows future directions.

2   Cooperative Coevolution with Recursive Differential Grouping

CC framework was first proposed by [15] in 1994. The main two steps of the general CC framework can be summarized as follows: 1. *Decomposition*: Decompose the problem into several subproblems, by dividing a given high-dimensional problem into a number of low-dimensional subcomponents and 2. *Optimisation*: Optimise each subproblem cooperatively with the use of an optimizer.

The existing decomposition methods are classified by [18] as manual or automatic (or blind and intelligent as proposed later in [20] as more appropriate terminology). The manual (or blind) decomposition method ignores the underlying structure of variable interaction, and the number and the size of the subcomponents are manually designed. Examples of such methods is uni-variable grouping [15], S_k grouping [2] and random grouping [21], and have been proved to work well in fully separable problems. In the automatic decomposition, the variable interactions are identified and the problem is decomposed accordingly.

The Recursive Differential Grouping (RDG) is one of the most effective automatic methods, capable of quickly grouping variables based on interaction. The grouping is done recursively and requires $\mathcal{O}(d \log d)$ function evaluations. There are several versions of RDG and the most recent is RDG3 [17]. Compared to previous versions, the RDG3 scheme puts emphasis on handling overlapping variables. The differential grouping schemes usually put groups with overlapping variables into a single, big group. This means that there are many variables that are not directly interacting (also termed "weak interactions") in the group.

In RDG3, when groups have overlapping variables, a size-limit-threshold is imposed. When the threshold is exceeded, no further overlapping variables are grouped together. This allows some overlapping variables to be grouped together, while also preventing the groups to grow too big. A small size-threshold will prevent variables with weak interactions from being grouped together, while a larger size-threshold will allow more weak interactions.

The RDG3 has been used in the CC framework in CC-RDG3 [17], paired with the covariance matrix adaptation-evolution strategy (CMA-ES) [8] as the solver. The algorithm shows exceptional results on the CEC2013 problems for LSGO [9], especially on overlapping problems.

3 Proposed Algorithm

The proposed modifications to the CC-RDG3 algorithm are described in this section. Each modification can be applied separately.

3.1 CMA-ES with Increasing Population

The CMA-ES algorithm explore the search space using the multivariate normal distribution $\mathcal{N}(\mu, \Sigma)$. The search at generation $g + 1$ follows the equation

$$x^{(g+1)} = \mathcal{N}(x^{(g)}, (\sigma^{(g)})^2 \mathbf{C}^{(g)}), \tag{1}$$

where $x^{(g+1)}$ is the offspring, $x^{(g)}$ is the current best point, while $\sigma^{(g)}$ and $\mathbf{C}^{(g)}$ are the step size (scaling factor) and the covariance matrix at current generation g, respectively. The CMA-ES adapts the σ and $\mathbf{C}$.

The performance of CMA-ES on multi-modal functions depends strongly on population size [7]. To address this, Auger, et al. [1] proposed a restart strategy with increasing population. When some stopping criteria is triggered, the CMA-ES is restarted and the population size is increased hence promoting exploration of the search space. In this work, the same stopping criteria as in [1] are used, except that the *equalfunvalhist* stopping criterion only check for flat fitness.

In regards with the CC framework, when any stopping criteria is triggered, the optimization on the current group is stopped and it will be restarted in the next cycle with double population size up to 8 times the original size (see Algorithm 1). The size limit is imposed to prevent the population size growing too large. When the size limit is reached, the step size σ is doubled instead. For brevity, algorithms that use the IPOP-CMA-ES strategy will be marked with "IPOP" in the name.

Algorithm 1. CC-RDG3-IPOP

$G \leftarrow$ Group variables using RDG3
Set initial population size $\lambda = \lambda_0$ and CMA-ES step size $\sigma = \sigma_0$
while Budget still available **do**
   for $i = 1 : |G|$ **do**
      Use CMA-ES with step size σ, other parameters at default on $f(\mathbf{x}_i)$
      Update $\mathbf{x}_i$
      Check termination code
      if CMA-ES terminated due to IPOP restart criterion **then**
         if $\lambda \leq \lambda^8$ **then** $\lambda \leftarrow 2\lambda$
         else $\sigma \leftarrow 2\sigma$
         end if
      end if
   end for
end while

3.2   Persistent Covariance Matrix

The CMA-ES algorithm will continuously adapt the covariance matrix, step size, and also records the evolution path through cumulation. Every time the algorithm is restarted, these information are usually lost and only the initial values of $\mathbf{x}$ are updated. With regards to the CC framework, a restart would happen after each cycle finishes.

We propose to use a persistent covariance matrix and step size. Persistent means that the covariance matrix, step size, and also the evolution path are not reset at each restart (see Algorithm 2). All values are retained and the next restart will start with these values. The function landscape may change after each cycle, but the information retained may help to kick-start the optimization in the subsequent cycles. The procedure will promote exploitation of potential areas in the search space.

Due to the conflicting nature between the persistent covariance matrix strategy against the IPOP-CMA-ES strategy, they are set to be mutually exclusive when used together (see Algorithm 3). The covariance matrix (and other values) are only retained if the stopping criteria in Sect. 3.1 are not triggered and the CMA-ES ends because it reaches maximum number of iterations. When any stopping criteria in Sect. 3.1 is triggered, the IPOP-CMA-ES will be used instead. Algorithms that use the persistent covariance strategy are marked with "KC" (keep covariance) in the name.

Algorithm 2. CC-RDG3-KC

$G \leftarrow$ Group variables using RDG3
Set initial CMA-ES step size $\sigma = \sigma_0$, and covariance matrix $\Lambda = \mathbb{1}$
while Budget still available **do**
    for $i = 1 : |G|$ **do**
        Use CMA-ES with σ and Λ, other parameters at default on $f(\mathbf{x}_i)$
        Update $\mathbf{x}_i, \sigma$, and Λ
    end for
end while

Algorithm 3. CC-RDG3-IPOP-KC

$G \leftarrow$ Group variables using RDG3
Set $\lambda = \lambda_0$, $\sigma = \sigma_0$, and $\Lambda = \mathbb{1}$
while Budget still available **do**
    for $i = 1 : |G|$ **do**
        Use CMA-ES with step size σ, other parameters at default on $f(\mathbf{x}_i)$
        Update $\mathbf{x}_i$
        Check termination code
        if CMA-ES terminated due to IPOP restart criterion **then**
            if $\lambda \leq \lambda^8$ **then** $\lambda \leftarrow 2\lambda$
            else $\sigma \leftarrow 2\sigma$
            end if
        else
            Update σ, and Λ
        end if
    end for
end while

3.3 Sensitivity Analysis Based Budget Allocation

Equation 2 is an example where the variables have imbalanced effects. A small perturbation on x_1 has much larger effects on $f(\mathbf{x})$ compared to a perturbation on x_2 (10^4 times larger).

$$f(\mathbf{x}) = 10^6 x_1 + 10^2 x_2 \tag{2}$$

The differential analysis (DA), also known as Morris method, is a sensitivity analysis (SA) method based on the first order differential. Sensitivity analysis methods assess the extent of the variables' effect on the objective function. The DA has been used previously for LSGO problem in [10,11].

For DA, the search space is divided into p intervals in each variable. A grid jump $\Delta = N * \frac{1}{(p-1)}$, with $N \in \mathbb{Z}_{>0} < p - 1$. Elementary effect (EE) for each variable can then be calculated using Eq. 3

$$EE_j(\mathbf{x}) = \frac{f(x_1, \ldots, x_{j-1}, x_j + \Delta, \ldots) - f(\mathbf{x})}{\Delta}, j = 1, \ldots, d \tag{3}$$

The $\mathbf{x}$ is picked randomly within the search space such that $\mathbf{x} + \Delta$ is still within the search space. Several EE_j are sampled with sample size r. The distributions of EE_j can be obtained. Further, we compute the mean of the absolute value of EE_j, μ^*, to rank the importance of each variable following Eq. 4, with s the sample number. Higher μ^* signifies higher impact/contribution to the objective value [3]. The budget allocated to a group can then be allocated based on μ^*. In this work, the portion p_s for group s follows Eq. 5.

$$\mu_j^* = \frac{\sum_{s=1}^{r} |EE_j(\mathbf{x})|_s}{r} \tag{4}$$

$$p_s = \begin{cases} 1 + \log \sum_{i \in S} \mu_i^*, & \text{if} \sum_{i \in s} \mu_i^* > 1 \\ 1, & \text{otherwise} \end{cases} \tag{5}$$

In [8], the maximum number of iterations is set at $30 \times d$. In this study, d is the number of variables in the main problem (without decomposition). The p_s is used to scale the number of iteration for each group with respect to $30 \times d$, i.e. each group will have a budget of $30 p_s \times d$ in each cycle. Algorithms that use the sensitivity analysis budget allocation strategy will be marked with "SA" in the name. Algorithms without "SA" assume μ^* for all variables are equal to 1.

4   Numerical Experiments

4.1   Setup of Experiments

To analyze the performance of the proposed algorithms, we compared the algorithms with the base CC-RDG3 algorithm. For each function, all algorithms are run 15 times and compared to the CC-RDG3 algorithm using the pairwise Wilcoxon test.

The test functions used in this study are a subset of the CEC2013 LSGO benchmark suite [9] $f_1 - f_{14}$. Problem f_{15} is omitted from this study because the algorithm implementation used in this study cannot find a feasible solution, most likely due to step size divergence. The problems use 1 000 input variables, except $f_{13} - f_{14}$ with only 905 variables. The budget is set at 3 000 000 function evaluations for each run for these functions.

Moreover, the test functions $f_{16} - f_{19}$ and $f_{21} - f_{24}$ from BBOB-largescale benchmark suite [5] are used to further assess the algorithms' performances on multimodal functions. The BBOB benchmark functions are configured to accept 160 input variables and each optimization run cannot use more than 1 600 000 function evaluations. In Table 1, the test functions and their properties are reported. Note that we keep the original numbering of each benchmark suite.

4.2   Numerical Results

Performances of the algorithms on the test problems can be observed in Table 2 and Table 3 and boxplots Fig. 1 to Fig. 4. For the boxplots, the data ranges are normalized to the range [0,1]. Due to the normalization, small differences may be exaggerated, and vice versa. Additionally, in Table 2 it can be seen that for f_3,

Table 1. Test Functions and their properties. Properties listed are modality (U = Unimodal, M = Multimodal), additive separability, number of input variables d, and special features of the functions.

CEC2013	Modality	Add. Sep.	d	Features
f_1: Elliptic	U	Separable	1 000	
f_2: Rastrigin	M	Separable	1 000	
f_3: Ackley	M	Separable	1 000	
f_4: 7 Elliptic	U	Partial	1 000	
f_5: 7 Rastrigin	M	Partial	1 000	
f_6: 7 Ackley	M	Partial	1 000	Deceptive
f_7: 7 Schwefel 1.2	U	Partial	1 000	
f_8: 20 Elliptic	U	Partial	1 000	
f_9: 20 Rastrigin	M	Partial	1 000	
f_{10}: 20 Ackley	M	Partial	1 000	Deceptive
f_{11}: 20 Schwefel 1.2	U	Partial	1 000	
f_{12}: Rosenbrock	M	Non-Separable	1 000	Overlapping
f_{13}: Schwefel 1.2	U	Non-separable	905	Overlapping, conforming
f_{14}: Schwefel 1.2	U	Non-separable	905	Overlapping, conflicting
BBOB	**Modality**	**Add. Sep.**	d	**Features**
f_{16}: Weierstrass	M	Non-separable	160	
f_{17}: Schaffers	M	Non-separable	160	
f_{18}: Schaffers	M	Non-separable	160	Ill conditioned
f_{19}: Griewank-Rosenbrock	M	Non-separable	160	
f_{21}: Gallagher's 101 Peaks	M	Non-separable	160	
f_{22}: Gallagher's 21 Peaks	M	Non-separable	160	
f_{23}: Katsuura	M	Non-separable	160	
f_{22}: Lunacek bi-rastrigin	M	Non-separable	160	

f_6 and f_{10} (Ackley functions), all algorithms have similar performances which are not far off from their starting points. This is because the Ackley function has a landscape similar to the needle-in-haystack problem where directed search strategies are expected to fail [1].

From Table 2 and Table 3, it can be seen when an algorithm with SA strategy performs well, the corresponding algorithm without SA strategy also shows a significant advantage over CC-RDG3. The SA strategy does not provide a significant improvement to the algorithms.

On unimodal functions, the KC strategy shows its superiority. In Fig. 1, Fig. 3, and Fig. 4, the CC-RDG3, and CC-RDG3-IPOP algorithms perform much worse on all unimodal functions. The KC strategy will consistently push the search to a local optima wherein in unimodal functions, any local optima is also a global optimum. Combined with the high grouping accuracy of RDG3, the performance of these algorithms on unimodal functions will be boosted.

However, on the highly multimodal f_2, f_5 and f_9 functions (see Fig. 2), the RDG-KC and RDG-KC-SA algorithms are not performing so well. On these

Table 2. Median of the best values obtained by the algorithms on CEC2013 test problems. Each algorithm is run 15 times on each function. Bold texts indicate the best results, • indicates better performance than the base CC-RDG3 algorithm, while ▽ indicates worse performance.

Fn	CC-RDG3	IPOP	KC	IPOP-KC	KC-SA	IPOP-KC-SA
f_1	1.16+07	1.16E+07	**3.68+05** •	**3.68+05** •	**3.68+05** •	3.68+05 •
f_2	6.01E+03	**1.28E+03** •	6.21E+03	**1.28E+03** •	6.21E+03	**1.28E+03** •
f_3	2.05E+01	2.05E+01	2.04E+01	2.04E+01	2.04E+01	2.04E+01
f_4	1.61E+08	1.49E+08	**1.41E+06**•	3.64E+06 •	1.42E+06 •	3.330E+06 •
f_5	1.66E+06	5.17E+05 •	2.46E+06 ▽	4.90E+05 •	2.52E+06 ▽	**4.74+05** •
f_6	1.00E+06	1.01E+06	9.96E+05 •	9.96E+05 •	9.96E+05 •	9.96E+05 •
f_7	1.44E+04	1.84E+04	**2.06E-19** •	2.07E-07•	4.13E-18 •	2.62E-07 •
f_8	1.23E+12	3.20E+12 ▽	2.03E+06 •	3.09E+07 •	**1.73E+06** •	3.81E+07 •
f_9	1.18E+08	**4.40E+07**•	1.54E+08 ▽	4.87E+07 •	1.70E+08 ▽	4.56E+07 •
f_{10}	9.12E+07	9.12E+07	9.05E+07 •	9.05E+07 •	9.05E+07 •	9.05E+07 •
f_{11}	1.99E+08	2.05E+08	1.56E+00 •	1.07E+02 •	**1.54E+00** •	1.06E+01 •
f_{12}	1.57E+03	1.58E+03	9.50E+02 •	8.93E+02 •	8.54E+02 •	**8.42E+02** •
f_{13}	4.57E+09	4.32E+09	1.90E+05 •	3.33E+06 •	**1.77E+05** •	1.76E+06 •
f_{14}	2.27E+09	2.56E+09	1.36E+08 •	2.92E+08 •	**1.09E+08** •	2.74E+08 •

Table 3. Median of the difference-to-optimum values obtained by the algorithms on BBOB-largescale test problems. Each algorithm is run 15 times on each function. Bold text indicate the best performance. Bold texts indicate the best results, • indicates better performance than the base CC-RDG3 algorithm, while ▽ indicates worse performance.

Fn	CC-RDG3	IPOP	KC	IPOP-KC	KC-SA	IPOP-KC-SA
f_{16}	**7.404E-01**	8.113E-01	1.258E+00 ▽	1.347E+00 ▽	1.318E+00 ▽	1.200E+00 ▽
f_{17}	**3.707E-01**	4.062E-01	1.173E+00 ▽	8.908E-01 ▽	1.043E+00 ▽	1.175E+00 ▽
f_{18}	1.778E+00	**1.737E+00**	4.067E+00 ▽	3.798E+00 ▽	3.162E+00 ▽	2.944E+00 ▽
f_{19}	2.503737e-01	2.503737e-01	1.659E-02 •	**1.659E-02** •	1.659E-02 •	2.291E-02 •
f_{21}	2.922E-08	**1.198E-08**	6.730E+00 ▽	1.451E-08	6.740E+00 ▽	1.340E-08
f_{22}	2.596E+00	3.299E+00	4.640E+00	2.448E+00	**2.438E+00**	3.114E+00
f_{23}	1.897E-02	**1.884E-02**	2.138E-02	2.452E-02 ▽	2.392E-02	2.040E-02
f_{24}	9.999E+01	**9.316E+01**	1.511E+02 ▽	1.445E+02 ▽	1.479E+02 ▽	1.445E+02 ▽

functions, the KC strategy will likely lead to early convergence which may trap the search at local optima. This can be observed in Fig. 7 for f_9 where the algorithms with KC strategy become flat very early. In multimodal functions, algorithms with IPOP strategy show better performances. This indicates that the observation in [7] holds true in large scale settings, a larger population will improve CMA-ES performance on multimodal functions.

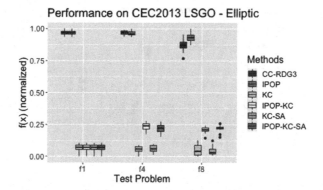

Fig. 1. Boxplot of the best values obtained on CEC2013 elliptic test problems.

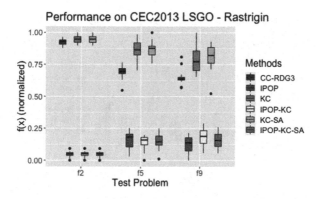

Fig. 2. Boxplot of the best values on CEC2013 test problems based on Rastrigin function.

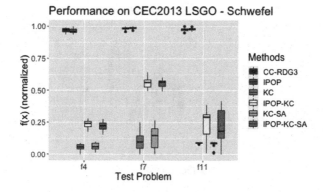

Fig. 3. Boxplot of the best values obtained on CEC2013 test problems based on Schwefel function.

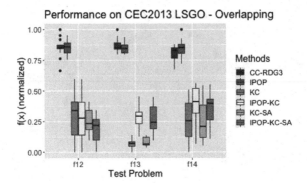

Fig. 4. Boxplot of the best values obtained on CEC2013 test problems with overlapping variables.

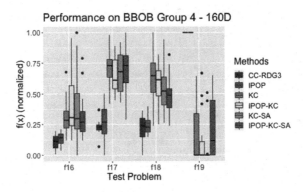

Fig. 5. Boxplot of the distance-to-optimum values obtained by the algorithms on BBOB-largescale test problems with adequate global structure.

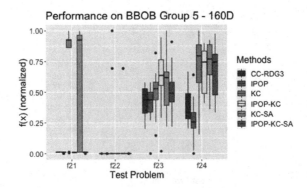

Fig. 6. Boxplot of the distance-to-optimum values obtained by the algorithms on BBOB-largescale test problems with weak global structure.

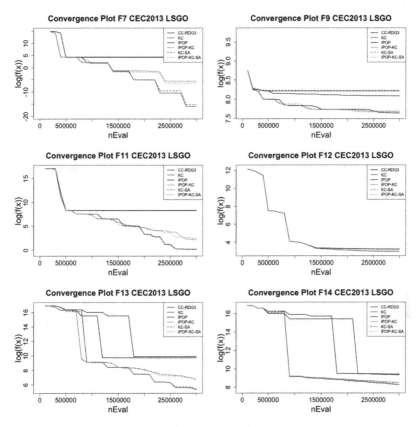

Fig. 7. Convergence plots for CEC2013 test problems. Each line is the mean achieved values for different algorithms after certain numbers of function evaluations.

The test results presented in Table 3 further confirm the dread of KC strategy and potency of IPOP strategy for multimodal functions. In most of the multimodal BBOB functions, the IPOP strategy has an advantage over the KC strategy. However, unlike on the f_3, f_5, and f_{10}, the improvement obtained from the IPOP strategy is insignificant on the BBOB problems. This may be because the restart is triggered too late and a too small budget to see the effect of increasing population. In a similar study for smaller problems, Hansen [6] used CMA-ES with a different population adaptation scheme called BIPOP-CMA-ES. The study in [6] uses more stopping criteria (hence it may stop earlier) and number of function evaluations up to $3 \times 10^5 d$.

Looking at Fig. 6, the CC-RDG3, and CC-RDG3-IPOP algorithms seem to perform terribly on f_{19}. If we look into Table 3, although they are indeed worse, the distance-to-optimum value on both algorithms are actually very low. However, we can still analyze why it performs worse than other algorithms.

By assessing the convergence history, we found that the two algorithms cannot find better solutions than the initial samples, hence the flat line in Fig. 8

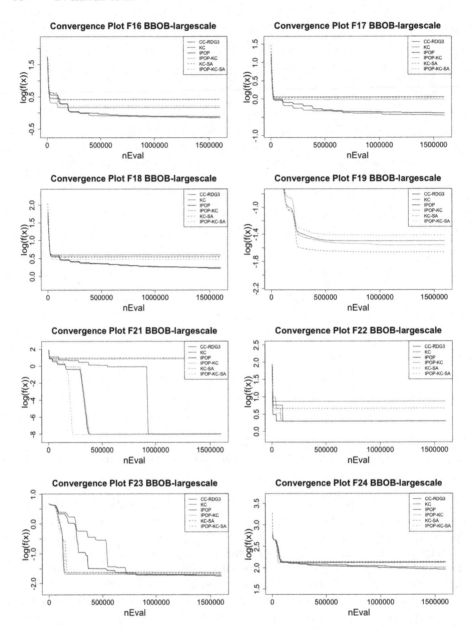

Fig. 8. Convergence plots for BBOB test problems. Each line is the mean distance-to-optimum values for different algorithms after certain numbers of function evaluations.

for f_{19}. In such a case, the search is restarted from the same initial point and the CMA-ES is also restarted with the same covariance matrix and step size as the previous cycle, repeating a failed search over and over. The problem with such restart is that the step size resets to a large value while what is needed in this case is a local search. The IPOP strategy also promotes a more global search instead of a local search hence the CC-RDG3-IPOP also does not perform well. On the other hand, with the introduction of the KC strategy, the step size will normally decrease in every cycle leading to a local search. The KC strategy clearly improves performance in such cases. However, the risk of early convergence to local optima still holds for the KC strategy.

In general, control over whether the search should be local or global is crucial in solving multimodal function. The two strategies provide a way to control it. The IPOP strategy will lead to a more global search, while the KC strategy will lead to a local search. To take full advantage of the strategies, a fitness landscape analysis can be conducted before choosing the strategies.

5 Conclusion and Future Work

In this study, three strategies to improve the CC-RDG3 algorithm are proposed and tested: persistent covariance, increasing population, and budget allocation based on sensitivity analysis. The budget allocation based on sensitivity analysis does not seem to provide significant improvement.

For unimodal functions, a persistent covariance strategy will improve performance while the IPOP strategy does not produce improvement on such functions. On multimodal functions, on the other hand, the persistent covariance could be detrimental as it leads to early convergence. On these functions, the IPOP strategy could potentially improve performance as the restart strategy prevents local entrapment. However, more tests on larger problems are needed. Furthermore, we identified a special case where the KC strategy is good for multimodal function: when a good candidate solution is found early and a local search is needed. To fully take advantage of the proposed strategies, a fitness landscape analysis should be conducted. How the landscape analysis will be integrated into the CC framework and the algorithms are left as future work.

Acknowledgment. This work is partly funded by the European Commission's H2020 program, UTOPIAE Marie Curie Innovative Training Network, H2020-MSCA-ITN-2016, under Grant Agreement No. 722734. The authors also acknowledge the financial support from the Slovenian Research Agency (research core funding No. P2-0098) as well as the DAAD (German Academic Exchange Service), Project-ID: 57515062 "Multi-objective Optimization for Artificial Intelligence Systems in Industry".

References

1. Auger, A., Hansen, N.: A restart CMA evolution strategy with increasing population size. In: Congress on Evolutionary Computation, vol. 2, pp. 1769–1776. IEEE (2005)
2. Van den Bergh, F., Engelbrecht, A.P.: A cooperative approach to particle swarm optimization. Trans. Evol. Comput. **8**(3), 225–239 (2004)
3. Campolongo, F., Cariboni, J., Saltelli, A., Schoutens, W.: Enhancing the Morris method. In: Sensitivity Analysis of Model Output, pp. 369–379 (2005)

4. Chen, W., Tang, K.: Impact of problem decomposition on cooperative coevolution. In: Congress on Evolutionary Computation, pp. 733–740. IEEE (2013). https://doi.org/10.1109/CEC.2013.6557641
5. Elhara, O., et al.: COCO: the large scale black-box optimization benchmarking (BBOB-largescale) test suite. arXiv preprint arXiv:1903.06396 (2019)
6. Hansen, N.: Benchmarking a BI-population CMA-ES on the BBOB-2009 function testbed. In: Proceedings of the 11th Annual Conference Companion on Genetic and Evolutionary Computation Conference: Late Breaking Papers, GECCO 2009, pp. 2389–2396. ACM, New York (2009). https://doi.org/10.1145/1570256.1570333
7. Hansen, N., Kern, S.: Evaluating the CMA evolution strategy on multimodal test functions. In: Yao, X., et al. (eds.) PPSN 2004. LNCS, vol. 3242, pp. 282–291. Springer, Heidelberg (2004). https://doi.org/10.1007/978-3-540-30217-9_29
8. Hansen, N., Ostermeier, A.: Completely derandomized self-adaptation in evolution strategies. Evol. Comput. $9(2)$, 159–195 (2001)
9. Li, X., Tang, K., Omidvar, M.N., Yang, Z., Qin, K., China, H.: Benchmark functions for the CEC 2013 special session and competition on large-scale global optimization. Gene $7(33)$, 8 (2013)
10. Mahdavi, S., Rahnamayan, S., Shiri, M.E.: Cooperative co-evolution with sensitivity analysis-based budget assignment strategy for large-scale global optimization. Appl. Intell. $47(3)$, 888–913 (2017)
11. Mahdavi, S., Rahnamayan, S., Shiri, M.E.: Multilevel framework for large-scale global optimization. Soft Comput. $21(14)$, 4111–4140 (2017). https://doi.org/10.1007/s00500-016-2060-y
12. Omidvar, M.N., Kazimipour, B., Li, X., Yao, X.: CBCC3 – a contribution-based cooperative co-evolutionary algorithm with improved exploration/exploitation balance. In: Congress on Evolutionary Computation, pp. 3541–3548, July 2016. https://doi.org/10.1109/CEC.2016.7744238
13. Omidvar, M.N., Li, X., Mei, Y., Yao, X.: Cooperative co-evolution with differential grouping for large scale optimization. Trans. Evol. Comput. $18(3)$, 378–393 (2014). https://doi.org/10.1109/TEVC.2013.2281543
14. Omidvar, M.N., Yang, M., Mei, Y., Li, X., Yao, X.: DG2: a faster and more accurate differential grouping for large-scale black-box optimization. Trans. Evol. Comput. $21(6)$, 929–942 (2017). https://doi.org/10.1109/TEVC.2017.2694221
15. Potter, M.A., De Jong, K.A.: A cooperative coevolutionary approach to function optimization. In: Davidor, Y., Schwefel, H.-P., Männer, R. (eds.) PPSN 1994. LNCS, vol. 866, pp. 249–257. Springer, Heidelberg (1994). https://doi.org/10.1007/3-540-58484-6_269
16. Salomon, R.: Re-evaluating genetic algorithm performance under coordinate rotation of benchmark functions. a survey of some theoretical and practical aspects of genetic algorithms. Biosystems $39(3)$, 263–278 (1996). https://doi.org/10.1016/0303-2647(96)01621-8
17. Sun, Y., Li, X., Ernst, A., Omidvar, M.N.: Decomposition for large-scale optimization problems with overlapping components. In: Congress on Evolutionary Computation, pp. 326–333. IEEE (2019). https://doi.org/10.1109/CEC.2019.8790204
18. Sun, Y., Kirley, M., Halgamuge, S.K.: A recursive decomposition method for large scale continuous optimization. Trans. Evol. Comput. $22(5)$, 647–661 (2017)
19. Sun, Y., Kirley, M., Halgamuge, S.K.: Extended differential grouping for large scale global optimization with direct and indirect variable interactions. In: Proceedings of the 2015 Annual Conference on Genetic and Evolutionary Computation, GECCO 2015, pp. 313–320. ACM, New York (2015). https://doi.org/10.1145/2739480.2754666

20. Sun, Y., Omidvar, M.N., Kirley, M., Li, X.: Adaptive threshold parameter estimation with recursive differential grouping for problem decomposition. In: Proceedings of the Genetic and Evolutionary Computation Conference, pp. 889–896 (2018)
21. Yang, Z., Tang, K., Yao, X.: Large scale evolutionary optimization using cooperative coevolution. Inf. Sci. **178**(15), 2985–2999 (2008)

Reinforcement Learning for N-player Games: The Importance of Final Adaptation

Wolfgang Konen$^{(\boxtimes)}$ (ID) and Samineh Bagheri (ID)

Cologne Institute of Computer Science, TH Köln, Gummersbach, Germany
{wolfgang.konen,samineh.bagheri}@th-koeln.de

Abstract. This paper covers n-tuple-based reinforcement learning (RL) algorithms for games. We present a new algorithm for temporal difference (TD) learning which works seamlessly on various games with arbitrary number of players. This is achieved by taking a player-centered view where each player propagates his/her rewards back to previous rounds. We add a new element called Final Adaptation RL (FARL) to this algorithm. Our main contribution is that FARL is a vitally important ingredient to achieve success with the player-centered view in various games. We report results on seven board games with 1, 2 and 3 players, including Othello, ConnectFour and Hex. In most cases it is found that FARL is important to learn a near-perfect playing strategy. All algorithms are available in the GBG framework on GitHub.

Keywords: Reinforcement learning · TD-learning · Game learning · N-player games · n-tuples

1 Introduction

1.1 Motivation

It is desirable to have a better understanding of the principles how computers can learn strategic decision making. Games are an interesting test bed and reinforcement learning (RL) is a general paradigm for strategic decision making. It is however not easy to devise algorithms which work seamlessly on a large variety of games (different rules, goals and game boards, different number of players and so on). It is the hope that finding such algorithms and understanding which elements in them are important helps to better understand the principles of learning and strategic decision making.

Learning how to play games with neural-network-based RL agents can be seen as a complex optimization task. It is the goal to find the right weights such that the neural network outputs the optimal policy for all possible game states or a near-optimal policy that minimizes the expected error. The state space in board games is usually discrete and in most cases too large to be searched exhaustively.

© Springer Nature Switzerland AG 2020
B. Filipič et al. (Eds.): BIOMA 2020, LNCS 12438, pp. 84–96, 2020.
https://doi.org/10.1007/978-3-030-63710-1_7

These aspects pose challenges to the optimizer which has to generalize well to unseen states and has to avoid overfitting.

In this paper we describe in detail a new n-tuple-based RL algorithm. N-tuples were introduced by Lucas [13] to the field of game learning. Our new learning algorithms extend the work described in [1,8,19] and serve the purpose to be usable for a large variety of games. More specifically we deal here with discrete-time, discrete-action, one-player-at-a-time games. This includes board games and card games with $N = 1, 2, \ldots$ players. Games may be deterministic or nondeterministic.

N-tuple networks are shown to work well in a variety of games, (e.g. in ConnectFour [1,19], Othello [13], EinStein würfelt nicht [3], 2048 [18], SZ-Tetris [7] etc.) but the algorithms described here are not tied to them. Any other function approximation network (deep neural network or other) could be used as well.

All algorithms presented here are implemented in the General Board Game (GBG) learning and playing framework [9,10] and are applied to several games. The variety of games makes the RL algorithms a bit more complex than the basic RL algorithms. This paper describes the algorithm as simple as possible, yet as detailed as necessary to be precise and to follow the implementation in GBG's source code, which is available on GitHub[1].

A work related to GBG [9,10] is the general game systems Ludii [14]. Ludii is an efficient general game system based on ludeme library implemented in Java, allowing to play as well as to generate a large variety of strategy games. Currently all AI agents implemented in Ludii are tree-based agents (MCTS variants or AlphaBeta). GBG on the other hand offers the possibility to train RL-based algorithms on several games.

The main contributions of this paper are as follows: (i) It presents a unifying view for RL algorithms applicable to different games with different number of players; (ii) it demonstrates that a new element, named Final Adaptation RL (FARL), is vital for having success with this new unifying view; (iii) it incorporates several other elements (afterstates, n-tuples, eligibility with horizon, temporal coherence) that are useful for all games. To the best of our knowledge, this is the first time that these elements are brought together in a comprehensive form for game-learning algorithms with arbitrary number N of players.

1.2 Algorithm Overview

The most important task of a game-playing agent is to propose, given a game state s_t, a good next action a_t from the set of available actions in s_t. TD-learning (Sect. 2.5) uses the value function $V(s_t)$ which is the expected sum of future rewards when being in state s_t.

It is the task of the agent to learn the value function $V(s)$ from experience (interaction with the environment). In order to do so, it usually performs multiple self-play training episodes, until a certain training budget is exhausted or a certain game-playing strength is reached.

---

[1] https://github.com/WolfgangKonen/GBG.

The nomenclature and algorithmic description follows as closely as possible the descriptions given in [6,18]. But these algorithms are for the special case of the 1-player game 2048. Since we want to use the TD-n-tuple algorithm for a broader class of games, in this paper we present a unified TD-update scheme inspired by [15] which works for 1-, 2-, ..., N-player games.

Our new RL-algorithm is partly inspired by [6,15] and partly from our own experience with RL-n-tuple training. The key elements of the new RL-logic – as opposed to our previous RL-algorithms [1,8] – are:

- New afterstate logic [6], see Sect. 2.2.
- Eligibility method with horizon [6], see Sect. 2.3.
- Generalization to N-player games with arbitrary N [15], see Sect. 2.4.
- Final adaptation RL (FARL) for all players, see Sect. 2.6.
- Weight-individual learning rates via temporal coherence learning (TCL) [1,2].

More details are described in an extended technical report [11].

2   Algorithms and Methods

2.1   N-tuple Systems

N-tuple systems coupled with TD were first applied to game learning by Lucas in 2008 [13], although n-tuples were introduced already in 1959 for character recognition purposes. The remarkable success of n-tuples in learning to play Othello [13] motivated other authors to benefit from this approach for a number of other games. The main goal of n-tuple systems is to map a highly non-linear function in a low dimensional space to a high dimensional space where it is easier to separate 'good' and 'bad' regions. This can be compared to kernel trick in Support Vector Machines (SVM). An n-tuple is defined as a sequence of n cells of the board. Each cell can have m values representing the possible states of that cell. Therefore, every n-tuple will have a (possibly large) look-up table indexed in form of an n-digit number in base m. An n-tuple system contains multiple n-tuples.

2.2   Afterstate Logic

For nondeterministic games, Jaśkowski et al. [6,18] describe a clever mechanism to reduce the complexity of the value function $V(s)$.

Consider a game like 2048 (Fig. 1): An exemplary action is to move all tiles to the right, this will cause the environment to merge adjacent same-value tiles into one single tile twice as big. This is the deterministic part of the action and the resulting state is called the **afterstate** s'. The second part of the action *move-right* is that the environment adds a random tile 2 or 4 to one of the empty tiles. This results in the **next state** s''.

The naive approach for learning the value function would be to observe the next state s'' and learn $V(s'')$. But this has the burden of increased complexity: Given a state-action pair (s, a) there is only *one* afterstate s', but $2n$ possible

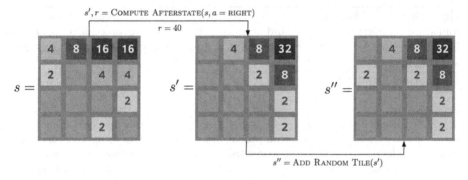

Fig. 1. For nondeterministic games it is better to split a state transition from s to s'' in a deterministic part, resulting in **afterstate** s', and a random part resulting in **next state** s'' (taken from [18]).

next states s'', where n is the number of empty tiles in afterstate s'.[2] This makes it much harder to learn the value of an action a in state s. And indeed, it is not the specific value of $V(s'')$ which is the value of action a, but it is the expectation value $\langle V(s'') \rangle$ over *all* possible next states s''.

It is much more clever to learn the value $V(s')$ of an afterstate. This reduces the complexity by a factor of $2\bar{n}$, where $\bar{n}$ is the average number of empty tiles. It helps the agent to generalize better in all phases of TD-learning.

For deterministic games there is no random part: afterstate s' and next state s'' are the same. However, afterstates are also beneficial for deterministic games: For positional games (like TicTacToe, ConnectFour, Hex, ...) the value of taking action a in state s depends only on the resulting afterstate s'. Several state-action pairs might lead to the same afterstate, and it often reduces the complexity of game learning if we learn the mapping from afterstates to game values (as we do in TD-learning, Sect. 2.5).

2.3 Eligibility Method

Instead of Sutton's eligibility traces [17] we use in this paper Jaśkowski's eligibility method [6]. This method is efficiently computable even in the case of long RL episodes and it can be made equivalent to eligibility traces in the case of short episodes. For details the reader is referred to Appendix A.3 of the extended technical report [11] or to [6].

2.4 N Players

We want to propose a general TD(λ) n-tuple algorithm which is applicable not only to 1- and 2-player games but to arbitrary N-player games.

---

[2] In the example of Fig. 1 we have $n = 9$ empty tiles in afterstate s', thus there are $2n = 18$ possible next states s''. The factor 2 arises because the environment can place one of the two random tiles 2 or 4 in any empty tile.

Algorithm 1. TDFROMEPISODE: Perform one episode of TD-learning, starting from state s_0. States s'_{t-1}, s_t, s'_t and actions a_t are for **one** specific player p_t. r_t is the delta reward for p_t when taking action a_t in state s_t. A_t is the set of actions available in state s_t.

1: **function** TDFROMEPISODE(s_0)
2:    $t \leftarrow 0$
3:    **repeat**
4:        Choose for player p_t action $a_t \in A_t$ from s_t using policy derived from V
5:            ▷ e.g. ϵ-greedy: with probability ϵ random, with prob. $1 - \epsilon$ using V
6:        Take action a_t and observe reward r_t, afterstate s'_t and next state s''.
7:        $V^{new}(s'_{t-1}) = r_t + \gamma V(s'_t)$ ▷ target value for p_t's previous afterstate
8:        Use NN to get the current value of previous afterstate: $V(s'_{t-1})$
9:        Adapt NN by backpropagating error $\delta = V^{new}(s'_{t-1}) - V(s_{t-1})$
10:       $t \leftarrow t + 1$
11:       $s_t \leftarrow s''$
12:   **until** s'' is terminal

The key difference to the TD-learning variants described in earlier work [1,8] is that there each state was connected with the next state in the episode. This required different concepts for TD-learning, depending on whether we had a 1-player game (maximize next state's value) or a 2-player game (minimize next state's value). Furthermore it has a severe problem for N-player games with $N > 2$: We usually do not know the game value for all other players in intermediate states, but we would need them for the algorithms in [1,8]. In contrast, van der Ree and Wiering [15] describe an approach where each player has a value function only for *his/her* states s_t or state-action-pairs (s_t, a_t). The actions of the opponents are subsumed in the reaction from the environment. That is, if s_t is the state for player p_t at time t, then s_{t+1} is the next state of the *same* player p_t on which (s)he has to act. This has the great advantage that there is no need to translate the value of a state for player p_t to the value for other players – we take always the perspective of the same player when calculating temporal differences.

In the next section we describe the application of these ideas to TD-learning, which will result in the (new) TD-FARL n-tuple algorithm valid for all N-player games.

2.5   TD Learning for N Players

We set up a TD-learning algorithm connecting moves to the last move of the **same** player. This is done in Algorithm 1 (TDFROMEPISODE). Algorithm 1 shows the TD-learning algorithm in compact form. It thus makes the general principle clear. But it has the disadvantage that it obscures one important detail: What is shown within the while loop is what has to be done by player p_t in state s_t. After completing this, we do however *not* move to the next state s_{t+1} of the same player p_t (one round away), but we let the environment act, get a new state

Algorithm 2. TD-FARL-EPISODE: Perform one episode of TD-learning, starting from state s_0. Similar to Algorithm 1, but with Final-Adaptation RL (FARL). We connect afterstate s' via player p_t with the previous afterstate $s_{last}[p_t]$ of this player. Note that s_{last} and r are vectors of length N (number of players).

```
 1: function TD-FARL-EPISODE(s_0)
 2:     t ← 0;
 3:     s_last[p] ← null  ∀ player p = 0, ..., N − 1              ▷ last afterstates
 4:     repeat
 5:         p_t = player to move in state s_t
 6:         Choose action a_t from s_t using policy derived from V     ▷ e.g. ε-greedy
 7:         (r, s', s'') ← MAKEACTION(s_t, a_t)           ▷ s': afterstate (after taking a_t)
 8:                            ▷ r is the delta reward tuple from the perspective of all players p
 9:         ADAPTAGENTV(s_last[p_t], r[p_t], s')
10:         s_last[p_t] ← s'         ▷ the afterstate generated by p_t when taking action a_t
11:         t ← t + 1
12:         s_t ← s''
13:     until (s'' is terminal)
14:     FINALADAPTAGENTS(p_t, r, s')      ▷ use final reward tuple to adapt all agents
15:
16:                               ▷ Update the value function (based on NN) for player p_t
17: function ADAPTAGENTV(s_last[p_t], r', s')
18:     if (s_last[p_t] ≠ null) then            ▷ Adapt V(s_last[p_t]) towards target T
19:         Target T = r' + γV(s') for afterstate s_last[p_t]
20:         Use NN to get V(s_last[p_t])
21:         Adapt NN by backpropagating error δ = T − V(s_last[p_t])
22:
23:                       ▷ Terminal update of value function for all players
24: function FINALADAPTAGENTS(p_t, r, s')
25:     for (p = 0, ..., N − 1, but p ≠ p_t) do
26:         if (s_last[p] ≠ null) then            ▷ Adapt V(s_last[p]) towards target r[p]
27:             Use NN to get V(s_last[p])
28:             Adapt NN by backpropagating error δ = r[p] − V(s_last[p])
29:                          ▷ Adapt V(s') → 0  (s': terminal afterstate of player p_t)
30:     Use NN to get V(s')
31:     Adapt NN by backpropagating error δ = 0 − V(s')
```

s_t'' for the **next** player, and then this next player does *his/her* pass through the while loop.

To make these details more clear, we write the algorithm down in a form where the pseudocode is closer to the GBG implementation. This is done in Algorithm 2 (TD-FARL-EPISODE). Some remarks on Algorithm 2:

- Now the sequence of states $s_0, s_1, ..., s_f$ is really the sequence of consecutive moves in an episode. The players usually vary in cyclic order, $0, 1, ..., N − 1, 0, 1, ...$, but other turn sequences are possible as well.
- In each state the connection to the last afterstate of the same player p is made via $s_{last}[p]$. Thus the update step is equivalent to Algorithm 1.

– In contrast to Algorithm 1, this algorithm has the final adaptation step FARL (function FINALADAPTAGENTS) included. FARL is covered in more detail in Sect. 2.6.

Algorithm 2 is simpler and at the same time more general than our previous TD-algorithms [1, 8] for several reasons:

1. Each player has its own value function V and each player seeks actions that **maximize** this V. This is because each V has in its targets the rewards from the perspective of the acting player. So there is no need to set up complicated cases distinguishing between minimization and maximization as it was in [1, 8].
2. The same algorithm is viable for **arbitrary** number of players.
3. There is no (or less) unwanted crosstalk because of too frequent updates (as it was the case for some variants in [1, 8]).[3]
4. Since states are connected with states one round (and not one move) earlier, positive or negative rewards propagate back faster.

2.6   Final Adaptation RL (FARL)

Once an episode terminates, we have a delta reward tuple for all players. A drawback of the plain TD-algorithm is that only the current player (who generated the terminal state) uses this information to perform an update step. But the other players can also learn from their (usually negative) rewards. This is what the first part of FINALADAPTAGENTS (lines 26–28 of Algorithm 2) does: Collect for each player *his/her* terminal delta reward and use this as target for a final update step where the value of the player's state one round earlier is adapted towards this target.[4]

One might ask whether it is not a contradiction to Sect. 2.4 where we stated that the value for other players is not known for $N > 2$. This is not a contradiction: Although intermediate *values* are usually not known for all players, the final *reward* of a game episode – at least for all games we know of – *is available* for all players. It is thus a good strategy to use this information for all players.

Second part of FINALADAPTAGENTS, lines 29–31: A terminal state is by definition a state where no future rewards are expected. Therefore the value of that state should be zero. However, crosstalk in the network due to the adaptation of other states may lead to non-zero values for terminal states. Jaśkowski [6] proposes to make an adaptation step towards target 0 for all terminal states.

---

[3] With crosstalk we mean the effect that the update of the value function for one state has detrimental effects on the learned values for other states.

[4] The target has only the delta reward $r[p]$ and does not need the value function $V(s')$ because the value function for a terminal s' is always 0 (no future rewards are expected).

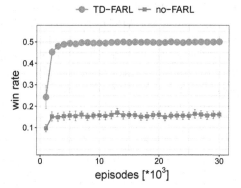

Fig. 2. Different versions of TD-learning on TicTacToe. Each agent is evaluated by playing games from different start positions in both roles, 1st and 2nd player, against the perfect-playing Max-N agent [12]. The best achievable result is 0.5, because Max-N will win at least in one of the both roles. Shown is the mean over 25 training runs. The error bars depict σ_{mean}.

3 Results

We show detailed results of our algorithms on two games. In preliminary experiments we tested various settings for parameters, namely the learning rate α, the random move rate ϵ and the eligibility rate λ. We selected for TicTacToe parameter α linearly decreasing from 1.0 to 0.5 and the n-tuple system consisted just of one 9-tuple. For ConnectFour we used $\alpha = 3.7$ and an n-tuple system consisting of initially randomly chosen but then fixed 70 8-tuples. For both games we had ϵ linearly decreasing from 0.1 to 0.0, $\lambda = 0.0$ and we used the TCL scheme as described in [1,11]. Note that due to TCL the effective learning rate adopted by most weights can be far smaller than α. The detailed parameter settings for all other games are given in the extended technical report [11].

3.1 TicTacToe

Figure 2 shows the learning curves of TD-learning. The red curve shows the full Algorithm 2 (TD-FARL-EPISODE). The blue curve shows the results when we switch off FINALADAPTAGENTS: The decrease in performance is drastic.

3.2 ConnectFour

Figure 3 shows learning curves of our TD-FARL agent on the non-trivial game ConnectFour. Two modes of evaluation are shown: The red curves evaluate against opponent AlphaBeta (AB), the blue curves against opponent AlphaBeta-Distant-Losses (AB-DL). The AlphaBeta algorithm extends the Minimax algorithm by efficiently pruning the search tree. Thill et al. [19] were able to implement AlphaBeta for ConnectFour in such a way that it plays perfect in situations where it can win. AB and AB-DL differ in the way they react on losing states: While AB just takes a random move, AB-DL searches for the move which postpones the loss as far (distant) as possible. It is tougher to win against AB-DL since it will punish every wrong move. The final results for our TD-FARL agent are however very satisfying: 49.5% win rate against AB, 46.5% win rate against AB-DL. It is worth noting that two perfect-playing opponents (AB and AB-DL) are not necessarily equally strong.

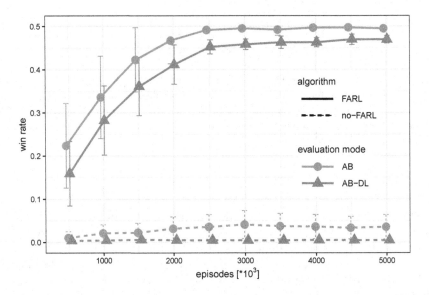

Fig. 3. TD-learning on ConnectFour. During training, agent TD-FARL is evaluated against the perfect-playing agents AlphaBeta (AB) and AlphaBeta-with-distant-losses (AB-DL). Both agents play in both roles (first or second). Since ConnectFour is a theoretical win for the starting player, the ideal win rates against AB and AB-DL are 0.5. The solid lines show the mean win rates from 10 training runs with FARL. The dashed curves *no-FARL* show the results when FARL is turned off. Error bars depict the standard deviation of the mean.

It is a remarkable success that TD-FARL learns only from training by self-play to defeat the perfect-playing AlphaBeta agents in 49%/46% of the cases. Remember that TD-FARL has never seen AlphaBeta before during training. The result is similar to our previous work [1]. But the difference is that the new algorithm can be applied without any change to other games with any N.

There is also a striking failure visible in Fig. 3: If we switch off FINALADAPT-AGENTS (curves *no-FARL*), we see a complete break-down of the TD agent: It loses nearly all its games. We conclude that the part propagating the final reward

of the other player back to the other player's previous state is vitally important.[5]
If we analyze the *no-FARL*-agent we find that it has only 0.9% active weights
while the good-working TD-FARL agent has 8% active weights. This comes
because the other player (that is the one who loses the game since the current
player created a winning state) has never the negative reward propagated back to
previous states of that other player. Thus the network fails to learn threatening
positions and/or precursors of such threatening positions.

Table 1. Results for Algorithm 2 (TD-FARL-Episode) on various games. In Nim(3P)
hxs, there are initially h heaps with s stones. For each game, 10 training runs with
different seeds are performed and the resulting TD agent is evaluated by playing against
opponents as indicated in column 3 (two such opponents in the case of Nim3P). Each
agent plays all roles. Shown are the TD agent's win rates or scores (rewards): mean
from 10 runs plus/minus one standard deviation of the mean.

Game	N	evaluated vs.	win rates or scores		other RL research	
			FARL	no-FARL		
2048	1		$142\,000 \pm 1\,000$	$122\,000 \pm 900$	[6]	$80\,000$
TicTacToe	2	Max-N_{10} [12]	$49\% \pm 5\%$	$18\% \pm 6\%$		
ConnectFour	2	AB [19]	$49.5\% \pm 0.5\%$	$3.5\% \pm 0.1\%$	[4]	$0.0\% \pm 0.0\%$
		AB-DL [19]	$46.5\% \pm 0.5\%$	$0.0\% \pm 0.1\%$		
Hex 6x6	2	MCTS$_{10000}$	$81\% \pm 5\%$	$0.0\% \pm 0.2\%$		
Othello	2	Edax$_{d1}$ [5]	$55\% \pm 1\%$	$53\% \pm 1\%$		
		Bench [15]	$95\% \pm 0.3\%$	$96\% \pm 0.2\%$	[15]	$87.1\% \pm 0.9\%$
Nim 3x5	2	Max-N_{15} [12]	$50\% \pm 1\%$	$12\% \pm 6\%$		
Nim3P 3x5	3	Max-N_{15} [12]	0.33 ± 0.03	0.03 ± 0.01		
		MCTS$_{5000}$	0.78 ± 0.02	0.09 ± 0.02		

3.3 A Variety of Games

In Table 1 we show the results for seven games with varying number of players
(1, 2, or 3). While there exist many well-known games for 1 and 2 players, it
is not easy to find 3-player games which have a clear winning strategy. Nim3P,
the 3-player-variant of the game Nim, is such a game. Each player can take any
number of pieces from one heap at his/her turn. The player who takes the last
piece loses and gets a reward of 0.0, then the successor is the winner and gets
a reward of 1; the predecessor gets a reward of 0.2. This smaller reward helps
to break ties in otherwise 'undecided' situations. The goal for each player is to
maximize his/her average reward. Nim3P cannot end in a tie.

All games are learned by exactly the same TD-FARL/no-FARL algorithm.
The strength of the resulting agent is evaluated by playing against opponents,

---

[5] It is really the first part of FARL which is important: We conducted an experiment
where we switch off only the second part of FARL and observed only a very slight
degradation (1% or less).

where all agents play in all roles. The opponents are in many cases perfect-playing or strong-playing agents. If all agents play perfect, the best possible result for each agent is a win rate of 50% for 2-player games and a score of 0.4 for the game Nim3P (one third of the total reward 1.2 distributed in each episode). Max-N_d is an N-Player tree search with depth d [12], being a perfect player for the games TicTacToe, Nim, Nim3P. For ConnectFour, AB and AB-DL [19] are perfect-playing agents introduced in Sect. 3.2. Edax$_{d1}$ [5] is a strong Othello program, played here with depth 1. BENCH [15] is a medium-strength Othello agent. MCTS$_a$ is a Monte Carlo Tree Search with a iterations.

As can be seen from Table 1, TD-FARL reaches near-perfect playing strength in most competitions against (near-)perfect opponents and it dominates non-perfect opponents. The most striking feature of Table 1 is its column 'no-FARL': it is in all games much weaker, with one notable exception: In Othello the results for TD-FARL and TD-no-FARL are approximately the same. This is supported by the results from van der Ree and Wiering [15] who had good results on Othello with their no-FARL algorithms. We have no clear answer yet why Othello behaves differently than all other games.

3.4   Comparison with Other RL Research

For some games we compare in Table 1 with other RL approaches from the literature. Jaśkowski [6] achieves for the game 2048 with a similar amount of training episodes and a general-purpose baseline TD agent scores around 80 000. It has to be noted that Jaśkowski with ten times more training episodes and algorithms specifically designed for 2048 reaches much higher scores around 600 000, but here we only want to compare with general-purpose RL approaches.

Dawson [4] introduces a CNN-based and AlphaZero-inspired [16] RL agent named ConnectZero for the game ConnectFour, which can be played online. Although it reaches a good playing strength against MCTS$_{1000}$, it cannot win a single game against our AlphaBeta agent. We performed 10 episodes with ConnectZero starting (which is a theoretical win), but found that instead AlphaBeta playing second won all games. This is in contrast to our TD-FARL which wins nearly all episodes when starting against AlphaBeta.

Finally we compare for the game Othello with the work of van der Ree and Wiering [15]: Their Q-learning agent reaches against BENCH (positional player) a win rate of 87% while their TD-learning agent reaches 72%. Both win rates are a bit lower than our 95%.

3.5   Discussion

Looking at the results for ConnectFour, one might ask the following question: If FARL is so important for RL-based ConnectFour, why could Bagheri et al. [1] learn the game when their algorithm did not have FARL? – The reason is, that both algorithms have different TD-learning schemes: While the algorithm in [1] propagates the target from the current state back to the previous state (one *move* earlier), our N-player RL propagates the target from the current state back to the previous move of the same player (one *round* earlier). The N-player FARL is more general (it works for arbitrary N). But it has also this consequence: If for example a 2-player game is terminated by a move of player 1, the value of the previous state $s_{last}[p_2]$ of player 2 is never updated. As a consequence, player 2 will never learn to avoid the state preceding its loss. Exactly this is cured, if we activate FARL.

4 Conclusion and Future Work

In summary, we collected evidence that Algorithm 2 (TD-FARL-EPISODE) produces good results on a variety of games. It has been shown that the new ingredient FARL (the final adaption step) is vital in many games to get these good results.

Compared to [1], TD-FARL has the benefit that it can be applied unchanged to all kind of games whether they have one, two or three players. The algorithm of [1] cannot be applied to games with more than two players.

We see the following lines of direction for future work: (a) More 3-player games. Although Nim3P with a clear winning strategy provided a viable testbed for evaluating our algorithm, taking more 3-player or N-player games into account will help us to investigate how well our introduced methods generalize. (b) Can we better understand why Othello is indifferent to using FARL or no-FARL? Are there more such games? If so, an interesting research question would be whether it is possible to identify common game characteristics that allow to decide whether FARL is important for a game or not.

References

1. Bagheri, S., Thill, M., Koch, P., Konen, W.: Online adaptable learning rates for the game Connect-4. IEEE Trans. Comput. Intell. AI Games **8**(1), 33–42 (2015)
2. Beal, D.F., Smith, M.C.: Temporal coherence and prediction decay in TD learning. In: Dean, T. (ed.) International Joint Conference on Artificial Intelligence (IJCAI), pp. 564–569. Morgan Kaufmann (1999)
3. Chu, Y.R., Chen, Y., Hsueh, C., Wu, I.: An agent for EinStein Würfelt Nicht! using n-tuple networks. In: 2017 Conference on Technologies and Applications of Artificial Intelligence (TAAI), pp. 184–189, December 2017
4. Dawson, R.: Learning to play Connect-4 with deep reinforcement learning (2020). https://codebox.net/pages/connect4. Accessed 21 Aug 2020
5. Delorme, R.: Edax, version 4.4 (2019). https://github.com/abulmo/edax-reversi. Accessed 1 Aug 2020
6. Jaśkowski, W.: Mastering 2048 with delayed temporal coherence learning, multistage weight promotion, redundant encoding, and carousel shaping. IEEE Trans. Games **10**(1), 3–14 (2018)
7. Jaśkowski, W., Szubert, M., Liskowski, P., Krawiec, K.: High-dimensional function approximation for knowledge-free reinforcement learning: a case study in SZ-Tetris. In: Conference on Genetic and Evolutionary Computation, pp. 567–573 (2015)

8. Konen, W.: Reinforcement learning for board games: the temporal difference algorithm. Technical report, TH Köln (2015). http://www.gm.fh-koeln.de/ciopwebpub/Kone15c.d/TR-TDgame_EN.pdf

9. Konen, W.: General board game playing for education and research in generic AI game learning. In: Perez, D., Mostaghim, S., Lucas, S. (eds.) Conference on Games (London), pp. 1–8 (2019). https://arxiv.org/pdf/1907.06508

10. Konen, W.: The GBG class interface tutorial V2.1: general board game playing and learning. Technical report, TH Köln (2020). http://www.gm.fh-koeln.de/ciopwebpub/Konen20a.d/TR-GBG.pdf

11. Konen, W., Bagheri, S.: Final adaptation reinforcement learning for N-player games. Technical report, TH Köln - Cologne University of Applied Sciences (2020). http://www.gm.fh-koeln.de/ciopwebpub/Konen20_TR.d/TR-FARL.pdf

12. Korf, R.E.: Multi-player alpha-beta pruning. Artif. Intell. **48**(1), 99–111 (1991)

13. Lucas, S.M.: Learning to play Othello with n-tuple systems. Aust. J. Intell. Inf. Process. **4**, 1–20 (2008)

14. Piette, É., Soemers, D.J.N.J., Stephenson, M., Sironi, C.F., Winands, M.H.M., Browne, C.: Ludii - the ludemic general game system. CoRR abs/1905.05013 (2019). http://arxiv.org/abs/1905.05013

15. van der Ree, M., Wiering, M.: Reinforcement learning in the game of Othello: learning against a fixed opponent and learning from self-play. In: Adaptive Dynamic Programming and Reinforcement Learning (ADPRL), pp. 108–115 (2013)

16. Silver, D., et al.: Mastering the game of Go without human knowledge. Nature **550**(7676), 354–359 (2017)

17. Sutton, R.S., Barto, A.G.: Reinforcement Learning: An Introduction. MIT Press, Cambridge (1998)

18. Szubert, M., Jaśkowski, W.: Temporal difference learning of n-tuple networks for the game 2048. In: 2014 IEEE Conference on Computational Intelligence and Games (CIG), pp. 1–8. IEEE (2014)

19. Thill, M., Bagheri, S., Koch, P., Konen, W.: Temporal difference learning with eligibility traces for the game Connect-4. In: Preuss, M., Rudolph, G. (eds.) International Conference on Computational Intelligence in Games (CIG), Dortmund (2014)

An Interactive Framework for Offline Data-Driven Multiobjective Optimization

Atanu Mazumdar[1]([✉]) [iD], Tinkle Chugh[2] [iD], Jussi Hakanen[1] [iD],
and Kaisa Miettinen[1] [iD]

[1] University of Jyvaskyla, Faculty of Information Technology,
P.O. Box 35 (Agora), FI-40014 University of Jyvaskyla, Finland
atanu.a.mazumdar@student.jyu.fi, {jussi.hakanen,kaisa.miettinen}@jyu.fi
[2] Department of Computer Science, University of Exeter, Exeter, UK
t.chugh@exeter.ac.uk

Abstract. We propose a framework for solving offline data-driven multiobjective optimization problems in an interactive manner. No new data becomes available when solving offline problems. We fit surrogate models to the data to enable optimization, which introduces uncertainty. The framework incorporates preference information from a decision maker in two aspects to direct the solution process. Firstly, the decision maker can guide the optimization by providing preferences for objectives. Secondly, the framework features a novel technique for the decision maker to also express preferences related to maximum acceptable uncertainty in the solutions as preferred ranges of uncertainty. In this way, the decision maker can understand what uncertainty in solutions means and utilize this information for better decision making. We aim at keeping the cognitive load on the decision maker low and propose an interactive visualization that enables the decision maker to make decisions based on uncertainty. The interactive framework utilizes decomposition-based multiobjective evolutionary algorithms and can be extended to handle different types of preferences for objectives. Finally, we demonstrate the framework by solving a practical optimization problem with ten objectives.

Keywords: Decision support · Decision making ·
Decomposition-based MOEA · Metamodelling · Surrogate · Kriging ·
Gaussian processes

1 Introduction

Sometimes while solving data-driven multiobjective optimization problems (or MOPs) additional data can not be acquired during the solution process. Instead, we may have pre-collected data of the phenomenon of interest that was obtained beforehand, e.g. by conducting physical experiments. This type of optimization problems are termed as *offline* data-driven MOPs [3,8,17]. For formulating the optimization problem, we can build surrogate models using the given data to approximate the behaviour of the phenomenon. Optimization can then be

© Springer Nature Switzerland AG 2020
B. Filipič et al. (Eds.): BIOMA 2020, LNCS 12438, pp. 97–109, 2020.
https://doi.org/10.1007/978-3-030-63710-1_8

performed utilizing these surrogates as objective functions e.g. by a multiobjective evolutionary algorithm (MOEA). However, approximation error in the surrogates' prediction can not be avoided. Certain surrogate models such as Kriging also provide information about the uncertainty (e.g. as standard deviation) in predictions. This uncertainty information can be utilized in the optimization process to improve the quality of the solutions [11].

Previous works on offline multiobjective optimization such as [3,8,11,17] approximate the entire Pareto front. This makes decision making a difficult task as the decision maker (DM) has to choose from a large set of solutions. Interactive multiobjective optimization approaches allow the DM to find solutions in an interesting region of the Pareto front and learn about the problem and the feasibility of one's preferences and adjust the latter. They also provide limited amount of information at a time thereby reducing the cognitive load (see [13] for more information). There have been many developments in interactive MOEAs [14] and decomposition based MOEAs have become quite popular because of their capability of solving MOPs with a large number of objectives [2,4,20]. Hence, interactive approaches such as [7,10,21] have been proposed for decomposition-based MOEAs. However, as far as we know, addressing DM's preferences while solving offline MOPs in decomposition-based MOEAs has not been considered.

Utilizing the uncertainty information in interactive optimization may be quite valuable to the DM for a better understanding of the solutions and better decision making while solving offline MOPs. The major challenge in utilizing uncertainty in an interactive optimization process is conveying this extra information to the DM as (s)he may not be familiar with it.

In this paper, we propose a framework for solving offline data-driven MOPs interactively using decomposition-based MOEAs. It enables the DM to understand and make decisions based on the uncertainties present in the approximated solutions. The framework does not increase the cognitive load of the DM significantly while providing preference information for uncertainties along with the preferences for objectives.

2   Background

We consider the underlying MOP that has to be solved of the following form:

$$\text{minimize } \{f_1(\mathbf{x}), \ldots, f_K(\mathbf{x})\},$$
$$\text{subject to } \mathbf{x} \in S, \tag{1}$$

where $K \geq 2$ is the number of objectives and S is the feasible region in the decision space $\mathbb{R}^n$. For a feasible decision vector $\mathbf{x}$, the corresponding objective vector $\mathbf{f}(\mathbf{x})$ comprises of the underlying objective (function) values $(f_1(\mathbf{x}), \ldots, f_K(\mathbf{x}))$.

A solution $\mathbf{x}^1 \in S$ dominates another solution $\mathbf{x}^2 \in S$ if $f_k(\mathbf{x}^1) \leq f_k(\mathbf{x}^2)$ for all $k = 1, \ldots, K$ and $f_k(\mathbf{x}^1) < f_k(\mathbf{x}^2)$ for at least one $k = 1, \ldots, K$. If a solution of an MOP is not dominated by any other feasible solutions, it is called nondominated. Solving an MOP using an MOEA typically produces solutions that are nondominated within the set of solutions it has found. The solutions of Eq. (1) that are nondominated in S are also called Pareto optimal solutions. Next, we discuss a generic approach to solve an offline data-driven MOP.

2.1 Generic Approach for Offline Data-Driven Multiobjective Optimization

A generic way for offline data-driven optimization using an MOEA described in [8,18] is shown in Fig. 1. The solution process can be divided into three parts: a) data collection, b) formulating the MOP and building surrogate models, and c) running an MOEA. The first step involves performing experiments to acquire the data and pre-processing it if necessary. Next, surrogate models are built to approximate the behaviour of the underlying objective functions using the provided data. The prediction vector of the fitted surrogate models can be represented as $\hat{\mathbf{f}}(\mathbf{x}) = (\hat{f}_1(\mathbf{x}), \ldots, \hat{f}_K(\mathbf{x}))$, where $\hat{f}_k$ is the surrogate's prediction for f_k. Surrogate models such as Kriging also provide the uncertainty in the model's prediction generally in the form of standard deviation. The predicted uncertainty vector is represented as $\hat{\boldsymbol{\sigma}}(\mathbf{x}) = (\hat{\sigma}_1(\mathbf{x}), \ldots, \hat{\sigma}_K(\mathbf{x}))$, where $\hat{\sigma}_k$ is the uncertainty in prediction for the kth objective function. In the third step, an MOEA is run to solve the optimization problem with the surrogates as objective functions.

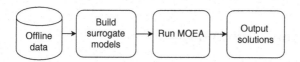

Fig. 1. A generic approach for offline data-driven multiobjective optimization.

Next, we briefly discuss an interactive approach for decomposition-based MOEAs which is a building block of the framework proposed in this paper.

2.2 Interactive Decomposition-Based MOEA

Decomposition-based MOEAs use reference (or weight) vectors to decompose the objective space into a number of sub-spaces. In general, they solve several simpler sub-problems that represent an aggregate of the objective functions by using a scalarizing function. Some examples of the scalarizing functions used are Chebyshev [20], penalty based boundary intersection distance (PBI) [20] and angle penalized distance (APD) [2]. The solutions obtained by solving these sub-problems jointly represent the approximated Pareto front of the MOP in the objective space.

Interactive decomposition-based MOEAs find solutions only in certain regions of the Pareto front. These approaches utilize preference information from the DM in the form of, e.g. a reference point, weights and preferred ranges for objectives. For more details, see, e.g. [14,19]. In this paper, we adopt the interactive approach proposed in [7] for decomposition-based MOEAs and briefly describe its main ideas as follows.

Converting Preference Information to Reference Vectors: One of the ways to incorporate preference information into decomposition-based MOEAs is by adapting the reference vectors to follow the DM's preferences [14]. We here demonstrate how to utilize a reference point which consists of the DM's desired value for each objective. However, the framework proposed later in this paper is not limited to only this type of preference information.

Consider a set of uniformly distributed reference vectors $V = \{\mathbf{v}^i \in \mathbb{R}^k | i = 1, \ldots, m\}$, where m is the total number of reference vectors, and $\bar{\mathbf{z}} \in \mathbb{R}^k$ is a single reference point provided by the DM. Each reference vector can be adapted as follows [2,7]:

$$\overline{\mathbf{v}^i} = \frac{r \cdot \mathbf{v}^i + (1-r) \cdot \mathbf{v}^c}{\|r \cdot \mathbf{v}^i + (1-r) \cdot \mathbf{v}^c\|}, \tag{2}$$

where $\mathbf{v}^c = \bar{\mathbf{z}} / \|\bar{\mathbf{z}}\|$ and $r \in (0,1)$. The central vector $\mathbf{v}^c$ is the projection of $\bar{\mathbf{z}}$ on a unit hypersphere and the spread of the adapted reference vectors is determined by the parameter r. The adapted reference vectors are close to $\mathbf{v}^c$ if r is close to zero and if r is close to one, the reference vectors are not changed much.

3   The Proposed Framework

As mentioned, since no new data is available in offline data-driven optimization, the approximation accuracy of the surrogate models determines the quality of solutions. In reality, the surrogate models' approximation involve uncertainty. As mentioned, Kriging surrogates [6] also provide an estimate of the uncertainty in its prediction. A solution with a higher uncertainty indicates that the objective values predicted by the surrogates have a lower probability of being close to the values of the underlying objective function. In other words, the uncertainty predicted by the surrogate models can represent the accuracy of the solutions when evaluated using the underlying objective functions. In [11], utilizing the predicted uncertainties from the surrogates as additional objective(s) produced solutions with a better hypervolume and accuracy in root mean squared error (RMSE) compared to the generic approach. This was because the approach simultaneously minimized the objective functions and their respective uncertainties. The solutions generated represented the trade-off between objective values and uncertainties. However, this results in an increase in both computational and cognitive load with a large number of objectives. Overall, it is desirable for the DM to get solutions that have a low uncertainty in order to achieve better accuracy.

As explained before, interactive approaches are quite advantageous as the DM can guide the optimization process through preferences for *objectives* and also learn about the problem. To incorporate preferences for *uncertainties* while solving an MOP interactively, the DM should first understand what uncertainty really means in regards to the MOP. Giving the DM an opportunity to provide preferences for uncertainties is desirable but may increase cognitive load.

The proposed framework aims at solving offline data-driven MOPs interactively by considering preferences for both objectives and uncertainties. The framework is based on a decomposition-based MOEA and preference information for objectives in the form of reference points. The first and primary challenge faced is the DM's understanding of uncertainty, specifically the uncertainty in the surrogates' approximation. Secondly, the cognitive load should not drastically increase when the DM wants to provide preferences for uncertainties along with the preferences for objectives. The proposed framework tackles both of the challenges and aims at providing an improved decision support for the DM during the solution process. Next, we discuss two steps which are the primary building blocks of the proposed framework.

3.1   Pre-filtering Solutions Following DM's Preferences

Generally, in offline data-driven MOPs, there exists a trade-off between the quality of solutions (e.g. hypervolume) and the accuracy of the solutions (e.g. RMSE) [11]. To have a diverse range of uncertainty and objective values, we first store the solutions from all the generations of an MOEA in an archive. This allows us to filter and make decisions from a pool of solutions having various objective and uncertainty values. However, only the solutions representing the DM's preferences for objectives are interesting to him/her. Hence, the archive needs some amount of pre-filtering before we can present it to the DM. We have to further filter these solutions such that only the solutions that simultaneously achieve the best objective values and the lowest uncertainties are shown to the DM. Hence, we propose a two-stage pre-filtering approach as follows.

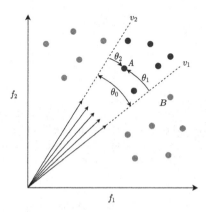

Fig. 2. Pre-filtering solutions: green dots are kept and red dots are rejected. (Color figure online)

The first stage is to find solutions in the archive that follow the DM's preferences for objectives, i.e., reference points. As described in Sect. 2.2, at first, the uniformly distributed set of reference vectors are adapted using Eq. (2) that reflects the DM's preferences for objectives. Next, we find the adapted reference vectors that have the highest component in one of the objectives and call them *edge vectors*. Initially, the set of reference vectors are uniformly distributed and have just one vector at each axis (objective). As the adaptation in Eq. (2) is linear; we find just one reference at every extreme or edge. Thus, the total number of edge vectors is K. The multidimensional volume enclosed by the edge vectors is termed as the *hypercone*. A solution is accepted by the first stage pre-filter if it lies inside the hypercone. Figure 2 shows the idea of the pre-filtering for a bi-objective minimization problem. The edge vectors are v_1 and v_2 and the angle between the edge vectors is θ_0. The angle between solution A and the edge vectors v_1 and v_2 is θ_1 and θ_2, respectively. A solution is accepted for the next pre-filtering stage if both θ_1 and θ_2 are smaller than θ_0. In the figure, the solutions in green (e.g. A) are accepted by this pre-filtering stage, and the solutions shown in red (e.g. B) are rejected. The rejected solutions do not follow the preferences and hence are not of interest to the DM. In general, with K objectives, the angle θ_0 between any two edge vectors is the same. This is because the set of uniformly distributed reference vectors is adapted by using a linear transformation. Hence, a solution is inside the hypercone if $\theta_k^i < \theta_0$ for all $k = 1, \ldots, K$, where θ_k^i is the angle between the kth edge vector and the ith solution.

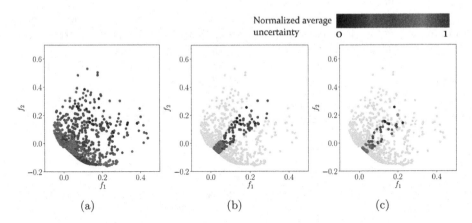

Fig. 3. The sub-figures show the solutions in different pre-filtering stages while solving a bi-objective minimization problem. The grey solutions are the ones filtered out at each stage. The red point denotes the reference point provided by the DM. (Color figure online)

The archive contains objective vectors and their respective uncertainties from all the generations. However, only the solutions with the smallest uncertainties and objective values are interesting for the DM. Hence, we propose a second pre-filtering stage that performs nondominated sorting on the solutions filtered by the first stage and include uncertainties as additional components in the vectors while sorting (as done in [11]). Considering uncertainty while performing nondominated sorting finds the solutions representing the trade-off between objective values and uncertainty.

These two stages are applied sequentially in the pre-filtering stage of our proposed framework. The functioning of the pre-filtering stage can be understood from Fig. 3, which shows solutions in the archive for a bi-objective minimization problem. The colour code represents the normalized average of the uncertainty vector for the solutions. Sub-figure (a) shows all the solutions in the archive before the pre-filtering. Sub-figure (b) shows the solutions after the first stage pre-filtering. It can be observed that only the solutions following the preferences for objectives (here the reference point in red) are filtered. Sub-figure (c) shows the solutions obtained after the second stage pre-filtering. The solutions after the pre-filtering stage follow the DM's preferences for objectives and represent the trade-off between objective values and uncertainties in the solutions. The grey solutions are the ones that are rejected at each pre-filtering stage.

3.2 DM's Understanding of Uncertainty

As discussed before, knowledge of uncertainty is an essential aspect while solving offline optimization problems. However, while solving real-life problems, the DM is not always familiar with uncertainty in the solutions. Depending on the problem, the DM can be assumed to have an idea of permissible tolerances in objective values. For example, in the welded beam problem [5], cost and end deflection are minimized. Considering just the DM's preference regarding cost, (s)he has an idea of the highest permissible cost. Here, the permissible deviation in the objective value is referred to as one-sided *tolerance* of the DM [9]. In other words, one-sided tolerance information can be considered as a cutoff over the probable variation in the objective values. In our case, the variation in objective values is available in the form of uncertainty in the surrogates. Preferred one-sided tolerances are *preferences for uncertainties* provided by the DM and represent the maximum permissible variation in the solutions when they are evaluated by the underlying objectives. In this paper, we refer to one-sided tolerance as tolerance for simplicity.

For the proposed framework (and later in the tests), we consider indifference tolerances. They are provided as a percentage for every objective and represent the 95% tolerance interval [9]. Let us consider the indifference tolerance provided by the DM for the kth objective function as $\tau_k\%$, where $k = 1, \ldots, K$. The distribution of the predicted objective value is Gaussian while using Kriging surrogates and the predicted standard deviation of the kth objectives' surrogate is $\hat{\sigma}_k(\mathbf{x})$. Thus, *cutoff tolerance functions* can be formulated such that the solutions do not violate the DM's preferences for uncertainties and thus are of interest to the DM. The kth cutoff tolerance function is:

$$g_k(\mathbf{x}) = 1.96\hat{\sigma}_k(\mathbf{x}) - \tau_k \cdot \hat{f}_k(\mathbf{x})/100 \le 0, \tag{3}$$

where **x** is the decision vector and $k = 1, \ldots, K$. A solution is interesting to the DM if the objective value of the kth objective function does not exceed $1.96\hat{\sigma}_k(\mathbf{x})$ or 95% confidence interval of the Gaussian distribution. Thus, the DM can change the preferences for uncertainties and visualize the solutions that do not violate the cutoff tolerance functions in Eq. (3). However, it has to be noted that the cutoff tolerance function can be modified depending on the prediction distribution of the surrogate.

3.3   Steps of the Framework

Figure 4 shows the simplified structure of the proposed interactive offline data-driven MOEA framework. The framework can be broadly divided into five steps:

1. Building surrogate models and initializing the MOEA.
2. Running the MOEA and storing the solutions in an archive.
3. Applying two-stage pre-filtering on the archive.
4. Interactively visualizing the solutions based on the preferences for uncertainties provided by the DM.
5. Asking for preference information for objectives from the DM and adapting the reference vectors.

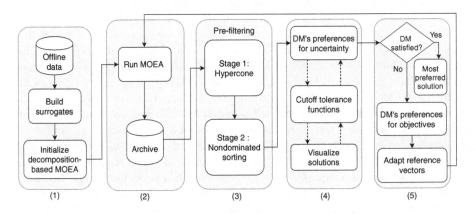

Fig. 4. The proposed framework for interactive offline data-driven multiobjective optimization.

Step 1: We formulate the MOP by utilizing the provided data. The expertise of the DM may be required in this. We build Kriging surrogate models for every objective function using the data (as in the generic approach in Sect. 2). Next, we initialize a decomposition-based MOEA and generate a uniformly distributed set of reference vectors and create the initial population.

Step 2: We run an MOEA for a fixed number of generations. The objective values and uncertainties for the individuals from every generation are stored in an archive that serves as a database for Step 3.

Step 3: At the end of Step 2, we have an archive containing objective vectors and uncertainties of different individuals. We apply the pre-filtering techniques as in Sect. 3.1. Note that for the first iteration, we do not have any preferences for objectives, and the reference vectors (that includes the edge vectors) are not adapted. Hence, the hypercone constitutes the entire objective space and the first pre-filtering stage accepts all the solutions.

Step 4: The DM provides preferences for uncertainties (indifference tolerances) $\tau_k\%$ and the pre-filtered solutions from Step 3 qualifying the cutoff tolerance functions in Eq. (3) are shown.

The DM can provide preferences for uncertainties as many times (s)he wishes thereby enabling him/her to view different solutions within the provided tolerances. For a better understanding of uncertainties while visualizing, solutions can be colour coded. This can be done by the normalized average of the uncertainty vector (in percentage) or by the maximum uncertainty of a solution for any of the objective functions. The DM may skip this step entirely if solution uncertainties are not interesting. As this step consists of just filtering solutions obtained after Step 3, it can be repeated with a very low computational cost.

Step 5: In this step, the DM can stop the optimization process if (s)he has found a satisfactory solution. Otherwise, (s)he is asked for new preference information. We adapt the reference vectors according to Eq. (2) so that solutions follow the preferences for objectives. After adapting the reference vectors, we go to Step 2.

The interaction process is split into Steps 4 and 5, where the DM provides preferences for uncertainties and objectives, respectively. Due to this, the cognitive load on the DM does not increase significantly. The DM can provide different preferences for uncertainties and view the corresponding solutions and repeat this as long as one wishes. The proposed way of providing preferences for uncertainties does not modify the selection process of the MOEA. Hence, the solution process is not affected.

4   Numerical Results

Assessing and comparing the performance of interactive approaches is still a research challenge. Hence, we demonstrate and discuss the advantages of the proposed framework by solving the general aviation aircraft (GAA) [15,16] design problem. Due to space limitations, further analysis on benchmark problems is available at http://www.mit.jyu.fi/optgroup/extramaterial.html as additional material.

The GAA problem refers to designing an aircraft for recreational pilots to business executives. We solved the problem as in [15] with 27 decision variables, ten objectives and one constraint. As we are dealing with offline optimization problems, we generated data using the implementation [1]. We used Latin hypercube sampling [12] to generate 1000 samples for decision variables and evaluated them using the GAA functions to obtain the offline data. To approximate the underlying objective functions, we used Kriging with a radial basis function kernel as our surrogate models. We used RVEA as the MOEA with standard parameter settings as in [2] and executed it for 100 generations in each iteration with standard crossover and mutation parameters. The spread parameter r was set as 0.2. However, it can be increased if the DM's wants a more diverse set of solutions. As our framework does not support constraint handling, we considered the constraint violation as an additional objective function for the demonstration.

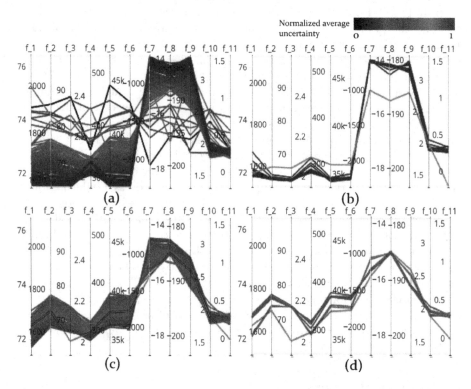

Fig. 5. The solutions obtained for two iterations of the interactive framework (all objectives are minimized). (a): solutions in the archive after the first iteration. (b) & (c): solutions after pre-filtering in the first and second iteration respectively with different reference points (red line). (d): solutions after DM provides preferences for uncertainties. (Color figure online)

Figure 5 shows solutions produced by the framework for two iterations. The colour coding represents the normalized average of the uncertainty vector for the solutions (blue is lowest and yellow is highest). Sub-figure (a) shows the solutions in the archive at the first iteration when there are no preferences for objectives available. In sub-figure (b) the DM provides the reference point (in red) and gets the pre-filtered solutions. It can be observed that the solutions produced follow the DM's preferences for objectives. However, (s)he chooses to skip the step of providing preferences for uncertainties as none of the solutions has a low uncertainty (as represented by the colour). In the next iteration, the DM changes the preferences for objectives. The solutions after pre-filtering, as shown in sub-figure (c) not only follow the DM's preferences for objectives but also have a lower uncertainty. We now provide hypothetical tolerances to demonstrate the framework's ability to consider preferences for uncertainties. In sub-figure (d) only a few solutions that are within the preferred uncertainty of the DM are shown. Finally, one of the solutions that matches the preferences for objectives and uncertainties may be chosen by the DM. (S)he may choose to reset the cutoff tolerances again to view a different set of solution to make decisions. Alternatively, if the DM is not satisfied with any of the solutions, (s)he may choose to change the preferences for objectives and continue the optimization.

If the DM is unaware of the uncertainties in the solutions, (s)he may be deprived of valuable knowledge regarding the acceptability of the solutions. In certain situations such as Fig. 5(b), judging the goodness of a solution based on the objective values alone may be misleading. By observing the uncertainties, the DM avoids making a worse decision and can modify preferences for objectives. The DM may choose to provide preferences for uncertainties and see solutions within different tolerances with a low computational cost. As the DM can see the solutions pre-filtered from the archive that have various uncertainties, (s)he has a wide range of solutions to make decisions if so desired.

5   Conclusions

In this paper, we proposed a framework for interactively solving offline data-driven MOPs. It enabled the DM to understand and provide preferences for uncertainties during an interaction. By using preferences for objectives, the DM can guide the solution process. The solutions generated follow the DM's preferences for objectives and have a variety of uncertainties. By preferences for uncertainties, the DM can control which solutions (s)he can see. The two-step interaction proposed in the framework does not significantly increase the cognitive load on the DM. We also demonstrated it by solving the GAA problem that proved its capability in solving many-objective problems. The visualization in the framework enabled the DM to provide preferences for uncertainties interactively. However, more work should be done in the field of reference vectors adaptation and development of comparison metrics for interactive approaches. We also need to perform tests with different types of preferences for objectives. Furthermore, the framework is not designed to handle constraints. Handling constraints for offline data-driven problems deserves further attention.

Acknowledgements. This research was partly supported by the Academy of Finland (grant number 311877) and is related to the thematic research area DEMO (Decision Analytics utilizing Causal Models and Multiobjective Optimization, http://www.jyu.fi/demo) of the University of Jyväskylä. This work was partially supported by the Natural Environment Research Council [NE/P017436/1].

References

1. Castro-Gama, M.: Mariocastrogama/GAA-Problem-MATLAB (2017). https:// github.com/mariocastrogama/GAA-problem-MATLAB. Accessed 21 Apr 2020
2. Cheng, R., Jin, Y., Olhofer, M., Sendhoff, B.: A reference vector guided evolutionary algorithm for many-objective optimization. IEEE Trans. Evol. Comput. **20**(5), 773–791 (2016)
3. Chugh, T., Chakraborti, N., Sindhya, K., Jin, Y.: A data-driven surrogate-assisted evolutionary algorithm applied to a many-objective blast furnace optimization problem. Mater. Manuf. Process. **32**(10), 1172–1178 (2017)
4. Deb, K., Jain, H.: An evolutionary many-objective optimization algorithm using reference-point-based nondominated sorting approach, part I: Solving problems with box constraints. IEEE Trans. Evol. Comput. **18**(4), 577–601 (2014)
5. Deb, K.: Evolutionary algorithms for multi-criterion optimization in engineering design. In: Miettinen, K., Neittaanmäki, P., Mäkelä, M.M., Périaux, J. (eds.) Evolutionary Algorithms in Engineering and Computer Science. Wiley (1999)
6. Forrester, A., Sobester, A., Keane, A.: Engineering Design via Surrogate Modelling. John Wiley and Sons, Hoboken (2008)
7. Hakanen, J., Chugh, T., Sindhya, K., Jin, Y., Miettinen, K.: Connections of reference vectors and different types of preference information in interactive multiobjective evolutionary algorithms. In: Proceedings of the 2016 IEEE Symposium Series on Computational Intelligence (SSCI), pp. 1–8 (2016)
8. Jin, Y., Wang, H., Chugh, T., Guo, D., Miettinen, K.: Data-driven evolutionary optimization: an overview and case studies. IEEE Trans. Evol. Comput. **23**(3), 442–458 (2019)
9. Krishnamoorthy, K., Mathew, T.: Statistical Tolerance Regions: Theory, Applications, and Computation. John Wiley and Sons, Hoboken (2009)
10. Li, K., Chen, R., Min, G., Yao, X.: Integration of preferences in decomposition multiobjective optimization. IEEE Trans. Cybern. **48**(12), 3359–3370 (2018)
11. Mazumdar, A., Chugh, T., Miettinen, K., López-Ibáñez, M.: On dealing with uncertainties from Kriging models in offline data-driven evolutionary multiobjective optimization. In: Deb, K., et al. (eds.) EMO 2019. LNCS, vol. 11411, pp. 463–474. Springer, Cham (2019). https://doi.org/10.1007/978-3-030-12598-1_37
12. McKay, M.D., Beckman, R.J., Conover, W.J.: A comparison of three methods for selecting values of input variables in the analysis of output from a computer code. Technometrics **21**(2), 239–245 (1979)
13. Miettinen, K.: Nonlinear Multiobjective Optimization. Kluwer Academic Publishers, Boston (1999)
14. Purshouse, R.C., Deb, K., Mansor, M.M., Mostaghim, S., Wang, R.: A review of hybrid evolutionary multiple criteria decision making methods. In: Proceedings of the IEEE Congress on Evolutionary Computation (CEC), pp. 1147–1154 (2014)
15. Shah, R.A., Reed, P.M., Simpson, T.W.: Many-objective evolutionary optimisation and visual analytics for product family design. In: Wang, L., Ng, A., Deb, K. (eds.) Multi-objective Evolutionary Optimisation for Product Design and Manufacturing, pp. 137–159. Springer, London (2011). https://doi.org/10.1007/978-0-85729-652-8_4
16. Simpson, T.W., Allen, J.K., Chen, W., Mistree, F.: Conceptual design of a family of products through the use of the robust concept exploration method. In: 6th AIAA/NASA/ISSMO Symposium on Multidisciplinary Analysis and Optimization, pp. 1535–1545 (1996)

17. Wang, H., Jin, Y.: A random forest-assisted evolutionary algorithm for data-driven constrained multiobjective combinatorial optimization of trauma systems. IEEE Trans. Cybern. **50**(2), 536–549 (2020)

18. Wang, H., Jin, Y., Sun, C., Doherty, J.: Offline data-driven evolutionary optimization using selective surrogate ensembles. IEEE Trans. Evol. Comput. **23**(2), 203–216 (2019)

19. Wang, H., Olhofer, M., Jin, Y.: A mini-review on preference modeling and articulation in multi-objective optimization: current status and challenges. Complex Intell. Syst. **3**(4), 233–245 (2017). https://doi.org/10.1007/s40747-017-0053-9

20. Zhang, Q., Li, H.: MOEA/D: a multiobjective evolutionary algorithm based on decomposition. IEEE Trans. Evol. Comput. **11**(6), 712–731 (2007)

21. Zheng, J., Yu, G., Zhu, Q., Li, X., Zou, J.: On decomposition methods in interactive user-preference based optimization. Appl. Soft Comput. **52**, 952–973 (2017)

Communication Optimization for Efficient Dynamic Task Allocation in Swarm Robotics

Nadia Nedjah[1]([✉])[iD], Luigi Maciel Ribeiro[1][iD],
and Luiza de Macedo Mourelle[2][iD]

[1] Department of Electronics Engineering and Telecommunications,
State University of Rio de Janeiro, Rio de Janeiro, Brazil
{nadia,luigimaciel}@eng.uerj.br
[2] Department of Systems Engineering and Computation,
State University of Rio de Janeiro, Rio de Janeiro, Brazil
ldmm@eng.uerj.br

Abstract. The interest in solving high complexity problems has been growing in recent years, intensifying the use of swarm robotics. Cooperation is a central idea to the usage of swarm robotics because it enables the solution of complex problems with a coordinated execution of basic tasks, which together lead to the achievement of the swarm common goal. This coordination is only possible with an efficient task allocation. Inspired by the strategy of the particle swarm optimization algorithm, we propose a novel algorithm called the Clustered Dynamic Task Allocation (CDTA). This algorithm performs task allocation to swarm robots in a fully distributed manner. It performs a guided search of the solution spaces using the concept of adaptive speed. However, this process requires an intense exchange of information between robots, which hinders the efficiency of the task allocation process for large swarms. This paper proposes the use of a clustered communication topology between the swarm robots, aiming to optimize the underlying communication processes, and thus enabling efficient task allocation for large robotic swarms. The results obtained with the cluster-based topology are compared to those obtained with the full mesh-based topology.

Keywords: Task allocation · Swarm robotics · Swarm intelligence

1   Introduction

Swarm intelligence [9] when applied to a physical robotic platforms is usually called as swarm robotics [1,8,10]. Composed of multiple interacting autonomous robots, swarm robotics can solve complex problems through cooperation between robots that, by performing simple basic tasks can often lead to reach the common goal, which is the emergence of an intelligent good solution of the problem. Task allocation is a fundamental process for using swarm robotics to solve high

© Springer Nature Switzerland AG 2020
B. Filipič et al. (Eds.): BIOMA 2020, LNCS 12438, pp. 110–124, 2020.
https://doi.org/10.1007/978-3-030-63710-1_9

complexity problems [8]. It defines the way tasks are assigned to the robots of the swarm. Dynamic task allocation is done on-the-fly, adapting to new configuration of the swarm in terms of size and composition. The solution of the task allocation process guarantees the execution of all tasks to achieve the overall goal of the robotic swarm.

This paper proposes a distributed algorithm to solve the dynamic task allocation problem while optimizing the communication process in order to be able to work with large robot swarms. This work is a continuation that aims at improving the results obtained by the Global approach for Dynamic Task Allocation algorithm (GDTA) proposed in [7]. GDTA achieves the task allocation by approaching it as an optimization problem. Inspired by the well-known Particle Swarm Optimization (PSO) algorithm [4]. In this approach, each robot represents a particle that has a position corresponding to a feasible allocation. At each iteration of the algorithm, allocations are evaluated according to their ability to meet the objective proportion. Allocations are adaptive, so the swarm task allocation is continually updated through information exchange between robots of the swarm. For this purpose, each robot of the swarm sends its current allocation and receives the allocations constructed by all the other members of the swarm. However, this type of approach has a large flow of information between robots, which leads to a loss of performance or even impossibility to be used when the swarm grows beyond certain size.

As such, the GDTA [7] uses the full mesh communication topology, in which all robots communicate with each other, generating exponential growth of the data flow due to the number of robots. When the swarm is of reduced size, i.e. up to 20 robots, the GDTA works fine. However, beyond this swarm size, the approach proposed in [7] does not converge and the task allocation process cannot be completed. As it was shown, the bottleneck is the exponential growth of the amount of information exchange between the robots to adjust their task allocation. So, it is worth to investigate the impact of other communication topologies that reduce the flow of information between swarm robots, allowing for a performance improvement and making it possible to work with larger swarms. The Clustered Dynamic Task Allocation (CDTA) algorithm has the same approach and methodology as that used by GDTA, but instead of communication through a full mesh topology, it uses the clustered communication topology as it will be explained in details throughout this paper. We show that this clustered communication strategy allows for a significant improvement in terms of the performance and allowed us to exploit swarms larger swarms. It is noteworthy to point out that this proposed approach can be used to allocate tasks dynamically for larger swarms. Here we experimented with swarms consisting of up to the 32 robots.

The remainder of this paper is structured into 4 sections. In Sect. 2, we present the formal definition of the Dynamic Task Allocation problem. In Sect. 3, we explain the steps of the proposed algorithm, demonstrating how communication is performed and optimized. In Sect. 4, we present and analyze of the results obtained. In Sect. 5, we draw some useful conclusions regarding the achieved improvement and point out some directions for future work.

2 Dynamic Task Allocation

Dynamic Task Allocation (DTA) is the process that manages and organizes a robot swarm to correctly execute a set of tasks, aiming at a unique global objective. This process consists of identifying and assigning, in a organized and distributed fashion, the task that each robot of the swarm must execute. There are many tasks, and two or more robots of the swarm may be allocated to execute the same task. The DTA process must be dynamic because the allocation changes in accordance with the environment and the swarm composition.

Seeking a formal representation of the DTA problem, let τ be the total number of valid tasks, $\mathbb{T} = \{t_1, t_2, \ldots, t_\tau\}$ the task identifier set to be allocated to ρ robots of the swarm. Note that τ and ρ are independent quantities.

Let us assume that the overall task decomposition generates the proportions $\mathbb{P} = \{p_1, p_2, \ldots, p_\tau\}$, which is defined by a set of positive integers $p_j \in \,]0, 1]$. Each p_j represents the percentage of the ρ robots, required to perform task t_j. Note that all $p_j \in \mathbb{P}$ sum up to 1. From the desired $\mathbb{P}$ ratio, we can calculate the number of robots that ought to be allocated to each task, represented by a set of counters $\mathbb{C} = \{c_1, c_2, \ldots, c_\tau\}$, such that each counter is the product of the ratio and the number of robots $c_j = p_j \times \rho$. Note that all counters $c_j \in \mathbb{C}$ sum up to ρ.

In a swarm, each robot has a unique identifier. The set of identifiers is represented by $\mathbb{I} = \{id_1, id_2, \ldots, id_\rho\}$. The task allocation of the swarm robots is represented by $\mathbb{A} = \{a_1, a_2, \ldots, a_\rho\}$, where a_j identifies the task to be performed by the robot id_j. From allocation $\mathbb{A}$, we can compute the number of robots allocated to each of the tasks represented by $\mathbb{C}_\mathbb{A} = \{c_1, c_2, \ldots, c_\tau\}$, as in (1):

$$c_j = \mathbb{C}_\mathbb{A}[t_j] = \sum_{r=1}^{\rho} \theta(a_r, t_j), \tag{1}$$

wherein function θ is defined as in (2):

$$\theta(a, t) = \begin{cases} 1 & \text{if } a = t; \\ 0 & \text{otherwise.} \end{cases} \tag{2}$$

It is noteworthy to emphasize that there are many possible optimal allocations, such as $\mathbb{A}^*$, that verifies the requirements of Eq. 3. So, the solution of the DTA problem is to find and allocation $\mathbb{A}^* = \{a_1^*, a_2^*, \ldots, a_\rho^*\}$ that meets the desired ratio as shown in (3):

$$\forall t_j \in \mathbb{T} \text{ and } \forall p_j \in \mathbb{P}, \quad \mathbb{C}_{\mathbb{A}^*}[t_j] = p_j \times \rho. \tag{3}$$

In order to find a solution of the DTA problem using an optimization algorithm, an objective function is required. This function should evaluate the error introduced by the found allocation $\mathbb{A}$ in relation to the sought allocation $\mathbb{A}^*$. The cost function should provide a metric to quantify a given allocation's quality, and used to optimize the DTA problem, is shown in (4):

$$f(\mathbb{A}) = \frac{\sum_{j=1}^{\tau} |\mathbb{C}[j] - \mathbb{C}_{\mathbb{A}}[j]|}{\tau}, \tag{4}$$

wherein τ is the number of valid tasks, $\mathbb{C}[j]$ is the correct number of robots that ought to be allocated to task j according to pre-defined proportion $\mathbb{P}$ and $\mathbb{C}_{\mathbb{A}}[j]$ is the number of robots, which are allocated to task j according to the evaluated allocation $\mathbb{A}$.

It is noteworthy to point out that, by analyzing the search space, we can find out about the complexity of the DTA problem thus formulated. Actually, we are dealing with a total of feasible allocations of τ^{ρ}. For instance, in a swarm of 25 robots with 5 tasks to be allocated, we have 298 quadrillion feasible allocations.

The academic community has come up with numerous task allocation algorithm proposals under the influence of different inspirations and approaches such as that based on market laws [6], behavioral [11], bio-inspired [12] and communication-oriented [2]. The different solutions for DTA in the state-of-the-art literature are classified according to the taxonomy presented in [13]. The DTA problem can be classified as either instantaneous assignment or time-extended assignment based on either the information is limited, allowing instant allocations or complete, allowing future planning, respectively [5].

3   Proposed DTA Algorithm

In order to optimize the results presented in [7], we developed the Clustered Dynamic Task Allocation (CDTA) algorithm. It is a distributed stochastic algorithm that performs dynamic task allocation. It can be categorized as a multi-task robots and time-extended approach. It exploits a search strategy that is inspired by Particle Swarm Optimization (PSO) technique, proposed in [4], but is fully distributed, as each PSO particle is physically represented by a robot.

The clustered communication topology has communication stages with well-defined characteristics. Each stage has a robot organization and communication structure that must be respected by all swarm robots. It uses $\mathbb{M}$ communication matrix that establishes the robot organization and communication topology structure, defining which cluster each robot is a member of, how many clusters there are in the swarm, how many robots there are in each cluster, and which robots are informers. Note that in the clustered topology, a member of the cluster may be a non-informant or informant member. The former type can communicates only with the robots that are also members of its proper cluster while the latter can also communicate with members of other clusters than its own. It is through these informant members that the partial information that emerges with a given cluster can flow through the swarm traversing clusters. Figure 1 presents an example of 3-cluster communication topology and its equivalent communication matrix, wherein the white nodes represent the informants. It is noteworthy to point out that, in this example, links between non-informants are represented simply by their cluster identifier. Moreover, links between informants, which can be either with members of their cluster, and thus are represented by the cluster identifier or with members of other clusters, and hence are represented by number 9. Without loss of generality, we assume here that there are always up to 8 different clusters, since with 8 clusters we can test a multitude of clustered robot swarms, and we can use a single digit to denote a given cluster.

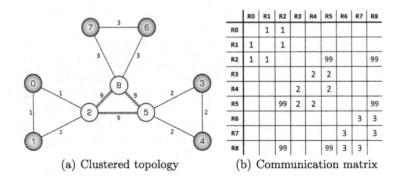

	R0	R1	R2	R3	R4	R5	R6	R7	R8
R0		1	1						
R1	1		1						
R2	1	1				99			99
R3					2	2			
R4				2		2			
R5			99	2	2				99
R6								3	3
R7							3		3
R8			99			99	3	3	

(a) Clustered topology   (b) Communication matrix

Fig. 1. Clustered communication organization within a swarm of 9 robots

The cluster communication process is divided into three steps. The first step is similar to mesh communication, where information is shared within each cluster, as shown in Fig. 2(a). During this communication step, we are able to identify the robot that has the best solution within the cluster, which we will denote by robot $Cbest$. The second step is a special communication made only between informants. During this communication step, all informant robots send and receive the best solutions found in each cluster and determine, at that moment, the robot that has the best solution of the whole swarm, which we will denote by robot $Gbest$. Figure 2(b) exemplifies this step. The third and last step is the communication that allows the informants to send the members of their respective clusters the best allocation, which we will denote by A_{Gbest}. Figure 2(c) illustrates this step.

The proposed CDTA algorithm is structured into five sequential stages: initialization; tuning; identification; updating and stopping. Algorithm 1 demonstrates how the connection between the stages is performed. The algorithm's steps enable robots to repeat the steps over and over again until a suitable solution of the DTA problem is found. Each of the stages is detailed in the sequel.

3.1   Initialization Stage

During the initialization stage, the initial configuration of CDTA is performed, allowing for the configuration of the algorithm's parameters. The CDTA's parameters consist of the number of robots ρ, the number of tasks τ; the target task distribution $\mathbb{P}$ and the communication matrix $\mathbb{M}$. It is noteworthy to already emphasize that this stage as run by robot i will also initialize the robot allocation A_i; its so-far best quality allocation A_{Pbest_i}; its so-far best cluster allocation A_{Cbest_i}; the so-far best swarm allocation A_{Gbest}; the ideal task counter $\mathbb{C}$; the

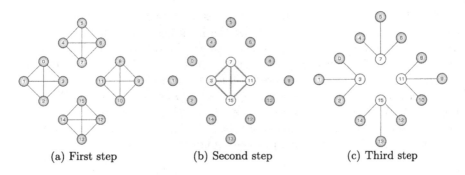

(a) First step	(b) Second step	(c) Third step

Fig. 2. The communication steps used in the clustered topology

---

Algorithm 1. CDTA main steps as executed by any given robot of the swarm

---
1: Initialization
2: **repeat**
3:     Tuning;
4:     **if** informant **then**
5:         Identification;
6:     **end if**
7:     Updating; Stopping;
8: **until** A valid allocation is found;
9: Execute assigned task

---

robots current task counter $\mathbb{C}_{\mathbb{A}i}$ and its current velocity v_i. These initializations are required by the stages of the main loop of the CDTA algorithm. The basic steps of the initialization stage are shown in Algorithm 2. Note that for a swarm of ρ robots, there are ρ such initializations running in parallel, one per robot.

Algorithm 2. Actions during the initialization stage

Require: ρ, τ , $\mathbb{P}$ and $\mathbb{M}$;
Ensure: $\mathbb{A}_i$, $\mathbb{A}_{Pbest_i}$, $\mathbb{A}_{Cbest_i}$, $\mathbb{A}_{Gbest}$, $\mathbb{C}$, $\mathbb{C}_{\mathbb{A}i}$ and v_i;
 1: **Generate** randomly $\mathbb{A}_i$ and v_i;
 2: **Compute** o $\mathbb{C}$ and $\mathbb{C}_{\mathbb{A}i}$;
 3: $\mathbb{A}_{Pbest_i} := \mathbb{A}_i$;
 4: $\mathbb{A}_{Cbest_i} := \mathbb{A}_i$;
 5: $\mathbb{A}_{Gbest} := \mathbb{A}_i$;

3.2   Tuning Stage

In the tuning stage, the best allocation $\mathbb{A}_{Cbest_j}$ for a given cluster j is updated. Allocation $\mathbb{A}_{Pbest_i}$ is the best allocation achieved so far by the robot i. To be up-to-date, robot i needs to compute the current allocation quality $f(\mathbb{A}_i)$, whenever the current allocation quality is better. Thus quality $Pbest_i$ is replaced by the quality of current allocation and allocation $\mathbb{A}_{Pbest_i}$ is replaced by current allocation $\mathbb{A}_i$ as shown in Algorithm 3. For the identification of the robot $Cbest_j$, an information exchange is carried out between the robots of the same cluster. So, each robot of the cluster sends to the other robots in its cluster its identifier id_i and the quality of its best allocation quality $Pbest_i$. As the messages from the other robots are being received, vector $\mathbb{V} = \{Pbest_1, Pbest_2, \ldots, Pbest_\rho\}$ is populated. Whenever this process is completed, this vector will be up-to-date, hence permitting the identification of robot $Cbest_j$. Note that for a swarm of γ clusters there are γ such tuning processes going on in parallel.

Algorithm 3. Actions during the tuning stage

Require: ρ, $\mathbb{A}_i$, $\mathbb{A}_{Pbest_i}$ and $\mathbb{M}$;
Ensure: id_{Cbest_j}, $Cbest_j$ and $\mathbb{A}_{Cbest_j}$;
1: **if** $f(\mathbb{A}_i) \leq Pbest_i$ **then**
2:     $Pbest_i := f(\mathbb{A}_i)$; $\mathbb{A}_{Pbest_i} := \mathbb{A}_i$;
3: **end if**
4: $msg \leftarrow \langle id_i, Pbest_i \rangle$;
5: **repeat**
6:     **Send** msg to all the robot of cluster j;
7:     **Receive** msg from all the robot of cluster j; $\mathbb{V}[i] := Pbest_i$;
8: **until** all messages are received/sent from/to all robot of cluster j
9: **Identify** robot $Cbest_j$ (id_{Cbest_j} and $Cbest_j$);
10: $msg1 \leftarrow \langle id_i, \mathbb{A}_i \rangle$; $msg2 \leftarrow \langle id_i \rangle$;
11: **repeat**
12:     **if** $id_i = id_{Cbest}$ **then**
13:        **Send** $msg1$ to all the robot of cluster j;
14:        **Receive** $msg2$ from all the robot of cluster j;
15:     **end if**
16:     **if** $id_i \neq id_{Cbest_j}$ **then**
17:        **Receive** $msg1$ from robot id_{Cbest_j};
18:        **Send** $msg2$ to robot id_{Cbest_j}; $\mathbb{A}_{Cbest_j} := \mathbb{A}_i$;
19:     **end if**
20: **until** all the cluster robots have received all messages

---

3.3   Identification Stage

During the identification stage, the identification of the robot $Gbest$, which is the robot with the best global allocation, is performed. For the purpose, it is necessary to compare all the best allocations $Cbest_j$ found within all clusters $j \in [1, \gamma]$. This stage is performed only by the informant robots, which represent the access points of their respective clusters. For identification purposes, vector $\mathbb{V}^* = \{Cbest_1, Cbest_2, \ldots, Cbest_\gamma\}$ has to be updated with the emerging $Cbests_j$ for $j \in [1, \gamma]$, which were found in the swarm clusters during the tuning stage. Informants exchange messages containing the $Cbest_j$ found in their respective clusters. Once vector $\mathbb{V}^*$ is up-to-date, the robot $Gbest$ is identified. The dynamics of the identification stage are presented in Algorithm 4.

Algorithm 4. Actions during the identification stage

Require: ρ, $Cbest_j$, $\mathbb{A}_{Cbest_j}$ and $\mathbb{M}$;
Ensure: $Gbest$ and $\mathbb{A}_{Gbest}$;
1: $msg3 \leftarrow \langle id_i, Gbest \rangle$;
2: **repeat**
3:     **Send** $msg3$ to all informant robots;
4:     **Receive** $msg3$ from all informant robots; $\mathbb{V}^*[j] := Cbest_j$;
5: **until** Receive/send from/to all informant robots
6: **Identify** robot $Gbest$ (id_{Gbest} and $Gbest$); $msg4 \leftarrow \langle id_i, \mathbb{A}_{Cbest} \rangle$; $msg5 \leftarrow \langle id_i \rangle$;
7: **repeat**
8:     **if** $id_i = id_{Gbest}$ **then**
9:         **Send** $msg4$ to all informant robots;
10:         **Receive** $msg5$ from all informant robots;
11:     **end if**
12:     **if** $id_i \neq id_{Gbest}$ **then**
13:         **Send** $msg5$ to robot id_{Gbest};
14:         **Receive** $msg4$ from robot id_{Gbest}; $\mathbb{A}_{Gbest} := \mathbb{A}_{Cbest}$;
15:     **end if**
16: **until** all informant have received all messages

3.4 Updating Stage

In the upgrade stage, informants send messages to the other robots within their respective cluster bearing the identifier id_{Gbest} of the robot that obtained the so-far swarm best solution as well as the allocation $\mathbb{A}_{Gbest}$. Robots receiving the informant message replace the old $\mathbb{A}_{Gbest}$ allocation with the updated new emerged one. Throughout this stage, non-informant robots remain in a waiting loop, waiting for the up-to-date information to be sent by the informant robots. Upon completion of the updating work, the entire swarm is hence allowed to proceed to the Stopping stage. The dynamics of the updating stage are presented in Algorithm 5.

Algorithm 5. Actions during the updating stage

Require: ρ, $Gbest$, $\mathbb{A}_{Gbest}$ and $\mathbb{M}$;
Ensure: $Gbest$ and $\mathbb{A}_{Gbest}$;
1: **repeat**
2:     $msg6 \leftarrow \langle id_i, \mathbb{A}_{Gbest} \rangle$; $msg7 \leftarrow \langle id_i \rangle$;
3:     **if** informant **then**
4:         **Send** $msg6$ to all robots of the cluster;
5:         **Receive** $msg7$ from all robots of the cluster;
6:     **else**
7:         **Send** $msg7$ to informant robot;
8:         **Receive** $msg6$ from informant robot; $\mathbb{A}_{Gbest} := \mathbb{A}_{Gbest}$;
9:     **end if**
10: **until** all robot of the cluster have received all messages

3.5 Stopping Stage

The stopping stage determines whether the optimization goal has been achieved and hence the main loop of CDTA should be terminated. Thus, if the A_{Gbest} allocation satisfies the $\mathbb{P}$ target task distribution, all robots are allowed to enter the execution state, wherein they keep executing the tasks, which they were allocated considering A_{Gbest}. However, if the best task allocation does not satisfy task proportion $\mathbb{P}$, *i.e.* we still have $A_{Gbest} \neq \mathbb{P}$, all robots iterate once again the main steps of the main loop as to infer a new position in the search space.

Algorithm 6 presents the dynamics of the stopping stage. First, the quality of the best global allocation $f(A_{Gbest})$ is evaluated. So, if this quality is equal to 0, this means that the allocation is valid. In this situation the robots enters the task execution loop to which they are allocated according to the found task allocation. Otherwise, if $f(A_{Gbest}) \neq 0$, then a new position, which corresponds to a new allocation, in the search space must be sought. After the new position has been obtained, a new cycle is performed, in which each robot of the swarm returns to the tuning stage.

Algorithm 6. Actions during stopping Stage

Require: ρ, τ, A_i, A_{Pbest}, A_{Gbest} and M ;
Ensure: A_i;
1: **if** $f(A_{Gbest}) = 0$ **then**
2:     **repeat**
3:         **Execute** assigned task $A_{Gbest}[i]$;
4:     **until** a new task distribution is sensed
5: **else**
6:     **for** $k := 1 \rightarrow \rho$ **do**
7:         **Generate** random r_1 in $[0\ldots1]$; **Generate** random r_2 in $[0\ldots1]$;
8:         $A_{cognitive} := c_1 \times r_1 \times (A_{Pbest_i}[k] - A_i[k])$; $A_{social} := c_2 \times r_2 \times (A_{Gbest}[k] - A_i[k])$;
9:         $A_{inertia} := w \times velocity[k]$; $velocity[k] := A_{inertia} + A_{cognitive} + A_{social}$;
10:        **if** $(velocity[k] - \lfloor velocity[k] \rfloor) \leq 0.5$ **then**
11:            $velocity[k] := \lfloor velocity[k] \rfloor$;
12:        **else**
13:            $velocity[k] := \lceil velocity[k] \rceil$;
14:        **end if**
15:        $A_i[k] := A_i[k] + velocity[k]$;
16:        **if** $A_i[k] < t_1$ **then**
17:            $A_i[k] := t_1$;
18:        **else**
19:            **if** $A_i[k] > t_\tau$ **then**
20:                $A_i[k] := t_\tau$;
21:            **end if**
22:        **end if**
23:    **end for**
24: **end if**

---

4   Performance Results

The implementation of the CDTA algorithm requires a robot that is autonomous, programmable and has a communication structure. In this case, ELISA-3 is the swarm robot used [3]. It has the required characteristics, along with a compact structure, allowing for the implementation of large groups of robots. Elisa-3 is of 5 cm in diameter and 3 cm high. It has a number of embedded devices that enables it to communicate with other ELISA-3 robots or the user and to move, among other functionalities [3]. The embedded communication takes place via a radio base station (nRF24L01+) connected to a computer via a USB cable, which transfers the data to the robots over a wireless connection. Each robot of the swarm has a unique identifier id ($RFID$) stored in the factory-programmed EEPROM memory.

The methodology used to perform the experiments allowed us to evaluate the results obtained regarding different swarm configurations that are characterized by the number of robots ρ and the number of tasks τ. Each of the experiment iterates dynamically the aforementioned task assignment process until it finds a new allocation $\mathbb{A}^*$ that meets the requirements of the target distribution $\mathbb{P}$. In all experiments, the swarm is initialized to an initial state, in which all robots are assigned task 0. So, the swarm will start in all experiments with the same initial allocation $\mathbb{A}_0 = \{0, 0, \ldots, 0\}$. The analysis is concerned with obtaining statistically valid results, so each of the tests performed is repeated 10 times. The final results to be analyzed are the average of the thus obtained results. It is noteworthy to point out that the results were robust throughout the different runs and the standard deviations were insignificant. Three factors are analyzed in these experiments. The first is the convergence time, which represents the time the implemented algorithm takes to find allocation $\mathbb{A}^*$ that satisfies the objective task proportion. The second and third analyzed factors allow for the evaluation of the communication process. The number of messages sent by the robots to the base and the number of messages sent from the base to the robots are analyzed.

4.1   CDTA's Performance

The tests use cluster communication topology configurations as explained in the previous sections, wherein the number of clusters is a function of the total number of robots. As shown in Fig. 3, tests are performed with 6 different configurations.

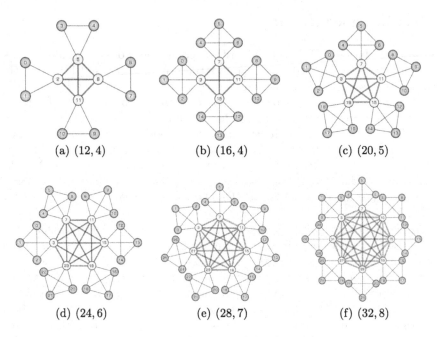

(a) $(12, 4)$ (b) $(16, 4)$ (c) $(20, 5)$

(d) $(24, 6)$ (e) $(28, 7)$ (f) $(32, 8)$

Fig. 3. Communication topology configurations (ρ, γ) used to evaluate CDTA's performance

Figure 4(a) shows the average convergence times regarding the 6 considered configurations for robot swarms, ranging from 12 to 32 robots when allocating of 2 to 5 tasks. Figure 4(b) shows the average of the total number of messages received while Fig. 4(c) exhibits the average of total number of messages sent.

The results presented in this section demonstrate that CDTA's performance regarding convergence time and message exchange (number of messages sent and received) have similar behavior on average. This characterizes a direct relationship of the communication process on the final result of such an implementation.

CDTA was successful in all the performed experiments. Nonetheless, it was noted that the swarm configuration with more than 50 robots achieves convergence for some task configurations only. This behavior occurred due to the fact that the chosen platform (ELISA-3) has some physical limitations, which in this case is the battery charge capacity, which limits the working time of the robots. With a 50-robot swarm, for the allocation of 4 tasks, the robot charge battery charge was exhausted before the solution is reached. Hence, we do not report these results in this paper as we have to verify exhaustively all experiment settings.

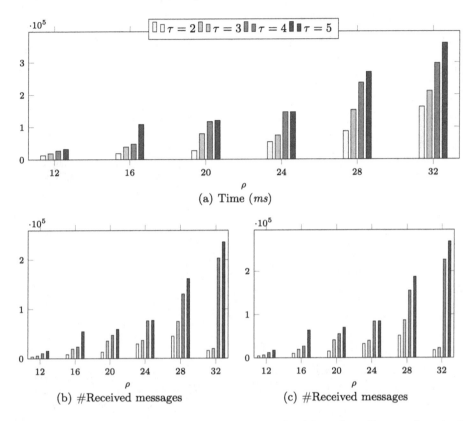

Fig. 4. CDTA's performance: convergence times and total number of sent and received messages

4.2   Comparison of CDTA's and GDTA's Performances

The results presented in this section are direct comparisons between the results obtained in the work [7] with the results obtained in this alternative proposal. GDTA is an algorithm used to search for a solution for DTA problem using distributed PSO based on a full mesh communication topology. It is noteworthy to emphasize that CDTA is distinct from GDTA regarding the exploited communication topology. CDTA uses a clustered topology. An initial understanding is that CDTA reduces information flow between robots and thus should improve the performance. Hence, this allows us to handle larger swarms of the same kind of physical robots.

Figure 5(a) shows the average convergence time, Fig. 5(c) shows the average total number of sent messages and Fig. 5(b) exhibits the averages total number of received messages for algorithms GDTA and CDTA. The presented results refer to 4 experiments with robot swarms ranging from 12 to 24 robots for an allocation of tasks ranging from 2 to 5 tasks.

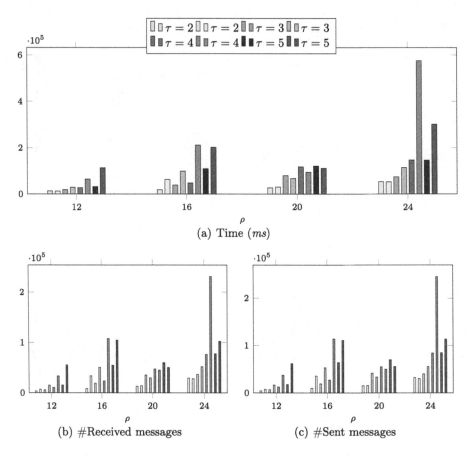

Fig. 5. GDTA's and CDTA's performance comparison, wherein red bars are for GDTA and blue ones are for CDTA (Color figure online)

The CDTA proposal achieved an average convergence time reduction of 30.03%. Its best performance yielded a reduction of 77.39% while its worst performance occasioned an increase of 24.73%. The average number of received messages decreased by 41.92%. Its best performance yielded a reduction of 78.21% while its worst performance occasioned an increase of 19.16%. On average, the number of sent messages dropped by 38.26%. Its best performance yielded a reduction of 76.44% while its worst performance occasioned and increase of 26.08%.

5   Conclusions

This work proposes CDTA, a novel stochastic distributed algorithm (CDTA) to optimize the communication used to solve the dynamic task allocation in a robotic swarm. It builds on the previous GDTA algorithm proposed in [7], wherein the communication is performed in a broadcast manner. Both CDTA and GDTA are PSO-inspired optimization algorithms. Nonetheless, in CDTA the communication is taking advantage of a clustered topology, and allows and significant improvement in terms of convergence time requirements thanks to the reduction of the total number of exchanged message between the robots. The cluster-based communication topology used by CDTA demonstrates its ability to allow the optimization of the communication process, yielding better results than the full mesh communication topology used by GDTA.

In the proposed CDTA algorithm, the robots do not wander around the environment. So, the configuration of the clusters within the robotic swarm is kept static. In the near future, we intend to improve the algorithm to allow for a online clustering of the robots, which would adjust the clusters' configuration dynamically as robot wander around, using closeness in terms of distance, as one of the main criteria to establish cluster formation. Furthermore, a new proposal could evaluate the impact of other communication topology configurations, such as a ring or a tree. Both the ring topology and the tree topology would further reduce the flow of information between robots, but both would delay the flow of the information among robots, which could impact negatively on the convergence of the task allocation process. Moreover, we suspect these communication topology configurations would require a complex internal structure for the communication process.

References

1. Brambilla, M., et al.: Swarm robotics: a review from the swarm engineering perspective. Swarm Intell. **7**(1), 1–41 (2013). https://doi.org/10.1007/s11721-012-0075-2
2. Caraballo, L., et al.: The block-information-sharing strategy for task allocation: a case study for structure assembly with aerial robots. Eur. J. Oper. Res. **260**(2), 725–738 (2017)
3. GCTronic, Elisa-3 (2019). http://www.gctronic.com/doc/index.php/Elisa-3
4. Eberhart, R., Kennedy, J.: A new optimizer using particle swarm theory. In: 1995 IEEE Proceedings of the 6th International Symposium on Micro Machine and Human Science, MHS 1995, pp. 39–43 (1995)
5. Gerkey, B.P., Matric, M.J.: A formal analysis and taxonomy of task allocation in multi-robot systems. Int. J. Robot. Res. **23**(9), 939–954 (2004)
6. Luo, L., Chakraborty, N., Sycara, K.: Distributed algorithms for multirobot task assignment with task deadline constraints. IEEE Trans. Autom. Sci. Eng. **12**(3), 876–888 (2015)
7. Mendonça, R.M., Nedjah, N., Mourelle, M.: PSO-based distributed algorithm for dynamic task allocation in a robotic swarm. Procedia Comput. Sci. **51**, 326–335 (2015)
8. Nedjah, N., Silva Jr., L.: Review of methodologies and tasks in swarm robotics towards standardization. Swarm Evol. Comput. **50**, 100565 (2019). https://doi.org/10.1016/j.swevo.2019.100565
9. Nedjah, N., Morais, G.R., Mourelle, L.: Inspiration-wise swarm intelligence metaheuristics for continuous optimization: a survey – part I. Int. J. Bio-inspired Comput. **15**(4), 207–223 (2019)

10. Tan, Y., Zheng, Z.-Y.: Research advance in swarm robotics. Defense Technol. **9**(1), 18–39 (2013)
11. Tang, F.; Parker, L. E. ASyMTRe: automated synthesis of multi-robot task solutions through software reconfiguration. In: 2005 IEEE Proceedings of the Robotics and Automation, IEEE ICRA, pp. 1501–1508 (2005)
12. Wang, J., Gu, Y., Li, X.: Multi-robot task allocation based on ant colony algorithm. J. Comput. **7**(9), 2160–2167 (2012)
13. Zhang, Y., Liu, S.-H.: Survey of multi-robot task allocation. CAAI Trans. Intell. Syst. **3**(2), 115–120 (2008)

Migration Guided by a Performance Index in Heterogeneous Island Models

Rodrigo C. A. F. Pontes[1], Grasiele R. Duarte[2], and Leonardo Goliatt[1(✉)]

[1] Computational Modeling Program, Federal University of Juiz de Fora,
Juiz de Fora, Brazil
rodrigofajardopontes@yahoo.com.br, leonardo.goliatt@ufjf.edu.br
[2] Civil Engineering Program, COPPE/Federal University of Rio de Janeiro,
Rio de Janeiro, Brazil
grasiele.duarte@coc.ufrj.br

Abstract. Evolutionary Algorithms are efficient alternatives to solve complex optimization problems. The high computational cost of these algorithms commonly motivates their implementation to run in parallel computational environments. Island Model enables the parallel implementation of Evolutionary Algorithms relatively easily to incorporate the migration operation into the evolutionary process. The inclusion of new solutions in a population, previously evolved in another population, can contribute positively to the problem's solution quality. In this work, a performance index was added to the Island Model, aiming to indicate how efficiently each island's population is in solving the problem according to its algorithm. Islands with higher performance indexes receive more individuals in migrations. In this way, these algorithms become more active in the evolutionary process. The experiments demonstrated that the new model solutions were as good as the solutions from each problem's best algorithm. We also noticed that even if we remove the most efficient algorithm from the model, it still adapts and provides efficient solutions.

Keywords: Island Model · Performance index · Evolutionary Computation

1 Introduction

Evolutionary Computation is an area of artificial intelligence that presents ways to find solutions to problems, usually formulated as optimization problems. It is a family of different algorithms called Evolutionary Algorithms (EA). They are characterized by implementing biological evolution mechanisms, such as reproduction, mutation, and selection. The first records of the use of EAs to solve problems started around the 1950s [10].

Several alternatives for implementing EAs have already been proposed in the literature. In the search for better performance, the Island Model (IM) was

© Springer Nature Switzerland AG 2020
B. Filipič et al. (Eds.): BIOMA 2020, LNCS 12438, pp. 125–134, 2020.
https://doi.org/10.1007/978-3-030-63710-1_10

created. In the IM, the population is divided between islands that evolve separately and communicate periodically through the migration operator's exchange of solutions. One of the main IM characteristics is the possibility of parallelization of EAs. For example, each island can be assigned to a processor. This can significantly reduce the simulation time.

Usually, the IM is implemented by applying different EAs between islands. In this type of IM, each island can follow a different trajectory in the search space, producing different solutions based on its EA characteristics. This can be interesting for the preservation of genetic diversity between individuals during the evolutionary process.

The migration occurs between iterations of EAs on the islands. In this operation, the individuals move from one island to another according to the topology applied to the IM, in order to share genetic material between populations. In the traditional IM, the migration rate between the two islands is fixed. That is, the number of individuals going from one island to another is always the same during the entire simulation.

This work aims to present and test a new IM, which is characterized by the variation in the migration operator. In the proposed IM, some islands receive more individuals than others in migrations, according to their EAs. The choice of these islands will be based on a performance index, which shows how well the island is doing at solving the problem.

2   Adaptive Island Model

The use of EAs to solve optimization problems is increasing due to their efficiency already demonstrated extensively in the literature. However, their behavior may vary according to the problem. Thus, it is not easy to choose an EA to solve a given problem to produce a good quality solution.

Another characteristic of EAs is the high computational cost required for their execution. For this reason, commonly, they are implemented to run in parallel computational environments. The IM is an alternative often used for this purpose [1]. There are several approaches to parallel implementations of EAs. Some distributed approaches were published by Derbel [6] and Jankee [14].

In the IM, the population is distributed in subsets called islands, which evolve their solutions individually in a parallel way. A certain topology connects the islands and, during the execution of their EAs, exchange solutions through the migration operation. In this case, the topology has a notable impact on the final IM result. Several topologies can be used, the most common being the ring topology [22,23].

In addition to the topology, the migration also depends on a set of rules to be defined by the user. These rules involve, for example, how often the migration will be applied, how many and what solutions in each island will migrate, and which among other available islands will be the destination islands [20,24,26].

The IM can also be homogeneous or heterogeneous. In the homogeneous IM, the same EA is applied to all islands. On the other hand, in the heterogeneous

IM, different EAs are applied between islands. Thus, in the heterogeneous IM, it is possible to combine different evolutionary strategies to solve the problem [15,17].

In a heterogeneous IM, the migration becomes a mechanism by which it is possible to establish cooperation between EAs. Solutions received by an island, coming from others with other EAs, can point unexplored regions in the search space. This effect can positively impact the quality of the final solution. In addition to the use of different EAs, the cooperation between EAs in IM also requires a convenient set of rules for migration. It is also important to observe that some EAs may be more suitable for solving a given problem in a heterogeneous IM than others.

An interesting way to explore the possibilities of a heterogeneous IM is through the use of dynamic topologies. In this type of implementation, the connections between islands change during the execution of their EAs, usually in the migrations and in an adaptive way. In these IMs, the topology and/or population distribution between islands is adjusted according to information obtained along the evolutionary process. The articles published by Lardeux et al. [5,16] are examples of this approach.

Different strategies for adaptive adjustment of topology in IM were proposed in the literature. In [2], it was proposed an approach based on the speciation concept, by which the population is grouped and distributed periodically according to their similarities. In [13] it was also considered the speciation concept to propose the Speciating Island Model (SIM), a Genetic Programming methodology in which the population is distributed in islands based in the identification of new species by outlier solutions in the population. In [21] it was proposed a procedure called ECO, based on the ecosystem concept, by which similar islands according to population quality are grouped in habitats. In [8] and [9] were proposed the dynamic adjustment of the IM topology according to the attractiveness between pairs of islands. The difference between strategies proposed in [8] and [9] is the definition of attractiveness based on the convergence rate of the EAs in the islands or in the quality of their populations. The IM appears in [19] among multi-population strategies, where also was presented some of its applications in solving problems in different areas.

2.1   Island Model with Performance Index

This work proposes a new approach based on IM, in which the migration operator is modified, aiming for the dynamic distribution of solutions between islands. In the proposed IM, the islands are fully connected by uni-directional connections. Each island is associated with a performance index, corresponding to its migration rate, which indicates how efficient it is in solving the problem. At each migration operation, islands with a high-performance index will receive more individuals, causing their populations increasing, while decreases the population in islands with lower performance index (less efficient islands).

In the proposed IM, each island also has a connection to itself. In this case, the migrant solutions can also consider remaining on the island on which they are already located, according to its performance index. Figure 1 illustrates the connections that each migrant solution from each island in the proposed IM has as alternatives to use a path to the chosen island.

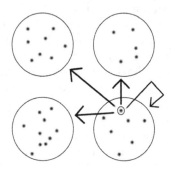

Fig. 1. Decision on the destination island by each migrant individual. The figure exemplifies the alternatives of the path for each migrant solution from each island according to the proposed IM, through the solution highlighted by a circle.

Islands with high-performance indexes indicate good EAs to solve the problem. These islands will increase the individual's chances of choosing. However, a minimum number of individuals has been established for the populations to prevent a particular island having fewer individuals than necessary. This value equals 5, which is the same for all islands.

When carrying out the migration, the best individuals in each island will choose the destination island first. This means that, for the islands that produce good results, after each migration, their quality populations may depreciate if their migrant solutions choose to leave them. On the other hand, despite losing their best individuals in migration, islands that produce no good results may receive better individuals from better islands, improving their populations.

In face of all these information, at each iteration n, the performance index R_n of each island is given by

$$R_n = R_{n-1} + \log\left(\frac{\hat{f}_{n-1}}{\hat{f}_n}\right) \qquad (1)$$

where R_{n-1} is the performance index until previous generation $n-1$, $\hat{f}_{n-1}$ and $\hat{f}_n$ are the average fitness in generations $n-1$ and n respectively. Note that $\hat{f}_{n-1}/\hat{f}_n$ is a measure of how much the population on the island has improved (or worsened) between iterations. Thus, it estimates the island gain in terms of solution quality if an individual migrates to it.

When the migration is carried out, the performance index from the generation before the migration is not calculated. This could cause a very sudden change in the result or even obtain a negative value. Additionally, in this work, the selection operator used in the algorithm is elitism, so the average of the solutions in each island never gets worse from one generation to the next. If there was no elitism, the variation could generate positive and negative returns. Since the performance index is based on return, it will never decrease from one generation to the next.

When applying the migration operator, a portion of the best individuals from an island migrate, using a roulette wheel to determine where they're going, taking into account the returns R_n of each island. Elitism was chosen to apply the selection operator in the algorithms. Consequently, we have only positive returns (R_n) since the average fitness of the population always decreases in minimization. If there was no elitism, the population average could vary up and down, generating positive and negative returns. As the performance index is based only on return, the island's performance index will never decrease from one generation to the next.

3   Assessing the Proposed Island Model

To check if the proposed IM produces competitive results, the test problems proposed in [18] to the competition CEC-2014 (Conference on Evolutionary Computation) were used. This set comprises 30 mono-objective minimization problems produced from 14 basic functions, divided into four groups. The three first problems are classified as Unimodal Functions, followed by the next thirteen problems identified as Simple Multimodal Functions. Six problems combine basic functions and because of this are classified as Hybrid Functions. Finally, the last eight functions compose the fourth group called Composition Functions and they are defined by weighted combinations of problems from other three groups. The domain for all problems is the range $[-100, 100]$.

In this work the proposed IM was evaluated with 4 islands. A different EA was applied in each island, each one with its own characteristics such as diversity of solutions, operators, selection mechanisms. Each EA could perform a different path in the solution space, contributing to each other through migration. The algorithms used in this work were: SGA (Simple Genetic Algorithm) [12], DE (Differential Evolution) [25], HS (Harmony Search) [11] and ES (Evolution Strategies) [3]. The values used to the parameters of the algorithms are shown in Table 1.

Table 1. Parameter setting of the algorithms used in the experiments.

Algorithm	Parameters
DE	F = 0.8, CR = 0.9, variant = DE/rand/1/exp, stop criteria on f = 1e−6, stop criteria on x = 1e−6
SGA	CR = 0.95, mutation probability = 0.05, selection strategy = "truncated"
HS	Rate of choosing from memory = 0.85, minimum pitch adjustment rate = 0.35, maximum pitch adjustment rate = 0.99, minimum distance bandwidth = 1e−5, maximum distance bandwidth = 1
ES	Starting step (σ) = 0.5. The other algorithm parameters are calculated during the simulation

For the implementation of the simulation code, the pygmo tool was used, the Python version of the pagmo [4], a scientific library based on IM, with several optimization problems and algorithms.

First, the EAs chosen for the experiments were evaluated individually. Each one of them was executed in a single population of 100 individuals, under the total of 100 generations. For this evaluation, according to the respective EAs, the experimental scenarios were identified as: C-01: DE, C-02: SGA, C-03: HS, C-04: ES.

For the second stage of experiment, the proposed IM was compared with the best EA identified in the first evaluation. The tested scenarios involving the IM are shown in Table 2. In scenario C-06, the DE algorithm was not used because it is considered to be one of the best algorithms in general, among the algorithms used in this work. It was checked if the proposed IM would work well without this EA in one of its islands.

Table 2. Description of the experimental scenarios C-05 and C-06, involving the proposed IM. The parameters used in the EAs are shown in Table 1.

Scenario	Algorithms (Islands)	Population size	Generations	Migration frequency
C-05	DE, SGA, ES e HS	100 (randomly divided between 4 islands with 25 individuals)	100	10 generations
C-06	SGA, ES e HS	100 (randomly divided between 2 islands with 33 individuals and 1 island with 34 individuals)	100	10 generations

During the IM execution, the best and average values of the objective function in population, the population size and the R_n value of each island were stored. Figure 2 shows the variation of the data along generations of scenario C-05 for one of the problems.

Table 3 shows the average results obtained in 30 runs of the best EA identified for each problem and the proposed IM. In table, the lowest values obtained for the two metrics for each problem were highlighted in boldface. The proposed IM obtained similar solutions to the best EA for most of the 30 tested problems.

For each problem, the Tukey's range test was performed to determine if there is significant difference between the best EA and the proposed IM. The results in Table 3 show that no significant difference was found for any problem. On the EAs performance, DE and HS were identified as the best ones, mainly DE, which produced best solution for a larger number of problems.

To compare the performance difference between all scenarios considered in this work, it was used the technique called Performance Profiles, proposed in [7]. This technique is applicable in evaluations where there are a set of algorithms

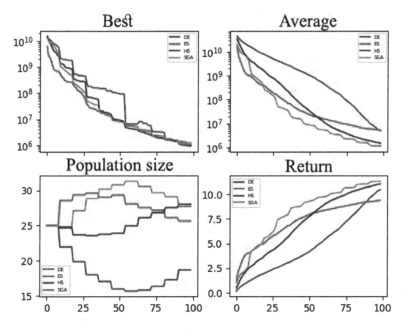

Fig. 2. Simulation details for problem F_2, under using the scenario C-05 to solve it.

and a set of problems. The results in Fig. 3 show that the scenario C-05 has the larger area under the curve, meaning that it was more efficient to reach a satisfactory solution.

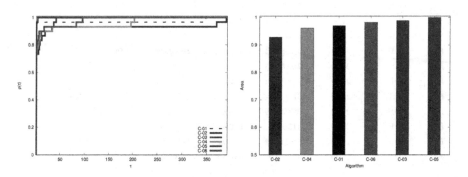

Fig. 3. Performance profiles of the 30 problems, running all scenarios C-01 to C-06 with 100 generations over 30 runs.

Table 3. Comparison of the best algorithm and the proposed IM. The second column presents the algorithm that showed the best average result in 30 runs. Column Optimum is the known optimal solution for each problem according [18], Solution Alg. and Solution IM are the solutions obtained by the best EA and proposed IM respectively, Standard deviation Alg. and Standard deviation IM are the standard deviation between solutions obtained in 30 runs of the best EA and the proposed IM respectively.

Problem	Best algorithm	Optimum	Average of solutions (Alg)	Standard deviation (Alg)	Average of solution (IM)	Standard deviation (IM)	Significant difference
F_1	DE	100	248.61	39.63	**118.12**	**36.85**	No
F_2	DE	200	200.49	0.18	**200.02**	**0.02**	No
F_3	DE	300	**300.00**	1.57	**300.00**	**0.00**	No
F_4	DE	400	**400.00**	**0.0007**	403.48	10.43	No
F_5	DE	500	**519.92**	0.61	520.00	**0.0002**	No
F_6	DE	600	600.11	**0.08**	**600.10**	0.27	No
F_7	HS	700	**700.08**	0.07	**700.08**	**0.05**	No
F_8	DE	800	**800.00**	8.89	**800.00**	**0.00**	No
F_9	HS	900	**905.93**	2.18	908.58	**2.17**	No
F_{10}	SGA	1000	1000.07	**0.03**	**1000.03**	0.04	No
F_{11}	HS	1100	**1190.19**	**46.38**	1226.09	107.42	No
F_{12}	ES	1200	1200.11	0.03	**1200.02**	**0.02**	No
F_{13}	HS	1300	1300.15	0.03	**1300.12**	**0.02**	No
F_{14}	DE	1400	**1400.15**	**0.02**	1400.16	0.06	No
F_{15}	HS	1500	**1500.13**	**0.20**	1501.13	0.53	No
F_{16}	HS	1600	**1601.25**	**0.32**	1601.70	0.59	No
F_{17}	DE	1700	1750.45	**11.15**	**1719.56**	25.17	No
F_{18}	DE	1800	1805.15	**0.88**	**1803.25**	2.42	No
F_{19}	ES	1900	1900.73	0.37	**1900.43**	**0.34**	No
F_{20}	DE	2000	2002.55	**0.41**	**2001.69**	0.97	No
F_{21}	DE	2100	**2103.29**	**1.07**	2105.85	8.02	No
F_{22}	HS	2200	2200.76	**0.66**	**2201.63**	3.82	No
F_{23}	DE	2300	**2629.46**	1.39	**2629.46**	**0.00**	No
F_{24}	HS	2400	**2515.43**	**3.90**	2515.59	4.66	No
F_{25}	DE	2500	2637.34	**3.27**	**2635.30**	7.29	No
F_{26}	HS	2600	2700.14	0.03	**2700.10**	**0.02**	No
F_{27}	DE	2700	**2703.30**	**0.31**	2792.58	136.68	No
F_{28}	DE	2800	3156.88	**0.05**	**3141.54**	81.22	No
F_{29}	DE	2900	**3061.34**	18.92	3117.90	24.66	No
F_{30}	DE	3000	3576.19	**30.58**	**3534.11**	36.91	No

4   Conclusions

In this paper, a migration strategy guided by a performance index was developed to heterogeneous Island Models. A set of 30 problems was used to assess the model performance compared to individual evolutionary approaches.

As the proposed model presented similar solutions to the best algorithms, it can be concluded that this model is a good option for most problems. If instead of this model, only one algorithm is used, one would have to test the algorithms one by one until the best one is found, which would require more effort.

Acknowledgment. The authors acknowledge the financial support of CNPq (429639/2016-3), FAPEMIG (APQ-00334/18), and CAPES - Finance Code 001.

References

1. Alba, E.: Parallel Metaheuristics: A New Class of Algorithms. Wiley, Hoboken (2005)
2. Bessaou, M., Pétrowski, A., Siarry, P.: Island model cooperating with speciation for multimodal optimization. In: Schoenauer, M., et al. (eds.) PPSN 2000. LNCS, vol. 1917, pp. 437–446. Springer, Heidelberg (2000). https://doi.org/10.1007/3-540-45356-3_43
3. Beyer, H.G., Schwefel, H.P.: Evolution strategies - a comprehensive introduction. Nat. Comput. **1**(1), 3–52 (2002)
4. Biscani, F., Izzo, D., Yam, C.H.: A global optimisation toolbox for massively parallel engineering optimisation. arXiv abs/1004.3824 (2010)
5. Candan, C., Goeffon, A., Lardeux, F., Saubion, F.: A dynamic island model for adaptive operator selection. In: Proceedings of the 14th Annual Conference on Genetic and Evolutionary Computation, GECCO 2012, pp. 1253–1260. Association for Computing Machinery, New York, NY, USA (2012)
6. Derbel, B., Verel, S.: DAMS: distributed adaptive metaheuristic selection. In: Proceedings of the 13th Annual Conference on Genetic and Evolutionary Computation, GECCO 2011, pp. 1955–1962. Association for Computing Machinery, New York, NY, USA (2011)
7. Dolan, E.D., More, J.J.: Benchmarking optimization software with performance profiles. Math. Program. **91**(2), 201–213 (2002)
8. Duarte, G., Lemonge, A., Goliatt, L.: A dynamic migration policy to the island model. In: 2017 IEEE Congress on Evolutionary Computation (CEC), pp. 1135–1142 (June 2017)
9. Duarte, G., Lemonge, A., Goliatt, L.: A new strategy to evaluate the attractiveness in a dynamic island model. In: 2018 IEEE Congress on Evolutionary Computation (CEC), pp. 1–8 (July 2018)
10. Friedberg, R.M.: A learning machine: part I. IBM J. Res. Dev. **2**(1), 2–13 (1958)
11. Geem, Z.W., Kim, J.H., Loganathan, G.: A new heuristic optimization algorithm: harmony search. SIMULATION **76**(2), 60–68 (2001)
12. Goldberg, D.E.: Genetic Algorithms in Search, Optimization and Machine Learning, 1st edn. Addison-Wesley Longman Publishing Co., Inc., Boston (1989)
13. Gustafson, S., Burke, E.K.: The speciating island model: an alternative parallel evolutionary algorithm. J. Parallel Distrib. Comput. **66**(8), 1025–1036 (2006). Special Issue: Parallel Bioinspired Algorithms
14. Jankee, C., Verel, S., Derbel, B., Fonlupt, C.: Distributed adaptive metaheuristic selection: comparisons of selection strategies. In: Bonnevay, S., Legrand, P., Monmarché, N., Lutton, E., Schoenauer, M. (eds.) EA 2015. LNCS, vol. 9554, pp. 83–96. Springer, Cham (2016). https://doi.org/10.1007/978-3-319-31471-6_7

15. Kurdi, M.: A new hybrid island model genetic algorithm for job shop scheduling problem. Comput. Ind. Eng. **88**(Suppl. C), 273–283 (2015)
16. Lardeux, F., Goëffon, A.: A dynamic island-based genetic algorithms framework. In: Deb, K., et al. (eds.) SEAL 2010. LNCS, vol. 6457, pp. 156–165. Springer, Heidelberg (2010). https://doi.org/10.1007/978-3-642-17298-4_16
17. Li, C., Yang, S.: An island based hybrid evolutionary algorithm for optimization. In: Li, X., et al. (eds.) SEAL 2008. LNCS, vol. 5361, pp. 180–189. Springer, Heidelberg (2008). https://doi.org/10.1007/978-3-540-89694-4_19
18. Liang, J.J., Qu, B.Y., Suganthan, P.N.: Problem definitions and evaluation criteria for the CEC 2014 special session and competition on single objective real-parameter numerical optimization. Technical report (December 2013)
19. Ma, H., Shen, S., Yu, M., Yang, Z., Fei, M., Zhou, H.: Multi-population techniques in nature inspired optimization algorithms: a comprehensive survey. Swarm Evol. Comput. **44**, 365–387 (2019)
20. Märtens, M., Izzo, D.: The asynchronous island model and NSGA-II: study of a new migration operator and its performance. In: Proceedings of the 15th Annual Conference on Genetic and Evolutionary Computation, GECCO 2013, pp. 1173–1180. ACM, New York, NY, USA (2013)
21. Parpinelli, R.S., Lopes, H.S.: An ecology-based heterogeneous approach for cooperative search. In: Barros, L.N., Finger, M., Pozo, A.T., Gimenénez-Lugo, G.A., Castilho, M. (eds.) SBIA 2012. LNCS (LNAI), pp. 212–221. Springer, Heidelberg (2012). https://doi.org/10.1007/978-3-642-34459-6_22
22. Ruciński, M., Izzo, D., Biscani, F.: On the impact of the migration topology on the island model. Parallel Comput. **36**(10–11), 555–571 (2010). Parallel Architectures and Bioinspired Algorithms
23. Skolicki, Z., De Jong, K.: The influence of migration sizes and intervals on island models. In: Proceedings of the 7th Annual Conference on Genetic and Evolutionary Computation, GECCO 2005, pp. 1295–1302. Association for Computing Machinery, New York, NY, USA (2005)
24. Skolicki, Z.M.: An Analysis of Island Models in Evolutionary Computation. Ph.D. thesis, Fairfax, VA, USA (2007)
25. Storn, R., Price, K.: Differential evolution - a simple and efficient heuristic for global optimization over continuous spaces. J. Glob. Optim. **11**(4), 341–359 (1997)
26. Tanabe, R., Fukunaga, A.: Evaluation of a randomized parameter setting strategy for island-model evolutionary algorithms. In: 2013 IEEE Congress on Evolutionary Computation, pp. 1263–1270 (2013)

Bio-inspired Optimization Based on Biological Growth Method and Mesh Morphing Surface Sculpting

Stefano Porziani$^{(\boxtimes)}$ and Marco E. Biancolini

Università degli Studi di Roma "Tor Vergata",
Via del Politecnico 1, 00133 Rome, Italy
porziani@ing.uniroma2.it

Abstract. The Biological Growth Method (BGM) is an efficient optimization approach suitable for the surface stress reduction in a specific mechanical component and allows us to obtain a more homogeneous stress distribution. This method mimics the way in which biological structures, such as tree trunks, bones and horns, evolve during their growth. The effectiveness of the BGM methodology, coupled with mesh morphing technique based on Radial Basis Functions (RBF), is presented here. Two cases are illustrated: the first referring to the growth of tree trunks under specific loads; the second referring to the optimization of an after-market component for high performances motorbikes.

Keywords: Radial basis functions · Finite element method · Optimization · Mesh morphing · Biological growth method

1 Introduction

In mechanical design, the optimal configuration of components has to be pursued, so that both costs and failure risks can be minimized. Nowadays, designer can take advantage of the introduction and widespread adoption of numerical simulations: this allows to virtually test different configurations using Finite Element Method (FEM) and optimization techniques. The research of an optimal configuration, however, requires the designer to build a numerical model for each configuration to be tested and this can become a very time-consuming task, specially dealing with complex shape models. Mesh morphing ([3,8] and [18]) is a powerful tool that allows to obtain different numerical model configurations by operating on the mesh nodes spatial position, with no need to rebuild the model geometry or mesh. This tool proved its reliability in several challenging engineering fields, such as Fluid Structure Interaction (FSI) problems, as described in [11,13] and [5], or crack front propagation prediction [9], as reported in [10] and [6].

Mesh morphing action can be driven in different ways: user can decide which displacement impose to which point, or it is possible to use numerical results

© Springer Nature Switzerland AG 2020
B. Filipič et al. (Eds.): BIOMA 2020, LNCS 12438, pp. 135–147, 2020.
https://doi.org/10.1007/978-3-030-63710-1_11

data to decide which point has to be moved and the amplitude of the displacement. Biological Growth Method (BGM) belongs to this second approach. BGM is a bio-inspired approach that is based on the behaviour observed in the biological tissue under stress: higher stress area usually promote an high growth rate so that the stress peaks can be mitigated. This method can be successfully employed to optimize mechanical component shape[16]; resulting organic shapes could be too complex to be built and specific manufacturing constraints can be added as demonstrated in [15]. In this latter work ([15]), the BGM and mesh morphing surface sculpting optimization (which can be considered a parameterless method) is compared with a parameter-based optimization strategy: the last one strategy, applied on a simple mechanical component, allowed a maximum stress reduction of 21.8%, whilst the proposed optimization strategy allowed a 30.7% maximum stress reduction on the same mechanical component, under the same load and constraint conditions. Industrial interest in parameter-less methods is increasing nowadays, in [16] the BGM based mesh morphing is compared with an adjoint based surface sculpting in an industrial component optimization. It is worth to remark that adjoint based parameter-less optimization can fail in obtaining optimized shapes if is not possible to evaluate the observable adjoint matrix for a specific numerical analysis, whilst BGM can be always applied since relays only on the local surface results of the numerical analysis.

In the present work, the result of the proposed methodology to optimize mechanical component shape [17] is first presented by showing how it works in nature, i.e., by modelling a tree trunk growth, and then it is applied to a motorsport application, i.e., showing the shape optimization of a front wheel support of a high performance motorcycle.

The methodology has been developed in the framework of ANSYS Workbench Finite Element Analysis (FEA) tool [1], using the mesh morpher RBF Morph ACT extension [2], which is based on Radial Basis Functions (RBFs), to manage both the mesh morphing and the BGM algorithms employed.

1.1   RBF Background

RBFs are a set of scalar functions introduced in the early 60s to interpolate multidimensional scattered data ([7]). They allow to interpolate a scalar field everywhere in the definition space, starting from known values at discrete points, also called source points. Given that data to be interpolated is in the form of scattered scalar values at source points $\boldsymbol{x}_{k_i}$ in the space $\mathbb{R}^n$, the interpolating function can be written as in Eq. (1).

$$s(\boldsymbol{x}) = \sum_{i=1}^{N} \gamma_i \varphi \left(\| \boldsymbol{x} - \boldsymbol{x}_{k_i} \| \right) + h(\boldsymbol{x}) \tag{1}$$

The points $\boldsymbol{x}$ at which the function is evaluated are the target points. φ is the radial function, which is a scalar function of the Euclidean distance between each source point and the target point considered; typical radial functions are shown in Table 1, considering $r = (\| \boldsymbol{x} - \boldsymbol{x}_{k_i} \|)$. γ_i are the weights of the radial basis which are to be evaluated solving a linear system of equations, whose order is equal to the number of source points introduced and the polynomial part h is added to guarantee the existence and the uniqueness of the solution. In mesh morphing applications, a linear polynomial can be used:

$$h(\boldsymbol{x}) = \beta_1 + \beta_2 x + \beta_3 y + \beta_4 z \tag{2}$$

in which β coefficients are to be evaluated together with γ weights in the solving RBF system resulting from orthogonality and uniqueness conditions (see for reference [17]). Once solved, the RBF system is used to interpolate each imposed displacement component as an independent scalar field:

Table 1. Most common radial functions.

RBF type	Equation
Spline type (Rn)	r^n, n odd
Thin plate spline	$r^n log(r)$, n even
Multiquadric (MQ)	$\sqrt{1+r^2}$
Inverse multiquadric (IMQ)	$\dfrac{1}{\sqrt{1+r^2}}$
Inverse quadric (IQ)	$\dfrac{1}{1+r^2}$
Gaussian (GS)	e^{-r^2}

$$
\begin{cases}
s_x(\boldsymbol{x}) = \sum_{i=0}^{N} \gamma_i^x \varphi\left(\|\boldsymbol{x} - \boldsymbol{x}_i\|\right) + \beta_1^x + \beta_2^x x + \beta_3^x y + \beta_4^x z \\[2em]
s_y(\boldsymbol{x}) = \sum_{i=0}^{N} \gamma_i^y \varphi(\|\boldsymbol{x} - \boldsymbol{x}_i\|) + \beta_1^y + \beta_2^y x + \beta_3^y y + \beta_4^y z \\[2em]
s_z(\boldsymbol{x}) = \sum_{i=0}^{N} \gamma_i^z \varphi(\|\boldsymbol{x} - \boldsymbol{x}_i\|) + \beta_1^z + \beta_2^z x + \beta_3^z y + \beta_4^z z
\end{cases}
\tag{3}
$$

In mesh morphing, source points are the mesh nodes on which the displacement is imposed, whilst the target nodes are the whole set of nodes that have to be morphed in order to obtain the new numerical model configuration.

1.2 BGM Method

The Biological Growth Method (BGM) is a shape optimization method which adopts as a driving force the entity of surface stresses of structural components. This method is based on the observation that biological structures, such as tree trunks and animal bones, can evolve at surfaces by adding biological material layers on areas where an activation stress acts. In [12] and in [14] it is proposed to extend this concept: material can be added on surfaces with high stresses and can be removed from surfaces where stresses are low. [12] demonstrated that combining photo-elastic techniques and BGM approach, a uniform stress along the boundary of a stress raiser can be obtained. In [14] a 2D study capable to predict the shape evolution observed in natural structures is presented and proposed to be used in CAE based optimization. In their work, the authors computed the volumetric growth $(\dot{\varepsilon})$ according to the von Mises stress (σ_{Mises}) and a threshold stress (σ_{ref}); the latter one was chosen according to the allowable stress for the specific design.

$$\dot{\varepsilon} = k \left(\sigma_{Mises} - \sigma_{ref} \right) \tag{4}$$

Waldman and Heller [19] proposed a more complex model for layer growth, suitable for shape optimization of holes in air-frame structures with multiple stress peak locations. The formula is more complex than Eq. (4), as reported in Eq. (5):

$$d_i^j = \left(\frac{\sigma_i^j - \sigma_i^{th}}{\sigma_i^{th}} \right) \cdot s \cdot c \ , \ \sigma_i^{th} = max(\sigma_i^j) \text{ if } \sigma_i^j > 0 \text{ or } \sigma_i^{th} = min(\sigma_i^j) \text{ if } \sigma_i^j < 0 \tag{5}$$

The model by Waldman and Heller moves the i-th boundary node of the j-th region by a distance d_i^j, computed using (5), where σ_i^j is the normal stress in the tangential direction, σ_i^{th} is the stress threshold, c is and arbitrary characteristic length and s is a step size scaling factor.

In the present work a different implementation of BGM is used. As stated before, the framework used to perform numerical simulations is ANSYS Mechanical exploiting the RBF Morph ACT Extension. The capability of RBF Morph in performing BGM optimization were already presented in [4]. The BGM implemented prescribes the node displacement (S_{node}) in the direction normal to the surface according to Eq. (6), where σ_{node} is the stress evaluated at each node, σ_{th} is a threshold value for stress defined by user, σ_{max} and σ_{min} are respectively the maximum and the minimum value of stress in the current set. d is the maximum offset between the nodes on which the maximum and the minimum stress are evaluated; this parameter is defined by the user to control the nodes displacement whilst limiting the possible distortion of the mesh.

$$S_{node} = \frac{\sigma_{node} - \sigma_{th}}{\sigma_{max} - \sigma_{min}} \cdot d \tag{6}$$

According to Eq. (6), nodes on the surface to be optimized can be moved either inward, if the stress on node is lower than the threshold value, or outward, if the evaluated stress is higher than the threshold value. In RBF Morph BGM implementation the Eq. (6) has been improved by adding the capability to use as driver different equivalent stress and strain definitions, as summarized in Table 2.

Table 2. Stress and strain types available in the RBF Morph implementation of BGM.

Stress/Strain type	Equation
von Mises stress	$\sigma_e = \sqrt{(\sigma_1 - \sigma_2)^2 + (\sigma_2 - \sigma_3)^2 + (\sigma_3 - \sigma_1)^2}$
Maximum Principal stress	$\sigma_e = max(\sigma_1, \sigma_2, \sigma_3)$
Minumum Principal stress	$\sigma_e = min(\sigma_1, \sigma_2, \sigma_3)$
Stress intensity	$\sigma_e = max(|\sigma_1 - \sigma_2|, |\sigma_2 - \sigma_3|, |\sigma_3 - \sigma_1|)$
Maximum Shear stress	$\sigma_e = 0.5 \cdot (max(\sigma_1, \sigma_2, \sigma_3) - min(\sigma_1, \sigma_2, \sigma_3))$
Equivalent Plastic strain	$\varepsilon_e = [2(1 + \nu')]^{-1} \cdot \left(0.5\sqrt{(\varepsilon_1 - \varepsilon_2)^2 + (\varepsilon_2 - \varepsilon_3)^2 + (\varepsilon_3 - \varepsilon_1)^2} \right)$

1.3   RBF and BGM Coupling

The above described mesh morphing technique and BGM can be successfully coupled in a optimization approach. This approach has been integrated in the RBF Morph ACT extension for ANSYS Mechanical and is based on the following steps:

1. the baseline geometry is discretized into finite elements; load and constraints are applied and FEM solution evaluated;
2. from FEM solution, nodal stress on surfaces to be optimized are retrieved, σ_{th} and d are set by user and S_{node} displacement along surface normal for each node is evaluated according to Eq. (6) for each selected node;
3. evaluated displacement are used to set up the RBF problem by imposing them as values to be interpolated (values on source points), user can optionally set additional source points values to complete the morphing set-up (i.e., points to be maintained fixed);
4. FEM model mesh is morphed and FEM solution evaluated again;
5. stress values on surface to be optimized are analyzed: if the new stress levels can be further optimized, the procedure is iterated from point 2; otherwise, the geometry can be considered optimized.

In the above described methodology, the user is required to set two BGM parameters: the threshold stress σ_{th} and maximum displacement d. The first parameter represents the stress level value on which the optimization procedure will try to converge; the second parameter represents the maximum displacement allowed within an individual optimization step: the smaller is its value the higher will be the number of steps to reach the optimum and the lower will be the risk of mesh distortions that could invalidate FEM model.

In the following sections, two applications of the proposed methodology will be illustrated: a first application involving a natural structure, i.e. a tree trunks junction in which loads applied have induced a particular tissue growth; a second application in which surface shape optimization of a high-performances motor-bike component is driven by BGM and mesh morphing.

2   Natural Application

As stated before, BGM was developed in 90's, and among main contributors it is possible to cite Mattheck and Burkhardt [14]. In their study, the tissue growth of a particular zone of a tree is described and reproduced numerically using a two-dimensional numerical model (see Fig. 1).

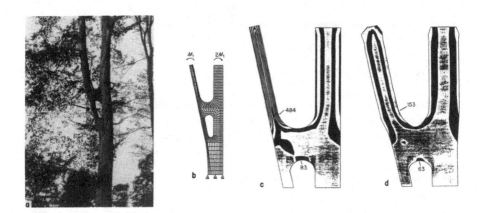

Fig. 1. Example of natural structures growth [14].

Adopting the proposed methodology, a three-dimensional model of the same natural structure has been modeled and analysed in order to investigate the model shape optimization. The modeling activities were realized taking into account the geometry depicted in Fig. 2a. Two-dimensional boundary conditions shown in Fig. 2b and reported in the above mentioned paper ([14]) were translated in the three-dimensional model, so that this latter was loaded and constrained as in the reference paper. Material used to modelling wood was considered as transversely isotropic, and material data used referred to a wood belonging to the *Pinacee* family (see Table 3).

The BGM driven surface sculpting was set to iterate 40 times, setting the threshold value to $50000Pa$ for the equivalent von Mises stress and the d parameter to $0.0005m$ (see Eq. (6)). The maximum and mean von Mises equivalent stress reduction is plotted in Fig. 3: the maximum value was reduced by 61%, whilst the mean value was reduced by 44% at the end of the 40th iteration.

The shape evolution at 0, 20 and 40 iterations is depicted in Fig. 4: in the left column the shape evolution is shown, whilst in the right column it is possible to notice how the surface portion interested by the highest stress value decreases and the area is subject to a more homogeneous stress distribution. As for the final shape achieved in [14] and shown in Fig. 1, the shape of left trunk is modified so that its diameter is increased just above the knee, in order to reduce surface stresses in this area.

Table 3. Wood elastic property used in numerical modelling.

Elastic property	Value
E_x, E_z	1.000 $[GPa]$
E_y	11.520 $[GPa]$
G_{xy}, G_{yz}	0.810 $[GPa]$
G_{xz}	0.355 $[GPa]$
ν_{xy}, ν_{zy}	0.0301 $[-]$
ν_{xz}, ν_{zx}	0.4080 $[-]$
ν_{yz}, ν_{yx}	0.3470 $[-]$

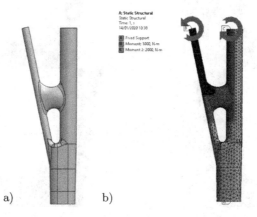

a)   b)

Fig. 2. a) tree CAD model; b) loads and constraints applied

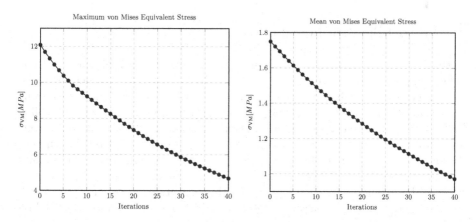

Fig. 3. Values of maximum and mean von Mises equivalent stress during the iterative surface sculpting.

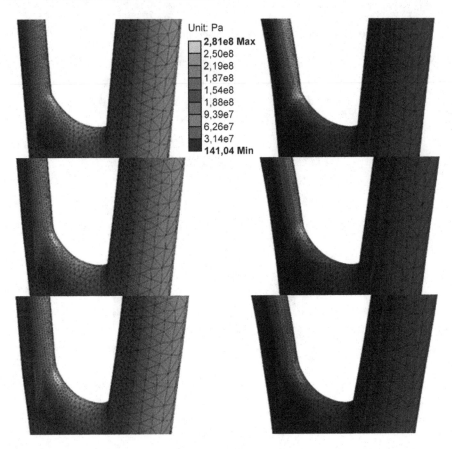

Fig. 4. Evolution of the tree geometry and stress distribution at (from the top) 0, 20, 40 iterations.

3   Motorbike Application

In this section an optimization study performed on the Ducati Panigale V4 front wheel support is presented. This component has an important function in the overall motorbike cycling: it represents the connection between front wheel, front suspension (fork) and front braking system. In a high performances motorbike, loads acting on this component are extremely high and the component needs an accurate design and optimization process. Highest loads act on the support during a overturning-limit brake, which is a condition when, due to the braking action applied, inertia forces acting on the motorbike lead to nullify contact between back wheel and road surface. In this condition, forces transmitted by braking system to threads are summed with vehicle inertial force transmitted by front wheel hub to the tightening clump (see Fig. 5).

Fig. 5. Load and constraints on the front wheel support

The scope of calculus is the shape optimization of the front wheel support and its consequent structural validation. The proposed optimised configuration will be realised using an aeronautical derivation aluminium alloy, EN AW 7075. A preliminary sensitivity analysis on the grid spacing has been performed in the baseline configuration representing the aftermarket geometry and the overturning-limit brake condition. Applied constraints and loads configuration is shown in Fig. 5, numerical values are not disclosed because are confidential information of the industrial partner. Von Mises stress distribution in the baseline configuration is depicted in Fig. 6.

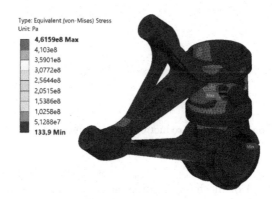

Fig. 6. Equivalent von Mises stress on the whole body

Analyzing this stress distribution two set of surfaces were selected to perform the surface sculpting adopting BGM and mesh morphing techniques. These surfaces, with von Mises stress distributions, are those highlighted in Fig. 7: a set of planar surfaces (Fig. 7 left) and a set of cylindrical ones (Fig. 7 right).

 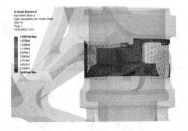

Fig. 7. Equivalent von Mises Stress on the sculpted surfaces

Three different approaches were pursued: BGM applied on planar surfaces (Setup 1), BGM applied on circular surfaces (Setup 2), BGM applied on both zones (Setup 3). The sculpting action has been set to iterate 10 times, obtaining the maximum von Mises stress variation and volume variation reported in Fig. 8. According to these graphs, Setup 1 is the solution providing more volume reduction (−0.6%), but maximum equivalent stress is increased at the end of the iterations (+0.3%). With Setup 2 the maximum value of von Mises stress decreases (−16.1%), with an increased volume (+1.5%). Setup 3 provides higher stress reduction (−20.8%) at the cost of an higher volume increase (+2.5%).

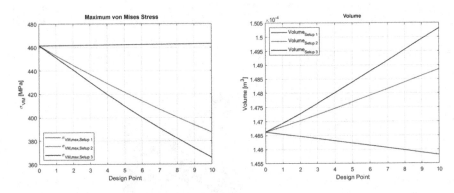

Fig. 8. Maximum von Mises stress reduction and Volume increase for the three BGM setup investigated

Since in this kind of mechanical components maximum stress value reduction is the most important performance index, as it can affect fatigue life of components themselves, Setup 3 can be considered as the optimal solution. The stress distribution obtained at the end of the surface sculpting optimization are depicted in Fig. 9, whilst the final shape is shown in Fig. 10.

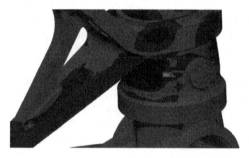

Fig. 9. Equivalent von Mises stress distribution after 10 iterations

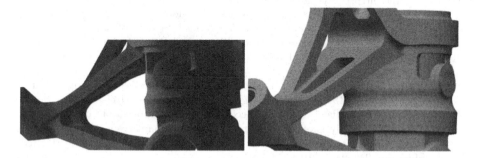

Fig. 10. Final shape obtained with 10 surface sculpting iterations

4 Conclusions

In the present work a new approach toward parameter-less shape optimization through surface sculpting has been presented, which is based on the combination of two mathematical tools: the biological growth method and the radial basis functions mesh morphing. The first one is based on the observation and imitation of growth mechanisms for natural tissues, and is coupled with an innovative and effective shape modification technique, RBF based mesh morphing. In the present paper, after giving theoretical background to both methods and a comparison with other parameter-less optimization solutions, two applications were presented.

In the first application, a test case from a fundamental paper on BGM has been analysed. In this application a natural structure, a tree trunk junction, was modeled using three-dimensional elements and the same two-dimensional loads and constraints applied to the literature case were translated and applied the three-dimensional model. Results gave a good agreement with literature case, both in terms of shape evolution and in terms of stress reduction (61% maximum stress reduction and 44% mean stress reduction).

In the second application, an industrial application was presented: the shape optimization of an after-market front wheel support for a high-performances motorbike. In this case three different strategies were applied, choosing and combining the surfaces of the component to be optimized. The final optimized shape reported a 20.8% maximum equivalent stress reduction, at the cost of 2.5% volume increase.

Acknowledgements. The authors would like to thanks Motocorse San Marino for sharing the geometry files of the presented study and Eng. Andrea Ridolfi for supervising numerical analysis execution and results and for sharing his noticeable experience with us.

References

1. ANSYS, Inc. http://www.ansys.com/products/structures. Accessed 29 July 2020
2. RBF Morph srl. http://www.rbf-morph.com/act-module/. Accessed 29 July 2020
3. Biancolini, M.E.: Mesh morphing and smoothing by means of radial basis functions (RBF): a practical example using Fluent and RBF Morph. In: Handbook of Research on Computational Science and Engineering: Theory and Practice, pp. 347–380. IGI Global (2011)
4. Biancolini, M.E.: Fast Radial Basis Functions for Engineering Applications. Springer, Cham (2018). https://doi.org/10.1007/978-3-319-75011-8
5. Biancolini, M.E., Cella, U.: An advanced RBF morph application: coupled CFD CSM aeroelastic analysis of a full aircraft model and comparison to experimental data. In: MIRA International Vehicle Aerodynamics Conference, Grove, United Kingdom, pp. 243–258 (2010)
6. Biancolini, M.E., Chiappa, A., Giorgetti, F., Porziani, S., Rochette, M.: Radial basis functions mesh morphing for the analysis of cracks propagation. Procedia Struct. Integr. **8**, 433–443 (2018)
7. Davis, P.J.: Interpolation and Approximation. Blaisdell Publishing Company, New York (1963)
8. De Boer, A., Van der Schoot, M., Bijl, H.: Mesh deformation based on radial basis function interpolation. Comput. Struct. **85**(11–14), 784–795 (2007)
9. Galland, F., Gravouil, A., Malvesin, E., Rochette, M.: A global model reduction approach for 3D fatigue crack growth with confined plasticity. Comput. Methods Appl. Mech. Eng. **200**(5–8), 699–716 (2011)
10. Giorgetti, F., et al.: Crack propagation analysis of near-surface defects with radial basis functions mesh morphing. Procedia Struct. Integr. **12**, 471–478 (2018)
11. Groth, C., Cella, U., Costa, E., Biancolini, M.E.: Fast high fidelity CFD/CSMfluid structure interaction using RBF mesh morphing and modal superposition method. Aircr. Eng. Aerosp. Technol. (2019). https://doi.org/10.1108/AEAT-09-2018-0246
12. Heywood, R.B.: Photoelasticity for Designers. Pergamon Press, Oxford (1969)
13. Lombardi, M., Parolini, N., Quarteroni, A.: Radial basis functions for inter-grid interpolation and mesh motion in FSI problems. Comput. Methods Appl. Mech. Eng. (2013). https://doi.org/10.1016/j.cma.2012.12.019
14. Mattheck, C., Burkhardt, S.: A new method of structural shape optimization based on biological growth. Int. J. Fatigue **12**(3), 185–190 (1990)
15. Porziani, S., Groth, C., Biancolini, M.E.: Automatic shape optimization of structural components with manufacturing constraints. Procedia Struct. Integr. **12**, 416–428 (2018)
16. Porziani, S., Groth, C., Mancini, L., Cenni, R., Cova, M., Biancolini, M.E.: Optimisation of industrial parts by mesh morphing enabled automatic shape sculpting. Procedia Struct. Integr. **24**, 724–737 (2019)

17. Porziani, S., Groth, C., Waldman, W., Biancolini, M.E.: Automatic shape optimisation of structural parts driven by BGM and RBF mesh morphing. Int. J. Mech. Sci., 105976 (2020). https://doi.org/10.1016/j.ijmecsci.2020.105976. http://www.sciencedirect.com/science/article/pii/S0020740320306184

18. Staten, M.L., Owen, S.J., Shontz, S.M., Salinger, A.G., Coffey, T.S.: A comparison of mesh morphing methods for $3D$ shape optimization. In: Quadros, W.R. (ed.) Proceedings of the 20th International Meshing Roundtable, pp. 293–311. Springer, Berlin (2011). https://doi.org/10.1007/978-3-642-24734-7_16

19. Waldman, W., Heller, M.: Shape optimisation of holes in loaded plates by minimisation of multiple stress peaks. Technical report DSTO-RR-0412, Aerospace Division, Defence Science and Technology Organisation, Melbourne, Australia (2015)

Understanding the Behavior of Reinforcement Learning Agents

Jörg Stork[1]([✉])[iD], Martin Zaefferer[1][iD], Thomas Bartz-Beielstein[1][iD], and A. E. Eiben[2][iD]

[1] TH Köln, Steinmülerallee 1, 51643 Gummersbach, Germany
{joerg.stork,martin.zaefferer,thomas.bartz-beielstein}@th-koeln.de
[2] Vrije Universiteit Amsterdam, De Boelelaan 1105,
1081 HV Amsterdam, Netherlands
a.e.eiben@vu.nl

Abstract. Reinforcement Learning (RL) is the process of training agents to solve specific tasks, based on measures of reward. Understanding the behavior of an agent in its environment can be crucial. For instance, if users understand why specific agents fail at a task, they might be able to define better reward functions, to steer the agents' development in the right direction. Understandability also empowers decisions for agent deployment. If we know why the controller of an autonomous car fails or excels in specific traffic situations, we can make better decisions on whether/when to use them in practice. We aim to facilitate the understandability of RL. To that end, we investigate and observe the behavioral space: the set of actions of an agent observed for a set of input states. Consecutively, we develop measures of distance or similarity in that space and analyze how agents compare in their behavior. Moreover, we investigate which states and actions are critical for a task, and determine the correlation between reward and behavior. We utilize two basic RL environments to investigate our measures. The results showcase the high potential of inspecting an agents' behavior and comparing their distance in behavior space.

Keywords: Reinforcement Learning · Behavior · Understandable AI

1 Introduction

In Reinforcement Learning (RL), agents are learning policies to solve a specific task. For example, we can consider a robot as an agent who has to navigate a particular environment and react to certain obstacles. At first, a user is interested in these robots' performance, which is commonly evaluated by their ability to solve the task and further based on a user-defined reward function. Besides this performance assessment, the trained robot's behavior, such as the action it takes for individual states, is the only observable part, as the internals of the policy remain indistinguishable by an external observer. Thus, users desire to analyze

© Springer Nature Switzerland AG 2020
B. Filipič et al. (Eds.): BIOMA 2020, LNCS 12438, pp. 148–160, 2020.
https://doi.org/10.1007/978-3-030-63710-1_12

and compare the behavior to exploit how the robot reacts in certain situations or if it behaves as intended. Even a well-performing robot may have developed a specialized behavior not intended by the user, such as only driving backward.

This paper compares agents based on their behaviors, which span a new space, the behavior space. This paper's primary motivation is to create a better understanding of this behavior space and develop useful measures for the comparisons of agents without knowing the inner details of their policies. Moreover, these measures could allow us to identify how agents in a learning set differ, not concerning their reward, but with regard to their behavior. It is particularly interesting to identify situations (states) in which an agent behaves differently than expected. As this is a broad topic, we will start by tackling the following research questions:

Q-1. How does an agent's behavior with good performance compare to similarly performing agents or inferior agents?
Q-2. Which input states are important or problematic for the task?
Q-3. Is there a correlation between an agent's reward and behavior, and how do changes in the behavior affect their reward?

Comparing agents in the behavior space has some prerequisites: For most RL environments, individual agents will not visit the entire state space and thus not learn the optimal action for these unobserved states. Unobserved states are, for instance, present in environments with continuous state spaces or exclusive paths. Nevertheless, as we investigate agents that map a policy from state to action space (i.e., Artificial Neural Network (ANN) policy controllers), we can compute an agent's behavior to any state, even if not observed or observable by the agent itself. This property allows us to compare two agents in the behavior space on a mutual state set and investigate differences. However, state sets are usually not initially known but based on processing the RL tasks and discovered during each agent's learning process. Thus, the individual state sets' contents are based on the state trajectory each agent follows, for example, an absolute path for a robot in a maze. Each agent in a learning set will likely have different trajectories, which renders it challenging to select input states to compute a useful behavior space to compare many agents.

Behavior spaces have previously been investigated in the RL literature. Most frequently, they were utilized to measure diversity and enforce explorative search strategies. For instance, Doncieux and Mouret used behavioral similarity measures to encourage the diversity of evolved agents in an evolutionary search [1]. Ollion and Doncieux suggested to measure and enforce exploration in the behavioral space [12]. Meyerson et al. [9] investigated how behavior characterizations can be learned automatically for novelty search. Quality diversity algorithms also depend on effective behavior comparison [13]. Similar directions have been investigated in the field of surrogate model-based optimization. Here, the term *phenotypic* space has been used, defining a space that encompasses behaviors and outcomes of individuals, rather than their encoding (genotype). Distances in the phenotypic space are used to train surrogate models. For instance, this has been investigated in the context of tree-coded genetic programming [5,11,16].

Similar work focused on graph-coded representations of neural networks. Here, phenotypic spaces and distance measure have been investigated for tasks like classification, reinforcement learning, or for evolving neural network controllers for robotic navigation [4,14].

Unlike these previous investigations, we aim to look at the behavior space not primarily to improve the performance of optimization or modeling algorithms. Instead, we aim for the understandability of agents' behavior. To do so, we utilize two RL environments, a designed maze with different mutual exclusive paths and the inverted pendulum, with a large real-valued state space.

2   Methods

2.1   Behavior Space in Reinforcement Learning

The *behavior* of an RL agent encompasses its (re-)actions, based on its environment and observed input states. The actions an agent takes for a specific state $s \in S$ is defined by a *policy* $\pi : S \rightarrow B$. The agents get a reward $r \in R$ for each state transition. The discussed methods apply to a wide range of RL agents. The only prerequisite is their ability to calculate a behavior for states that have not been observed by those agents themselves. More precisely, we define the behavior as the set of actions for a set of input states. For an agent A, we denote its behavior as B_A, with $B_A = \pi_A(\mathbf{S})$. Here, $\mathbf{S}$ is a set containing n input state vectors, $\pi_A(\mathbf{S})$ is the policy function computing the actions of agent A for all states in $\mathbf{S}$. Consequently, the behavior space $\mathcal{B}$ is the set of all possible behaviors (or the behavior of all possible agents) for a RL task, that is, $B_A \in \mathcal{B}$.

2.2   Behavior Comparison and State Importance

For the comparison of two agents A and A', we can calculate the distance of their behaviors, which can then be denoted by $\mathrm{d}(B_A, B_{A'})$. Because the distance depends on the state space, we consider the distance of two behaviors concerning the same state set $\mathbf{S}$. The employed distance function can be chosen according to the data type of $B_A, B_{A'}$. That is, if they contain continuous values, we might use the Euclidean distance. If they are ordinal integers, we can choose the Manhattan distance instead, with $\mathrm{d}(B_A, B_{A'}) = \sum_i^n |\pi_A(\mathbf{S_i}) - \pi_{A'}(\mathbf{S_i})|$. The comparison of actions for individual states can provide interesting insights into the specific behavior of an agent and further the importance of that state for the task. In particular, we analyze the effects of unobserved states (UOS), which are not present in the state set of a specific agent, and the influence of states with degrees of freedom (DFS), where several actions lead to the same or similar reward. In general, we consider a state as important (or problematic), if the correct action for this state is essential for getting a good reward (or challenging to learn, e.g., a majority of agents in a learning set fails to learn the correct action). For the impact of states on the reward, we utilize the *Action Reward Rank*: For each state, all performed actions of the agents are compared, and the best ranking agent who took this action is outlined. Hence, this action is related to the final best performing agent in the set.

2.3   Reward Behavior Correlation

To understand the benefits of comparisons in the behavior space, the correlation between reward distance and behavior distance is interesting. Therefore, we investigate a set of m agents $\{A_1, ..., A_m\}$, their behaviors $\{B_{A_1}, ..., B_{A_m}\}$, and their accumulated rewards $\{R_{A_1}, ..., R_{A_m}\}$. We compute the Reward Behavior Correlation (RBC) for all pairwise comparisons

$$\text{RBC}_{\text{all}} = \text{cor}\Big(\text{d}(\{B_{A_1}, ..., B_{A_m}\}), \text{d}(\{R_{A_1}, ..., R_{A_m}\})\Big).$$

Here, $\text{d}(\{B_{A_1}, ..., B_{A_m}\})$ calculates all pairwise distances of the present agents using the behavioral distance $\text{d}(B_{A_i}, B_{A_j})$. Correspondingly, $\text{d}(\{R_{A_1}, ..., R_{A_m}\})$ calculates all pairwise distances of the present agents using a distance of their accumulated rewards $\text{d}(R_{A_i}, R_{A_j})$. The correlation $\text{cor}(., .)$ may be computed rank-based, if desired, or with standard linear correlation (Pearson correlation). Similarly to RBC_{all}, we can also compare each agent to the optimum agent A_{opt} (the agent with the largest reward), instead of performing all pairwise comparisons. We denote this as RBC_{opt}. A large RBC means that small/substantial differences in reward coincide with small/significant differences in behavior. Hence, a large RBC is a good indicator that the behavior space is easier to traverse for search algorithms and easier to learn for surrogate models.

This property has a close connection to the Fitness Distance Correlation (FDC) used in evolutionary computation to rate problem difficulty [6]. There, differences in fitness are correlated with distances in the search space. RBC_{all} considers all pairwise distances while RBC_{opt} and FDC consider distances only between candidate solutions and the global optimum (or best-known solution [7]).

3   Experiments

3.1   Deterministic Maze

The deterministic maze was designed with *mazelab* [17] as a comprehensible problem where correct actions are known, and behavior is manually rateable. The environment, visualized in Fig. 1(a), consists of a 10×7 matrix (shown in figures as 9×6, excluding external walls) with different encoding for accessible ways, walls, the agent and goal. The target is to find the shortest path to the goal. The agent is allowed to take only deterministic actions for each observed agent position in each cardinal direction. Thus they can get stuck against a wall. Agents get a small negative reward for each movement, a larger negative reward if running against a wall or moving backward, and a positive reward for reaching the goal. The maximum step size of each agent is fixed to 30, whereas only 11 are needed to follow the shortest path. We manually designed the maze to feature DFS and UOS: The maze has a total of four paths to the goal and 22 unique agent positions, but these are partly exclusive, and successful agents have always UOS. Moreover, the lower fork is a DFS, while the upper one is not. The intention was to construct a problem where agents with the same reward

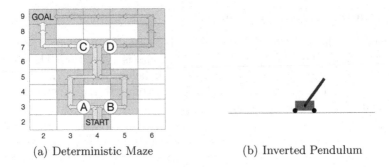

(a) Deterministic Maze   (b) Inverted Pendulum

Fig. 1. Environments. For the maze environment, external walls are not displayed. Different ways: A and B are equal in reward, while D is slightly worse than C.

can have different behavior, cause of the forks, and different paths. Moreover, to analyze the effect of different exclusive paths and the UOS on the pairwise behavior comparison.

3.2 Continuous Inverted Pendulum

The inverted pendulum is a time-dependent physics simulator with a continuous input space (Fig. 1(b)). The target is to balance the pendulum on a car in the upright position for most time steps, starting at a random downwards position by moving the car. The environment is evaluated over 500 timesteps but discontinues if the base car moves out of designated limits. The action space was made deterministic for more comprehensible behavior comparisons. The pendulum environment has no exclusive paths, i.e., all states are observable, but agents will have an enormous number of UOS because of the real-valued input space. We also consider the environment to include multiple DFS, e.g., multiple correct behaviors are possible. The environment allows a large number of behaviors and different sized sets of observed states per agent.

3.3 Generating Reinforcement Learning Agents by Neuroevolution

The RL agents' policies are created and trained by utilizing Neuroevolution to learn ANN policies in an evolutionary process. The underlying algorithm is the graph-based *cartesian genetic programming* CGP by A. Turner[1] [8,15]. For the maze problem, ANNs with 70 inputs and 4 outputs were evolved, where the softmax function computes the resulting action. The pendulum ANN has 6 inputs (5 + 1 bias) and a single output. For an output value >0.5, the action is drive left, otherwise, drive right. The ANNs are evolved in terms of connection weights and structure, i.e., the number and placing of connections, nodes, and transfer functions. The maximum number of nodes and connections for each ANN was set to 100 (maze) and 1000 (pendulum). This leads to a vast amount

---

[1] http://www.cgplibrary.co.uk - v2.4 - accessed: 2018-01-12.

Table 1. Parameters and results of the neuroevolution run for both environments

	maze	pendulum		maze	pendulum
repeated runs	12	1	total agents	48e3	4020
evaluations per run	4020	4020 × 30	unique agents	43	3648
observed states per agent	30	max 15e3	unique states	22	30e6

of different ANN topologies. The inner workings of the ANNs are complex and very difficult to compare [3,14]. Thus, only the reward and the behavior of the agents using these ANNs are considered observable.

Table 1 summarizes the parameters and outcomes of the Neuroevolution. The pendulum agents' rewards were aggregated over 30 different instances for reducing the impact of the random start positions; all states and actions from these instances are included in the agents' state sets. The agents of each environment were merged into one data set. Agents with equal state-input sets (i.e., those following precisely the same path) were filtered to acquire a feasibly sized data set. Due to the small number of input states for the maze environment, its amount of agents is significantly reduced. Conversely, the majority of trajectories in the pendulum experiment is unique. The cleaned-up data for each environment consist of all unique agents; the input states they observed, the corresponding actions, and their rewards. The agents were ranked, where equal performance leads to a shared rank. The maze problem has two best-ranked (rank 1) agents. For the following experiments, we arbitrarily chose one of these two as a reference agent (denoted as "best agent").

3.4 Experimental Setup for Analyzing the Behavior Measures

Behavior Comparison: First, explorative data analysis is conducted to analyze the behaviors and visualize them in the environment. We analyze the behavior for individual input states in particular for the maze problem, as we can manually identify wrong actions and understand their impact on the reward. Furthermore, we use a one-to-one comparison of agents with similar rewards to see the influence of UOS and DFS. For the pendulum problem, we analyze and reveal different behavior based on specific inputs and compare the influence of using different state sets as input for the behavior comparison. The denoted "best agent" for this problem is the best found.

State Importance: The maze environment has designed DFS and UOS, i.e., the forks with different importance and different exclusive paths to reach the goal. The goal of the importance analysis is to discover these states by comparing the behavior of all agents. We take a best-ranked agent as the reference for correct actions and calculate the percentage of different actions for each state by one-to-many comparisons, weighted by the difference in rank for these agents, by $d(B_A, B_{A'}) \times d(rank_A, rank_{A'})/sum(rank_A, rank_{A'})$. Further, we calculate and visualize the action reward rank (Sect. 2.2) for each state.

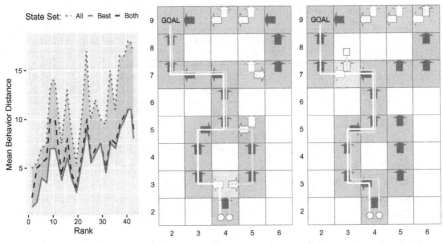

(a) Behavior Distance,   (b) 2x Rank 1 Comparison, (c) Best vs Rank 13,
Aggregated Mean by Rank d= All 5, Both 2, Best 1   d= All 4, Both 1, Best 1

Fig. 2. One-to-one behavior comparison of the best agent against all agents, computed with different state input sets (a) and two selected examples (b,c) Green: differences on Input set C (BEST). Blue: differences on Input set D (BOTH, includes C). Red: differences on Input set B (ALL, includes C and D). Grey cells: agents act the same. a) Summary of behavior distance of best against all. Shaded areas illustrate the input set differences. b) Trajectories: best rank 1 (white) vs. another rank 1 (yellow) c) Trajectories: best (white) vs. Rank 13 (yellow) (Color figure online)

Reward Behavior Correlation: The main challenge in computing the RBC_{all} and RBC_{opt} is selecting a suitable state set to compare the behavior. With the previous experiments' experience, we defined different options to select a suitable state set and analyze which of them leads to the best overall RBC:

- Input set A: Random states sampled from all known states of all agents.
- Input set B: All known states of an environment.
- Input set C: The observed states of the best agent.
- Input set D: The observed states of both compared agents.
- Input set E: The observed states of one compared agent.

For the pendulum problem, we calculate the RBC_{all} on an equidistant sampled (each 15th) subset of agents to significantly reduce the computation time.

4   Results and Discussion

4.1   Behavior Comparison

The comparison of the best agent against all and selected inferior agents for the maze environment on different state sets (B, C, D) is illustrated in Fig. 2.

Interestingly, the best agent does not choose the best action in all states. It only chooses correctly for the states it observed by itself. The agent would run into walls if placed in certain positions (e.g., 5,5 or 4,9).

The behavior distance is amplified by different actions for states that were not observed by the compared agents, i.e., UOS lead to a larger distance, in particular visible in Fig. 2(b) and (c), where red cells highlight the UOS. If the state input set of both agents are used instead of all, the influence of UOS is smaller, as at least one of the agent has observed these states (blue line/cells). However, it is still evident for the higher ranks. A remarkable observation is shown in Fig. 2(c), for a comparison between the best agent and a medium-rank agent (rank 13). They have a behavior distance of only 1 if compared on their mutual state set and 4 with UOS considered. Their behavior on their mutual state set is nearly identical, despite the significant difference in rank.

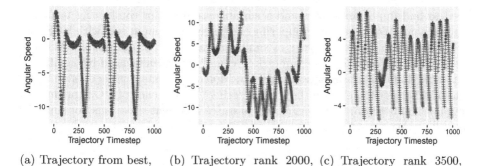

(a) Trajectory from best, total difference is 33%   (b) Trajectory rank 2000, total difference is 24%   (c) Trajectory rank 3500, total difference is 4%

Fig. 3. Behavior comparison for the pendulum. The behavior difference from best versus rank 1000 is shown (Green cross = same action, red dot = different action) for the *angular speed* value over the first 1000 states of state sets from best, rank 2000, and rank 3500. As visible, the behavior difference is influenced by the state sets. Particularly, the dissimilarity in (c) is smaller. (Color figure online)

The number of acquired states for the pendulum is enormous and not suitable for complete comparisons as we visualized for the maze. However, we computed behavior differences of smaller state subsets and visualized them using a selected input, the *angular speed* of the pendulum, which is nearly zero if the pendulum is balanced in the upright position. Fig. 3(a) shows the behavior of the best agent against the rank 1000 (of 3648) agent by calculating it on best, as well as on rank 2.000 (b) and rank 3500 (c) input sets. Fig. 3(a) shows that for time-steps 250–300 and 750–800, the rank 1000 agent behaves consequently differently. These time-steps illustrate a situation of a falling pendulum, shortly after it was balanced. While the best agent countersteers this movement, the rank 1000 agent accelerates it. Consequently, we were able to identify a situation where the lower-ranked agent fails to learn the correct actions. However, as the actions are based on all inputs and the angular speed is just one of them, finding these situations manually remains challenging. Figure 3(c) shows what happens if the behavior of the two agents is compared on the input set of a distant ranked agent. The state input set of the rank 3500 is considerably different: Each recorded trajectory is only some time steps long, presumably caused by the agent quickly driving the base car to the horizontal limit, which leads to termination. For such extreme situations, both compared agents (best vs. rank 1000) seem to behave similarly. Conversely, their difference in reward seems to be related to smaller differences in critical situations. We can summarize these observations to identify some properties of the behavior space:

I) Agents with the same reward/rank can have a considerable behavior distance, mainly if compared on state input sets with UOS and DFS.
II) Small behavior differences (e.g., $d < 3$) can cause significant rank changes.
III) The input set has a huge impact on the behavioral distance comparison.

These observations reflect a central challenge of behavioral comparisons: We need to find important states and a suitable state set for conducting behavior comparisons. We argue that comparing the behavior on input sets with UOS can help distinguish between agents of similar reward, but is presumably overestimating their behavior distance on task level and further influenced by significant variances due to random actions in UOS. Moreover, comparing agents on state sets of other agents, even without considering the influence of UOS, might not reveal useful behavior distances, as these states represent situations not suitable for telling apart good behavior.

4.2   State Importance

For the state importance, we illustrate the percentage of agents with behavior differing from the best agent for each state, weighted by their differences in rank. In case of the maze, Fig. 4(a) shows this statistic only for agents reaching the goal, while Fig. 4(b) concerns all agents. Here, highly valued states are considered to be more important, as most agents behave dissimilarly to the presumed 'correct' action. For the comparison between the best agents, many states show no importance, i.e., similar behavior in this set. The maze was designed such that the importance of the DFS fork in (4,3), should be less than the no-DFS fork in (4,7). This is represented by our importance measure, as (4,7) has a twice as high value in Fig. 4(a) and (b). However, the importance measure also provides other states with a high importance value, particularly visible in the maze's upper part. This can be explained by the type of behavior comparison (all states) and the influence of UOS for each agent. Agents can have 'wrong' behavior for these states, even if they can solve the environment. This is observable in Fig. 4(c), where for each state, the best agent choosing a specific action is shown. While for the state (4,3) and also for (4,7), we see a correct identification of different ways, (5,5), (4,9), and (5,9) give the wrong idea of correct actions, as the supposedly best-outlined action is surprisingly to run against a wall. This effect of UOS is amplified if all agents are considered. For example, the lowest-ranked agent runs directly against a wall. However, we compute and

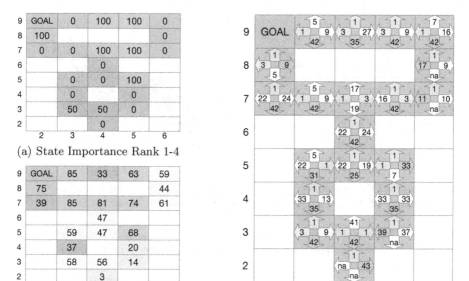

Fig. 4. (a) State importance calculated using either the best agents or (b) all agents. Higher values depict higher importance, colored by value quarters for easier comparison. (c) Action reward rank. Shows the best rank choosing each action for each state. Green = rank 1, blue = rank 3, red = worst action rank. The two rank 1 agents choose different actions in (4,3) and (5,5). (4,3) is DFS, and (5,5) an UOS for the best agent. (Color figure online)

compare its behavior (intensified by its low rank) on all states. We assume that if we compare a broad set of agents, the UOS, with their presumably random actions, do not affect the importance as strongly. Thus, the shown importance is presumably higher in the states of the upper part of the maze, as only a minority of agents reach this part of the maze. For the rest, we are just comparing their behavior on UOS. Thus, our importance measures could also help identify states of an environment rarely reached by any agent in a set.

4.3   Reward Behavior Correlation

For the RBC analysis, the previous results have shown that it is essential to choose a suitable state set for each pairwise comparison. The results are displayed in Fig. 5 and Table 2. Figure 5(a) and (b) shows the resulting RBC_{all} and RBC_{opt} values, respectively. For both, the overall correlation is notably positive. In 5(b) it differs between good agents (rank 1–800), medium agents (800–3100), and poor agents (3100–3600). The other input sets (A, B, C, and E) lead to an inferior RBC_{opt} for both problems. Moreover, set D and E lead to the highest RBC_{all}, with a very significant difference for the maze problem. We assume that

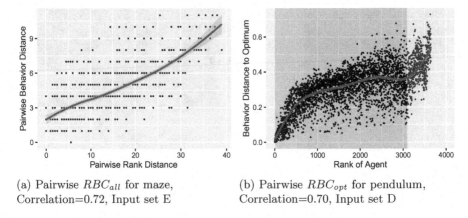

(a) Pairwise RBC_{all} for maze,
Correlation=0.72, Input set E

(b) Pairwise RBC_{opt} for pendulum,
Correlation=0.70, Input set D

Fig. 5. (a) RBC_{all} plot for the maze environment (b) RBC_{opt} plot for the pendulum problem. Computed on input set E and D, respectively. A decent correlation is visible.

the best correlation would be achieved if agents are compared in their mutual behavior space. The presumed cause for the higher RBC_{all} is the reduction of the influence of unobserved states in the comparison. In particular, the maze environment agents have less UOS where they likely act random, if set D or E are considered. Including UOS in a comparison does thus not lead to a more detailed behavior distance, but one with higher overall variance, thus leading to an inferior RBC. This is visible for the pendulum, which for all sets, has a large amount of UOS due to the continuous state space, which leads to a smaller difference in the variants to compute the RBC_{all}. The overall positive RBC_{all} outlines the high potential of agent comparisons in the behavior space to improve the search for good ranking agents.

Table 2. RBC_{all} of all agents for different input sets

environment	A) random	B) all	C) reference	D) both observed	E) one observed
maze	0.27	0.29	0.28	0.62	**0.72**
pendulum	0.36	na	0.34	**0.45**	0.36

5   Conclusion

In this work, we investigated the properties of the behavior space of RL agents and how this space can help to compare agents in learning sets to gain valuable insights. Regarding our research questions, we can conclude for Q-1, that even small changes in the behavior can have considerable effects on the reward. At the same time, agents achieving the same reward can show quite different behavior. We believe that focusing only on the reward of an agent might not be the optimal choice. Instead, the agents' behavior can give valuable insights into how agents achieve that reward. This can reveal agents with surprising behavior or help to improve the learning process. For instance, reward functions can be designed to enforce or suppress specific behavior.

The analysis of Q-2 has shown that accessing the variable importance is challenging and highly dependent on the underlying set of agents and the environment. These challenges are mainly caused by comparing an agent on states, which were not observed by it, or are even not observable by this agent due to environment restrictions, e.g., mutually exclusive paths. For these cases, an agent's behavior can be random, even for the ones with the best reward. A comparison of behavior on these states might deliver misleading results. Only if multiple agents observed states, we could access their real importance.

This finding is further stressed when considering Q-3. The RBC is highest if we consider pairwise behavior comparisons on those states that have been observed by both compared agents. The reasonable positive RBC shows that the behavior space is a promising concept. We suggest that searching in that space may be beneficial.

For future work, we aim to take a close look at how the understanding of behavioral spaces can be exploited, e.g., by new reward measures, direct search in the behavior-space, and specialized search operators:

Reward Measures: Ideally, reward measures help to steer the search into desirable areas of the search space. Understanding which states are critical to receiving a good match between behavior and reward may help design better reward measures. The importance of developing useful reward measures for RL is stressed in a review by Doncieux and Mouret [2].

Search in Behavior Space: The usage of agents' behavior distance as an additional search criterion seems very attractive. It can be used to preserve diversity in evolutionary search procedures [1]. Further, the search for a specific behavior may be of interest, independent or in addition to reward-driven search, e.g., by modeling the reward to behavior space with surrogate models. An example application would be *inverse reinforcement learning* [10]. The search in behavior space allows the use of completely different agent topologies or even comparing agents trained by different algorithms.

Search Operators: Finally, a good understanding of the latent, behavioral space may help to define better search operators. For instance, search operators could be designed to search directly in the behavior space, rather than the policy or topology space.

References

1. Doncieux, S., Mouret, J.: Behavioral diversity measures for evolutionary robotics. In: IEEE Congress on Evolutionary Computation, pp. 1–8 (2010)
2. Doncieux, S., Mouret, J.-B.: Beyond black-box optimization: a review of selective pressures for evolutionary robotics. Evol. Intell. **7**(2), 71–93 (2014). https://doi.org/10.1007/s12065-014-0110-x

3. Gaier, A., Asteroth, A., Mouret, J.-B.: Data-efficient neuroevolution with kernel-based surrogate models. In: Genetic and Evolutionary Computation Conference (GECCO) (2018)
4. Hagg, A., Zaefferer, M., Stork, J., Gaier, A.: Prediction of neural network performance by phenotypic modeling. In: Proceedings of the Genetic and Evolutionary Computation Conference Companion - GECCO 2019, Prague, Czech Republic, pp. 1576–1582. ACM (2019)
5. Hildebrandt, T., Branke, J.: On using surrogates with genetic programming. Evol. Comput. 23(3), 343–367 (2015)
6. Jones, T., Forrest, S.: Fitness distance correlation as a measure of problem difficulty for genetic algorithms. In: Proceedings of the 6th International Conference on Genetic Algorithms, Pittsburgh, PA, USA, July 1995, pp. 184–192. Morgan Kaufmann (1995)
7. Kallel, L., Schoenauer, M.: Fitness distance correlation for variable length representations. Technical Report 363, CMAP, Ecole Polytechnique (1996)
8. Khan, M.M., Khan, G.M., Miller, J.F.: Evolution of neural networks using cartesian genetic programming. In: IEEE Congress on Evolutionary Computation, pp. 1–8, July 2010
9. Meyerson, E., Lehman, J., Miikkulainen, R.: Learning behavior characterizations for novelty search. In: Proceedings of the Genetic and Evolutionary Computation Conference 2016, GECCO 2016, pp. 149–156. Association for Computing Machinery, New York (2016)
10. Ng, A.Y., Russell, S.J., et al.: Algorithms for inverse reinforcement learning. In: Icml vol. 1, pp. 663–670 (2000)
11. Nguyen, S., Zhang, M., Tan, K.C.: Surrogate-assisted genetic programming with simplified models for automated design of dispatching rules. IEEE Trans. Cybern. 47(9), 2951–2965 (2016)
12. Ollion, C., Doncieux, S.: Why and how to measure exploration in behavioral space. In: Proceedings of the 13th Annual Conference on Genetic and Evolutionary Computation, GECCO 2011, pp. 267–274. Association for Computing Machinery, New York (2011)
13. Pugh, J.K., Soros, L.B., Stanley, K.O.: Searching for quality diversity when diversity is unaligned with quality. In: Handl, J., Hart, E., Lewis, P.R., López-Ibáñez, M., Ochoa, G., Paechter, B. (eds.) PPSN 2016. LNCS, vol. 9921, pp. 880–889. Springer, Cham (2016). https://doi.org/10.1007/978-3-319-45823-6_82
14. Stork, J., Zaefferer, M., Bartz-Beielstein, T., Eiben, A.E.: Surrogate models for enhancing the efficiency of neuroevolution in reinforcement learning. In: Proceedings of the Genetic and Evolutionary Computation Conference - GECCO 2019, Prague, Czech Republic, pp. 934–942. ACM (2019)
15. Turner, A.J., Miller, J.F.: Cartesian genetic programming encoded artificial neural networks: a comparison using three benchmarks. In: Proceedings of the GECCO 2013, pp. 1005–1012. ACM (2013)
16. Zaefferer, M., Stork, J., Flasch, O., Bartz-Beielstein, T.: Linear combination of distance measures for surrogate models in genetic programming. In: Auger, A., Fonseca, C.M., Lourenço, N., Machado, P., Paquete, L., Whitley, D. (eds.) PPSN 2018. LNCS, vol. 11102, pp. 220–231. Springer, Cham (2018). https://doi.org/10.1007/978-3-319-99259-4_18
17. Zuo, X.: mazelab: a customizable framework to create maze and gridworld environments (2018). https://github.com/zuoxingdong/mazelab

Time Series Encodings with Temporal Convolutional Networks

Markus Thill[1]([✉]) [ID], Wolfgang Konen[1] [ID], and Thomas Bäck[2] [ID]

[1] TH Köln – University of Applied Sciences, Gummersbach, Germany
{markus.thill,wolfgang.konen}@th-koeln.de
[2] LIACS, Leiden University, Leiden, The Netherlands
t.h.w.baeck@liacs.leidenuniv.nl

Abstract. The training of anomaly detection models usually requires labeled data. We present in this paper a novel approach for anomaly detection in time series which trains unsupervised using a convolutional approach coupled to an autoencoder framework. After training, only a small amount of labeled data is needed to adjust the anomaly threshold. We show that our new approach outperforms several other state-of-the-art anomaly detection algorithms on a Mackey-Glass (MG) anomaly benchmark. At the same time our autoencoder is capable of learning interesting representations in latent space. Our new MG anomaly benchmark allows to create an unlimited amount of anomaly benchmark data with steerable difficulty. In this benchmark, the anomalies are well-defined, yet difficult to spot for the human eye.

Keywords: Time series representations · Temporal convolutional networks · Autoencoder · Anomaly detection · Unsupervised learning · Mackey-Glass time series · Chaos

1 Introduction

For the operation of large machines in companies or other critical systems in society, it is usually necessary to record and monitor specific machine or system health indicators over time. In the past, the recorded time series were often evaluated manually or by simple heuristics (such as threshold values) to detect abnormal behavior. With the more recent advances in the fields of ML (machine learning) and AI (artificial intelligence), ML-based anomaly detection algorithms are becoming increasingly popular for many tasks such as health monitoring and predictive maintenance. Supervised algorithms need labeled training data, which are often cumbersome to get and to maintain in real-world applications. Yet, unsupervised anomaly detection remains up to now a challenging task.

In this paper we propose a novel autoencoder architecture for sequences (time series) which is based on temporal convolutional networks [3] and shows its efficacy in unsupervised learning tasks. Our experiments show that the architecture can learn interesting representations of sequences in latent space. The idea of

© Springer Nature Switzerland AG 2020
B. Filipič et al. (Eds.): BIOMA 2020, LNCS 12438, pp. 161–173, 2020.
https://doi.org/10.1007/978-3-030-63710-1_13

unsupervised anomaly learning is based on the assumption that in real-world tasks the overwhelming part of the time-series data will be normal. Without the need to label the data, we train a model that learns the normal behavior, i.e. assigns a low score to normal and a higher score to anomalous data. Finally, only a small fraction of labeled data is needed to find a suitable threshold for the anomaly score. This can also be fine-tuned in operation, with an already trained model.

For the initial benchmarking and comparison of our algorithm, we introduce a new synthetic benchmark based on Mackey-Glass (MG) time series [21]. In its current form, the Mackey-Glass Anomaly Benchmark (MGAB) consists of 10 MG time series in which anomalies were inserted using a clearly defined procedure. Although the anomalies are inserted synthetically, spotting them is rather difficult for the human eye. Due to the structured insertion process and the clear labeling of nominal and anomalous data, no domain knowledge is required to correctly label the data. Additionally, the difficulty of the anomaly detection task is steerable by simply adjusting a few parameters of the MGAB generation process (e.g. time delay, smoothness parameters).

2   Related Work

Other well known time series anomaly benchmarks are Yahoo Webscope S5 [16] and NAB [17]. The Webscope S5 benchmark mostly contains simple/trivial spatial anomalies. In NAB [17], the labeling process is not always immediately comprehensible without having domain-dependent knowledge of the time series. Furthermore, the amount of data is often too small for many deep learning approaches. In [29], we introduce an anomaly benchmark based on electrocardiogram recordings of the MIT-BIH ECG dataset [10].

In recent years a lot of effort was put into the design of time series anomaly detection algorithms and many new methods have been proposed: A common approach is to use the prediction error of a time series regression model as anomaly score [23,29,30]. Commonly, also autoencoder-based approaches are used [11,22], where the reconstruction error of the time series serves as an indicator for anomalous behaviour. Other approaches are based on generative adversarial networks (GANs) [13,18] or variational-based networks/autoencoders [26,27,32]. There exists also an architecture [33] where the parameters of a deep autoencoder and of a Gaussian mixture model are simultaneously learned during training. Most of the aforementioned algorithms are unsupervised.

In this work we will compare several state-of-the-art algorithms on MGAB: The first one is DNN-AE, an anomaly detection algorithm based on a regular deep neural network autoencoder [11]. DNN-AE takes short sequences from a time series and attempts to encode and reconstruct these. Large reconstruction errors indicate anomalous behavior. Similar to DNN-AE, the algorithm LSTM-ED [22] uses an encoder-decoder approach, but now based on LSTM networks [12] to encode short sub-sequences taken from a time series. A third algorithm, Numenta's anomaly detection algorithm NuPIC [28] is based on the hierarchical temporal memory (HTM) algorithm [9] which is biologically inspired by the neocortex of the brain. Finally, the LSTM-AD algorithm [29] uses stacked LSTM networks to predict a time series for several prediction horizons and learns a statistical model of normal behavior in order to detect anomalous events. All algorithms compared in this work are unsupervised, since no anomaly labels are passed to the algorithms during training. Only during the test phase a small fraction of the labels are used to determine a suitable anomaly threshold.

3   TCN Autoencoder

In computer vision architectures, convolutional neural networks (CNN) are very popular due to their equivariance properties and sparse interactions. Temporal convolutional networks (TCN) translate these convolutional advantages from computer vision into the time domain, as we will detail in Sect. 3.1 and Sect. 3.2.

The central idea of the TCN autoencoder (TCN-AE) is to encode a sequence of length T into a significantly shorter sequence of length T/s (where $s \in \mathbb{Z}^+$ is a sampling factor) and subsequently to reconstruct the original sequence from the compressed sequence (using a decoder network). The idea is similar to a classical (deep) autoencoder, where fixed-sized inputs are encoded into a latent space representation and the latent variables are used to reconstruct the original input. Similarly, the TCN-AE encodes sequences along the temporal axis into a compressed representation and then attempts to reconstruct the original sequence. However, it differs from a regular autoencoder in so far that it replaces the dense layer architecture of a regular autoencoder with the more powerful convolutional architecture. Due to this, it is also more flexible with respect to the input length. Our TCN autoencoder consists of two temporal convolutional neural networks (TCNs) [3], one for encoding and one for decoding. Additionally, a downsampling and upsampling layer are used in the encoder and decoder, respectively. The individual components will be described in more detail in the following.

3.1   Discrete Dilated Convolutions

The dilated acausal convolution of a d-dimensional sequence $\mathbf{x} : \{0, 1, \ldots, T - 1\} \rightarrow \mathbb{R}^d$, and a discrete filter with a finite impulse response (FIR filter) $\mathbf{h}[n]$, $\mathbf{h} : \{0, 1, \ldots, k - 1\} \rightarrow \mathbb{R}^d$, can be defined as:

$$y[n] = (\mathbf{x} *_q \mathbf{h})[n] = \sum_{i=0}^{k-1} \mathbf{h}[i]^\mathsf{T} \cdot \mathbf{x}[n - q \cdot (i - k/2)], \tag{1}$$

where $y[n] \in \mathbb{R}$ is the output of the filter with size $T - k + 1$, $q \in \mathbb{N}$ is the dilation rate, $\mathbf{h}[i] \in \mathbb{R}^d$ is the impulse response of the filter with kernel size k. While the regular convolution ($q = 1$) applies the filter to adjacent elements of the input sequence, the dilated convolution $*_q$ allows to skip several values in the input sequence before the next filter tap $\mathbf{h}[i]$ is applied. The convolution

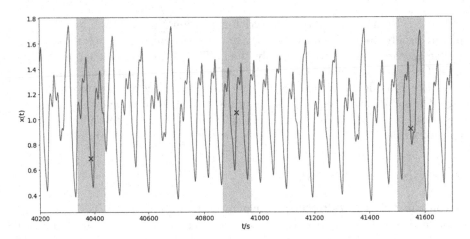

Fig. 1. A section of a Mackey-Glass time series containing three anomalies. For the human eye these anomalies would be very hard to spot, if we took the red bars away. (Color figure online)

operation slides a $k \times d$-dimensional filter stepwise over the input sequence $\mathbf{x}[n]$ and computes a weighted average of $\mathbf{x}[n]$ and the corresponding weights $\mathbf{h}[i]$ in each step. Since the filter is only sled along the (discrete) time-axis, the operation is commonly referred to as one-dimensional convolution. The convolution in Eq. (1) is slightly acausal due to the term $k/2$. In some applications it might also be reasonable to use causal convolutions (Fig. 1).

Many neural network architectures for sequence modeling utilize dilated convolutions in order to build a hierarchical temporal model with a large receptive field. These models are capable of learning long-term temporal patterns in the input data. The main idea is to construct a stack of dilated convolutional layers, where the dilation rate increases with every additional layer. A common choice is to start with a dilation rate of $q = 1$ for the first layer of the network and to double q with every new layer. This approach allows to increase the receptive field of the model exponentially.

3.2   Temporal Convolutional Networks

The temporal convolutional network (TCN) [3] is inspired by several convolutional architectures [6,8,14,24], but differs from these approaches, according to the authors, insofar as it combines simplicity, auto-regressive prediction, residual blocks and very long memory. A full description of TCN would be out of scope for this paper, the reader is referred to [3] for the details. Its main elements are however the dilated convolutions of Sect. 3.1. A TCN can be basically described by three elements: a list of dilation rates $(q_1, q_2, \ldots, q_{n_r})$, the number of filters n_{filters}, and the kernel size k, which is the same for all filters in a TCN.

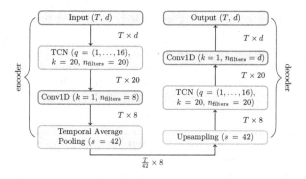

Fig. 2. Architecture of TCN-AE. Each layer is described by its parameters inside the box. The input of the TCN-AE is a sequence $\mathbf{x}[n]$ with length T and dimensionality d.

3.3 An Autoencoder Using TCNs

The novel element we propose in this paper is an autoencoder (AE) for time series *which employs TCNs* as building blocks. This architecture, which we name TCN-AE, is sketched in Fig. 2. Like any autoencoder, TCN-AE consists of an encoder and a decoder. The encoder initially processes the input sequence $\mathbf{x}[n]$ of length T and dimension d using a TCN. Subsequently, in order to reduce the size of the feature map (dimensionality) of the TCN's output, a one-dimensional convolutional layer (1×1 convolution [19]) is used with $q = 1$, $k = 1$ and a smaller number of filters (i.e., $n_{\text{filters}} = 8$). The temporal average pooling layer is the last layer in the encoder and responsible for downsampling the series by a factor s. It does so by averaging groups of size s along the time axis.

Right afterwards, the downsampled sequence is passed to the decoder module and brought back to its original length using an upsampling layer which simply performs a nearest neighbor interpolation. The upsampled sequence is passed through a second TCN, which is parameterized in the same way as the encoder-TCN, but has independent weights. Finally, the reconstruction of the input sequence is generated with a Conv1D layer which ensures (by setting $k = 1$ and $n_{\text{filters}} = d$) that the dimensionality of the input is matched. Once TCN-AE is trained, the input sequence and its reconstruction will be used for detecting anomalies, as described in the next section.

3.4 Anomaly Detection with TCN-AE

A natural application of TCN-AE is the anomaly detection in time series. When TCN-AE is trained on time series containing predominantly nominal data, the network will attempt to minimize the reconstruction error for these nominal patterns. At the same time, the reconstruction error for anomalous patterns or patterns which differ significantly in their characteristics should be larger. One possibility to identify these unusual patterns is to estimate a distribution for the reconstruction error. In our approach, we decide to slide a window of length ℓ over our reconstruction error and compute a mean vector $\boldsymbol{\mu}$ and covariance matrix $\boldsymbol{\Sigma}$. Subsequently, the Mahalanobis distance can be used as anomaly score. The unified algorithmic description of the anomaly detection procedure in combination with TCN-AE is listed in Algorithm 1. Only for determining the anomaly threshold, 10% of the true labels are used, as described in Sect. 5.3.

Algorithm 1. Anomaly detection algorithm using the TCN-AE architecture.

1: **Adjustable parameters**:
2:      $\mathcal{M}_\tau$: anomaly threshold, obtained as described in Section 5.3
3:      ℓ: window length for constructing the error vectors
4:      T_{train}: length of training sub-sequences
5:
6: **function** ANOMALYDETECT($\mathbf{x}_{tr}[n], \mathbf{x}[n]$) ▷ time series $\mathbf{x}_{tr}, \mathbf{x} : \mathbb{N} \to \mathbb{R}^d$ of length T
7:      **Construct** model TCNAE() and **Initialize** the trainable parameters
8:      **for** $\{1 \ldots n_{\text{epochs}}\}$ **do**
9:           Extract training sub-sequences $\mathbf{X}_{\text{train}}^{(i)} \in \mathbb{R}^{T_{\text{train}} \times d}$ from $\mathbf{x}_{tr}[n]$, $i = 1, \ldots, B$
10:          $\forall i \in \{1, \ldots, B\} : \text{TRAIN}(\text{TCNAE}, \mathbf{X}_{\text{train}}^{(i)})$ ▷ Train net on mini-batches
11:     **end for**
12:     $\hat{\mathbf{x}}[n] \leftarrow \text{TCNAE}(\mathbf{x}[n])$ ▷ Encode and reconstruct whole sequence
13:     $\mathbf{e}[n] \leftarrow \mathbf{x}[n] - \hat{\mathbf{x}}[n]$ ▷ reconstruction error $\mathbf{e} : \mathbb{N} \to \mathbb{R}^d$ of length T
14:     $\mathbf{E}[n] \leftarrow \text{SLIDINGWINDOW}(\mathbf{e}[n], \ell)$ ▷ $\mathbf{E} : \mathbb{N} \to \mathbb{R}^{T \times \ell \times d}$
15:     $\mathbf{E}'[n] \leftarrow \text{RESHAPE}(\mathbf{E}[n])$ ▷ $\mathbf{E}' : \mathbb{N} \to \mathbb{R}^{T \times \ell \cdot d}$
16:     $\boldsymbol{\mu}, \boldsymbol{\Sigma} = \text{ESTIMATE}(\mathbf{E}'[n])$ ▷ $\boldsymbol{\mu} \in \mathbb{R}^{\ell \cdot d}$,
17:     $M[n] \leftarrow (\mathbf{E}'[n] - \boldsymbol{\mu})^\mathsf{T} \boldsymbol{\Sigma}^{-1} (\mathbf{E}'[n] - \boldsymbol{\mu})$ ▷ Mahalanobis distance for each point
18:     $a[n] \leftarrow \begin{cases} 0 & \text{if } M[n] < \mathcal{M}_\tau \\ 1 & \text{else} \end{cases}$ ▷ Binary anomaly flags
19:     **return** $a[n]$ ▷ Return anomaly flag for each time series point
20: **end function**

---

4   The Mackey-Glass Anomaly Benchmark

In this work we will compare various anomaly detection algorithms on a non-trivial synthetic benchmark, named Mackey-Glass anomaly benchmark (MGAB) in the following. Mackey-Glass time series are known to exhibit chaotic behavior under certain conditions. MGAB contains 10 MG time series of length $T = 10^5$. Into each time series 10 anomalies are inserted with a procedure described in Sect. 4.1. In contrast to other synthetic benchmarks, the introduced anomalies are for the human eye very hard to distinguish from the normal (chaotic) behavior. Overall, we generate 100 anomalies in 10^6 time series points. The benchmark data and the detailed procedure for generating these and similar benchmark data are publicly available at GitHub [31].[1]

---

[1] GitHub repository: https://github.com/MarkusThill/MGAB/.

4.1 Generating Anomalies in Mackey-Glass Time Series

In order to create the Mackey-Glass Anomaly Benchmark, we first generate a sufficiently long time series having a dimension of $d = 1$ using the JiTCDDE [2] solver with the parameters $\tau = 18, n = 10, \beta = 0.25, \gamma = 0.1, h = 0.9$. The integration step size is set to 1. The maximal Lyapunov exponent (MLE) of $\lambda_{mle} = 0.0061 \pm 0.0002$ suggests that the generated time series is (mildly) chaotic. Subsequently, we split this series into ten same-sized individual time series and insert 10 anomalies into each time series.

5 Results

5.1 Experimental Setup

Anomaly Detection Algorithms. All training algorithms are unsupervised, i.e. they do not need the true anomaly labels during the training process. Only in order to find a suitable anomaly threshold, a small fraction of labels is used, as described in Sect. 5.3. Otherwise, the anomaly labels are only used at test time to evaluate the performance of the individual algorithms. In one run, each algorithm is trained for 10 rounds: in the i-th round the algorithms are trained on the i-th time series and evaluated on the time series $\{1, \ldots, 10\} \setminus \{i\}$. In total, we perform 10 runs with different random seeds. In order to find suitable hyper-parameters for each algorithm, we use the HYPEROPT library [4] and optimize the F_1-score on a separate MG time series.

For all neural networks we use the Adam optimizer [15] to train the weights by minimizing the MSE loss. Additionally, all time series (having a dimension of $d = 1$) are standardized to zero mean and unit variance.

DNN-AE [7]: we use a PyTorch [25] implementation for the anomaly detection algorithm based on a deep autoencoder [11]. The algorithm requires several parameters, which we choose as follows: batch size $B = 100$, number of training epochs $n_{\text{epochs}} = 40$, sequence length $T_{\text{train}} = 150$ and a hidden size of $h = 10$ for the bottle neck (which results in a compression factor of $T_{\text{train}}/h = 15$ for each sequence). Finally, we set $\%_{Gaussian} = 1\%$, which specifies that 99% of the data is used to estimate a Gaussian distribution for the anomaly detection task.

LSTM-ED [22] is also implemented using PyTorch and uses the following parameter setting: batch size $B = 100$, number of training epochs $n_{\text{epochs}} = 20$, sequence length $T_{\text{train}} = 300$, hidden size $h = 100$ and $\%_{Gaussian} = 1\%$. Both, encoder and decoder use a stacked LSTM network with two layers.

NuPIC [28]: Numenta's anomaly detection algorithm has a large range of hyper-parameters which have to be set. We use the parameters recommended by the authors in [17]. It is possible to tune the parameters with an internal swarming tool [1]. However, this is a time-expensive process which is not feasible for the large MGAB dataset.

LSTM-AD [29]: here we select the following parameters: batch size $B = 1024$, number of training epochs $n_{\text{epochs}} = 30$, and sequence length $T_{\text{train}} = 128$. A 2-layer LSTM network with 256 units in the first layer and 128 units in the second layer is used. The target horizons are chosen to be $H = (1, 3, \ldots, 51)$.

TCN-AE: The main TCN-AE parameters are given in Fig. 2. Additionally we use the sequence length $T_{\text{train}} = 1050$, batch size $B = 32$ and $n_{\text{epochs}} = 40$.

5.2   Learning Time Series Representations

In our first experiment we want to assess the capabilities of the TCN-AE architecture to learn representations of time series. For this purpose we train a TCN-AE model using many different MG time series with a varying time delay parameter τ. Ideally, TCN-AE should be able to learn the main characteristics of

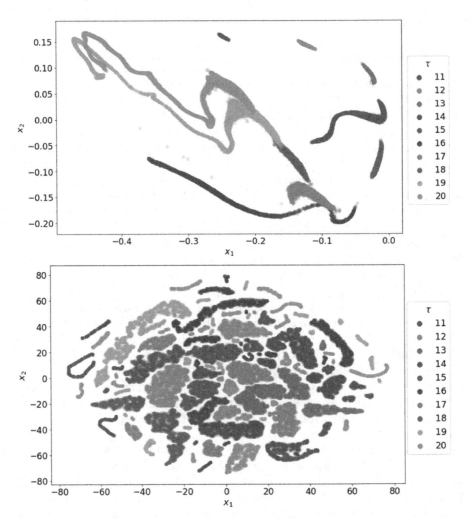

Fig. 3. Top: 2d-representation of 10^5 (10^4 for each τ) different Mackey-Glass time series using TCN-AE. The (unsupervised) algorithm is capable of learning an encoding which separates the MG time series fairly well according to their τ value. **Bottom**: 2d-representation of the same MG time series, but now using t-SNE [20] to find suitable encodings.

the individual time series and find suitable compressed representations. In our experiment we use TCN-AE on 10^5 different Mackey-Glass time series (10^4 for each τ in the range of $\tau = 11 \ldots 20$). Each time series of length 256 is encoded into a 2-dimensional compressed representation. The algorithm is trained in an unsupervised manner, hence, τ is not passed to the algorithm at any time. Surprisingly, even with this large compression rate of 128, TCN-AE can find an interesting embedding for the MG time series, as depicted in Fig. 3 (top). For a certain τ, all samples are placed in *only one* connected cluster (with the exception of a few satellites) and these clusters are mostly – with a few small exceptions – *non-overlapping*.

For comparison, we repeated the same experiment with the popular t-SNE [20] clustering algorithm. We executed t-SNE on a GPU with the help of a certain CUDA implementation [5]. We tried different parameter settings and finally fixed the perplexity parameter to 200, the learning rate to 10 and the number of iterations to 10^4. The results for t-SNE in Fig. 3 (bottom) indicate that it is not a trivial task to find suitable representations for MG time series. t-SNE has in comparison to TCN-AE more difficulties to cluster all sequences with a certain time delay parameter τ in only *one* connected region.

5.3   Algorithm Evaluation

Determining the Anomaly Threshold. All algorithms output an anomaly score for each point of the time series. A low anomaly score indicates nominal behavior and high scores suggest that anomalies are present. In order to classify each point as nominal or anomalous a so-called anomaly threshold is required. Points with a score above the threshold are classified as anomalous, all other points are classified as nominal. We determine this threshold for all algorithms as follows: A sub-sequence containing 10% of the data is taken and the anomaly threshold is optimized on this short sequence, such that the F_1-score is maximized. The optimal threshold is then fixed for the complete time series and the overall results are obtained. Since the results can vary depending on which sub-sequence is used for the threshold adjustment, we repeat the above procedure, similarly to k-fold cross validation, for 10 different 10% sub-sequences of the considered time series and record the results for the 10 different sub-sequences.

Performance Measures. In order to assess the performance of all algorithms and to be able to compare the results, we use several common performance metrics in this paper. Analogously to typical classification problems, a confusion matrix can be constructed for time series anomaly detection tasks, containing the number of true-positives (TP), false-positives (FP), false-negatives and true-negatives (TN). TP indicates the number of anomalies, which were correctly identified within an anomaly window (a small range around the actual anomaly point). Only the first detection in an anomaly window is counted. On the other hand, a missed anomaly window (no point inside the window is flagged) will be judged as a FN. If a point is incorrectly presumed to be anomalous (detection outside any anomaly window), this will be considered as a FP. All other points, which are not marked as anomalous, are considered as true-negatives (TN). From these four quantities the well known performance measures precision, recall and F_1-score can be derived.

5.4   Anomaly Detection on the Mackey-Glass Anomaly Benchmark

In a second experiment, we compare TCN-AE to several state-of-the-art anomaly detection algorithms on the Mackey-Glass Anomaly Benchmark. For each algorithm, except NuPIC, 10 runs were performed. Hence, for each algorithm and time series 10 different models are trained and each model is evaluated on the other nine time series. NuPIC is completely deterministic and does not require several runs. Additionally, as described in Sect. 5.1, the anomaly threshold for each algorithm and time series is tuned on 10 different sub-sequences. We add up the TP, FN and FP over all 10 time series and summarize the results in Table 1. Up to 100 anomalies can be detected in total. We can see that the (deep) DNN-AE detects most of the anomalies (approx. 92), missing only about 8 on average. However, this result is achieved at the expense of producing many false-positives. Overall, DNN-AE produces more than 60 false positives on average, while TCN-AE produces less than one. Hence, DNN-AE achieves the highest recall among all algorithms but ranks only 3rd in F_1-score, due to its low precision. TCN-AE scores best in F_1-score and precision. NuPIC has the poorest performance in all measures.

Table 1. Results for MGAB. The results shown here (mean and standard deviation of 10 runs and 10 sub-sequences, Sect. 5.3) are for the sum of TP, FN and FP over all 10 time series. For each algorithm and time series the anomaly threshold was tuned on 10% of the data using a cross-validation approach: the threshold is tuned on 10 different 10%-sequences of the data.

Algorithm	TP	FN	FP	Precision	Recall	F_1-score
NuPIC [28]	3.00 ± 0.00	97.00 ± 0.00	132.00 ± 0.00	0.02 ± 0.00	0.03 ± 0.00	0.03 ± 0.00
LSTM-ED [22]	14.6 ± 5.86	85.4 ± 5.86	57.0 ± 20.43	0.21 ± 0.08	0.15 ± 0.06	0.17 ± 0.06
DNN-AE [11]	91.79 ± 1.22	8.21 ± 1.22	62.58 ± 13.65	0.6 ± 0.06	0.92 ± 0.01	0.72 ± 0.04
LSTM-AD [29]	88.8 ± 2.59	11.20 ± 2.59	0.62 ± 0.61	0.99 ± 0.01	0.89 ± 0.03	0.94 ± 0.01
TCN-AE [this work]	90.54 ± 1.72	9.46 ± 1.72	0.20 ± 0.47	1.00 ± 0.01	0.91 ± 0.02	0.95 ± 0.01

5.5   Discussion

The initial results that we obtained with our new TCN-AE architecture are promising. The learned representations (Fig. 3) on different MG time series appear to be useful and may reveal interesting insights. For anomaly detection we achieve with TCN-AE and LSTM-AD the highest F_1-score on the non-trivial

MG benchmark. Remarkably, all algorithms except NuPIC require many trainable weights. TCN-AE had 164 451 parameters, DNN-AE 241 526, LSTM-ED 244 101 and LSTM-AD 464 537. That is, the other high-performing algorithms require 50%–300% more trainable weights than TCN-AE.

6   Conclusion and Future Work

In this work, we proposed with TCN-AE a novel autoencoder architecture for multivariate time series and evaluated it on various Mackey-Glass (MG) time series with respect to two relevant tasks: representation learning and anomaly detection. TCN-AE could learn a very interesting representation in only two dimensions which accurately distinguishes MG time series differing in their time delay values τ (Sect. 5.2). On the Mackey-Glass Anomaly Benchmark (MGAB), which was introduced in this paper, TCN-AE achieved better anomaly detection results than other state-of-the-art anomaly detectors (Sect. 5.4).

Possibilities for future work on TCN-AE include: (a) Gaining more insights from the representations that TCN-AE learns unsupervisedly (Fig. 3). (b) Since the network architecture allows to train TCN-AE with training sequences of arbitrary length, another improvement could be to start the training process with short sequences and then successively increase the sequence length after each epoch. This approach could enable a faster learning progress in the beginning and allow fine tuning of the weights towards the end of the training. (c) We are planning to evaluate TCN-AE on other real-world anomaly detection benchmarks containing (multi-variate) time series. Possible options are electrocardiogram signals [10] or industrial monitoring tasks [16,17].

References

1. Ahmad, S.: Running swarms (2017). http://nupic.docs.numenta.org/0.6.0/guide-swarming.html. Accessed 29 June 2020
2. Ansmann, G.: Efficiently and easily integrating differential equations with JiTCODE, JiTCDDE, and JiTCSDE. Chaos **28**(4), 043116 (2018)
3. Bai, S., Kolter, J.Z., Koltun, V.: An empirical evaluation of generic convolutional and recurrent networks for sequence modeling. CoRR abs/1803.01271 (2018)
4. Bergstra, J., et al.: Hyperopt: a Python library for model selection and hyperparameter optimization. Comput. Sci. Discov. **8**(1), 014008 (2015)
5. Chan, D.M., Rao, R., Huang, F., Canny, J.F.: GPU accelerated T-distributed stochastic neighbor embedding. JPDC **131**, 1–13 (2019)
6. Dauphin, Y.N., Fan, A., Auli, M., Grangier, D.: Language modeling with gated convolutional networks. In: ICML 2017, p. 933–941 (2017)
7. Fischer, M., et al.: Anomaly Detection on Time Series: An Evaluation of Deep Learning Methods (2019). https://github.com/KDD-OpenSource/DeepADoTS
8. Gehring, J., Auli, M., Grangier, D., Yarats, D., Dauphin, Y.N.: Convolutional sequence to sequence learning. CoRR abs/1705.03122 (2017)
9. George, D., Hawkins, J.: Towards a mathematical theory of cortical micro-circuits. PLoS Comput. Biol. **5**(10), e1000532 (2009)

10. Goldberger, A.L., et al.: PhysioBank, PhysioToolkit, and PhysioNet: components of a new research resource for complex physiologic signals. Circulation **101**(23), e215–e220 (2000)

11. Hawkins, S., He, H., Williams, G., Baxter, R.: Outlier detection using replicator neural networks. In: Kambayashi, Y., Winiwarter, W., Arikawa, M. (eds.) DaWaK 2002. LNCS, vol. 2454, pp. 170–180. Springer, Heidelberg (2002). https://doi.org/10.1007/3-540-46145-0_17

12. Hochreiter, S., Schmidhuber, J.: Long short-term memory. Neural Comput. **9**(8), 1735–1780 (1997)

13. Jiang, W., Hong, Y., Zhou, B., He, X.: A GAN-based anomaly detection approach for imbalanced industrial time series. IEEE Access **7**, 143608–143619 (2019)

14. Kalchbrenner, N., Grefenstette, E., Blunsom, P.: A Convolutional neural network for modelling sentences. In: ACL, Baltimore, Maryland, pp. 655–665 (2014)

15. Kingma, D.P., Ba, J.: Adam: a method for stochastic optimization. arXiv preprint arXiv:1412.6980 (2014)

16. Laptev, N., Amizadeh, S.: Yahoo anomaly detection dataset S5 (2015). http://webscope.sandbox.yahoo.com/catalog.php?datatype=s&did=70

17. Lavin, A., Ahmad, S.: Evaluating real-time anomaly detection algorithms - the Numenta anomaly benchmark. In: ICMLA (2015)

18. Li, D., Chen, D., Jin, B., Shi, L., Goh, J., Ng, S.-K.: MAD-GAN: multivariate anomaly detection for time series data with generative adversarial networks. In: Tetko, I.V., Kůrková, V., Karpov, P., Theis, F. (eds.) ICANN 2019. LNCS, vol. 11730, pp. 703–716. Springer, Cham (2019). https://doi.org/10.1007/978-3-030-30490-4_56

19. Lin, M., Chen, Q., Yan, S.: Network in network. arXiv preprint arXiv:1312.4400 (2013)

20. van der Maaten, L., Hinton, G.: Visualizing data using t-SNE. J. Mach. Learn. Res. **9**, 2579–2605 (2008)

21. Mackey, M.C., Glass, L.: Oscillation and chaos in physiological control systems. Science **197**(4300), 287–289 (1977)

22. Malhotra, P., et al.: LSTM-based encoder-decoder for multi-sensor anomaly detection. CoRR abs/1607.00148 (2016)

23. Munir, M., et al.: DeepAnT: a deep learning approach for unsupervised anomaly detection in time series. IEEE Access **7**, 1991–2005 (2019)

24. van den Oord, A., et al.: WaveNet: a generative model for raw audio. CoRR abs/1609.03499 (2016)

25. Paszke, A., et al.: PyTorch: an imperative style, high-performance deep learning library. In: Wallach, H., et al. (eds.) NIPS, pp. 8024–8035. Curran Assoc. (2019)

26. Pereira, J., Silveira, M.: Unsupervised anomaly detection in energy time series data using variational recurrent autoencoders with attention. In: Wani, M.A., et al. (eds.) ICMLA, pp. 1275–1282. IEEE (2018)

27. Sölch, M., et al.: Variational inference for on-line anomaly detection in high-dimensional time series. CoRR abs/1602.07109 (2016)

28. Taylor, M., et al.: numenta/nupic: 1.0.5 (2018). https://doi.org/10.5281/zenodo.1257382

29. Thill, M., Däubener, S., Konen, W., Bäck, T.: Anomaly detection in electrocardiogram readings with stacked LSTM networks. In: ITAT. CEUR Workshop Proceedings, vol. 2473, pp. 17–25 (2019)

30. Thill, M., Konen, W., Bäck, T.: Online anomaly detection on the Webscope S5 dataset: a comparative study. In: EAIS, pp. 1–8. IEEE (2017)

31. Thill, M., Konen, W., Bäck, T.: MGAB: The Mackey-Glass Anomaly Benchmark (2020). https://doi.org/10.5281/zenodo.3762385
32. Xu, H., et al.: Unsupervised anomaly detection via variational auto-encoder for seasonal KPIs in web applications. In: WWW, pp. 187–196 (2018)
33. Zong, B., et al.: Deep autoencoding Gaussian mixture model for unsupervised anomaly detection. In: ICLR (2018)

Algorithms and Applications

On Formulating the Ground Scheduling Problem as a Multi-objective Bilevel Problem

Margarita Antoniou[1,2]([⊠]) [iD], Gašper Petelin[1] [iD], and Gregor Papa[1,2] [iD]

[1] Jožef Stefan Institute, Ljubljana, Slovenia
{margarita.antoniou,gasper.petelin,gregor.papa}@ijs.si
[2] Jožef Stefan International Postgraduate School, Ljubljana, Slovenia

Abstract. In this paper, a bilevel multi-objective formulation of the Ground Scheduling Problem is presented. First, the problem is formulated as a bilevel optimisation problem (BOP), wherein the upper level (UL) is a biobjective problem determining the pairs of Ground Station (GS) to Spacecraft (SC) and the starting time of each event with objectives the maximisation of the access windows and the minimisation of the communication clashes of each GS. These two objectives of the UL can be assumed as a measure of the violation of the feasibility of a schedule. The lower level (LL) consists of a single objective optimisation problem that determines the duration of each event, with objectives the communication time requirement of SCs with GS and the total ground station usage, combined together to a weighted sum function. The approach used to solve this multi-objective BOP is a nested approach, where the Pareto front of the upper level is obtained by a multi-objective optimisation algorithm (NSGA2) and the lower level is solved using a GA. The formulation is tested on one small test case from literature and the relevant results are reported.

Keywords: Bilevel optimisation · Multi-objective optimisation · Satellite scheduling

1 Introduction

The Ground Station Scheduling (GSS) refers to the problem of planning the communication between satellites (or spacecraft) and the ground stations. The importance of the GSS problem relies on finding optimal allocation of the communication of many satellites to a limited number of ground stations. The problem is very complex, highly constrained, and proved to be NP-hard [7]. Therefore, since only near-optimal solutions are expected to be found the use of EAs and other metaheuristics has become popular, e.g. [3,9]. The problem is most of the time formulated as a multi-objective problem, consisting of several and conflicting objectives [11,12]. Moreover, the optimisation of each of the objectives can be modeled in a hierarchical or simultaneous fashion [13]. In the simultaneous optimisation, the objectives are optimised at the same time, obtaining a

© Springer Nature Switzerland AG 2020
B. Filipič et al. (Eds.): BIOMA 2020, LNCS 12438, pp. 177–188, 2020.
https://doi.org/10.1007/978-3-030-63710-1_14

Pareto front of the solutions, ignoring their hierarchy. In this way, the solutions of the optimisation might not be representative of the final schedule, since some communications will be omitted as they don't satisfy some of the constraints.

The main scope of this paper is to present and test a bilevel multi-objective formulation of the Ground Scheduling Problem. The problem is formulated as a bilevel optimisation problem (BOP), wherein the upper level is a biobjective problem determining the pairs of Ground Station (GS) to Spacecraft (SC) and the starting time of each event with objectives the maximisation of the access windows and the minimisation of the communication clashes of each GS. These two objectives of the UL can be assumed as a measure of the violation of the feasibility of a schedule. The lower level consists of a single objective optimisation problem that determines the duration of each event, with objectives the communication time requirement of SCs with GS and the total ground station usage, formulated as a weighted sum function. The approach used to solve this multi-objective BOP is a nested approach, where the Pareto front of the upper level is obtained by NSGA2 and the lower level is solved using a GA. The expected results of this approach are to have more representative solutions to the optimization of the final schedule.

The remainder of this paper is organized as follows. In Sect. 2 the multi-objective bilevel optimisation problem is described along with its mathematical representation. In Sect. 3 the ground scheduling problem is presented, with the notations and the objective functions taken into account in this implementation, and the formulation as a multi-objective bilevel problem is defined. The nested evolutionary approach adopted for the optimisation is shortly described in Sect. 4. The experimental setup and the obtained results are discussed in Sect. 5. Finally, Sect. 6 concludes the paper, giving some future steps of the research.

2   Multi-objective Bilevel Optimisation Problem

The general bilevel optimisation problem (BOP) consists of two levels of optimisation problems referred to as the upper and lower level (UL and LL). The lower level works as a constraint to the upper, meaning that the feasible space of the upper level is determined by the optimal solution of the lower level problem. The mathematical representation of a BOP can be described as follows:

$$
\begin{aligned}
&\min_{x \in X} \quad F(x, y) \\
&\text{subject to} \quad G(x, y) \leq 0, \\
&\qquad\qquad \min_{y \in Y} \quad f(x, y) \\
&\qquad\qquad \text{subject to} \quad g(x, y) \leq 0
\end{aligned}
\tag{1}
$$

where y is the solution of the LL problem from the set of solutions $Y \subseteq R^n$, with regard to the solution from UL, x from the set of solutions $X \subseteq R^m$. This means that the LL problem is optimised only with respect to y, while x is kept fixed. The highest level of the hierarchy is the UL optimisation problem where F is its objective, while f corresponds to the objective of the LL of the optimisation problem, the lowest level in the hierarchy [4]. Moreover, $G(x, y)$ and $g(x, y)$ correspond to the inequality constraints of the UL and LL respectively.

If F and f are vector functions ($F : R^n \times R^m \rightarrow R^N$ and $f : R^n \times R^m \rightarrow R^M$), then the problem is called a multi-objective bilevel problem. A general Multi-objective Bilevel Optimisation Problem (MBOP) can be described as follows [6]:

$$\min_{x \in X, y \in Y} \quad F(x, y) = (F_1(x, y), \dots, F_N(x, y))$$

$$\text{subject to} \quad G(x, y) \leq 0,$$

$$\min_{y \in Y} \quad f(x, y) = (f_1(x, y), \dots, f_M(x, y)) \tag{2}$$

$$\text{subject to} \quad g(x, y) \leq 0$$

In the above formulation, $F_1(x, y), \dots, F_N(x, y)$ and $f_1(x, y), \dots, f_M(x, y)$ are the UL and LL objective functions respectively. A solution is a feasible solution to the UL problem, only if it is a Pareto-optimal solution of the LL optimisation problem. More about the basic notations and theoretical results about the MBOP can be found in [2]. Note that in our formulation we make the optimistic assumption, meaning in case there is more than one optimal LL solution, we assume that is the one that is optimal for the UL as well [2].

3   Satellite and Ground Scheduling Problem

In this section, the satellite scheduling problem and more specifically the ground scheduling problem are described shortly. Then, the mathematical formulation and notation of the problem are presented, defining its parameters, variables and objective functions used. Last, the interpretation of a bilevel multi-objective problem and its mathematical formulation is given.

3.1   Problem Description

The Ground Station Scheduling optimises the plan of the communication between satellites (or spacecraft) and the ground stations. The problem can be formulated with many different objectives. In this paper, a benchmark instance of the ground station scheduling generated with the STK simulation toolkit from Xhafa et al. [12,13] is used. Therefore, the same formulation of objectives is implemented –with some small modifications of the quantification of some objectives– to correspond to the same input and output parameters. The main objectives taken into account in this formulation are 1. maximising the visibility windows of SCs and GSs 2. minimising the clashes of the time windows between different SCs to the same GS, 3. satisfying the required communication time between SC with GSs, 4. minimising the idle time of the GSs.

3.2 Mathematical Formulation

The notation and the mathematical problem is presented as follows:

Parameters

- $s \in 1, \ldots, S$ satellite set, index s
- $g \in 1, \ldots, G$ ground station set, index g
- $h \in 1, \ldots, H$ set of available Access Windows for a specific g and a specific s for all days of the schedule, index h
- $d \in 1, \ldots, D$ & set of days, index d
- tw_{sg}^h: h^{th} time window between a specific g and a specific s
- $T_{AOS}(tw_{sg}^h), T_{LOS}(tw_{sg}^h)$ are the visibility and losing signal times of a g from a s
- $\forall g \in G, s \in S \ AW_{s,g} = \bigcup\limits_{h=1}^{H} [T_{AOS}(tw_{sg}^h), T_{LOS}(tw_{sg}^h)]$ where AW defines all the time periods s and g can communicate
- $k_s^d \in 1, \ldots, K$ are requirements for each s each day d
- $T_{beg}(k_s^d), T_{end}(k_s^d)$ are the beginning and ending time of a requirement where connection has to be established for at least $T_{req}(k_s^d)$ during a specified period d.

Decision Variables

- $n_{sg}^m \in N$ an event of the schedule, where $m \in M$ is the consecutive number of event when a specific g communicates with a specific s, N is the total number of events of the schedule
- $T_{start}(n_{sg}^m), T_{dur}(n_{sg}^m)$ Starting and Duration time between s and g.

Objective Functions

Access Windows Fitness Function: Access windows or visibility windows are the time windows during which a g can establish communication with an s. Therefore in the schedule, we want to maximize the number of events that fall into these time windows. $\forall g \in G, s \in S, m \in M$

$$f_{AW}(n_{sg}^m) = \begin{cases} 1 \text{ if } [T_{start}(n_{sg}^m), T_{start}(n_{sg}^m) + T_{dur}(n_{sg}^m)] \subseteq AW_{s,g} \\ 0 \text{ else} \end{cases} \tag{3}$$

$$Fit_{AW} = \frac{\sum_{m=1}^{M} \sum_{g=1}^{G} \sum_{s=1}^{S} f_{AW}(n_{sg}^m) * 100}{N} \tag{4}$$

Communication Clash Fitness Function: A communication clash occurs when two satellites are trying to communicate with the same Ground Station at the same time. In this case, the solutions are infeasible. The goal here is to minimise the clashes that are produced between the several SCs to one GS. Let from n_{gs}^m create the sets $\forall s : n_g^l \in N$ where $l \in L \subset N$ is the index of the mth

event of a specific g to all the s, after its events are sorted in ascending order for a fixed g and $\forall s$ according to their $T_{start}(n_s^m)$ Then:

$$f_{sc}(n_g^l) = \begin{cases} -1 \text{ if } T_{start}(n_s^{l+1}) < T_{start}(n_s^l) + T_{dur}(n_s^l) \\ 0 \text{ else} \end{cases} \tag{5}$$

$$Fit_{CS} = \frac{N + \sum_{g=1}^{G} \sum_{l=1}^{L} f(n_g^l) * 100}{N} \tag{6}$$

Communication Time Requirements Fitness Function: In order for TTC (Telemetry, Tracking, and Command) tasks to be completed, such as data download tasks, there exist some minimum time requirements. These periodical tasks are given as an input to the problem, in a matrix of their starting and ending times for each period (day) for each satellite. The objective is to satisfy as much as possible these requirements in the whole schedule. The fitness function is computed as follows: $\forall n \in N$ and $\forall k \in K$

$$f(k_s^d, n_{sg}^m) = \|[T_{start}(n_{sg}^m), T_{start}(n_{sg}^m) + T_{dur}(n_{sg}^m)] \cap [T_{beg}(k_s^d), T_{end}(k_s^d)]\| \tag{7}$$

In the reference paper, the problem was formulated as follows:

$$f_{TR}(k_s^d) = \begin{cases} 1 \text{ if } (\sum_{g=1}^{G} \sum_{m=1}^{M} f(k_s^d, n_{sg}^m)) \geq T_{Req}(k_s^d) \\ 0 \text{ else} \end{cases} \tag{8}$$

This formulation (Eq. 8), where the percentage of violation of the requirement is calculated, may pose a problem in some bilevel formulations. When this objective is optimized without any other constraints on the same level, it may happen that all of the event duration are increased to their maximum limit (here e.g. the maximum days of the schedule). To prevent this from happening, the fitness function was reformulated as follows:

$$f_{TR}(k_s^d) = \begin{cases} 0 \text{ if } (\sum_{g=1}^{G} \sum_{m=1}^{M} f(k_s^d, n_{sg}^m)) < T_{Req}(k_s^d) \\ T_{Req}(k_s^d)/(\sum_{g=1}^{G} \sum_{m=1}^{M} f(k_s^d, n_{sg}^m)) \text{ else} \end{cases} \tag{9}$$

$$Fit_{TR} = \frac{\sum_{s=1}^{S} \sum_{g=1}^{G} f_{TR}(k_s^d)}{K} * 100 \tag{10}$$

The new formulation assigns a small penalty to the events that establish communication for a period that is longer than the required amount of time. This penalty is proportional to the length of the requirement.

Ground Station Usage Fitness Function: This fitness function is maximizing the busy time of a GS (minimising its idle time). This is expressed as a percentage of the GSs busy time and the total available communication time of a GS.

$$Fit_{GU} = \frac{\| \bigcup_{m=1}^{M} \bigcup_{g=1}^{G} \bigcup_{s=1}^{S} [T_{start}(n_{gs}^m), T_{start}(n_{gs}^m) + T_{dur}(n_{gs}^m)]\|}{\sum_{g=1}^{G} T_{total}(g)} * 100 \tag{11}$$

where $T_{total}(g)$ is the total available time of a GS, in this case the number of days of the schedule.

3.3   Interpretation as a Bilevel Multi-objective Problem

In the reference paper, the problem was approached by combining the fitness objectives into one, by assigning weights to each fitness functions as follows:

$$Fit_{Total} = 1.5 * Fit_{AW} + Fit_{TR} + 0.1 * Fit_{CS} + 0.01 * Fit_{GU}$$

It should be noted that the fitness functions can be grouped into modules, of serial and parallel, according to the dependencies among the fitness functions. In this problem, Fit_{AW} and Fit_{CS} belong to the serial fitness module, while the rest two objectives to the parallel module. From a hierarchical point of view, the objectives of Access windows Eq. 4 and Communication Clash Eq. 6 (the serial module) are the ones that should be evaluated first, as they are also defining the violation of the feasibility of each event. Also, these two objectives are most of the time conflicting, making the problem difficult to find an optimal solution. In this paper, we take into account this hierarchy, by decoupling the problem into two levels. We define the UL as a biobjective optimisation problem and the LL as a single objective, defined by a weighted function of the rest two objectives. The mathematical representation of the problem is as follows:

$$\max_{x \in X, y \in Y} \quad F(x,y) = (F_{AW}(x,y), F_{CS}(x,y))$$

$$\text{subject to} \tag{12}$$

$$\max_{y \in Y} \quad f(x,y) = (F_{TR}(x,y) + 0.1 * F_{GU}(x,y))$$

where the decision variables of the upper level are $x = SC, GS, T_{start}$, and the decision variables of the lower level is $y = T_{dur}$.

Therefore, most of the variables of the scheduling problem are defined by the UL, while the LL defines only the duration of each event. The optimal $Tdur$ defined by the LL is then used to evaluate the Pareto front of the UL. The rationale behind this formulation lies in firstly the assumed hierarchy of the objectives and then the influence of the decision variables to each objective. One can notice that the ground station usage fitness (Eq. 11) and the communication time requirement fitness (Eq. 9) are mostly influenced by the variable T_{dur} of each event. Moreover, the objectives of the UL are actually a measure of the violation of the feasibility of the events. In this way, we take into account LL optimal objectives that are violating as less as possible these constraints, making the solution more representative to the final schedule. Finally, by keeping the number of decision variables low at the LL, the optimisation problem becomes of lower dimensionality and relatively easier to optimise. The general structure of the bilevel model is presented in Fig. 2.

4   Evolutionary Algorithms for MBOP

To solve the MBOP that we formulated, we adopt a nested optimisation approach [10]. A similar nested approach has been applied in [8], where they implemented a nested Genetic Algorithm (GA) for solving an integrated long-term
staffing and scheduling problem. In the UL, the biobjective problem is solved
with the NSGA-II multi-objective algorithm [1]. To evaluate each individual of
the UL, the LL is solved to optimality with a GA. Each optimisation of the
LL for each UL individual is independent, so these processes were parallelized
to reduce the computational cost. Finally, the result is a Pareto front of all
the non-dominated solutions of the upper-level. The general pseudocode of the
nested algorithm is shown in Algorithm 1. For solving the problem with GA
and NSGA2, the following representation of the chromosome was adopted. Each
chromosome encodes a schedule as a list of communication events, where each
event is represented by 5 binary variables, as seen in Fig. 1. I is a binary variable
that indicates whether the specific schedule is taken into account or not, while
the rest are representing the SCs with their corresponding GSs and their starting
and duration times. One chromosome consists of many of these tuples to create a whole schedule. As a crossover operator, HUX was selected, while BitFlip
mutation was used as a mutation strategy for the specific implementation, both
for NSGA2 and GA.

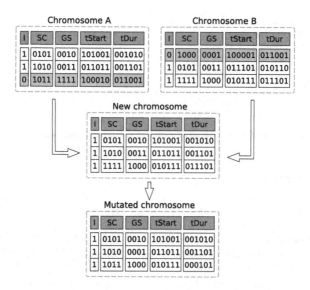

Fig. 1. Chromosome encoding and its mutation and crossover operators.

Algorithm 1. Nested MBOP

Input: $AW, S, G, Days, TReq$
Output: $GS - SC, n, fitness functions$

1: **procedure** NESTEDMBOP
2: *Initialize Population X_0*
3: *Best ← {}*
4:    **for** number of generations **do:**
5:        **for all** *Individuals $X_i \in X$* **do in parallel:**
6:            *call lower-level GA with X_i as an input, obtain Y_{ibest} as an output*
7:        **end for**
8:        *Evaluate Fitness(X)*
9:        *A ← Pareto Front(X) ∪ Best*
10:       *Best ← Pareto Front(A)*
11:       *reproduction (selection, mutation, recombination)*
        return *Best non dominated solutions*

Upper level Problem

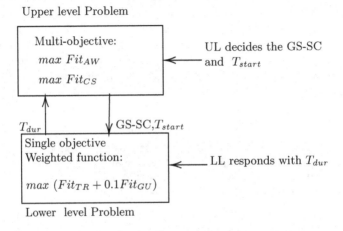

Lower level Problem

Fig. 2. Bilevel model structure of the Ground Scheduling Problem

5   Experiments

5.1   Experimental Setup and Problem Instance

For the implementation of the NSGA-II and GA, the platypus[1] framework in python is used. For the upper level, a population size of 30 and 500 generations was used, while for the LL a population size of 50 and 20 generations. The problem instance corresponds to the first small size of the benchmarks generated by Xhafa et al. from STK toolkit[2], where there are 5 Ground Stations, 10 Spacecraft and the number of days is 10. The preliminary results refer to one run of the nested approach to test the mathematical formulation of the problem. The

---

[1] https://platypus.readthedocs.io/en/latest/getting-started.html.
[2] https://www.researchgate.net/publication/260086344_GS_Scheduling_Inputs.

control parameters values used are reported in Table 1. Our implementation of the objective functions and the related code can be found at [5].

Table 1. Selected control parameters that are used in all of the reported results.

	UL	LL
HUX crossover rate	0.3	0.3
BitFlip mutation rate	0.001	0.001
Population size	30	50
Number of generations	500	20

5.2   Results and Discussion

In Fig. 3 the convergence of the hypervolume indicator of the UL NSGA-II is presented with respect to the number of generations. The results show that the algorithm converges as the generations evolve. In Fig. 4 the scatter plot of the solutions of the final UL generations is depicted. Orange dots represent the obtained Pareto front, while the blue dots are the dominated solutions of the population. In Fig. 5 the final objective values of the Pareto front solutions and their corresponding LL objective values are depicted. It is interesting to note, that the objective values of the Fit_{TR} seem to be concentrated with a small variance around 20. These low values are most probably an implication of the reformulation of the objective function that was implemented and described in Sect. 3 and is a topic for further research. Also with this formulation, we only accept solutions that violate as less as possible the constraints of the AW and Clashes and this explains further the low values of the lower level objective.

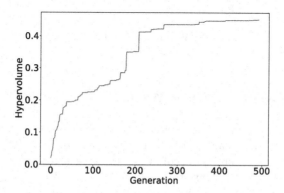

Fig. 3. Hypervolume indicator convergence of Upper Level NSGA-II.

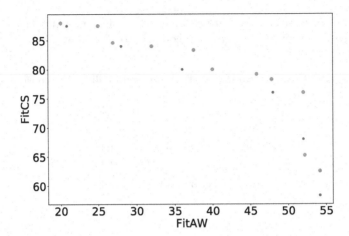

Fig. 4. Scatter plot of the non-dominated (orange) and dominated (blue) solutions of the final UL generation and the obtained Pareto front for case I_S_01. (Color figure online)

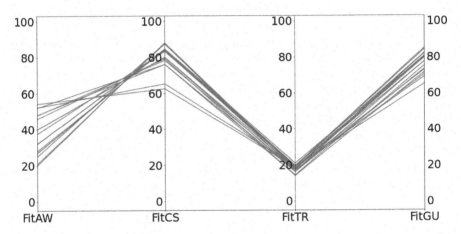

Fig. 5. Parallel coordinate plot of the approximate Pareto front on the case I_S_01 with bilevel algorithms (green). (Color figure online)

6   Conclusion and Future Work

We formulated for the first time the GSP as a multiobjective bilevel problem and tested in one benchmark instance. In the final schedule of a GSP, only the feasible solutions are taken into account and the values of some of the objectives are not optimal anymore. The proposed formulation of the GSP aims to give more representative results of this final schedule. It can take advantage of the hierarchy of the objectives, without using weights, giving more than a single optimal schedule at the end. Finally, the bilevel formulation can be useful for modeling the problem with other objectives as well, especially when the lower level is cheaper to evaluate.

In the next steps, the possible implications of the time requirement objective reformulation will be examined and improved. Moreover, a different formulation of the problem, meaning different UL and LL objectives and/or decision variables can be interesting, by exploring deeper the hierarchies of the problem. Last but not least, algorithmic-wise, ways to reduce further the computational cost of the bilevel approach will be examined, such as additional parallelization, use the knowledge of the previous runs by using them as an initial population of each lower level run, and the possibility of using approximation functions.

Acknowledgements. This work is funded by the European Commission's H2020 program, UTOPIAE Marie Curie Innovative Training Network, H2020-MSCA-ITN-2016, under Grant Agreement No. 722734 and from the Slovenian Research Agency (research core funding No. P2-0098).

References

1. Deb, K., Agrawal, S., Pratap, A., Meyarivan, T.: A fast elitist non-dominated sorting genetic algorithm for multi-objective optimization: NSGA-II. In: Schoenauer, M., Deb, K., Rudolph, G., Yao, X., Lutton, E., Merelo, J.J., Schwefel, H.-P. (eds.) PPSN 2000. LNCS, vol. 1917, pp. 849–858. Springer, Heidelberg (2000). https://doi.org/10.1007/3-540-45356-3_83
2. Eichfelder, G.: Multiobjective bilevel optimization. Math. Program. **123**(2), 419–449 (2010)
3. Globus, A., Crawford, J., Lohn, J., Pryor, A.: Scheduling earth observing satellites with evolutionary algorithms. Technical report 20030062898, NASA Technical reports, December 2003
4. Migdalas, A., Pardalos, P.M., Värbrand, P.: Multilevel Optimization: Algorithms and Applications, vol. 20. Springer, Boston (2013). https://doi.org/10.1007/978-1-4613-0307-7
5. Petelin, G.: Satellite scheduling repository (2019). https://repo.ijs.si/gpetelin/satellites-scheduling. Accessed 04 Sept 2020
6. Pieume, C.O., Marcotte, P., Fotso, L.P., Siarry, P., et al.: Generating efficient solutions in bilevel multi-objective programming problems. Am. J. Oper. Res. **3**(02), 289 (2013)
7. Scherer, W.T., Rotman, F.: Combinatorial optimization techniques for spacecraft scheduling automation. Ann. Oper. Res. **50**(1), 525–556 (1994)
8. Schulte, J., Günther, M., Nissen, V.: Evolutionary bilevel approach for integrated long-term staffing and scheduling. In: Proceedings of the 8th Multidisciplinary International Conference on Scheduling: Theory and Applications (MISTA 2017), pp. 144–157 (2017)
9. Spangelo, S., Cutler, J., Gilson, K., Cohn, A.: Optimization-based scheduling for the single-satellite, multi-ground station communication problem. Comput. Oper. Res. **57**, 1–16 (2015)
10. Talbi, E.G.: A taxonomy of metaheuristics for bi-level optimization. In: Talbi, E.G. (ed.) Metaheuristics for Bi-level Optimization. Studies in Computational Intelligence, vol. 482, pp. 11–39. Springer, Heidelberg (2013). https://doi.org/10.1007/978-3-642-37838-6_1

11. Wang, J., Jing, N., Li, J., Chen, Z.H.: A multi-objective imaging scheduling app-roach for earth observing satellites. In: Proceedings of the 9th Annual Conference on Genetic and Evolutionary Computation, pp. 2211–2218 (2007)

12. Xhafa, F., Herrero, X., Barolli, A., Takizawa, M.: Using STK toolkit for evaluating a GA base algorithm for ground station scheduling. In: 2013 Seventh International Conference on Complex, Intelligent, and Software Intensive Systems, pp. 265–273. IEEE (2013)

13. Xhafa, F., Ip, A.W.: Optimisation problems and resolution methods in satellite scheduling and space-craft operation: a survey. Enterp. Inf. Syst., 1–24 (2019). https://doi.org/10.1080/17517575.2019.1593508

Optimization of a Thermal Ice Protection System by Means of a Genetic Algorithm

Bárbara Arizmendi Gutiérrez$^{(\boxtimes)}$ (ID), Alberto Della Noce (ID),
Mariachiara Gallia (ID), and Alberto Guardone (ID)

Politecnico di Milano, Via Giuseppe La Masa, 34, 20156 Milano, Italy
barbara.arizmendi@polimi.it

Abstract. Ice accretion poses a major threat for performance and safety of aircraft. Electro-Thermal Ice Protection Systems (ETIPS) are a reliable and flexible alternative to protect critical parts against it. Their main drawback is the high power consumption, especially when operating in fully evaporative Anti-Ice mode. In this work, a Genetic Algorithm (GA) is deployed to optimize the heat flux distribution on the fixed heaters of a wing ETIPS that operates in Anti-Ice regime. The aim is to minimize the power consumption while ensuring safety, such that no runback ice is formed downstream the protected parts. A thermodynamic numerical model was deployed to assess runback ice formations for each layout of heat fluxes. A linear penalty method was selected to handle the constraint of no-runback ice formation. Crossover and Mutation operators for GA were investigated for a large population as well as a penalty factor. Higher penalties and Mutation-based GA presented the best optimization performance based on several runs. The optimal layout of fluxes was found to minimize as well the convective losses in several ways to increase the evaporative efficiency.

Keywords: In-flight icing · Ice Protection Systems · Optimization · Genetic Algorithms

Nomenclature

Parameters

Δl_i	Size of the heater i [m]	H	IPS Substratum thickness [m]
δ	Thickness [m]	h	Heat Transfer Coefficient[Wm^{-2}K^{-1}]
$\dot{m}$	Mass Rate [kgs^{-1}]	i_{l-s}	Solidification latent heat [Jkg^{-1}]
$\dot{Q}$	Thermal Power [Wm^{-1}]	i_{l-v}	Vaporization latent heat [Jkg^{-1}]
$\dot{q}''$	Heat Flux [Wm^{-2}]	k_{wall}	Effective Thermal Conductivity
P	Heat Fluxes vector	l	Number of chromosome gens
A	Control volume surface area [m^2]	p	Probability
		P_i	Heat Flux of the heater i [Wm^{-2}]

© Springer Nature Switzerland AG 2020
B. Filipič et al. (Eds.): BIOMA 2020, LNCS 12438, pp. 189–200, 2020.
https://doi.org/10.1007/978-3-030-63710-1_15

c	Chord [m]	s	Curvilinear Coordinate [m]
c_p	Specific Heat [Jkg^{-1}K^{-1}]	T	Temperature [K]
F	Wetness fraction	V	Velocity [ms^{-1}]
LWC	Liquid Water Content [kgm^{-3}]	imp	Impinging
MVD	Mean Volume Diameter [μm]	in	Incoming to a control volume
Subscripts		IPS	Ice protection system
0	Total	m	Mutation
∞	Free stream	out	Outgoing from a control volume
A	Average of runs	rec	Recovery
B	Best of all runs	ref	Reference Temperature, 273.15K
cr	Crossover	$wall$	External solid surface
f	Liquid film	$water$	Liquid film
ice	Freezing		

1   Introduction

Aircraft icing consists of the accumulation of ice on their surfaces when interacting with supercooled clouds. These contain water droplets that are at a temperature below the freezing point but they remain liquid in metastable equilibrium. When the droplets impact, they totally or partially freeze [9]. Among other effects, in-flight icing causes a reduction in the lift capability, increase in drag, decrease of the control surface effectiveness [10]. Furthermore, severe ice accretions have been the cause of several accidents in the past [14]. According to literature, "the average altitude of icing environments is around 3 000 m above mean sea level, with few encounters above 6 000 m" [15]. Commonly, aircraft operate at these altitudes and for this reason, the critical parts of aircraft must include Ice Protection Systems (IPS). Anti-Ice operational regime of IPS prevents the formation of ice and it includes two operating modes: fully evaporative and running wet. Electro-Thermal IPS (ETIPS) is a mature technology widely deployed to protect small critical parts due to its reliability. It consists of a substratum including resistors to transform electricity into heating power. One of its main drawbacks a high power consumption compared to other technologies, especially in fully evaporative operation for large protected areas in long icing encounters. Also, when operating in running wet regime, the water that is not evaporated might freeze downstream forming the so-called runback ice. Runback ice also compromises safety and performance. Wing ETIPS are deployed in several substratum heating bands that extend spanwise and can be controlled independently. Despite its drawbacks, there is room for improvement and motivation for such in the development of fully electric aircraft.

There is a very limited research effort available in open literature concerning ETIPS experimental studies, mainly due to high cost and confidentiality. A study conducted by Al-Khalil [1] consists of a set of icing wind tunnel tests of an ETIPS. However, there is a large research effort on the development of numerical models for the prediction of the performance of Thermal Anti-Ice ETIPS. Numerical models aim to support preliminary designs and to improve the understanding of the physics. These codes include ANTICE [1], FENSAP-ICE [2], the works by Silva [18,19] and many others. They are based on the formulation of mass and energy conservation equations in control volumes. With the development of numerical codes, there is a recent research effort on optimizing their power consumption. Pellisier [13] performed a surrogate-based numerical optimization study of the geometric parameters of Pneumatic wing IPS. The goal was to minimize the power consumption while ensuring all water was evaporated employing GA. Pourbagian performed a surrogate-based optimization study of a wing Anti-Ice ETIPS in both operational modes [16] utilizing Multi-Adaptive Direct Search. Further work of Pourbagian [17] included several formulations of objective functions and constraints for the optimization of an Anti-Ice ETIPS.

In this work, the minimization of the thermal power consumption of an Anti-Ice ETIPS working in fully evaporative regime was performed utilizing a GA. Several Genetic operators were investigated and compared to find the best performing one. The numerical framework of optimization of the IPS includes only in-house developed and open-source codes. It is aimed to obtain an understanding of the physics of optimized configurations compared to intuitive designs, hence the identification of the global minimum is only advantageous. In Sect. 2, the framework for numerical simulations is presented. Section 3 describes the optimization methodology including the objective function selected. In Sect. 4, the results obtained are presented and discussed. Finally in Sect. 5 the concluding remarks are explained.

2   Numerical Modelling

2.1   Model Equations

Several assumptions and simplifications were introduced to enable the model construction. Steady-state was assumed, given that generally, Anti-Ice systems deal with long exposures to icing conditions. The physical process was decomposed in several loosely coupled numerical steps. The discretization of the computational domain was performed utilizing the in-house software uhMesh [7]. The computation of the Aerodynamic field was performed through the CFD code SU2 [8]. The flow was modelled as inviscid and the resulting velocity field for the reference test case is presented in Fig. 1. The distribution of water impingement was computed by means of the in-house software PoliDrop [3]. It consists of a Lagrangian Particle Tracking solver that computes the trajectories of water droplets in an aerodynamic field. The distribution of water on the surface is quantified by the collection efficiency. The obtained profile for the reference test case is presented in Fig. 2. The thermal calculations were performed by the Anti-Ice module of PoliMIce. It solved mass and energy conservation equations. The model equations were based on the work of Silva [18,19] while the liquid film model is based on the work of Myers [12] adapted to the Anti-Ice problem. The equations are solved in a discrete domain divided into control volumes. The mass conservation equation reads:

$$\frac{\partial \delta_f \bar{u}_f(\delta_f, s)}{\partial s} = \frac{\dot{m}_{imp} - \dot{m}_{evap} - \dot{m}_{ice}}{A \rho_{H_2O}} \qquad (1)$$

From δ_f, $\dot{m}_{in}$ and $\dot{m}_{out}$ can be retrieved. The equation of the energy conservation in the solid substratum of the IPS is presented next:

$$\frac{d}{ds}\left(k_{wall}\ H\ \frac{dT_{wall}}{ds}\right) - F\ h_{water}\ (T_{wall} - T_{water}) + \dot{q}''_{IPS}$$
$$- (1 - F)\ [h_{air}\ (T_{wall} - T_{rec})] = 0 \qquad (2)$$

Finally, a second conservation equation in the liquid film is formulated:

$$F\ A\ h_{air}\ (T_{rec} - T_{water}) + F\ A\ h_{water}\ (T_{wall} - T_{water})$$
$$+ \dot{m}_{in}\ c_{p_{water}}\ (T_{in} - T_{ref}) - \dot{m}_{out}\ c_{p_{water}}\ (T_{out} - T_{ref})$$
$$+ \dot{m}_{imp}\left[c_{p_{water}}\ (T_\infty - T_{ref}) + \frac{V_\infty^2}{2}\right] \qquad (3)$$
$$- \dot{m}_e\ [i_{l-v} + c_{p_{water}}\ (T_{water} - T_{ref})]$$
$$+ \dot{m}_{ice}\ [i_{l-s} - c_{p_{water}}\ (T_{water} - T_{ref})] = 0.$$

The main heat fluxes in Eq. 3 are the evaporative and convective ones. The convective heat fluxes are inefficiencies as ideally all the thermal power supplied would be devoted to evaporation. The evaporative heat flux depends exponentially on the temperature whereas the convective heat flux is linear. It is assumed there is no temperature gradient across the height of the film. Terms to predict

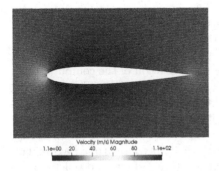

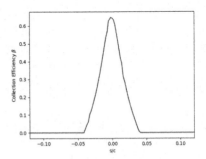

Fig. 1. Airflow velocity field computed by means of the CFD software SU2 for the test case 67A

Fig. 2. Water collection efficiency computed by means of PoliDrop. The 0 abscissa corresponds to the leading edge of the airfoil. Positive values of s/c correspond to the suction surface of the airfoil.

and account for mass and heat fluxes of the runback ice were introduced into the model formulation proposed by Silva [18]. The IPS substratum was modelled as a unique layer with an equivalent thermal conductivity and a fixed thickness.

2.2   Baseline Design

The layout of the ETIPS was taken from the experimental work of Al-Khalil [1]. The geometry consisted of an extruded NACA0012 profile with a chord of 0.9144 m. The IPS comprised a set of 7 multilayered heaters fitted at the leading edge expanding spanwise. Due to a manufacturing issue, the heaters have been shifted towards the suction side a total of 0.0145 m. Therefore, the geometry, depicted in Fig. 3, is not symmetric. The freestream velocity is equal to 89.4 ms^{-1}, the pressure is equal to 90 000 Pa, the angle of attack equal to 0° and the Static Air Temperature is equal to 251.33 K. As for the cloud properties the LWC is equal to 5.5e−4 kgm^{-3} and the MVD is equal to 20 μm.

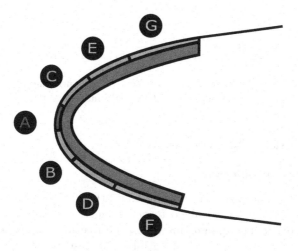

Fig. 3. Layout of the heaters of the ETIPS. Note that due to a manufacturing issue the heaters are shifted towards the CEG side

This layout and operation conditions were selected as the baseline test case for optimization because they represented a realistic problem for which actual improvements entailed by the optimization study would be quantified. The model validation results are shown in Fig. 4, where they are compared to experimental measurements reported in the work of Al-Khalil [1]. Computational results are in good agreement with experiments, in particular in the region of impingement. Due to fixed cloud and flight parameters, the mass impinging is computed only once through the Aerodynamic and Particle Tracking solvers. Therefore, each model evaluation included only the solution to the thermodynamic model. This rendered the computational cost per evaluation in the order of 20 s. The simulations were run in a single node from a cluster, which included two Intel Xeon

X5650 processors with a base frequency of 2.67 GHz. Each consists of 6 cores with 2 threads each, 24 threads in total.

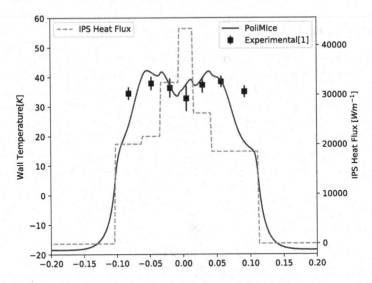

Fig. 4. Comparison of the experimental surface temperature readings from the work of Al-Khalil [1] and the predictions from the ETIPS numerical model

3 Optimization Methodology

3.1 Problem Formulation

The target of the optimization is the minimization of the thermal power consumption of the ETIPS constrained to no-runback ice formations downstream the protected parts. The designs for which the freezing mass rate was greater than 1e−7 kgs^{-1} were considered infeasible. The design vector **P** included the heat fluxes corresponding to each heater. A linear penalty method was chosen to handle the constraint. The amount of constraint violation was integrated into the objective function as a penalty. The penalty was chosen to be linearly proportional to the amount of extra-power that would be required to evaporate the freezing mass rate. Hence, the formulation of the optimization problem for a discrete domain reads:

$$\underset{\mathbf{P}\in\mathbb{R}^{7}}{\text{minimize}}\ \sum_{i=1}^{7} P_i \Delta l_i + k \sum_{i=1}^{N} \dot{m}_{ice}(s_i)i_{l-v} \tag{4a}$$

$$\text{subject to}\ \ P_i \geq 0 \text{Wm}^{-2} \tag{4b}$$

$$P_i \leq 45\ 000 \text{Wm}^{-2}, \tag{4c}$$

where k is an integer proportionality factor. Low k values drove the optimization algorithm to the infeasible region of the design space. High values stopped the exploration of the portions of the design space close to the constraint. Two different values were tested namely, $k = 3$ and $k = 10$. When the constraint was inactive, the objective function solely depended linearly on the heat fluxes. Further decrease of the heat fluxes lead to the formation of runback ice, activating the constraint. At that point, the monotony of the objective function changed due to the penalty. Consequently, the global minimum must lay at the feasibility boundary.

3.2 Optimization Algorithm Description

GAs were selected as the preferred optimization algorithm because the objective function included nonlinearities and multiple local minima. These features were associated with the inclusion of the penalty, which also introduced noise to the objective function. That was due to the coupling of several numerical models with their associated numerical errors. For these reasons, gradient-based algorithms could misperform here. In addition, GAs are easily scaled to multi-objective problems, allowing future problem exploitation. Finally, GAs are simple, mature, widely proven and versatile algorithms that have successfully optimized complex objective functions with different features when adequate parameters are set [4]. Their main drawback is the slow or no convergence to the exact global minimum and the requirement of parameter tunning. The computational cost per evaluation of the ETIPS numerical model is low, enabling numerous repeated samples.

GAs are inspired by the survival of the fittest individuals in a population. Each individual is represented by a chromosome containing the input parameters and by its fitness that accounts for its respective objective function value. The input parameters were encoded forming a binary string, the chromosome in which each bit mimics a gen. Bit encoding can perform equally well than real value encoding as reported by De Jong [5]. Among its benefits are the ease of performing the operations of Crossover and Mutation. A total of 23 bits per design variable were required to get an accuracy of 0.01. The selected generic operators for the evolution of the population were Roulette Selection, One-point Crossover, Bit-flip Mutation and Elitism for the single best individual of a population [11]. The selection of operator parameters and population size is of paramount importance for the adequate performance of the algorithm. In this work, they were extracted from the parameter study performed by Deb for a multiple peak function [6]. Selection operator performs the exploitation of local portions of the design space to find a minimum. Crossover and Mutation operators account for two different paradigms for exploration and exploitation. To investigate the suitability of each, their performance was investigated in Crossover-based GA (C-GA) and Mutation-based GA (M-GA) as well as combined (CM-GA). A constant population of 500 individuals was selected. In a preliminary study, a population of 100 individuals presented premature convergence as well as poor population diversity for C-GA, M-GA and CM-GA, Operators parameters p_{cr} and p_m were set to 0.9 and $\frac{1}{l}$ respectively as suggested by Deb [6]. The stopping criterion was set to 100 000 function evaluations per run. To cope with the characteristic randomness of the algorithm, each of the runs was repeated 5 times.

4   Results

A summary of results is depicted in Table 1, where the best objective function values H_b for each GA and k are reported with their respective constraint values $\dot{m}_{ice}$ and the arithmetic mean of the minimized power consumption of all the 5 runs H_A.

Table 1. Best and Average Performance of the 5 runs for each of the GA tested and different penalty factors. The values reported account only for the power consumption, not including constraint violation penalties.

k	C-GA			M-GA			CM-GA		
	H_b	$\dot{m}_{ice}$	H_A	H_b	$\dot{m}_{ice}$	H_A	H_b	$\dot{m}_{ice}$	H_A
3	4249	1.48e−6	4289	4329	2.75e−6	4369	4293	5.98e−7	4342
10	4286	0.00	4341	4249	0.00	4287	4328	0.00	4381

First, it was observed that for $k = 10$, the optimized solutions for each run were generally feasible. Hence, the exploration of the design space focused the search in the feasible and linear portion of the design space. The best performing GA on average and individually was M-GA for the parameters selected. It retrieved the overall best optimized solution, which decreased the thermal power consumption by 11.8%, pushing the design to the feasible space. Besides, it presented the minimal difference between H_A and H_b showing better consistence. Nevertheless, CM-GA was the poorest performing algorithm caused by an excess of exploration or sub-optimal parameter selection that slowed the convergence. On the other hand, for $k = 3$, penalties were small enough such that infeasible solutions were well-performing. As stated in Sect. 3, the landscape of the infeasible region is more complex. Because of that, more exploration was needed making C-GA and CM-GA more adequate choices for the parameters selected. The best performing GA was C-GA for both H_b and H_A. The Mutation operator performed exploration and exploitation actions even in a heterogeneous population whereas the Crossover operator conducted exploitation only for homogeneous populations. The selected large population and random Selection operator maintained diversity in the population. However, in the feasible space, further exploitation given by M-GA was suitable and thorougher exploration performed by CM-GA ill-performed.

The convergence histories for the 5 runs of M-GA and $k = 10$ are depicted in Fig. 5. Analogous results were found for the remaining GAs and runs. The computational cost per run was in the range of 2e5 s. One can see that the convergence rate was slow, not reaching it clearly in any of the runs. Besides, each run converged to a different value. This was due to the presence of several local minima, inherent inefficiency of the GA or sub-optimal parameter selection. Furthermore, the selective pressure was low. That was caused by the population size and the uniform Selection operator that maintained alive unfit individuals and their genetic information by chance. On a different note, any minimum must lie at the feasible boundary, dictated by the ice formation threshold. Otherwise, H_b could be further reduced manually by decreasing any P_i until reaching it. Consequently, in these runs no minimum was reached.

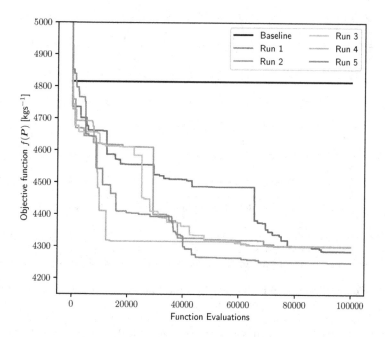

Fig. 5. Convergence history over the course of the simulations. Convergence was still not reached.

Next, the results obtained for the optimized design are presented in Fig. 6 and Table 2. It was found that the optimal design minimized as well the convective losses. In the baseline design, those accounted for 38% of the total thermal power and 31% in the optimized design. That was achieved by shortening the liquid film and nearly turning off heaters F and G. All the excess heat supplied to them would be dissipated by the air. At stagnation point, there is a prominent temperature drop. Large portion of heat is taken there to warm impinging droplets. Besides convective losses relative to the thermal power supply are maximum, hence keeping the heat flux low improved system performance. At the locations corresponding to heaters B, C, D and E, the relative convective losses were reduced. By raising the temperature there, the evaporation process was more efficient the mass evaporated increases exponentially with water temperature and convective losses depend linearly. In that way, a bigger portion of the thermal power supplied was devoted to evaporation, improving the efficiency of the ETIPS.

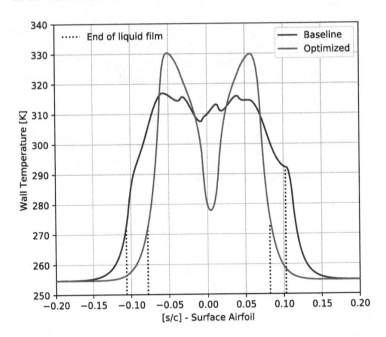

Fig. 6. Temperature predictions on the solid surface for baseline and optimized designs. Included additionally, the limits of the liquid film in each case for comparison

Table 2. Comparison of the heat fluxes and total power consumption per meter span protected for baseline and optimized designs.

Heat flux [Wm^{-2}]	Heater A	Heater B	Heater C	Heater D	Heater E	Heater F	Heater G	Power [Wm^{-1}]
Base	43 400	32 550	26 350	21 700	18 600	20 150	18 600	4 815
Opt	6 328	39 378	39 476	41 853	43 039	0	239	4 250

5   Final Remarks

Any of the GA alternatives was successful in finding the designs that outperformed the initial intuitive design within few function evaluations. However, convergence to a minimum was slow and frequently non reached. In addition, the global minimum was not identified either. This evidenced the shortcomings of GA under sub-optimal parameters selection. Nevertheless, it was concluded that deploying a more aggressive elitist strategy could speed up convergence. For instance, elitist parent-off spring survival to fill the population size, which provided promising results in preliminary runs. Moreover, the number of bits chosen for the binary encoding of each of the variables should be investigated as well for improved convergence. With regards to the allocation of heat fluxes, it was found that an optimal design presents minimal convective losses for the same amount of evaporative heat fluxes. This could be achieved by increasing the water temperature in locations of relatively low convective losses and shrinking the liquid film. Furthermore, the heat fluxes in dry parts should be low or otherwise, the convective losses would rapidly escalate. Due to the accuracy of the numerical model presented in Sect. 2, a mismatch is expected between the best solution here presented and reality. However, the qualitative design guidance can be helpful on the allocation of heat fluxes on the heaters of an ETIPS.

Acknowledgements. The work in this paper was supported by the H2020-MSCA-ITN-2016 UTOPIAE, grant agreement 722734.

References

1. Al-Khalil, K.M., Horvath, C., Miller, D.R., Wright, W.B.: Validation of NASA thermal ice protection computer codes. Part 3; The validation of ANTICE. In: 35th Aerospace Sciences Meeting and Exhibit, p. 51 (2001)
2. Beaugendre, H., Morency, F., Habashi, W.G.: FENSAP-ice's three-dimensional in-flight ice accretion module: ICE3D. J. Aircr. **40**(2), 239–247 (2003)
3. Bellosta, T., Parma, G., Guardone, A.: A robust 3D particle tracking solver of in-flight ice accretion using, arbitrary precision arithmetics. In: VIII International Conference on Coupled Problems in Science and Engineering (2019)
4. Cavazzuti, M.: Optimization Methods: From Theory to Design Scientific and Technological Aspects in Mechanics (2012)
5. De Jong, K.: Evolutionary Computation: A Unified Approach. MIT Press, Cambridge (2006)
6. Deb, K., Agrawal, S.: Understanding interactions among genetic algorithm parameters. In: Foundations of Genetic Algorithms, pp. 265–286 (1998)
7. Dussin, D., Fossati, M., Guardone, A., Vigevano, L.: Hybrid grid generation for two-dimensional high-Reynolds flows. Comput. Fluids **38**(10), 1863–1875 (2009)
8. Economon, T.D., Palacios, F., Copeland, S.R., Lukaczyk, T.W., Alonso, J.J.: SU2: an open-source suite for multiphysics simulation and design. AIAA J. **54**(3), 828–846 (2016)
9. Gent, R., Dart, N., Cansdale, J.: Aircraft icing. Philos. Trans. Roy. Soc. Lond. Ser. A Math. Phys. Eng. Sci. **358**(1776), 2873–2911 (2000)
10. Lynch, F.T., Khodadoust, A.: Effects of ice accretions on aircraft aerodynamics. Prog. Aerosp. Sci. **37**(8), 669–767 (2001)
11. Michalewicz, Z.: Genetic Algorithms + Data Structures = Evolution Programs. Springer, Heidelberg (2013)
12. Myers, T., Charpin, J., Chapman, S.: Modelling the flow and solidification of a thin liquid film on a three-dimensional surface. In: Di Bucchianico, A., Mattheij, R., Peletier, M. (eds.) Progress in Industrial Mathematics at ECMI 2004, pp. 508–512. Springer, Heidelberg (2006). https://doi.org/10.1007/3-540-28073-1_76
13. Pellissier, M., Habashi, W., Pueyo, A.: Optimization via FENSAP-ICE of aircraft hot-air anti-icing systems. J. Aircr. **48**(1), 265–276 (2011)
14. Petty, K.R., Floyd, C.D.: A statistical review of aviation airframe icing accidents in the US. In: Proceedings of the 11th Conference on Aviation, Range, and Aerospace Hyannis, pp. 623–628 (2004)
15. Politovich, M.: Aircraft icing. In: Encyclopedia of Atmospheric Sciences, vol. 358, no. 1776, pp. 68–75 (2003)

16. Pourbagian, M., Habashi, W.G.: Surrogate-based optimization of electrothermal wing anti-icing systems. J. Aircr. **50**(5), 1555–1563 (2013)
17. Pourbagian, M., Talgorn, B., Habashi, W.G., Kokkolaras, M., Le Digabel, S.: Constrained problem formulations for power optimization of aircraft electro-thermal anti-icing systems. Optim. Eng. **16**(4), 663–693 (2015)
18. Silva, G., Silvares, O., de Jesus Zerbini, E.: Numerical simulation of airfoil thermal anti-ice operation, Part 1: Mathematical modelling. J. Aircr. **44**(2), 627–633 (2007)
19. Silva, G., Silvares, O., Zerbini, E., Hefazi, H., Chen, H.H., Kaups, K.: Differential boundary-layer analysis and runback water flow model applied to flow around airfoils with thermal anti-ice. In: 1st AIAA Atmospheric and Space Environments Conference, p. 3967 (2009)

A Memetic Algorithm with Parallel Local Search for Flowshop Scheduling Problems

Pavel Borisovsky[1] and Yulia Kovalenko[1,2(✉)]

[1] Omsk Department, Sobolev Institute of Mathematics SB RAS,
13 Pevtsov Street, 644043 Omsk, Russia
borisovski@mail.ru, julia.kovalenko.ya@yandex.ru
[2] Institute of Scientific Information for Social Sciences RAS,
51/21 Nakhimov Avenue, 117997 Moscow, Russia

Abstract. We propose a new memetic algorithm to minimize the makespan for the flowshop scheduling problem in two variants: the classic permutation setting and the no-wait statement. Our algorithm hybridizes the local search technique into the framework of a steady-state genetic algorithm. A local search heuristic is applied on each iteration and explores the insertion neighborhood. The execution of the local search is parallelized using the CUDA framework for Graphics Processing Units. The initial population is constructed by means of greedy constructive heuristics. A computational experiment on the benchmark instances shows that the proposed algorithm yields results competitive to those of well-known algorithms for the flowshop problem.

Keywords: Local search · Genetic algorithm · Permutation · CUDA · GPU

1 Introduction

We consider the permutation flowshop scheduling problem with makespan criterion (FSSP) [7]. Let n be the number of jobs and m be the number of machines. Each of n jobs is to be sequentially processed on machines $1, \ldots, m$. The processing time p_{ji} of job j on machine i is given. Preemption of the execution of a job on a machine is disallowed. At any time, each machine can process at most one job and each job can be processed on at most one machine. The sequence in which the jobs are to be processed is the same for each machine. The aim is to find a permutation of jobs to minimize the maximum completion time, $C_{\max}$. The FSSP appears in various real-world situations, such as engineering problems, production and air transportation scheduling. We also consider the flowshop setting with no-wait environment [9], where a job must be processed from start to completion, without any interruption either on or between machines.

Due to the strong NP-hardness of the considered flowshop problems [7,23], heuristics and metaheuristics occupy an important place among the methods developed for them. In particular, single-solution based metaheuristics such as

© Springer Nature Switzerland AG 2020
B. Filipič et al. (Eds.): BIOMA 2020, LNCS 12438, pp. 201–213, 2020.
https://doi.org/10.1007/978-3-030-63710-1_16

iterative local search, tabu search, simulated annealing, variable neighborhood search (see, e.g., [8,22,24,26,31]), and hybrid population-based algorithms such as genetic algorithms, ant colony systems, particle swarm, differential evolution (see, e.g., [11,13,15,20,28]) have been developed. In order to construct an initial solution the NEH-algorithm [17] is often used, which is considered to be the best one among polynomial time constructive heuristics for the flowshop scheduling. For permutation-based optimization problems four neighborhoods are usually used: insertion, swap, shift and inversion. The experimental evaluation showed that the insertion neighborhood is the most efficient for various variants of the flowshop [8,22,26]. Some local search heuristics explore subsets of insertion and swap neighborhoods, and use problem-specific speed-up technics (see, e.g., [8,11,26,28,29]). Hybrid evolutionary algorithms as usual apply order-type crossovers, insertion-based local updates, greedy constructive heuristics [12,17], and various mechanisms for maintaining population diversity (migration of individuals between subpopulations, restarting procedures with updating all or part of individuals, adaptive learning strategies for multiple operators) [15,19,20].

A memetic algorithm is a method that combines a population-based search approach, and local search (LS) techniques and/or constructive heuristics (see, e.g., [18]). Such population-based search frameworks as genetic algorithms (GAs) and ant colony optimization are often used in the domain of combinatorial optimization, while differential evolution and particle swarm optimization are favored in continuous variable problems. Local improvements can be incorporated at different steps of the population-based search. It is possible to classify improvement at initialization step, post-processing integration, and procedures that are interleaved within population-based evolutionary operators. Coordination of the algorithmic components can be performed by means of fitness-based or distance-based diversity adaptive rules, adaptive hyper-heuristics, self-adaptive and co-evolutionary schemes, and learning processes [18]. Various memetic algorithms (also called hybrid algorithms) have been proposed and for problems on permutations, in particular for the flowshop settings (see, e.g., [2,5,18,19]).

Recently the use of graphics processing units (GPUs), CPU multi-core environments and heterogeneous approaches is popular to speedup optimization and provide a basis for parallel computing [24]. GPU computing is one of the powerful ways to achieve high-performance on various applications [6,25]. Parallelization strategies are classified according to the source of parallelism: low-level parallelism (evaluating neighbor solutions or computing the objective of a solution in parallel), domain decomposition (subproblems are solved simultaneously by applying the same sequential algorithm), independent and cooperative multi-search (explorations of the search space by different methods).

For variations of the flowshop scheduling the following parallel algorithms were developed: GPU-accelerated branch-and-bound algorithms [3,30] (bounding operators are performed on GPU), GPU-based local search methods with parallel execution of swap or insertion moves [10,29,31], a parallel version of NEH-algorithm [16], multi-search metaheuristics [20,24], and others. For example, several individuals or sub-populations are updated in parallel in such multi-search population-based methods as parallel simulated annealing, parallel tabu search, island genetic algorithm and hybrid memetic algorithm with iterated greedy heuristic [20,24]. We also note that hybrid population-based algorithms with GPU-based low-level parallelism have been proposed for various problems on permutations. In particular, the experimental evaluation showed applicability of the algorithms to routing and scheduling problems (see, e.g., [6,24,25]).

Our Results. We propose a unified memetic algorithm for the classic and no-wait flowshop scheduling problems. Our algorithm uses the randomized analog of NEH-heuristic [17] to generate the initial population. Moreover, this algorithm applies a local search method with insertion neighborhood. In order to reduce the computational time we provide parallel realization of the local search, where moves in a neighborhood are distributed between GPU-threads. The performance of our algorithm is evaluated with two standard benchmarks: Reeves's instances [21] and Taillard's instances [27]. Experimental results showed that the proposed memetic algorithm yields results competitive or superior to those of state-of-the-art algorithms.

The article is organized as follows. Section 2 presents our memetic algorithm and describes its operators. Section 3 provides the experimental evaluation on benchmark instances. Section 4 contains the concluding remarks.

2   Memetic Algorithm

Our memetic algorithm is implemented within the population-based framework of genetic algorithms. The genetic algorithm uses a population of individuals and reproduction operators to reach optimal/near optimal solutions, where each individual encodes some solution. We chose the natural representation of solutions for the flowshop scheduling, i.e. an individual is represented as a permutation of jobs. The components of the permutations are called genes. The initial population is built by the randomized analog of NEH-heuristic [17] and an insertion local search (which will be described below). The fitness function is equal to the objective function and calculated in $O(nm)$ time for the classic flowshop scheduling, and $O(n)$ time for the no-wait case (using the well-known reduction to the asymmetric traveling salesman problem, see, e.g., [14]). The basic scheme of the proposed memetic algorithm is outlined in Algorithm 1.

The randomized analog of NEH-heuristic includes the following two stages. Firstly we randomly sort all jobs (in the original NEH-algorithm jobs are ordered by decreasing sums of processing times on all machines), then take the first two jobs and find their order with the best makespan. Secondly we take the i-th job from the sequence obtained on the first stage, and construct the best partial solution by inserting this job into all possible i positions of the current schedule, $i = 3, 4, \ldots, n$. The computational complexity of this heuristic is $O(n^2 m)$.

We use the steady state replacement, in which one iteration means producing two offspring individuals. The choice of parents is made by the *tournament* selection operator, in which σ individuals are selected randomly and the best one is returned as a result. Parameter σ is defined manually. The first and second parents are selected by independent applications of this operator. When the new child individuals are generated, they are included in the population, replacing two existing individuals that are found by the "inverse" selection operator. It works as described above, but selects the worst individuals among the randomly selected ones.

Algorithm 1. Basic Scheme of the Memetic Algorithm

1: Build initial population Π using NEH and LS_{ins}.
2: Until a termination condition is satisfied do

  2.1 Choose two individuals p_1 and p_2 from Π.
  2.2 Apply reproduction operator: $(c_1, c_2) = R(p_1, p_2)$.
  2.3 Apply local search operator LS_{ins} to c_1 and c_2 and construct c'_1 and c'_2.
  2.4 Choose individuals q_1, q_2 from Π for replacement.
  2.5 Replace q_1 and q_2 by c'_1 and c'_2.

3: Return the best found individual.

The reproduction operator consists of crossover and mutation. Three crossovers, the *Order Crossover* (OX), the *Partially Mapped Crossover* (PMX), and the *Cycle Crossover* (CX), are implemented (see e.g. [4]), the choice between them is made randomly with equal probability. Note that we use order-based and position-based crossover operators: OX preserve the absolute positions in the sequence of elements of one parent individual and the relative positions of those from the other; PMX partially copies values of genes from parents, and the rest positions are filled by the pairwise exchanges between parents; in CX a value of each gene is copied from one of the values of this gene in the parent solutions. Two mutation operators are used. The first one, M_{swap}, selects two random positions and swaps the values in these positions. The second operator, M_{ins}, randomly selects a gene and inserts its value at a new randomly selected position shifting the middle part of the chromosome in the appropriate direction. Moreover, the mutation is applied to an offspring individual one or two or three times, the number of times is chosen randomly.

The local search procedure based on insertion neighborhood is used in the algorithm. We call it LS_{ins}. Note that here a move to the neighbor solution is the same as in the M_{ins} operator, i.e. two positions i and j are selected, and element at position i is inserted in position j. A one step of the LS consists in enumeration of all pairs i and j and performing a best improving move if it exists (best improvement strategy). The enumeration part is done in parallel and implemented for running on a Graphics Processing Unit. A GPU has a highly parallel processor with hundreds or thousands cores that is now widely used not only for graphics rendering but also for general purpose computing. The SIMD (Single Instruction, Multiple Data) architecture of the GPU suits well for tasks where the same function must be executed large number of times in many parallel threads.

In our implementation, each thread computes cost function for some pair i and j. Note that the program code of one step of LS_{ins} is different for the cases

$i < j$ (ForeInsertion) and $j < i$ (BackInsertion), so they are implemented as different procedures. The mapping between values i, j and the thread id is done in the most evident way illustrated below (considering the case $i > j$).

i \ j	0 1 2 3
1	0
2	1 2
3	3 4 5
4	6 7 8 9

For instance, the thread with $id = 7$ operates with $i = 4, j = 1$.

To keep the memory consumption and the transfer costs between the CPU and the GPU, all the threads share the same current solution $\pi = (\pi_1, \ldots, \pi_n)$. Since its size is relatively small, the time required to copy it to the GPU is negligible. The neighbor permutations are not generated explicitly, instead the required elements are obtained when necessary, i.e. in the case $i > j$ it holds $\pi'_j = \pi_i$, $\pi'_k = \pi_{k-1}$ if $j < k \leq i$, and $\pi'_k = \pi_k$ otherwise. For the case $i < j$, the correspondence is done similarly. The input data of the problem, i.e. the matrix of processing times is loaded to the constant memory at the beginning of the computations.

As a result of execution of all the threads, a set of cost values for all possible moves is obtained and the best one is selected. The search for the best move is also done in parallel using a *reduction* step, in which the whole set is divided in smaller parts, each part is searched for the minimal element, then a minimum is found among the obtained elements. When the best pair i, j is found, the improving neighbor solution is built on the CPU.

Unfortunately, the GPU approach requires to implement the objective function evaluation twice: in the CPU code of the fitness function, and in the GPU kernel, but these are mostly the same copy/paste parts of the code.

On each iteration of LS_{ins}, the case $i < j$ or $j < i$ is selected randomly, then the best move under this condition is found and applied. The search is stopped when neither of two cases improves the current solution. This approach helps to adjust the algorithm for the GPU architecture and introduces some randomness to the local search.

The LS_{ins} is widely used for the FSSP and many authors report its advantage. We also tested an adaptive LS in parallel version on a GPU, where three neighborhoods: insertion, swap and optimization of the subsequences are combined. However, a preliminary experiment did not demonstrate statistical significant improvements of such approach. So, we apply only LS_{ins} in our main computational experiment.

To prevent the algorithm to get stuck in the regions of poor local optima, the following restart rule is applied (see e.g. [1]): The memetic algorithm performs the first $Iter_{min}$ iterations unconditionally. After that, each time the algorithm finds a new record solution, the execution time since the last restart (i.e. the last rebuild of the population) is registered and the same amount of time is given for the algorithm to continue. In the experiments it was observed that in some rare cases this may lead to very long restarts, so the parameter $T_r^{\max}$ was introduced, which defines the limit of the amount of time given to the algorithm after the last record hitting.

3   Implementation Details and Experimental Results

For the computational evaluation, our memetic algorithm (denoted MA$_{PLS}$) was coded in C++ and compiled with g++ 5.5.0 with O3 optimization flag under 64 bit Ubuntu Linux 18.04. The GPU part of LS was implemented in C with CUDA toolkit 8.0 (https://developer.nvidia.com/cuda-80-ga2-download-archive). In the experiments the following equipment is used: CPU Intel i5-9400F 2.90 GHz and GPU Tesla C2075. We observed that for the largest considered instances (with 200 jobs) the local search on the GPU is about eight times faster than the similar sequential local search on one core of the CPU.

In the preliminary tests the algorithm settings were tuned as follows. The population size is 200, the tournament size for the selection operator is $\sigma = 10$, the minimal number of iterations is $Iter_{min} = 1000$. For each instance MA$_{PLS}$ made 20 independent runs consisting of three restarts. The experiments were done on the well known benchmarks of Reeves [21] and Taillard [27]. The considered instances and their sizes are given in Table 1. The values of parameter T_r^{max} (see Sect. 2) in seconds were adjusted manually depending on the problem size and are also given in this table.

Table 1. Problem sizes and time limits

Jobs	Machines	Instances	T_r^{max}	T_r^{max}(no wait)
50	10	rec31,...,rec35	7	3
75	20	rec37,...,rec41	20	6
50	20	ta51,...,ta60	10	3
100	10	ta71,...,ta80	20	5
100	20	ta81,...,ta90	30	7

3.1   Comparison to Known Algorithms for the Classic Flowshop

The proposed memetic algorithm MA$_{PLS}$ is initially evaluated on the permutation flowshop scheduling problem. For a comparison, three evolutionary algorithms from the literature are considered: the hybrid backtracking search algorithm (HBS) [13], the memetic algorithm (MA) [19], and the parallel hybrid method (MA+MIG) [20]. All the considered algorithms construct the initial population using NEH-based heuristics and randomly, and apply local search with the insertion neighborhood.

HBS [13] is an evolutionary algorithm using specific population management strategy with backtracking search. Initial population is constructed randomly, except for one individual, which is build by NEH-approach. The algorithm incorporates three order-based crossovers, random insertion local search, and swap-, insertion-, and inverse-type mutations. It was executed on Pentium Dule-Core 3 GHz processor, 4 Gb RAM.

MA [19] iteratively applies order crossover, shift mutation, and two problem-specific heuristics (gap filling and job shifting). The initial population is generated by Johnson's algorithm [12], NEH-based heuristics and randomly. A restart mechanism is also used. The algorithm [19] was executed on Intel Core i7 2.8 GHz, 4 Gb RAM.

MA+MIG [20] is a parallel hybrid method, that combines memetic algorithm and multi-CPU-threaded iterated greedy (MIG) algorithm (one thread is used for the MA and seven threads for MIG). The population in MA has the ternary tree structure. The initial population is constructed by NEH and greedy heuristics, and randomly. Each iteration of the MA includes optimal 1-point crossover, inversion mutation and local improvements. MIG is based on the insertion neighborhood, and runs concurrently with the MA. A restarting rule and a migration of individuals between the algorithms are applied. MA+MIG was tested on Dual Xeon E5405 (Quad core) 2.0 GHz, 32 Gb RAM (unfortunately, the authors did not report the running time of MA+MIG on the considered instances with 20 machines from [27]).

The results of four considered algorithms for the classic permutation flowshop problem are given in Table 2. The first column shows the instance name. Column C^* indicates the optimal or best-known objective values. The performance of the algorithms is evaluated by the relative error $r = (C - C^*)/C^* \times 100\%$, where C is the objective value of the solution, found by the algorithm. In the table, the minimal, average, and maximal errors are reported in the corresponding columns. Empty cells in the table mean that the results were not published for these instances. In addition, the test instances were solved by the general purpose local search based optimization package LocalSolver (https://www.localsolver.com/). For each instance, one run with the time limit equal to the average execution time of MA$_{PLS}$ was performed, the relative errors are shown in the last column. Table 3 demonstrates the relative errors and run times averaged over series. The full results for each individual run are available at https://github.com/pborisovsky/flowshop-gpu.

As we can see from Tables 2 and 3, the newly proposed MA$_{PLS}$ outperforms HBS and MA in terms of relative errors, The maximal relative error of MA$_{PLS}$ is less than the minimal error of HBS on all considered instances from [21]. The average relative error of the resulting solution for MA$_{PLS}$ is 0.6%, while that of MA is 0.8% over 30 tested instances from [27]. Note that the running time of MA and HBS was similar to the run time presented in this study for our algorithm.

We also carried out the statistical analysis of experimental data using the Wilcoxon test. The results indicate that the difference between the record values of MA$_{PLS}$ and MA is statistically significant at level $\alpha \leq 0.05$ on series from [27].

Table 2. Relative percentage error for the classic flowshop

Name	C^*	MA$_{\text{PLS}}$			HBS			MA		MA+MIG			Local
		r_{min}	r_{avg}	r_{max}	r_{min}	r_{avg}	r_{max}	r_{min}	r_{avg}	r_{min}	r_{avg}	r_{max}	Solver
rec31	3045	0.26	0.26	0.26	0.43	1.91	2.66						1.84
rec33	3114	0	0	0	0	0.59	1.28						0.0
rec35	3277	0	0	0	0	0	0						0.0
rec37	4951	0.3	0.76	1.19	1.92	2.93	4.2						4.97
rec39	5087	0.65	0.69	0.88	0.9	1.88	3.38						1.97
rec41	4960	0.3	0.63	1.17	1.69	2.72	3.55						2.88
ta51	3847	0.47	0.83	1.2				1.2	1.21	0.39	0.59	0.7	2.7
ta52	3704	0.24	0.31	0.59				0.3	0.44	0.11	0.24	0.35	3.46
ta53	3640	0.16	0.68	1.13				0.99	1.03	0.25	0.7	0.88	3.08
ta54	3719	0.43	0.69	0.91				0.56	0.75	0.38	0.66	0.86	1.91
ta55	3610	0.11	0.48	0.83				0.19	0.4	0.22	0.49	0.61	3.24
ta56	3679	0.33	0.61	1.06				0.43	0.68	0.14	0.49	0.71	2.94
ta57	3704	0.16	0.48	0.81				0.54	0.73	0.27	0.54	0.7	2.43
ta58	3691	0.51	0.78	1.11				0.57	1.14	0.27	0.81	1.03	2.36
ta59	3741	0.4	0.67	1.2				0.56	0.71	0.35	0.53	0.7	2.06
ta60	3756	0.29	0.47	0.67				0.67	0.83	0.29	0.32	0.37	1.28
ta71	5770	0	0.01	0.02				0	0.03				0.12
ta72	5349	0	0.19	0.24				0.24	0.24				0.24
ta73	5676	0.05	0.05	0.05				0.05	0.05				0.26
ta74	5781	0	0.47	0.78				0.19	0.24				0.78
ta75	5467	0	0.29	0.55				0.05	0.07				0.8
ta76	5303	0	0.08	0.09				0.09	0.09				0.34
ta77	5595	0.02	0.06	0.09				0.13	0.19				0.18
ta78	5617	0.11	0.34	0.41				0.2	0.26				0.82
ta79	5871	0.07	0.1	0.34				0.22	0.28				0.97
ta80	5845	0.05	0.05	0.05				0.05	0.05				0.62
ta81	6202	0.69	1.02	1.34				1.42	1.52	0.42	0.82	1.02	2.21
ta82	6183	0.55	0.91	1.33				1.34	1.36	0.73	0.91	1.1	2.35
ta83	6271	0.38	0.74	1.02				1.29	1.39	0.24	0.48	0.62	2.01
ta84	6269	0.49	0.83	1.55				1.37	1.43	0.16	0.48	0.54	2.71
ta85	6314	0.21	0.74	1.36				1.19	1.31	0.25	0.51	0.65	2.33
ta86	6364	0.03	1.42	1.93				1.37	1.46	0.17	0.71	0.94	1.98
ta87	6268	0.49	0.77	1.08				1.01	1.07	0.4	0.68	0.88	1.8
ta88	6401	0.53	0.81	1.41				1.45	1.57	0.61	0.81	1.03	2.55
ta89	6275	0.41	0.79	1.08				1.07	1.11	0.4	0.76	0.92	1.88
ta90	6434	0.19	0.82	1.51				1.15	1.29	0.3	0.62	0.79	1.63

Algorithms MA$_{\text{PLS}}$ and MA+MIG demonstrate competitive relative errors on problems of sizes 50×20 and 100×20. The results of LocalSolver look quite good for the general-purpose solver, but not superior to the considered evolutionary algorithms.

Table 3. Comparison of the algorithms for the classic flowshop

Size	MA$_{\text{PLS}}$			HBS			MA			MA+MIG		Local
	$r_{\min}$	r_{avg}	Time	$r_{\min}$	r_{avg}	Time	$r_{\min}$	r_{avg}	Time	$r_{\min}$	r_{avg}	Solver
50 × 10	0.09	0.09	15.67	0.14	0.83	36.7						0.61
75 × 20	0.42	0.69	127.33	1.5	2.51	216.3						3.27
50 × 20	0.31	0.6	49				0.6	0.79	65	0.27	0.54	2.55
100 × 10	0.03	0.16	49.1				0.12	0.15	70			0.51
100 × 20	0.4	0.89	194.8				1.27	1.35	142	0.37	0.68	2.15

3.2   Comparison to Known Algorithms for the No-Wait Flowshop

A similar experiment was carried out for the no-wait flowshop problem. No modifications of the algorithm were done except the fitness calculation. For the comparison, genetic algorithms HGA [28] and GA-VNS [11] were considered.

HGA [28] uses the population management strategy known as elitist recombination. The initial individuals are generated at random. The orthogonal-array-based crossover with three or six cut points, exchange mutation, and two reduced variants of insertion local search (α-range insertion search and insertion search with cut-and-repair) are utilized in the GA [28]. A perturbation is applied by means of mutation operators. The algorithm [28] was executed on Intel Pentium III 1266 MHz, 1 Gb RAM.

GA-VNS [11] uses the steady state replacement, Block Order Crossover and insertion mutation. Individuals are improved by a variable neighborhood search based on swap and insertion neighborhoods. The initial population is constricted by the same randomized analog of NEH-heuristic as in our algorithm. The algorithm [11] was executed on Intel Pentium IV 3.2 GHz, 512 Mb RAM.

The same test instances were used in the experiment for no-wait FSSP, the optimal makespan values were collected from [14]. The results are given in Tables 4 and 5 in the form identical to the classic flowshop. Negative deviations for HGA indicate that the records reported in [28] are less than the values given in column C^*, which contradicts with [14], where the authors claim that the provided solutions are exact optima. The average relative errors of GA-VNS presented in paper [11] were copied to Table 5 (marked by underline). These errors correspond to upper bounds from [11], which do not coincide with optimal makespans from [14]. So the relative deviations for GA-VNS will be greater than in [11] if instead of upper bounds we take the optimal values.

As seen from Tables 4 and 5 our algorithm MA$_{\text{PLS}}$ presents very competitive results in terms of relative errors. Optimal solutions were found on 13 out of 36 instances, and the maximal relative error is no more than 0.8%. The average relative error for MA$_{\text{PLS}}$ is approximately by the factor 4 smaller than that of HGA on 22 Taillard's instances, where the calculated deviations are non-negative for HGA (the difference between the record values is statistically significant at level $\alpha \leq 0.05$ on these problems). Notice that MA$_{\text{PLS}}$ is more time

Table 4. Relative percentage error for the no-wait flowshop

Name	C^*	MA$_{PLS}$			GA-VNS			HGA			Local
		r_{min}	r_{avg}	r_{max}	r_{min}	r_{avg}	r_{max}	r_{min}	r_{avg}	r_{max}	Solver
rec31	4307	0	0.13	0.35	0.18	0.51	0.76	0.14	0.5		1.49
rec33	4424	0	0.21	0.45	0.09	0.71	1.49	0.16	0.71		2.08
rec35	4397	0	0.08	0.18	0	0.4	0.72	0	0.48		2.25
rec37	8008	0.14	0.28	0.55	0.23	0.86	1.32	0.21	0.51		3.5
rec39	8419	0.08	0.22	0.42	0.11	0.76	1.2	0.32	0.76		3.88
rec41	8437	0.01	0.22	0.4	0.15	0.68	1.01	0.53	0.65		4.43
ta51	6129	0	0	0				0.15	0.34	0.7	6.04
ta52	5725	0	0.01	0.09				−0.07	0.46	1.14	5.66
ta53	5862	0	0.1	0.19				−0.26	0.38	1.14	5.41
ta54	5788	0	0	0.03				−0.12	0.29	0.67	4.22
ta55	5886	0	0.01	0.1				0.08	0.4	1.09	4.09
ta56	5863	0	0.13	0.2				0.2	0.47	0.82	3.38
ta57	5962	0	0.07	0.13				−0.42	0.2	0.65	3.02
ta58	5926	0	0.07	0.24				−0.12	0.42	0.76	3.68
ta59	5876	0	0	0				−0.63	−0.04	0.39	4.94
ta60	5957	0	0.02	0.12				−0.37	0.11	0.37	2.3
ta71	8055	0.26	0.4	0.53				0.74	1.47	2.17	3.34
ta72	7853	0.39	0.59	0.85				1.69	2.48	3.16	3.32
ta73	8016	0.21	0.38	0.64				0.51	1.57	2.48	3.44
ta74	8328	0.19	0.35	0.6				−0.01	1.31	2.13	3.41
ta75	7936	0.3	0.47	0.74				0.69	1.39	2.02	4.62
ta76	7773	0.23	0.47	0.72				0.64	1.42	2.24	4.53
ta77	7846	0.14	0.37	0.65				0.88	2.05	3	4.28
ta78	7880	0.28	0.45	0.63				0.75	2.15	2.86	4.31
ta79	8131	0.33	0.48	0.64				1.17	1.96	2.68	3.8
ta80	8092	0.28	0.51	0.77				1.16	2.02	3.06	4.45
ta81	10675	0.21	0.35	0.59				0.66	1.42	2.41	5.62
ta82	10562	0.3	0.44	0.8				0.88	1.9	2.7	4.66
ta83	10587	0.2	0.41	0.6				0.8	1.45	2.21	3.58
ta84	10588	0.2	0.33	0.51				0.4	0.87	1.97	4.88
ta85	10506	0.16	0.35	0.61				0.4	1.45	2.58	4.15
ta86	10623	0.17	0.45	0.71				0.72	1.22	2.17	5.23
ta87	10793	0.2	0.31	0.44				0.32	1.12	2.21	3.95
ta88	10801	0.12	0.35	0.54				0.57	0.96	1.77	3.73
ta89	10703	0.14	0.33	0.48				0.45	1.46	2.43	4.34
ta90	10747	0.25	0.43	0.69				0.44	1.69	2.98	4.62

consuming than GA-VNS, probably because it does not use some specific properties of the no-wait setting, but the solutions quality of MA$_{PLS}$ is much better. Again, general-purpose software LocalSolver shows good performance, but is still inferior to the considered evolutionary algorithms.

The proposed memetic algorithm is implemented in a very generic way using little knowledge of the particular problem, and it can be easily applied to any

Table 5. Comparison of the algorithms for the no-wait flowshop

Size	MA$_{\text{PLS}}$			GA-VNS			HGA			Local
	$r_{\min}$	r_{avg}	time	$r_{\min}$	r_{avg}	Time	$r_{\min}$	r_{avg}	Time	Solver
50 × 10	0	0.14	8	0.09	0.54	0.33	0.1	0.56	0.25	1.94
75 × 20	0.08	0.24	41.33	0.16	0.77	0.82	0.35	0.64	1.27	3.94
50 × 20	0	0.04	9.4	<u>0.07</u>	<u>0.47</u>	0.35	−0.16	0.3	3	4.27
100 × 10	0.26	0.45	56.5	<u>0.43</u>	<u>0.85</u>	2.18	0.82	1.78	67	3.95
100 × 20	0.19	0.38	75.3	<u>0.42</u>	<u>0.91</u>	2.18	0.56	1.35	83	4.48

other optimization problem on permutations. Of course the algorithm may be not competitive for such problems like TSP, for which many advanced methods were developed based on the property that the cost function can be fastly updated in local search moves. Besides, other types of neighborhoods are more appropriate for permutation problems with objective functions containing weights of adjacencies between elements. On the other hand, there are many problems that do not have this property (see, e.g., [9,24,25]), and the proposed MA$_{\text{PLS}}$ can be used for their solving.

4   Conclusion

We proposed and experimentally evaluated a unified memetic algorithm for two versions of the permutation flowshop scheduling. The algorithm does not essentially use any special knowledge of a particular problem except the objective function, and may be applied to other problems on permutations. The main feature of the algorithm is the parallel local search implemented for executing on GPU. This study allows to estimate the advantages of using GPUs in the design of metaheuristics. In our experiments, the proposed algorithm showed better or similar performance comparing to other evolutionary algorithms specially adjusted for solving only one variant of the considered problem. Note that unlike usual processors, GPUs are being rapidly improved, and much better performance can be expected using a newer device. The future research may concentrate on the improvement of parallel local search and its better adjustment for the GPU architecture, and further evaluation and development of this approach for other optimization problems.

Acknowledgements. The research was supported by the Russian Science Foundation, project number 17-18-01536 (Yu. Kovalenko). The experiments were performed using "Tesla" cluster at Omsk branch of Sobolev Institute of Mathematics.

References

1. Borisovsky, P., Dolgui, A., Eremeev, A.: Genetic algorithms for a supply management problem: MIP-recombination vs greedy decoder. Eur. Jour. Oper. Res. **195**(3), 770–779 (2009)

2. Borisovsky, P., Eremeev, A., Kallrath, J.: Multi-product continuous plant scheduling: combination of decomposition, genetic algorithm, and constructive heuristic. Int. J. Prod. Res. **58**, 2677–2695 (2019)
3. Chakroun, I., Melab, N., Mezmaz, M., Tuyttens, D.: Combining multi-core and GPU computing for solving combinatorial optimization problems. J. Parallel Distrib. Comput. **73**(12), 1563–1577 (2013)
4. Cotta, C., Troya, J.: Genetic forma recombination in permutation flowshop problems. Evol. Comput. **6**(1), 25–44 (1998)
5. Eremeev, A.V., Kovalenko, Y.V.: A memetic algorithm with optimal recombination for the asymmetric travelling salesman problem. Memetic Comput. **12**(1), 23–36 (2019). https://doi.org/10.1007/s12293-019-00291-4
6. Essaid, M., Idoumghar, L., Lepagnot, J., Brevilliers, M.: GPU parallelization strategies for metaheuristics: a survey. Int. J. Parallel Emergent Distrib. Syst **34**(5), 497–522 (2018)
7. Garey, M., Johnson, D., Sethi, R.: The complexity of flowshop and jobshop scheduling. Math. Oper. Res. **2**, 117–129 (1976)
8. Grabowski, J., Wodecki, M.: A very fast tabu search algorithm for the permutation flow shop problem with makespan criterion. Comput. Oper. Res. **31**(11), 1891–1909 (2004)
9. Hall, N., Sriskandarajah, C.: A survey of machine scheduling problems with blocking and no-wait in process. Oper. Res. **44**(3), 510–525 (1996)
10. Janiak, A., Janiak, W., Lichtenstein, M.: Tabu search on GPU. J. Univ. Comput. Sci. **14**(14), 2416–2427 (2008)
11. Jarboui, B., Eddaly, M., Siarry, P.: A hybrid genetic algorithm for solving no-wait flowshop scheduling problems. Int. J. Adv. Manuf. Technol. **54**, 1129–1143 (2011)
12. Johnson, S.: Optimal two- and three-stage production schedules with setup times included. Naval Res. Logistics Q. **1**, 61–68 (1954)
13. Lin, Q., Gao, L., Li, X., Zhang, C.: A hybrid backtracking search algorithm for permutation flow-shop scheduling problem. Comput. Ind. Eng. **85**, 437–446 (2015)
14. Lin, S.W., Ying, K.C.: Optimization of makespan for no-wait flowshop scheduling problems using efficient matheuristics. Omega **64**, 115–125 (2016)
15. Liu, B., Wang, L., Jin, Y.H.: An effective hybrid PSO-based algorithm for flow shop scheduling with limited buffers. Comput. Oper. Res. **35**(9), 2791–2806 (2008)
16. Metlicka, M., Davendra, D., Hermann, F., Meier, M., Amann, M.: GPU accelerated NEH algorithm. In: 2014 IEEE Symposium on Computational Intelligence in Production and Logistics Systems (CIPLS), pp. 114–119. IEEE (2014)
17. Nawaz, M., Enscore, E., Ham, I.: A heuristic algorithm for the m-machine, n-job flowshop sequencing problem. OMEGA **11**, 91–95 (1983)
18. Neri, F., Cotta, C., Moscato, P.: Handbook of Memetic Algorithms. Springer, Heidelberg (2012). https://doi.org/10.1007/978-3-642-23247-3
19. Rahman, H., Sarker, R., Essam, D.: A memetic algorithm for permutation flow shop problems. In: 2013 IEEE Congress on Evolutionary Computation, pp. 1618–1625 (2013)
20. Ravetti, M., Riveros, C., Mendes, A.: Parallel hybrid heuristics for the permutation flow shop problem. Ann. Oper. Res. **199**, 269–284 (2012)
21. Reeves, C.: A genetic algorithm for flowshop sequencing. Comput. Oper. Res. **22**(1), 5–13 (1995)
22. Reeves, C., Yamada, T.: Genetic algorithms, path relinking and the flowshop sequencing problem. Evol. Comput. **6**, 45–60 (1998)
23. Rock, H.: The three-machine no-wait flowshop problem is NP-complete. J. Assoc. Comput. Mach. **31**(2), 336–345 (1984)

24. Schryen, G.: Parallel computational optimization in operations research: a new integrative framework, literature review and research directions. Eur. J. Oper. Res. **287**, 1–18 (2020)

25. Schulz, C., Hasle, G., Brodtkorb, A.: GPU computing in discrete optimization. Part II: Survey focused on routing problems. EURO J. Transp. Logistics **2**, 159–186 (2013)

26. Taillard, E.: Some efficient heuristic methods for the flow shop sequencing problem. Eur. J. Oper. Res. **47**, 65–74 (1990)

27. Taillard, E.: Benchmarks for basic scheduling problems. Eur. J. Oper. Res. **64**, 278–285 (1993)

28. Tseng, L.Y., Lin, Y.T.: A hybrid genetic algorithm for no-wait flowshop scheduling problem. Int. J. Prod. Econ. **128**(1), 144–152 (2010)

29. Van Luong, T., Melab, N., Talbi, E.-G.: GPU-based approaches for multiobjective local search algorithms. A case study: the flowshop scheduling problem. In: Merz, P., Hao, J.-K. (eds.) EvoCOP 2011. LNCS, vol. 6622, pp. 155–166. Springer, Heidelberg (2011). https://doi.org/10.1007/978-3-642-20364-0_14

30. Vu, T.T., Derbel, B.: Parallel branch-and-bound in multi-core multi-CPU multi-GPU heterogeneous environments. Future Gener. Comput. Syst. **56**, 95–109 (2016)

31. Wei, K., Sun, X., Chu, H.: Reconstructing permutation table to improve the Tabu search for the PFSP on GPU. J. Supercomput. **73**, 4711–4738 (2017)

Optimizing Robotic Cheetah Leg Parameters Using Evolutionary Algorithms

Maxim Buzdalov$^{(\boxtimes)}$, Sergey Kolyubin, Artem Egorov, and Ivan Borisov

ITMO University, Saint Petersburg, Russia
{mbuzdalov,s.kolyubin,aaegorov,borisovii}@itmo.ru

Abstract. We present a new application suitable for evolutionary algorithms: geometry optimization for robotic applications. Our working example is a robotic cheetah leg, which uses simple control algorithms, but accurately crafted and tuned mechanics to maximize motion efficiency. In this paper we aim at tuning its parameters, such that the joints of the leg follow the desired trajectories as close as possible. Optimization is done in two stages involving just two parameters each.

Even this simply-looking problem presents a challenge to evolutionary algorithms, as it is both ill-conditioned and multimodal. However, we show that choosing a better fitness function that captures our desires in a different way can make the problem much easier.

Keywords: Robotic leg · Fitness function · Multimodal functions

1 Introduction

Development of generative (or computational) design methods and algorithms became a hot topic in CAD-system in general, and robotics in particular, several decades ago [2, 9, 23]. However, with recent developments in machine learning and numerical optimization techniques we expect a new wave to come, bringing not only theoretical achievements, but also a number of interesting implementation examples. Modern methods of structure synthesis are used in various robotic tasks in manufacturing, aquaculture and fishery, technical medicine, automated inspection, entertainment and film making, and others [3, 7, 8, 11, 13, 15, 16, 20–22].

On the other hand, working in different application areas requires understanding of specific design requirements and constraints, which will define the optimization problem framework, including cost function selection. For example, synthesis of the mechanism of the robot feeder was carried out in accordance with the condition of minimum acceleration and speed limits of the end-effector [20]. In [11] synthesis of a surgical robot was carried out according to the parameters of the instrument working area, depending on its position for a serial robot. Various methods have been developed and applied for legged robots in particular.

Supported by Russian Science Foundation grant (project no. 17-79-20341).

Fig. 1. The prototype of the Minitaur mechanism built in the BE2R Lab, ITMO University, based on the concept presented in [17]

In [15] the walking bilateral robot with flexible passive legs has been developed, where each joint has been optimized to ensure smooth movements similar to a human gait. In [8] dynamic synthesis was performed for the jumping robot to reduce the torque on the drivers.

Generative design in general includes topology optimization, nevertheless the problem of robot geometric parameters optimization addressed in this work is an essential part of it. Moreover, for many tasks, especially when we stick to certain manufacturing technologies, doing parametric optimization covers 90% of what is needed and gives more cost-efficient solutions.

This research is motivated by the task to synthesize a structure that would mechanically repeat the desired behaviour of the bio-inspired robotic cheetah leg mechanism (see Fig. 1 for an example of our experimental test-bed). Same goal can be achieved if we leave system design as is and force desired motion by means of control algorithms along, but this approach has its bottlenecks. At first, it is much less energy efficient and requires much more complicated control systems both in terms of hardware (sensors and actuators) and algorithms.

In this sense, our work is related to recent developments of the Disney-Research team in the field of mechanism optimization. Mainly, they are solving animatronics tasks [3,13,21], jumping and walking robots projects [5,14].

In our previous attempt, we used the Pattern Search optimizer [10] offered by the MATLAB environment. Since Pattern Search is an advanced form of continuous local search, which has good convergence properties but a lack of the global search ability, our next step, which we attempt in this paper, is to investigate how global optimizers perform on the same task. For this stage, we chose the representative continuous evolutionary optimizers from the two most prominent families which are known to perform well in various benchmarks: Differential Evolution [18] and Covariance Matrix Adaptation Evolution Strategy, or CMA-ES [6].

We should mention that even though this case study is related to legged robot design, the proposed approach is quite general to be applied for mechanism optimization of various robotic systems. On the other hand, these steps in rigid-body kinematics optimization can be a starting point for further studies including automatic elastic elements allocation and its elasto-static parameters adjustment, which was done manually in authors' preceding work [1].

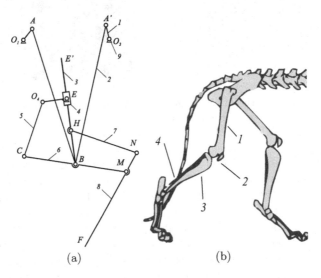

(a)   (b)

Fig. 2. a) The mechanism of the Cheetah Leg: (1) cranks, (2) connecting rods, (3) crank arm/femur, (4) brick, (5) rocker, (6) connecting rod/tibia, (7) rocker/fibula, (8) output link/ankle, (9) frame, F is a contact point with ground/feet. b) Cheetah skeleton: (1) femur, (2) patella, (3) tibia, (4) fibula

The rest of the paper is organized in the following way. Sect. 2 sets some preliminaries including mechanical design issues to be taken into account, framework of the proposed parametric optimization, and description of the cost function used in our previous studies. Section 3 presents main contribution of this work, which is improving parametric convergence by means of evolutionary algorithms along with a newly suggested cost function. We also put here optimization results together with our observations on what properties the mechanism optimization problem has to make it an interesting challenge for evolutionary algorithms implementation. Section 4 concludes.

2   Preliminaries

2.1   Leg Mechanism Description

Topology of our robotic leg is inspired by the animal cheetah's muscle-skeletal structure (see Fig. 2(b)). But completely copying the legs' structure makes not much sense, instead we want a mechanism that will reproduce desired animal-like motions, which is of interest for animatronic designs.

The leg can be divided in three parts: the hip, the knee, and the foot. The Minitaur mechanism (Fig. 2(a)) is a good choice for the robotic hip because of the following reasons. It can produce a large range of different gaits, controlling the difference in the angles of the input links and their speed. It is compact so the height and length of the jump does not depend on the width of the mechanism [17]. The input shafts O_1 and O_2 are rotating cranks O_1A and O_3A' to actuate leg mechanism. The mechanism of the Minotaur is responsible for moving the patella (see B on Fig. 2(a)).

The knee mechanism (see EO_4CB on Fig. 2(a)) controls the angle between the femur and the tibia within the specified range (see $E'B$ and 6 on Fig. 2(a)). The knee mechanism is attached to the output link of the Minitaur mechanism (thigh) and to the brick (see EH on Fig. 2(a)).

The last group of the leg are tibia, fibula and ankle and they execute pantograph functions (see BM, 7 and 8 on Fig. 2(a)).

2.2   Decomposition and Constraints

Capturing rigid-body kinematics only, the mechanism can be described as a function transforming the input values like rotating cranks' angles to output values like contact point coordinates in Cartesian space. This function exists in the kinematic state space, which can be represented as all possible output values. This space can be narrowed depending on constraints imposed on kinematic parameters of the mechanism.

In our case, this transformation is indeed the forward kinematics nonlinear function, and lengths of the links are its parameters. So, in order to set the optimization problem first we need to decide, which parameters should be *a priori* fixed and which can be optimized, and what are upper and lower bounds for the latter ones. This choice is mostly based on mechanical design limitations.

Since the multi-link mechanism under consideration has quite many parameters that can be optimized, we decided to divide it to subsystems, define constraints and desired behaviour for each one, and therefore split optimization procedure into stages. This decomposition is illustrated in Fig. 3.

In order to save space and do not bother the reader with mechanical details we will not elaborate here on imposed design constraints, but mention that is were reasoned by conditions for the existence of linkages, overall mechanism dimensions' and structural strength's limitations. As the result, for example, for the hip subsystem length's of rods AB and $A'B$ (upper bounded by 260 mm) and phase difference between input shafts $0° < \beta < 180°$ were chosen as parameters for optimization, while the rest of subsystem's geometric parameters were fixed to pre-defined values. The choice of parameters allows to use basic box constraint handling techniques.

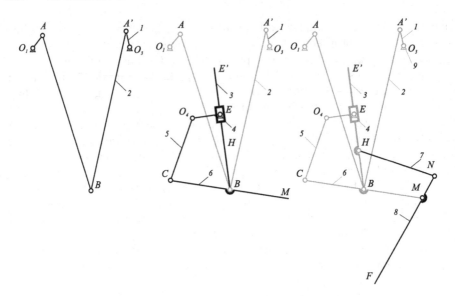

Fig. 3. Leg mechanism decomposition for optimization, from left to right: the hip, the knee, and the foot structures. Active black indicates a structure to be optimized.

2.3   Existing Cost Function

Our goal is to find geometric parameters values such that characteristic points of our mechanism will follow a desired trajectory, while the latter one is defined by certain key features important for locomotion like stride length and height, path curvature, and so on.

Driven by intention to minimize computational load, in our previous study we used the following optimization cost function (see [4] for details). We compared perimeters and areas for the calculated cyclic path and the desired ones as major metrics for curve-fitting. But since these two aggregated measures are not enough to guarantee that curve shapes will be close to each other, we augmented it with matching heights and lengths of a stride, i.e. minimizing distances between most left, right, top, and down points of the desired and calculated trajectories respectively (see Fig. 4(b)). These points were selected as special, because they break the trajectory into phases of jerk, leg pull-up, leg extension, and landing.

To simplify calculations, we approximated path traced by a point as a polygon, specified by pairs of the planar coordinates of its vertices. In this case the area S and perimeter P of the polygon were calculated by splitting it into segments, which are defined based on the polygon vertices locations (see Fig. 4(a)):

$$S = S_{N,1} + \sum_{i=1}^{N-1} S_{i,i+1}, \quad P = L_{N,1} + \sum_{i=2}^{N} L_{i-1,i},$$

where $S_{i,j} = \frac{(x_j - x_i) \cdot (y_j + y_i)}{2}$ is the area of the trapezoid with indexes i and j denote respective points numbering, and $L_{j,i} = \sqrt{(x_i - x_j)^2 + (y_i - y_j)^2}$.

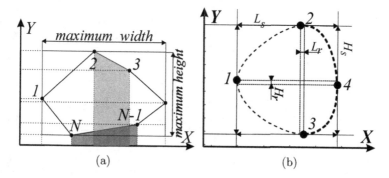

Fig. 4. a) A polygon that is constructed from an array of coordinates of a curve. b) 1, 4 are the leftmost and rightmost, and 2, 3 are the highest and lowest trajectory points respectively. L_s and H_s are stride length and height respectively

The resulting optimization cost function was calculated as

$$F = (S^\star - S)^2 + (P^\star - P)^2 + \sum_{i=1}^{4} ((x_i^\star - x_i)^2 + (y_i^\star - y_i)^2),$$

where S, $S^\star$, P and $P^\star$ denote the area and the perimeter of the polygons related to the calculated and the desired trajectories respectively (see Fig. 4(b)).

However, as it will be shown later in this paper, such cost function selection has certain disadvantages in terms of parametric convergence, especially when using evolutionary algorithms.

3 Experiments and Observations

In our experiments, we consider optimization of the first two stages: the hip (Fig. 3, left) and the knee (Fig. 3, middle). Both of them involve optimizing two variables, which gives an advantage of the convenient visual analysis of the behaviour of optimizers. We used the following optimizers:

- Pattern Search, proposed in [10]; the MATLAB implementation was used with the following parameters: maximum of 40 iterations (which was enough for complete convergence), mesh size 10^{-4}, mesh contraction factor 0.5, and the use of complete poll.
- Differential Evolution [18]: the DE/1/rand/bin variant with population size 40, crossover probability 0.5, differential weight sampled from [0.5; 1.5].
- CMA-ES [6]: the official implementation[1] with its default settings.

The computation budget was set to 400 for all the methods (however, Pattern Search tends to converge prematurely much earlier). As fitness functions involve modeling and hence are expensive, we performed only 10 runs for each optimizer.

---

[1] https://github.com/CMA-ES/pycma.

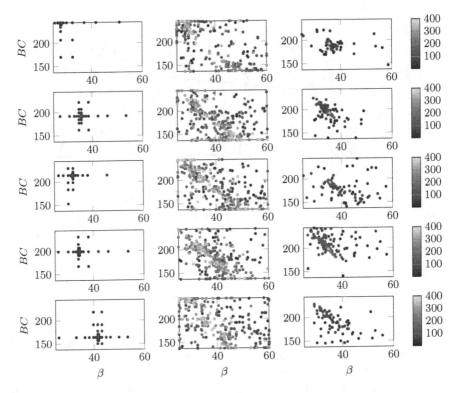

Fig. 5. Convergence in the search space: Pattern Search (left column), Differential Evolution (middle column) and CMA-ES (right column) on the old function for hip. Runs ranked 1, 3, 5, 7, 9 according to the final fitness value are shown. Point colors show the number of fitness evaluation

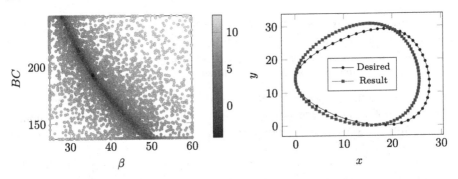

Fig. 6. Left: The fitness landscape of the old function for hip, with points colored according to the logarithm of fitness minus 8.88. Right: The best found trajectory for hip with fitness 8.8936 according to the old function

The considered problems have only basic box constraints, which Differential Evolution and Pattern Search can handle out of the box, so the only change was to use 10^9 plus the distance to the feasible region as a fitness value for infeasible queries made by CMA-ES.

We discuss the **hip stage** first. Figure 5 displays five out of ten runs for each optimizer, chosen based on the resulting fitness values in order to showcase more of the possible outcomes of these algorithms. The colors in this figure are based on the number of the fitness function evaluations corresponding to each point, so these plots visually illustrate the convergence behaviour of the optimizers. One can see that Pattern Search converges very quickly, CMA-ES tests a larger region of the search space before convergence, and Differential Evolution is still scattered very much across the search space after 10 iterations. More experiments show that, for the latter, a wide range of population sizes from 10 to 40 results in roughly the same behaviour.

The best fitness values out of these ten runs were 8.9644 for Pattern Search, 8.9639 for Differential Evolution and 8.8936 for CMA-ES, and the medians were 10.4478, 9.4342 and 9.5830, respectively. The Wilcoxon rank sum test [12,19] with the one-sided hypotheses based on these median values yields the following p-values:

- 0.0144 for Pattern Search vs CMA-ES,
- 0.0446 for Pattern Search vs Differential Evolution,
- 0.5733 for CMA-ES vs Differential Evolution,

which indicates that Pattern Search is worse on this problem than either of the evolutionary algorithms, whereas the latter perform similarly.

Figure 6 presents all the queries made by these algorithms combined on a single plot, where the color represents the logarithm of the fitness value (the darker the color, the better the fitness). As one can see, the fitness landscape of this problem resembles the Rosenbrock function with a number of local optima in the valley. It appears to be quite hard: in our case CMA-ES found a local optimum overlooked by other methods.

Figure 6 also presents the desired hip trajectory and the best found individual, according to the fitness function. We can see that, although the overall shape is captured correctly, there is still a visible difference between the trajectories.

In an attempt to escape from the complexities imposed by the fitness landscape of the existing fitness function, we have designed a **new one**, which is only marginally harder to compute, but captures the intended qualities better. This function is evaluated as follows:

- the desired trajectory and the one generated by the evaluated individual are represented as piecewise linear functions $D(t)$ and $A(t)$ of the parameter $t \in [0; 1]$ returning two-dimensional points, where $t = 0$ means the first trajectory point, $t = 1$ the last one, and other values are interpolated linearly;
- the value $\int_0^1 (D(t) - A(t))^2 dt$ is computed using the two-pointer approach.

For the new fitness function, Fig. 7 and 8 represent the same data as for the original function. Based on the presented scatter plots, the convergence properties of the algorithms appears to remain the same. The best fitness values out of

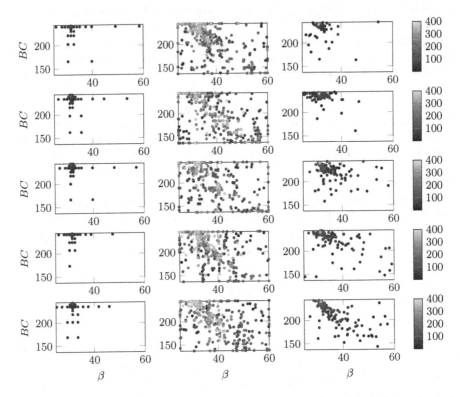

Fig. 7. Convergence in the search space: Pattern Search (left column), Differential Evolution (middle column) and CMA-ES (right column) on the new function for hip. Runs ranked 1, 3, 5, 7, 9 according to the final fitness value are shown. Point colors show the number of fitness evaluation

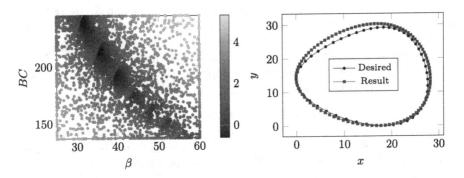

Fig. 8. Left: The fitness landscape of the new function for hip, with points colored according to the logarithm of fitness. Right: The best found trajectory for hip with fitness 0.545307 according to the new function

Table 1. Statistical summary of the results for the knee stage experiments

	Pattern search	Differential evolution	CMA-ES
Old function			
Min	22.5552	22.8797	22.5541
Median	33.2892	24.1715	28.1541
New function			
Min	6.3197	6.3180	6.3183
Median	7.9530	6.3197	6.6584

the ten runs are 0.54546 for Pattern Search, 0.56200 for Differential Evolution and 0.54531 for CMA-ES, whereas the respective medians are 0.58083, 0.60336 and 0.57958. The p-values produced by the Wilcoxon rank sum tests are:

- 0.2644 for Differential Evolution vs Pattern Search,
- 0.09516 for Differential Evolution vs CMA-ES,
- 0.05256 for Pattern Search vs CMA-ES,

so all the algorithms now perform quite similarly. Together with the landscape observation on the left of Fig. 8 this indicates that the fitness landscape appears to be much easier, although still multimodal. One can also see on the right of Fig. 8 that the approximation of the desired trajectory is now much better.

The same experiments with both functions performed for the **knee stage** demonstrate mostly the same trends (Fig. 9, 10, 11 and 12), although the fitness landscapes appear to be easier. Tables 1 and 2 present the basic statistical evaluation. They indicate, in particular, that all the algorithms are quite similar on the old function, whereas Differential Evolution performs somewhat better on the new function.

Table 2. The p-values by the Wilcoxon rank sum test for the knee stage experiments

Null hypothesis	P.S. $\geq$ CMA	CMA $\geq$ D.E.	P.S. $\geq$ D.E.
Old function	0.0615	0.1237	0.0828
New function	0.2644	0.0014	0.0057

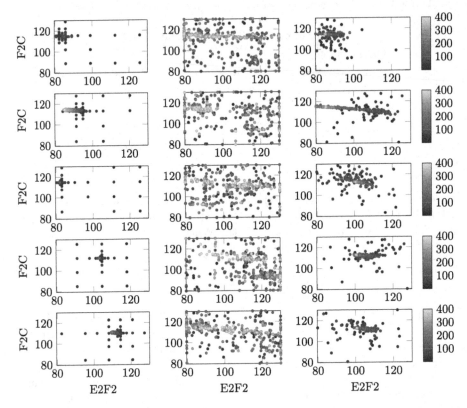

Fig. 9. Convergence in the search space: Pattern Search (left column), Differential Evolution (middle column) and CMA-ES (right column) on the old function for knee. Runs ranked 1, 3, 5, 7, 9 according to the final fitness value are shown. Point colors show the number of fitness evaluation

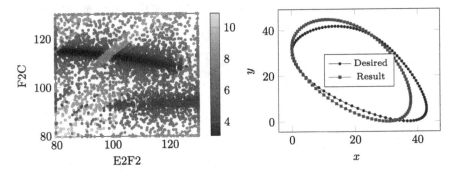

Fig. 10. Left: The fitness landscape of the old function for knee, with points colored according to the logarithm of fitness. Right: The best found trajectory for knee with fitness 22.5541 according to the old function

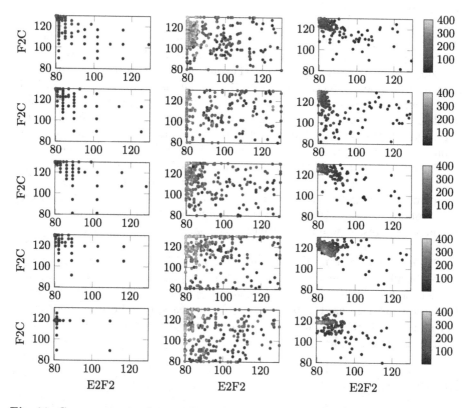

Fig. 11. Convergence in the search space: Pattern Search (left column), Differential Evolution (middle column) and CMA-ES (right column) on the new function for knee. Runs ranked 1, 3, 5, 7, 9 according to the final fitness value are shown. Point colors show the number of fitness evaluation

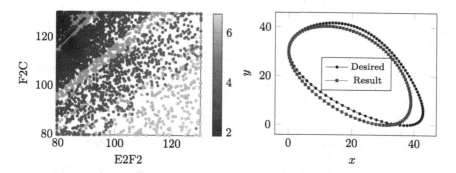

Fig. 12. Left: The fitness landscape of the new function for knee, with points colored according to the logarithm of fitness. Right: The best found trajectory for knee with fitness 6.31798 according to the new function

4   Conclusion

We have investigated the problem of parameter tuning for the robotic cheetah leg from the viewpoint of evolutionary computation. Regarding the considered methods, both CMA-ES and differential evolution tend to outperform the previously used local search method Pattern Search in terms of solution quality. Which of the considered evolutionary algorithms is better, depends on the particular problem variation in question. Based on the observed scatter plots, CMA-ES is typically better at exploitation, whereas Differential Evolution seems to be stronger at exploration, however, the overall difference is not very large.

The investigation of whether the recent advances in the corresponding algorithmic families have an impact in these problems is a possible future work. We also plan to investigate how the simultaneous optimization of all the parameters of the robotic cheetah leg relates to the already-considered chain of independent optimization runs, as well as to attempt the complete structure synthesis rather than just geometry optimization.

The most insightful part is that a choice of the fitness function, even among those which have the same global optimum and express the same desires, can significantly influence the quality of the solutions and the hardness of the problem. The fitness function used in previous studies appears to be both ill-conditioned and multimodal, which makes the problem especially hard, whereas the new function is much simpler.

References

1. Borisov, I.I., Larkina, A.E., Egorov, A.A., Kulagin, I.A., Kolyubin, S.A., Stramigioli, S.: Study on elastic elements allocation for energy-efficient robotic cheetah leg. In: Proceedings of IEEE/RSJ International Conference on Intelligent Robotics, pp. 1696–1701 (2019)
2. Cagan, J., Campbell, M.I., Finger, S., Tomiyama, T.: A framework for computational design synthesis: model and applications. J. Comput. Inf. Sci. Eng. **5**(3), 171–181 (2005)
3. Coros, S., et al.: Computational design of mechanical characters. ACM Trans. Graph. **32**(4), 1 (2013)
4. Egorov, A., Larkina, A., Borisov, I., Kolyubin, S., Stramigioli, S.: Cascaded constrained optimization for cheetah-inspired galloping robot leg mechanism design. In: IFAC World Congress (2020, accepted for publication)
5. Ha, S., Coros, S., Alspach, A., Kim, J., Yamane, K.: Task-based limb optimization for legged robots. In: IEEE/RSJ International Conference on Intelligent Robots and Systems (2016)
6. Hansen, N., Ostermeier, A.: Completely derandomized self-adaptation in evolution strategies. Evol. Comput. **9**, 159–195 (2001)
7. Hao, Q., Li, S., Liu, B.: The kinematic performance optimization of a 2-DoF parallel robot based on new variance indices. In: IEEE Advanced Information Management, Communicates, Electronic and Automation Control Conference (2016)
8. Heab, G., Geng, Z.: Dynamics synthesis and control for a hopping robot with articulated leg. Mech. Mach. Theory **46**(11), 1669–1688 (2011)

9. Heisserman, L.: Generative geometric design. IEEE Comput. Graphics Appl. **14**(2), 37–45 (1994)
10. Hooke, R., Jeeves, T.A.: "Direct search" solution of numerical and statistical problems. J. ACM **8**(2), 212–229 (1961). https://doi.org/10.1145/321062.321069
11. Lum, M.J.H., Rosen, J., Sinanan, M.N., Hannaford, B.: Optimization of a spherical mechanism for a minimally invasive surgical robot: theoretical and experimental approaches. IEEE Trans. Biomed. Eng. **53**(7), 1440–1445 (2006)
12. Mann, H.B., Whitney, D.R.: On a test of whether one of two random variables is stochastically larger than the other. Ann. Math. Stat. **18**(1), 50–60 (1947)
13. Megaro, V., et al.: Designing cable-driven actuation networks for kinematic chains and trees. In: Proceedings of the ACM SIGGRAPH/Eurographics Symposium on Computer Animation (2017)
14. Megaro, V., Zehnder, J., Bächer, M., Coros, S., Gross, M., Thomaszewski, B.: A computational design tool for compliant mechanisms. ACM Trans. Graph. **36**(4), 1–12 (2017)
15. Ogura, Y., et al..: Human-like walking with knee stretched, heel-contact and toe-off motion by a humanoid robot. In: IEEE/RSJ International Conference on Intelligent Robots and Systems (2006)
16. Shakiba, M., Shadmehr, M.H., Mohseni, O., Nasiri, R., Ahmadabadi, M.N.: An adaptable cat-inspired leg design with frequency-amplitude coupling. In: International Conference on Robotics and Mechatronics (2016)
17. Snippe, M.S.: Cheetah robot leg mechanism: analysis, design and cost of transport. Master's thesis, University of Twente, Netherlands (2017)
18. Storn, R., Price, K.: Differential evolution - a simple and efficient heuristic for global optimization over continuous spaces. J. Glob. Optim. **11**(4), 341–359 (1997)
19. Wilcoxon, F.: Individual comparisons by ranking methods. Biometrics Bull. **1**(6), 80–83 (1945)
20. Xi, Y., Xia, Y., Li, X., Sun, Y., Wang, H.: Kinematic analysis and parameter optimization of six-bar linkage based on ADAMS. In: International Conference on Mechanic Automation and Control Engineering (2010)
21. Xu, H., Knoop, E., Coros, S., Bächer, M.: Bend-it: design and fabrication of kinetic wire characters. ACM Trans. Graph. **37**(6), 239:1–239:15 (2018). https://doi.org/10.1145/3272127.3275089
22. Zhang, J., Jin, Z., Feng, H.: Type synthesis of a 3-mixed-DOF protectable leg mechanism of a firefighting multi-legged robot based on GF set theory. Mech. Mach. Theory **130**, 567–584 (2018)
23. Zhou, M., Rozvany, G.I.N.: The COC algorithm, part II: topological, geometrical and generalized shape optimization. Comput. Methods Appl. Mech. Eng. **89**(1), 309–336 (1991)

A Game Theory Approach for Crowd Evacuation Modelling

Carolina Crespi, Georgia Fargetta, Mario Pavone[(✉)], Rocco A. Scollo, and Laura Scrimali

Department of Mathematics and Computer Science, University of Catania,
Viale A. Doria 6, 95125 Catania, Italy
{georgia.fargetta,rocco.scollo}@phd.unict.it
{mpavone,scrimali}@dmi.unict.it

Abstract. In this paper, we introduce some new methodologies in a general path problem. Finding a good path is always a desirable task and it can be also crucial in emergency and panic situations, in which people tend to assume different and unpredictable behaviors. In this paper, we analyse an escape situation in which the environment is a labyrinth and people are agents that act as two different kinds of ant colonies. In particular, we assume that people act according to opposite behaviors: (*i*) cooperatively, helping each other and the group; (*ii*) non cooperatively, helping just themselves, and no caring about the rest of the group. So, we use in a path problem an Ant Colony Algorithm based on two breeds of colonies: a cooperative and a non-cooperative one. We imagine that their task is to find the exit of the labyrinth making decisions according to the ACO rules and according to their breed. Every breed has, in fact, two different strategies. Via a game theory approach, we investigate how these two strategies affect the final payoff of each breed.

Keywords: Game theory · Ant Colony Optimization · Swarm intelligence · Optimization · Metaheuristics

1 Introduction

Throughout history, humans have been interested in natural disasters and the topic of evacuation, because optimizing the evacuation's strategies has vital importance in reducing the human and social harm, and saving the aid time. During evacuation, there are more than a few decisions which have to be made in a very short period of time, and in the most appropriate way. Significant research efforts have been made in the literature, (see [9]), to deal with evacuation optimization on the basis of deterministic optimization model, nevertheless the cooperative or non-cooperative behavior's aspects of real-world evacuation have not been taken into account comprehensively. In [5] the authors focused their ideas on the evacuation routes; whereas, in our work we focused on the minimum path and also on the behavior of the crowd. A suitable way to find optimum evacuation routes, during an emergency, is using Ant Colony Optimization (ACO)

© Springer Nature Switzerland AG 2020
B. Filipič et al. (Eds.): BIOMA 2020, LNCS 12438, pp. 228–239, 2020.
https://doi.org/10.1007/978-3-030-63710-1_18

algorithms [6,7,16]. Indeed, humans have faced complex optimization problems such as finding the shortest path between various points, evacuation simulations and optimization, allocating the optimum amount of resources, determining the optimum sequence of the processes in a production line, among others. Ant Colony Optimization algorithms are approximate techniques, belonging to the Swarm Intelligence methods, which imitate the cooperative behavior of real ants to solve optimization problems. Each artificial ant is inspired by the behavior of a real ant and can be seen as an agent of a multi-agent system. Real ants are eusocial insects and use collective behavior to achieve complex task, such as finding shortest paths between food sources and their nest. Using a simple communication mechanism like a chemical trail (pheromone), an ant colony is able to find the shortest path between two points. Initially, ant colony optimization algorithms have been applied to many combinatorial optimization problems, achieving good results in solving different problems, such as graph coloring [2], scheduling [13,17] and assignment problems [1]. Nowadays, ACO algorithms have also been applied to problems belonging to the class of dynamic optimization problems, in which topology and costs can change during the execution of the algorithm. Routing in telecommunications networks is an example of such a problem [8]. Game theory has been widely used in the research of various scientific disciplines, from biological systems to economic and social networks [4]. With the help of game theory, researchers can conduct extensive studies on the pedestrian and evacuation dynamics [3,19]. However, game-theoretical models are focused on the study of the crowd's behavior in evacuation process. Indeed, in [18] the authors study a game-theoretical model to underline the relationship between cooperative and competitive agents in a crowd. Also, [12] discusses the basic principles of multiple robot cooperative system using Game Theory and Ant Colony Algorithms.

The aim of this research work is to study and analyse the collective behavior of a little social group that tries to escape from a disaster situation, such as earthquakes, volcanic eruptions, and/or hurricanes, trying to reach a safe location in the shortest possible time. Therefore, an ACO algorithm has been taken into account to study the behavior of different agents in strictly dynamic situations. Specifically, two different agents have been considered, which act differently: cooperative and non-cooperative agents. Ants colonies are recognized to be the best organized and cooperative social system, able to make their social community work at the best, and able to perform complex tasks, such as, for instance, discovering the shortest path between food and anthill, or defend the own anthill from attack by predators [11]. Moreover, any action of any ant, is related only to its local environment, local interactions with other ants, simple social rules, and in total absence of centralized decisions. These last features, that we find own in catastrophic situations, convinced us to consider ACO as the simulation model suitable for our study, because a sophisticated collective behavior based on local interactions, social rules, and in absence of centralized decisions, becomes crucial in reaching safe locations. Finally, the relationship between ACO and Game Theory aims to find a good solution in the case where agents with different ideas and strategies have to share a particular situation. As happens in an emergency scenario for the crowd, the same happens with a group of ants that tries to achieve the exit as safe as possible.

2   The Model

The Ant Colony Optimization algorithm is a well-known procedure that takes inspiration from the ants' behavior, when they look for a path between any food source and their anthill. It has been observed that they can identify the shortest path, and communicate it to the others through chemical signals released along the path, called pheromones. In recent years, this behavior has been translated into mathematical and computer language and used to solve different kinds of optimization problems through different versions of the algorithm itself. Despite the different contexts where it has been applied, the mathematical description of the algorithm is quite the same for most of the problems. In particular, the ant's environment is considered as a graph $G = (N, L)$, where N is the set of nodes and L is the set of links. A generic ant k is supposed to be placed on a node i, and she must choose a destination node according to her behavior in real life; that is, preferring a path with some pheromone traces. However, this behavior is not deterministic so a **proportional transition rule** $p_{ij}^k(t)$ is defined as in Eq. (1). It states that an ant k, on a node i and at a time t will choose a destination node j with a probability that is proportional to the quantity of pheromone on the link connecting i with j, if the link j belongs to the set of possible displacements for k. The probability is 0 otherwise. In formulas, we have:

$$p_{ij}^k(t) = \begin{cases} \frac{\tau_{ij}(t)^\alpha \cdot \eta_{ij}^\beta}{\sum_{l \in J_i^k} \tau_{il}(t)^\alpha \cdot \eta_{il}^\beta} & \text{if } j \in J_i^k \\ 0 & \text{if } j \notin J_i^k. \end{cases} \tag{1}$$

As said previously, J_i^k is the set of possible movements of the ant k. Moreover, η_{ij} is the visibility of node j (defined as the inverse of the distance between two nodes), $\tau_{ij}(t)$ is the pheromone intensity on a path at a given iteration, while α and β are two parameters that determine the importance of pheromone intensity with respect to the visibility of a path. Once the ant k arrives at a destination node j, she updates the pheromone trace by releasing at a time t an amount of it proportional to the inverse of the length of the path $L^k(t)$ (eventually multiplied by a Q-factor) if the link (i, j) belongs to the path $T^k(t)$ of the ant at time t. It is 0 otherwise. In this way, the greater the length of a path is, the less pheromone will be present on it. This feature is described by Eq. (2) in which $\Delta\tau_{ij}^k(t)$ represents the amount of pheromone deposited by the ant k.

$$\Delta\tau_{ij}^k(t) = \begin{cases} \frac{Q}{L^k(t)} & \text{if } (i, j) \in T^k(t) \\ 0 & \text{if } (i, j) \notin T^k(t). \end{cases} \tag{2}$$

Finally, a global updating rule $\tau_{ij}(t + 1)$ is applied as in Eq. (3). It states that the intensity of pheromone will be updated considering the intensity $\tau_{ij}(t)$ of it at a previous step, and decreasing it with an evaporation factor ρ.

$$\tau_{ij}(t+1) = (1-\rho) \cdot \tau_{ij}(t) + \sum_{k=1}^{m} \Delta\tau_{ij}^k(t). \tag{3}$$

Now, starting from this procedure we have modified and extended ACO rules to fit them in our model. In particular, we have tried to mix concepts of game theory with concepts of optimization, to explore and highlight some novel features still not completely understood. To do this, we have imagined a generic risk situation like the one a group of ants is forced to live if it must solve a labyrinth. In other words, we assume that ants must find the exit of the labyrinth from a certain entrance as soon as possible to survive. We have modelled this escape situation like a game in which every ant can adopt two different strategies to exit from the labyrinth. We have chosen a labyrinth structure, since it generalizes and makes more interesting and challenging the optimization problem of finding the shortest path in a graph. We have realized this model using *NetLogo* [15], an agent-based model software that allowed us not only to build materially the structure of the labyrinth itself and implement the algorithm, but also to see what was happening during the simulation thanks to an opportune dedicate tab. We have built the labyrinth modifying an existing model proposed in [14]. We have fixed the seed of the random numbers to regenerate, at each run, the same labyrinth. Then, we have created a network underneath the labyrinth and realized more complex labyrinths by strictly modifying the procedure proposed in [14]. This upgraded version can add other links between some nodes with at least two first neighbors and other nodes with at least two first neighbors, in order to prevent the loss of the dead ends. We have repeated this procedure for different kinds of labyrinths with different sets of nodes and links, and grouped them in order to increase complexity. Finally, we have selected for all of them one node on the left part of the labyrinth to be the entrance, and one node on the right part to be the exit. We underline that the entrance and the exit are chosen on the left and on the right, respectively, to give an example to focus on a sample of the labyrinth. In order to generalize the problem, we can put the exit wherever we want or we can rotate the labyrinth, as suitably as we need. Then, we have created two different kinds of ants that act differently, and each of them follow a different strategy to escape from the labyrinth. In particular, we have imagined what would happen if some ants acted cooperatively, while other ants acted non cooperatively. Thus, at first we initialize the set of the whole colony and then, by means of a cooperation parameter f, we establish the fraction of ants who will act cooperatively. It follows that the remaining fraction $(1-f)$ of ants will act non cooperatively. In detail, we set the two strategies, that cannot be changed once the fraction of cooperative ants is defined, as follows:

- Non-Cooperative: they block a random node of their path. In Fig. 1, non-cooperative ants are colored in blue, while a blocked node is represented as a fire.
- Cooperative: if they find a damaged node close to their path, they repair it. In Fig. 1, cooperative ants are colored in red.

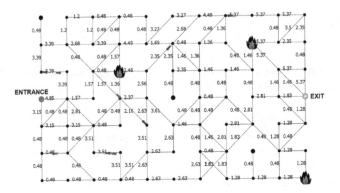

Fig. 1. In this model the entrance is fixed (always on the left part of the labyrinth), whilst the exit changes, in any position of the labyrinth, in according to the number of prizes on it. Bigger black nodes represent end nodes, i.e. dead ends roads; fires indicate the damaged nodes by the non-cooperative ants; and the black labels on the edges indicate the intensity of pheromone on that route. With red are showed the cooperative ants, and in blue the non-cooperative ones. (Color figure online)

Both of them become safe if and only they arrive at the exit. Every kind of ant is "equipped" with the same transition rule. In other words, each ant chooses the next target node according to the same rule, even if it belongs to different families and acts differently. In particular, the transition rule in (4) defines the probability $p_{ij}^k(t)$ of an ant to go from a starting node i to a destination node j as follows: during the first iteration, the ants explore randomly the labyrinth. They choose to visit a link according to the intensity of pheromone on it that, in the first iteration, is equal to 1 for all the links of the labyrinth.

The first ant of each kind that arrives at the exit releases a trace of pheromone $\Delta\tau_{ij}$ along every link of her path. For simplicity, in our model, the intensity of pheromone released by each ant on every link of her path is $\Delta\tau_{ij} = 1.5$. After that, the other ants of the same kind die, the global updating rule (5) is applied and a new generation is launched. In formulas, we define the transition rule as:

$$p_{ij}^k(t) = \begin{cases} \dfrac{\tau_{ij}(t)}{\sum_{l \in J_i^k} \tau_{il}(t)} & \text{if } j \in J_i^k \\ 0 & \text{otherwise}, \end{cases} \qquad (4)$$

with τ_{ij} intensity of pheromone on the link (i,j) and J_i^k is the set of allowed links. Finally, the global updating rule is defined as:

$$\tau_{ij}(t+1) = (1 - \alpha) \cdot \tau_{ij}(t) + \Delta\tau_{ij}, \qquad (5)$$

where α is the evaporation rate, τ_{ij} is the pheromone intensity on the link (i,j) at the previous step and $\Delta\tau_{ij}$ is the amount of deposited pheromone by the winning ant, at each turn, on the same link. In this model, we have also imposed that, once the quantity of pheromone falls below a certain threshold, it remains fixed and does not decrease further. This choice is to prevent the stagnation of the algorithm around a local optimum. Thus, within this situation, we want to analyze how two different strategies evolve in time during a critical situation, namely, in finding the shortest path from the entrance to the exit in the shortest possible time. In the next section, we will discuss about some game theory definitions used in the model. We decide not to consider the gain of a single link, but the aim of one ant is to reach the exit as soon as possible. In fact, the exit, or in our case the shelter, has a capacity that in the algorithm is represented by a prize in the exit. If there are no more prizes on the exit, i.e. capacity in the shelter, the exit will move (with the same budget of prizes) to another edge node of the graph, except the ones on the left part of the labyrinth. We are ruling out the possibility that the exit and the entrance are on the same side of the graph. It is a dynamic case in which not only the ants must be able to find the exit from the maze through the shortest path, but from time to time, they must also have the ability to organize themselves for a new objective that gives the opportunity to collect prizes.

2.1 Evacuees' Game

Game theory allows one to define how much an agent can gain from its actions and decisions. Indeed, agents are defined to be rational and intelligent and try to reach the highest value of the profit function. In game theory, the profit function models reality so as to give a value to the emotional or economic gain to the agent who adopts a certain strategy. A strategy space for a player is the set of all possible strategies of a player; whereas, a strategy is a complete plan of action for every stage of the game. Formally, we define a payoff function for a player as a map from the cross-product of players' strategy spaces to reals, i.e. the payoff function of a player takes as its input a strategy profile and yields a representation of payoff as its output.

In this model, we consider an N-players game ($N \geq 2$). The evacuees represent the players of the game, who have to reach a safe area. We suppose that evacuees can chose either to cooperate (C) or not to cooperate (NC), when attempting to arrive a desired safe area after or during a disaster. Each player starts from the same node and tries to reach an exit using the minimum path. A little group of evacuees tries to arrive in a safe area, which has a capacity K, but only one member of the group can reach that place. When the shelter is full or is not enough safe, we consider a new shelter, placed in another node of the graph, which the evacuees have to reach.

Let $G = (N, L)$ be the graph associated with the game, where N is the set of nodes and L the set of links. The payoff of the player that finally reaches the safe area depends on a parameter, the pheromone τ_{ij} on the edge (i, j) used in the Ant Colony Algorithm. According to the strategies we define two different payoff functions, which depend on the strategy that an agent chooses. As a consequence, we define the payoff function of an agent k, who chooses the cooperative strategy a_k^C:

$$u_k(a_k^C, a_{-k}) = \frac{f \cdot \sum_{i,j} \tau_{ij}}{n}, \quad 0 < f \leq 1. \tag{6}$$

We define the payoff function of an agent k, who chooses the non-cooperative strategy a_k^{NC}:

$$u_k(a_k^{NC}, a_{-k}) = \frac{(1-f) \cdot \sum_{i,j} \tau_{ij}}{n}, \quad 0 \leq f < 1. \tag{7}$$

We denote f as the percentage of cooperative players and n as the number of evacuees of a group. We consider $\sum_{i,j} \tau_{ij}$ as the sum of the pheromone on the links of the agent path. We underline that a_k is a generic strategy, that an agent k can choose from (C) or (NC) and we denote a_{-k} the strategies of all agents, except k.

We group for all k, the cooperative (C) and the non-cooperative ants (NC) respectively, as:

$$u^C = f \cdot \sum_{i,j} \tau_{ij}, \quad 0 < f \leq 1; \qquad u^{NC} = (1-f) \cdot \sum_{i,j} \tau_{ij}, \quad 0 \leq f < 1.$$

Finally, we denote the profit function of the game as the sum of the payoff of all cooperative ants plus the payoff of all non-cooperative ants, i.e. $U = u^C + u^{NC}$.

3   Experiments and Results

In our simulations, we use ant shape agents according to the implemented algorithm, but this is just a graphic feature that doesn't affect the correctness of the procedure. It follows that a generation of ants represents a group of people who try to arrive at a shelter or a safe area. At the end of each generation, only one ant of each kind survives. After several preliminary experiments, we choose a set of $n = 10$ agents and perform 10 different simulations for different values of f, starting from $f = 0$ to $f = 1$ and increasing f at a regular interval of 0.20. For our purposes, we consider the trend of ten generations. Figure 2 shows the trend of the average profit function over 10 simulations at different values of f (and correspondingly $(1 - f)$). In each plot, the x-axis indicates the generations number, while in the y-axis are displayed the average profits obtained, respectively, by the cooperative agents (Fig. 2a) and by the non-cooperative ones (Fig. 2b).   In particular, the figure represents the comparison of the values of the profit function for each evacuee referred to the percentage of cooperative agents (f). We notice that when the number of cooperative agents increases, the value of profit function increases too, following a linear trend. Furthermore, for $f = 0.8$ and $f = 1.0$, after a few generations, the average profit function grows similarly, reaching the same value after 10 generations. This suggests that a non-cooperative behavior of a few agents can increase the profit of the other ones. In the same way, the plot in Fig. 2b shows that a non-cooperative strategy is good if and only if a lot of agents choose that particular strategy. Also, in this

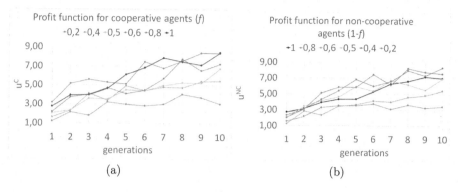

Fig. 2. Comparison of the average profit obtained by cooperative agents (plot (a)), compared to obtained one by non-cooperatives (plot (b)).

case, the average profit function reaches the best values for $f = 0.2$ and $f = 0.4$, leading to the same evaluation of the previous case.

In Fig. 3 we can see the average profit function comparison for $f = 0.2$ and $f = 0.8$, both for cooperative evacuees and non-cooperative evacuees. In Fig. 3a, we find the value of f for which are present 2 cooperative evacuees and 8 non-cooperative evacuees, and in Fig. 3e the symmetric situation. The same distinction is present also in Fig. 3 for $f = 0.4$ in Fig. 3b, and $f = 0.6$ in Fig. 3d, but with 4 and 6 different kinds of evacuees in two symmetric situations. For these plots, the average profit function is higher for the larger groups (non-cooperative for $f < 0.5$ and cooperative for $f > 0.5$). This can be explained because these plots are calculated for a percentage of cooperation less than $f = 0.5$. In fact, at $f = 0.5$ something special happens. In Fig. 3c the trend of the average profit function for cooperative evacuees starts to be lower than the one for the non-cooperative evacuees, but as the generations increase, the two functions tend to reach the same value.

The *Chicken Game* supports our considerations. Indeed, the main feature of this game is that players try to avoid appearing as a "chicken". So each player taunts the others to increase the risk of shame in giving up. However, when a player surrenders, the conflict is avoided and the game is mostly over. Furthermore, the fact that the profit function is the same when half of the population is cooperative and the other is not, leads to compare the *Chicken Game* with the particular case $f = 0.5$. In fact, the balance of the game is obtained when one player chooses strategy (C) and the other the strategy (NC), that is the opposite strategy. In this situation, no player is considered a "chicken" until the moment when the value of f decreases, and hence the competitive strategy takes advantage. We observe, however, that the game of chicken is considered as a social dilemma [10].

To better investigate the meaning of these data, we calculate the average values of the profit function over 10 simulations for each group of evacuees and for each value of f. Figure 4 shows what we have obtained. As we can see, as

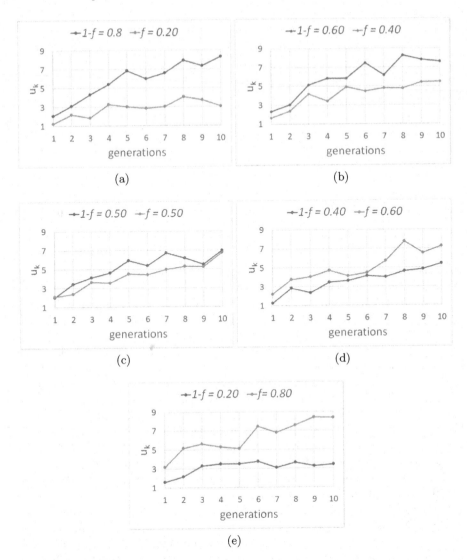

Fig. 3. Average profit function comparison obtained by the cooperative and non-cooperative agents, at different values of f and $(1 - f)$.

the percentage of f increases, the average value of the profit function has two different trends. The one for cooperative evacuees increases as f increases. The one for non-cooperative evacuees decreases. In particular, the average value of the profit function for $f \geq 0.50$ is higher than the ones for $f \leq 0.50$. This means that the average values calculated for two opposite and symmetric configurations are not the same. The two curves are not symmetrical. In fact, the two curves are not symmetrical because they are the outcome of different dynamic scenarios,

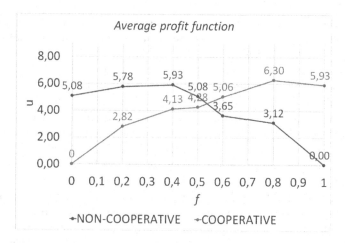

Fig. 4. Average profit function comparison over 10 simulations and over 10 generations for cooperative and non-cooperative evacuees.

where the two kinds of agents (cooperative and non-cooperative) act differently. Of course, these effects are strongly affected by the number of the former compared to the latter, and in particular, higher values of the profit function (u) are strictly related to higher values of the parameter f. This, in general, is not a surprising result since is quite common that cooperation means, in most cases, better performances. It is important to say that in game theory there are several examples in which players can choose whether to adopt a more or less cooperative strategy. Let's consider the classic game of hawks and doves as an example. These sample-animals represent couples of the same type of animals and same population that fly on a prey. Each animal can choose to behave like a hawk or a dove: hawk (strategy H) or dove (strategy D) behavior indicates aggressive or peaceful behavior, respectively. In this example, if the players choose the same strategy then they divide the loot, otherwise, if they both choose the same strategy, one will get the maximum profit the other the minimum profit. From this example we can see how in situations where there is total collaboration, a greater profit is obtained than in a situation in which only one can obtain a good profit. However, in this context, we imagine that better performances can be linked or explained with one evacuee's willing to improve its profit. It is presumable that in real-life escape situations people tend to act in the same way that is, trying to improve their profit function. Therefore, our results suggest that to do this they should prefer a cooperative strategy.

4   Conclusions

In this paper we analyse the affinity between the behavior of ants and people in a particular situation. Indeed, in an emergency situation, a crowd seems to move in a messy way but inside the crowd there are little groups that try to decide their behavior inside that group. As a consequence, we investigate the cooperative or non-cooperative agents' choice inside each single group. This original approach consists of correlation between ants and people, that give us the possibility to underline some interesting factors, as the importance of using the sum of the pheromone into the profit function. The payoff's values, for each agent, lead to significant observations regarding the cooperative and competitive behaviors of the agents, in a difficult situation, where an evacuee has to decide as fast as he can. Furthermore, the idea to insert the percentage of cooperative agents in the profit function represents another innovative aspect that allows us to better understand both the behavior of the agents and the profit they may have as we explain in Sect. 3. In fact, for the first time is used a game theory approach to an evacuation model using an ACO algorithm, to find the solution of the profit function of the game. The quality and safety of the chosen path is directly proportional to the sum of the pheromone along this path. This leads to a profit function that reflects the safety and efficiency of the path chosen by the evacuees. Moreover, during the comparison over 10 simulations and over 10 generations for cooperative and non-cooperative evacuees, we notice that if a lot of evacuees choose cooperative strategies, then the value of the function is higher than the same number of evacuees can gain playing a competitive strategy. The results presented in this paper are just a small part of a bigger study that is still under work. Further studies and simulations have to be made. Especially because our model considers just one winner at each run, which is not a desirable situation in real life.

References

1. Cai, Z., Wang, W., Zhang, S., Jiang, Z.: Ant colony optimization for component assignment problems in circular consecutive-k-out-of-n systems. In: 2017 IEEE International Conference on Industrial Engineering and Engineering Management (IEEM), pp. 954–958 (2017)
2. Consoli, P., Collerá, A., Pavone, M.: Swarm intelligence heuristics for graph coloring problem. In: IEEE Congress on Evolutionary Computation (CEC), vol. 1, pp. 1909–1916. IEEE Press (2013). https://doi.org/10.1109/CEC.2013.6557792
3. Dogbé, C.: Modeling crowd dynamics by the mean-field limit approach. Math. Comput. Modell. **52**(9–10), 1506–1520 (2010). https://doi.org/10.1016/j.mcm.2010.06.012
4. Fargetta, G., Scrimali, L.R.M.: Generalized Nash equilibrium and dynamics of popularity of online contents. Optim. Lett. 1–19 (2020). https://doi.org/10.1007/s11590-019-01528-4
5. Forcael, E., González, V., Orozco, F., Vargas, S., Pantoja, A., Moscoso, P.: Ant colony optimization model for tsunamis evacuation routes. Comput. Aided Civil and Infrastruct. Eng. **29**(10), 723–737 (2014). https://doi.org/10.1111/mice.12113
6. Hajjem, M., Bouziri, H., Talbi, E.G., Mellouli, K.: Intelligent indoor evacuation guidance system based on ant colony algorithm. In: IEEE/ACS 14th International Conference on Computer Systems and Applications (AICCSA), pp. 1035–1042 (10 2017). https://doi.org/10.1109/AICCSA.2017.47

7. Hongzhi Wang, C.W., Yifeng Guo, Y.Z., Zhu, M.: Emergency escape route planning for the louvre summary. Acad. J. Comput. Inf. Sci. **2**, 78–84 (2019). https://doi.org/10.25236/AJCIS.010041

8. Huang, S.H., Huang, Y.H., Blazquez, C.A., Paredes-Belmar, G.: Application of the ant colony optimization in the resolution of the bridge inspection routing problem. Appl. Soft Comput. **65**(C), 443–461 (2018). https://doi.org/10.1016/j.asoc.2018.01.034

9. Kotsireas, I.S., Nagurney, A., Pardalos, P.M. (eds.): DOD 2015 2016. SPMS, vol. 185. Springer, Cham (2016). https://doi.org/10.1007/978-3-319-43709-5

10. Macy, M.W., Flache, A.: Learning dynamics in social dilemmas. Proc. Nat. Acad. Sci. **99**(suppl 3), 7229–7236 (2002). https://doi.org/10.1073/pnas.092080099

11. O'Shea-Wheller, T., Sendova-Franks, A., Franks, N.: Differentiated anti-predation responses in a superorganism. PLoS ONE **10**(11), e0141012 (2015). https://doi.org/10.1371/journal.pone.0141012

12. Ping, Y., Chao, Y., Li, Z., Cuiming, L.: Based on game theory and ant colony algorithm's research on group robot cooperative system control. In: 2010 International Conference on Electrical and Control Engineering, pp. 532–535. IEEE (2010). https://doi.org/10.1109/iCECE.2010.137

13. Reddy, G., Phanikumar, S.: Multi objective task scheduling using modified ant colony optimization in cloud computing. Int. J. Intell. Eng. Syst. **11**, 242–250 (2018). https://doi.org/10.22266/ijies2018.0630.26

14. Steiner, J.: Maze maker (2004). http://ccl.northwestern.edu/netlogo/models/community/maze-maker-2004

15. Wilensky, U.: Netlogo. Center for Connected Learning and Computer-Based Modeling. Northwestern University, Evanston, IL (1999). http://ccl.northwestern.edu/netlogo/

16. Zarrinpanjeh, N., Javan, F., Naji, A., Azadi, H., Maeyer, P., Witlox, F.: Optimum path determination to facilitate fire station rescue missions using ant colony optimization algorithms (case study: City of Karaj). ISPRS Int. Arch. Photogram. Remote Sens. Spat. Inf. Sci. **XLIII-B3-2020**, 1285–1291 (2020). https://doi.org/10.5194/isprs-archives-XLIII-B3-2020-1285-2020

17. Zhang, X., Wang, S., Yi, L., Xue, H., Yang, S., Xiong, X.: An integrated ant colony optimization algorithm to solve job allocating and tool scheduling problem. Proc. Inst. Mech. Eng. Part B J. Eng. Manuf. **232** (2016). https://doi.org/10.1177/0954405416636038

18. Zheng, X., Cheng, Y.: Modeling cooperative and competitive behaviors in emergency evacuation: a game-theoretical approach. Comput. Math. Appl. **62**(12), 4627–4634 (2011). https://doi.org/10.1016/j.camwa.2011.10.048

19. Zheng, X., Zhong, T., Liu, M.: Modeling crowd evacuation of a building based on seven methodological approaches. Build. Environ. **44**(3), 437–445 (2009). https://doi.org/10.1016/j.buildenv.2008.04.002

A Hybrid Neural Network-Genetic Programming Intelligent Control Approach

Francesco Marchetti[(⊠)] and Edmondo Minisci

Intelligent Computational Engineering Laboratory,
University of Strathclyde, Glasgow, UK
{francesco.marchetti,edmondo.minisci}@strath.ac.uk

Abstract. The proposed work aims to introduce a novel approach to Intelligent Control (IC), based on the combined use of Genetic Programming (GP) and feedforward Neural Network (NN). Both techniques have been successfully used in the literature for regression and control applications, but, while a NN creates a black box model, GP allows for a greater interpretability of the created model, which is a key feature in control applications. The main idea behind the hybrid approach proposed in this paper is to combine the speed and flexibility of a NN with the interpretability of GP. Moreover, to improve the robustness of the GP control law against unforeseen environmental changes, a new selection and crossover mechanisms, called Inclusive Tournament and Inclusive Crossover, are also introduced. The proposed IC approach is tested on the guidance control of a space transportation system and results, showing the potentialities for real applications, are shown and discussed.

Keywords: Intelligent Control · Genetic Programming · Neural Networks · Optimal control · Space transportation system

1 Introduction

Many different Artificial Intelligence (AI) techniques have been used in the past decades for various IC applications [18], where the definition of IC can be summarized as follows: *a controller can be defined intelligent if it can deal autonomously with unforeseen changes in the environment, in the control system or in the goals, by relaying on techniques pertaining to the fields of Artificial Intelligence, Operations Research and Automatic Control* (Saridis [16] and Antsaklis [1]). Mainly three different classes of AI techniques have been used for IC both alone and hybridized: Fuzzy Logic (FL), Evolutionary Computing (EC) and Machine Learning (ML). Among these different techniques, NNs are certainly the most common, mainly due to their flexibility and their ability in being integrated in control systems of any kind, e.g. as was done in [7].

GP can be also used for control applications (Marchetti et al. [12], Chiang [2]) and as suggested by Koza et al. [9], it is particularly interesting for its ability to

© Springer Nature Switzerland AG 2020
B. Filipič et al. (Eds.): BIOMA 2020, LNCS 12438, pp. 240–254, 2020.
https://doi.org/10.1007/978-3-030-63710-1_19

produce interpretable control laws for nonlinear systems. In fact, GP possess two key advantages in comparison to NNs: 1) it can create a regression model from scratches by interacting with the environment, so without the need of providing a huge amount of training data; and 2) it produces a human-readable mathematical equation, which can be easily interpreted by the designer. Such interpretability is of particular importance for control applications, where in order to assess the reliability and behaviour of a control system the control equation must be known. Considering that an intelligent controller must possess the ability to learn and adapt online, hence the computational load of this adaptation or learning process must be very low, the main aim of this work is to propose an IC approach that combines GP and NN, which has the interpretability of GP without its excessive computational cost for online learning and adaptation.

In this respect, a novel hybrid approach to IC is introduced, where a NN is used to optimize online the GP control law found during the offline training process. Moreover, to increase the robustness of the proposed control method, two new features have been introduced in the considered GP algorithm: the Inclusive Tournament and the Inclusive Crossover. It is shown that these alternative heuristics allow for a greater robustness of the GP control law when varying environmental conditions and uncertainties are considered.

To the authors best knowledge, the control approach introduced in this work is not present in the literature. In fact, the classical approach to hybridize GP and NN is in a Neuroevolutionary manner where GP or another evolutionary algorithm to optimize the topology and weights of a NN which then is used for control purposes, as in [6,15] or inside a Reinforcement Learning (RL) control framework as in [5,8].

The paper is structured as follows: Sect. 2 introduces the concepts behind the NN Optimization of the GP control law; Sect. 3 introduces the new tournament and crossover mechanism employed in this work; in Sect. 4 the chosen test case is presented, and the obtained results are shown and discussed in Sect. 5; the final conclusions and future work directions are then presented in Sect. 6.

2   Neural Optimization of the Genetic Programming Control Law

The core of this work consists in the use of a feedforward NN to optimize online a control law obtained offline using GP. The idea of this hybrid approach comes from the need to keep the interpretability of a control law produced using GP, while having the advantages of a NN, namely the ability to perform learning and adaptation online with a much lower computational cost.

As schematised in Fig. 1, once the GP control law is obtained offline, the NN is used to optimize online the key coefficients of such control law, that are:

- The *weights* inserted as multiplying factors of the input variables of the GP control law. All the weights are independent and initialized to 1. The weights are inserted after the GP control law is created, as depicted in Fig. 2.

– The *real valued coefficients* inserted in the GP control law during its creation. Also for these values as for the weights, they are all independent. This means that if the same coefficient is used multiple times in the GP law, these are considered as different coefficients by the optimization process.

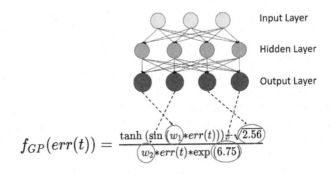

$$f_{GP}(err(t)) = \frac{\tanh\left(\sin\left(w_1 * err(t)\right)\right) + \sqrt{2.56}}{w_2 * err(t) * \exp(6.75)}$$

Fig. 1. Schematic of the genetic programming control law update

$$f_{GP}(err(t)) = \frac{\tanh(\sin(err(t)) + \sqrt{2.56}}{err(t) * \exp(6.75)}$$

$$\downarrow$$

$$f_{GP}(err(t)) = \frac{\tanh(\sin(w_1 * err(t)) + \sqrt{2.56}}{w_2 * err(t) * \exp(6.75)}$$

Fig. 2. How the GP control is modified to insert the multiplying factors. The red rectangles highlights where the weights are inserted (Color figure online)

The procedure to go from the offline creation of the GP control law to its online adaptation is described by the following three steps schematized also in Fig. 3:

1. The GP control law is obtained offline by simulating a control task where a disturbance is considered. The GP control law is created to control the plant against that particular disturbance scenario: noise is introduced in the form of uncertainties in the physical models and perturbations of the applied disturbances. The main goal of this phase is to find a robust GP control law, in order to perform well also on unseen disturbance scenarios.

2. Define a set of disturbance cases uniformly covering the whole domain of the possible disturbance scenarios (Fig. 4a), referred as "disturbance domain" from this point onward, and perform an optimization of the obtained GP control law on each of the disturbance points. The optimization is considered successful if the performed trajectory is the same or within a small range

defined by the user from the reference trajectory. The results obtained from the successful optimizations are stored to produce a training dataset for the NN. Such optimization of the GP control law performed on the training set is done using classical optimization techniques.

3. The NN is trained on the training dataset produced at the previous step and the created model is then tested on a predefined set of disturbance scenarios (Fig. 4b) considering also the uncertainties on the physical models.

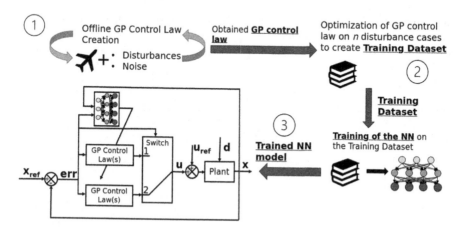

Fig. 3. Schematic of the process to obtain the proposed Hybrid Neural Network-Genetic Programming Intelligent Control Approach. The proposed control scheme is depicted in the lower left part.

According to the taxonomy presented in [18], the proposed control approach can be classified as G0, E2, C1, since the goal is predefined by the user and it is followed by minimizing the tracking error (G0); the environment is defined but subject to time varying disturbances, modelled by the introduction of environmental disturbances and uncertainties (E2); the GP control law parameters are updated online by the NN (C1).

3   Inclusive Genetic Programming

When using GP in a control environment, it is important to assess the robustness of the produced control law. In fact, it is desirable to obtain a control law, which is capable to control the desired plant also in the presence of uncertainties and unforeseen events. Since an intelligent controller is expected to work on nonlinear systems, to increase the robustness of the GP control law and describe their behaviour in a more accurate way, it is important for it to capture the nonlinear behaviour of the plant. In order to do so, the GP must maintain a certain degree of diversity in the population to preserve also complex structures

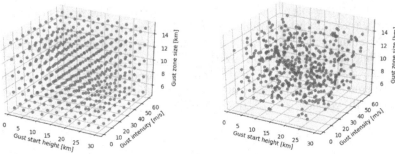

(a) Training Scenarios - Disturbance scenarios used to create the training dataset for the NN

(b) Test Scenarios - Disturbance scenarios used to test the proposed control approach

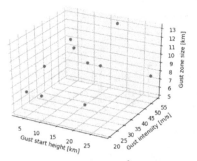

(c) Disturbance scenarios used to compare the control laws for the SPG and IGP comparison

Fig. 4. Different sets of disturbance scenarios considered in this work

able to capture nonlinearties, which would be discarded otherwise due to their excessive complexity.

To maintain the population diversity and improve the robustness of the GP control law, a new tournament and crossover mechanisms, which can be seen as approaches to create and exploit different niches [17], are introduced: the Inclusive Tournament (IncT) and the Inclusive Crossover (IncC).

The main concept behind the IncC and IncT is the following: the individuals in the population are divided into n categories (niches) according to their genotypic diversity, i.e. the number of nodes in an individual or individual length. The categories are created in an evenly distributed manner (linearly divided) between the maximum and minimum length of the individuals in the population, then the individuals are assigned to the respective category according to their length. The same number of categories is kept during the evolutionary process, but their size (the interval of individuals lengths that they cover) and the amount of individuals inside them change at every generation. Once the categories are created, both the crossover and tournament selection are performed considering individuals from different categories in order to maintain the population diversity. Finally, before starting the evolutionary process, a search for the population with the highest entropy [14] is performed, in order to start with a diversified initial population.

3.1 Inclusive Tournament

The IncT consists in performing a Double Tournament [10] on each category of the considered population as in Algorithm 1. Moreover, the selection mechanism applied to the considered individuals is modified in order to favour those individuals that respect the applied constraints (called Modified Double Tournament in Algorithm 1). The employed evolutionary strategy is based on the $\mu + \lambda$ algorithm.

Algorithm 1. Inclusive Tournament

1: Divide the population into n categories based on the length of the individuals
2: **while** Number of selected individuals $< \mu$ **do**
3:   **for** i in number of categories **do**
4:     **if** Number of selected individuals from i-th category $<$ total number of individuals in i-th category **then**
5:       Select one individual in i-th category with Modified Double Tournament selection
6:     **end if**
7:   **end for**
8: **end while**

3.2 Inclusive Crossover

Algorithm 2 describes the mechanism behind the IncC. A one point crossover is applied between two individuals which are selected from two different categories. The list of exploitable categories is continuously updated in order to avoid selecting always from the same categories. About the two individuals chosen, one is the best of the considered category, in order to pass the best performing genes to the future generation and the other is selected randomly in order to maintain a certain degree of diversity in the population. Moreover, a mechanism to avoid breeding between the same or very similar individuals is used (lines 7–14 in Algorithm 2). Here n_l is a preset constant defining the maximum number of loop iterations, needed to avoid possible infinite loops.

Algorithm 2. Inclusive Crossover

1: **if** *List of exploitable categories* is empty **then**
2:     *List of exploitable categories* ← list of all filled categories
3: **end if**
4: Select randomly two different categories from *List of exploitable categories*
5: Remove chosen categories from *List of exploitable categories*
6: Select the **best** individual from the first category and select a **random** individual from the second category
7: n = 0
8: **while** The selected individuals have the same fitness and n < n_l **do**
9:     Repeat lines 4 to 6
10:     **if** *List of exploitable categories* is empty **then**
11:         *List of exploitable categories* ← list of all filled categories
12:     **end if**
13:     n = n+1
14: **end while**
15: Apply crossover to the chosen individuals

3.3   Robustness Analysis

To quantify the improvements in the robustness of the obtained GP control law made possible by the IncT and IncC, a comparison between the Standard Genetic Programming (SGP) and the Inclusive Genetic Programming (IGP) was made on the creation of a control law for the test case introduced in Sect. 4, considering the uncertainties in the models and a perturbation of the design disturbance scenario. Such perturbation was introduced as a random variation of ±10% of the design gust v_g and gust range Δ_g at every generation of the evolutionary process. Such variation is not cumulative across generations and its magnitude is different at every generation. Regarding the disturbance scenario, more is explained in Sect. 4.1.

The creation of the GP control law was performed on 10 different disturbance scenarios (Fig. 4c), which were spread uniformly over the disturbance domain. Each line in Table 1 is a control law created on a different disturbance scenario. Both GP algorithms were set to create two control laws at the same time, since two control parameters were present in the considered test case (Individual 1 and 2 in Table 1). The SGP algorithm employs a Double Tournament selection and a single point crossover. The GP algorithms were set as follows:

- *Primitives*: $+, ++$ (ternary addition), $-, *, \tanh, \sqrt{\cdot}, \log, \exp, \sin, \cos$. All the primitives were modified in order to avoid numerical errors.
- *Fitness Functions*: two fitness functions were simultaneously considered

1. min $fitness_1 = RMSE(objectives)$ where:

$$objectives = \left(\int | e\hat{r}r_v(t) | \, dt, \int | e\hat{r}r_\chi(t) | \, dt, \right.$$

$$\int | e\hat{r}r_\gamma(t) | \, dt, \int | e\hat{r}r_h(t) | \, dt,$$

$$\left. orbital \ requirements \right)$$

where the considered errors are scaled with the maximum values of the states, and

$$orbital \ requirements = \left| \frac{h_{ref \, final} - h_{final}}{h_{max}} \right| + \left| \frac{v_{abs} - v_{orbit}}{v_{max}} \right|$$

$$+ \left| \frac{\chi_{abs} - \chi_{orbit}}{\chi_{max}} \right| + \left| \frac{\gamma_{ref \, final} - \gamma_{final}}{\gamma_{max}} \right|$$

2. min $fitness_2 = ||constraints \ violation||_2$
   - *Termination Criteria: generation number* = 150
   - *Double Tournament Parsimony size*: 1.6 for both algorithms
   - *Double Tournament Fitness size*: 2 for both algorithms
   - *Population Size*: 300 individuals for both algorithms
   - *Crossover Rate*: 0.2 for IGP, 0.7 for SGP
   - *Mutation Rate*: 0.7 for IGP, 0.2 for SGP
   - *Elitism Rate*: 0.1 for both algorithms

For the IGP, the mutation rate was set at 0.7 at the beginning of the evolutionary process in order to explore the search space. Then, when feasible individuals were found ($fitness_2 = 0$), the mutation rate was decreased by 0.01 and the crossover rate was increased by the same quantity at each generation, until the crossover rate reached the value of 0.65. Moreover, to avoid bloating, both the IGP and SGP make use of the bloat control operators implemented in the DEAP library.

After the creation of the control laws, these were tested on 500 disturbance scenarios evenly distributed in the disturbance domain (Fig. 4a), in order to asses the robustness of the obtained control laws. The results of this comparison are listed in Table 1.

The major highlights of this comparison are:

- From the column "Disturbance Cases Solved" in Table 1, it can be seen how the IGP control laws can perform successfully on average on 207/500 disturbance scenarios while the SGP ones on 81/500, hence a greater robustness is achieved.
- Looking at the columns from "Length Individual 1" to "Depth Individual 2" in Table 1, it can be seen how the SGP can always find substantially smaller individuals than IGP. Nonetheless, they outperform those found with IGP in terms of robustness (last column in Table 1) only two times out of 10. Moreover, in terms of fitness 1 values, the individuals created with SGP always

Table 1. Results of GP control law creation using the Inclusive GP and Standard GP. The highlighted values indicates which GP algorithm performed better on the considered disturbance scenario.

	Fitness 1	Fitness 2	Successful	Length Individual 1	Depth Individual 1	Length Individual 2	Depth Individual 2	Disturbance cases solved
IGP	**0.8688**	0	No	65	14	26	12	**20/500**
SGP	1.9712	0	No	2	1	6	4	0/500
IGP	**0.5427**	0	No	71	23	9	6	60/500
SGP	0.7811	0	No	2	1	8	2	**150/500**
IGP	**0.4832**	0	No	3	1	15	5	**73/500**
SGP	1.8142	0	No	2	1	5	4	1/500
IGP	**0.6076**	0	**Yes**	57	17	14	6	44/500
SGP	0.6603	0	No	2	1	2	1	**209/500**
IGP	**0.4986**	0	**Yes**	41	16	75	18	**436/500**
SGP	0.9315	0	No	2	1	4	3	45/500
IGP	**0.5272**	0	**Yes**	68	21	35	13	**248/500**
SGP	1.0006	0	No	6	4	2	1	57/500
IGP	**0.4985**	0	**Yes**	21	7	88	14	**428/500**
SGP	0.7328	0	No	2	1	4	3	104/500
IGP	**0.7218**	0	No	10	5	122	25	**276/500**
SGP	0.7888	0	No	2	1	5	3	186/500
IGP	**0.5520**	0	**Yes**	75	14	100	25	**434/500**
SGP	1.0065	0	No	2	1	2	1	50/500
IGP	**0.7602**	0	No	33	9	5	3	**52/500**
SGP	1.1208	0	No	2	1	2	1	8/500

perform worse than those created with IGP. These observations suggest that indeed more complex (e.g. bigger) individuals have better performances than smaller ones hence they are capable of capturing more efficiently the nonlinearties of the plant.

– Using the same number of maximum generations and population size, the SGP is never able to find a successful control law on the disturbance scenario of design, while the IGP is able to find a successful control law 50% of the time as reported in the column "Successful" in Table 1. Here successful means that the final values of the states are within 1% range of their reference values. This suggests that IGP can find better solutions than SGP with a smaller computational budget.

4   Test Case

The system considered to test the proposed controller is the FESTIP-FSS5 Single-Stage-to-Orbit vehicle (D'angelo et al. [3]). The main peculiarities of such vehicle are its lifting body shape and the use of an aerospike engine, which can be used during the entire ascent trajectory. This vehicle is very different from a standard multistage rocket, having greater control capability, and hence is an interesting framework for the design and testing of intelligent controllers. Here, only those aspects that influence the design of the controller will be described. For a more detailed description of this vehicle please refer to [3].

The aim of the considered controller is to perform the guidance of the vehicle by tracking a reference trajectory. In particular the reference trajectory obtained in [11] is considered.

4.1   Disturbance Scenario

The control capabilities of the proposed controller are tested by simulating different disturbance scenarios consisting in a gust acting in a certain altitude range with constant intensity and by considering uncertainties in the aerodynamic and atmospheric models. The uncertainties formulation was taken from [13].

Each disturbance scenario is described by three parameters as in Eq. (1)

$$disturbance\ scenario = (h_{start}, v_g, \Delta_g) \tag{1}$$

where $h_{start} \in [1, 30]$ km is the altitude at which the gust starts, $v_g \in [1, 60]$ m/s is its intensity and $\Delta_g \in [5, 15]$ km is the width of the gust zone. The gust is applied as in Eq. (2)

$$v = \begin{cases} v, & h < h_{start} \\ v - v_g, & h_{start} \leq h \leq h_{start} + \Delta_g \\ v, & h > h_{start} + \Delta_g \end{cases} \tag{2}$$

5   Results

The code for the algorithms and the models have been implemented in Python 3 and rely on the open source library DEAP [4] for the GP part, and Tensorflow for the NN. All the simulations were run on a Laptop with 16 GB of RAM and an Intel® Core™ i7-8750H CPU @ 2.20 GHz × 12 threads and multiprocessing was used. The code developed in this work is open source and can be found at https://github.com/strath-ace/smart-ml.

In this section, other than presenting the final results on the performances of the proposed controller, also the influence of the optimization algorithm used to create the training dataset and the architecture of the employed NN are analyzed in order to understand their influence on the whole controller creation process.

Note that the formulation of the test case used in this section does not consider the constraints that were implemented during the creation of the control law using GP in Sect. 3. This because the aim of the next steps of the proposed approach (the optimization of the GP control law and the control tests using also the NN) is to maintain the trajectory within 1% from the reference one, and then the constraints satisfaction is implied.

The training dataset for the NN was produced by performing an optimization of the best performing control law obtained with IGP (fifth row in Table 1) on 500 different disturbance scenarios evenly distributed in the disturbance domain (Fig. 4a). The goal of the optimization process is to find the optimal GP control law parameters explained in Sect. 2 in order to obtain a controlled trajectory which is within 1% range of the reference trajectory. The optimal GP parameters and the related trajectory are then stored to produce the training dataset for the NN. In order to understand the influence of the employed optimization algorithm on the whole process and on the training phase, a comparison of the Broyden–Fletcher–Goldfarb–Shanno (BFGS) and Nelder-Mead (NM) algorithms was made and the results are listed in Table 2. These two algorithms were chosen since both are implemented in the *scipy optimize* library and BFGS is a gradient based method, while NM is a direct search method.

From these results it can be seen that BFGS is six times faster and can converge better than NM since it can perform a successful optimization of the GP control law on 24.6% more disturbance scenarios than the latter. Such better performances can be explained by the fact that, by being gradient based, BFGS can converge faster to the local minimum, while NM makes use of the whole optimization budget at its disposal (greater computational time) but without using the information from the gradient it is not able to successfully converge to the minimum.

Table 2. Comparison of two different optimization algorithms

	BFGS	Nelder-Mead
Successes	439/500	316/500
Computational time	1 day 03h27m27s	6 days 12h33m19s

The results of the optimization using both algorithms were used to produce two different training datasets for the NN which were structured as the matrix in Eq. (3).

$$training\ dataset = \begin{bmatrix} t'_1 & x'_{11} & \dots & x'_{1s} & err'_x11 & \dots & err'_x1s & C_{11} & \dots & C_{1n} \\ t'_2 & x'_{21} & \dots & x'_{2s} & err'_x21 & \dots & err'_x2s & C_{21} & \dots & C_{2n} \\ \dots & \dots & \dots & \dots & \dots & \dots & \dots & \dots & \dots & \dots \\ t'_m & x'_{m1} & \dots & x'_{ms} & err'_xm1 & \dots & err'_xms & C_{m1} & \dots & C_{mn} \end{bmatrix} \quad (3)$$

The *training dataset* matrix in Eq. (3) has dimensionality $[m \times (2s + n + 1)]$, where m denotes the different optimizations performed, s is the number of the states parameters, and n refers to the optimized parameters typical of the considered GP equation. In this case, each component represented in Eq. (3) is a column vector containing 500 points of the performed trajectory, e.g. x'_{11} contains the trajectory of the state x_1 obtained using the optimized values of the GP control laws from C_{11} to C_{1n}. The same explanation is valid for the tracking errors, which are measured as the differences between the obtained trajectory and the reference one.

The training datasets obtained with both algorithms were used to train three different NN architectures with fully connected layers: A) one hidden layer with 30 neurons per layer (Configuration 30 with 1,629 trainable parameters); B) two hidden layers with 25 neurons per layer (Configuration 25 × 25 with 2,014 trainable parameters); C) two hidden layers with 30 neurons per layer (Configuration 30 × 30 with 2,559 trainable parameters). The NNs were then tested five times on a predefined set of 500 disturbance scenarios obtained randomly and uniformly distributed in the disturbance domain (Fig. 4b). These 500 disturbance scenarios are different than those used in the previous steps of the process in order to further test the robustness of the proposed controller. The three NN architectures were chosen in order to observe the effects of the variation of the number of trainable parameters on the overall performances. The obtained results are listed in Table 3.

Table 3. Success rates (%) of the three different NN configurations tested on five different runs on the same test points using the NN trained on the training datasets produced with the BFGS and Nelder-Mead optimization.

	BFGS						Nelder-Mead					
	Success rate (%)						Success rate (%)					
	Run 1	Run 2	Run 3	Run 4	Run 5	Mean ± σ	Run 1	Run 2	Run 3	Run 4	Run 5	Mean ± σ
	Configuration 30											
NN	71.0	70.2	68.2	71.2	68.0	(**69.72 ± 1.36**)	68.0	68.0	71.0	67.2	69.6	(**68.76 ± 1.13**)
GP	67.8	70.6	70.0	69.0	67.8	(**69.04 ± 0.43**)	65.6	65.6	66.6	65.6	66.8	(**66.04 ± 1.41**)
Global	84.8	84.6	83.6	84.0	84.2	(**84.24 ± 0.50**)	82.6	82.6	82.2	81.6	84.8	(**82.76 ± 0.92**)
	Configuration 25 × 25											
NN	69.0	69.4	69.6	72.6	71.6	(**70.44 ± 1.34**)	66.0	70.6	69.0	70.6	67.2	(**68.68 ± 1.72**)
GP	70.6	71.2	70.2	71.6	70.6	(**70.84 ± 0.97**)	62.4	69.4	66.2	70.2	68.0	(**67.24 ± 1.36**)
Global	86.2	84.8	83.8	85.6	86.2	(**85.32 ± 0.54**)	80.0	82.6	82.2	82.8	82.2	(**81.96 ± 1.08**)
	Configuration 30 × 30											
NN	71.2	71.6	68.2	70.8	72.0	(**70.76 ± 1.84**)	68.6	68.0	68.6	69.2	69.0	(**68.68 ± 2.78**)
GP	71.0	68.6	69.8	72.8	68.0	(**70.04 ± 1.00**)	68.8	68.0	69.4	67.0	68.8	(**67.24 ± 0.41**)
Global	85.0	84.8	83.0	84.4	86.0	(**84.64 ± 0.83**)	82.4	83.4	84.4	82.4	81.2	(**82.76 ± 1.08**)

In Table 3, *success rate* means how many successful trajectories (within 1% from the reference trajectory) were obtained over 500 different disturbance scenarios (Fig. 4b). The results in Table 3 were obtained by performing a control action on the selected disturbance scenario using in parallel: 1) the non optimized GP control law (GP approach, rows GP in Table 3); and 2) the GP control law always optimized by the NN (NN approach, rows NN in Table 3). *Global*, in Table 3, refers to the total success rate achieved when considering both the GP and NN approaches. This comparison highlighted how when using alone either the GP approach or the NN one, the success rate is ~70% (~68% for those obtained with NM) of the tested disturbance scenarios. While if the global amount of success is considered, the success rate gets to ~85% (~82% for those obtained with NM). This suggests that the two approaches NN and GP can be complementary, that is, the GP approach is successful on some disturbance scenarios where the NN approach fails and vice-versa. The observed complementarity indicates that a controller as depicted in Fig. 3 could be effective by enhancing the GP control law performances optimizing it online with a NN when the GP control law fails, which is, when the tracking error on the states becomes greater than a certain threshold. It can also be observed that, in line with the results obtained from the BFGS and NM comparison, the lower success rate of the NM algorithm translates into a smaller training dataset for the NN than the one obtained with the BFGS algorithm, which as a consequence influenced the precision and success rate of the NN.

6   Conclusion

In this work, a new hybrid approach to IC, consisting in an NN based online optimization of a GP control law produced offline, has been proposed. Results coming from tests with different settings of disturbances show that the approach is more robust that using only the GP trained offline.

Moreover, the creation of the training dataset using two different optimization algorithm showed the importance of this phase, highlighting how using different optimization methods can lead to different results. In fact, a gradient based method produced better results both in terms of accuracy (24.6% more successes) and of computational time (six times faster) than a direct search method. As a consequence, the controller trained with the dataset produced using the BFGS algorithm achieved a slightly greater robustness on test cases than the one trained with the NM algorithm.

To improve the performance of the GP, two new features were also devised, implemented and tested: Inclusive Tournament and Inclusive Crossover. The Inclusive Tournament and Inclusive Crossover were designed to improve the robustness of the GP control law since it is a key aspect in control applications. In comparison with a standard implementation of GP using standard single point crossover and Double Tournament selection, the control law created with IGP can control the plant successfully on average on 25.2% more disturbance cases than the one created with the SGP.

Different future research directions lie ahead: the creation of the training dataset for the NN requires further investigation in order to assess the possible benefits of using a global optimizer instead of a local one and also to understand if the creation of the training dataset could be avoided in order to speed up the process, for example by using a RL framework. Different NN architectures will be tested, e.g. a Radial Basis Function (RBF) network, in order to assess which could be the best NN configuration for this application. Finally a more in depth analysis of the Inclusive Crossover and Tournament will be performed in order to fully understand the extent of the introduced improvements in comparison to the SGP.

References

1. Antsaklis, P.J.: Defining intelligent control. Report to the task force on intelligent control. IEEE Control Syst. Soc. **58**, 1–31 (1993)

2. Chiang, C.H.: A genetic programming based rule generation approach for intelligent control systems. In: 3CA 2010–2010 International Symposium on Computer, Communication, Control and Automation, vol. 1, pp. 104–107 (2010). https://doi.org/10.1109/3CA.2010.5533882

3. D'Angelo, S., Minisci, E., Di Bona, D., Guerra, L.: Optimization methodology for ascent trajectories of lifting-body reusable launchers. J. Spacecraft Rockets **37**(6), 761–767 (2000)

4. Fortin, F.A., De Rainville, F.M., Gardner, M.A., Parizeau, M., Gagńe, C.: DEAP: evolutionary algorithms made easy. J. Mach. Learn. Res. **13**, 2171–2175 (2012)

5. Gomez, F., Schmidhuber, J., Miikkulainen, R.: Efficient non-linear control through neuroevolution. In: Fürnkranz, J., Scheffer, T., Spiliopoulou, M. (eds.) ECML 2006. LNCS (LNAI), vol. 4212, pp. 654–662. Springer, Heidelberg (2006). https://doi.org/10.1007/11871842_64

6. Gomez, F.J., Miikkulainen, R.: Active guidance for a finless rocket using neuroevolution. In: Cantú-Paz, E., et al. (eds.) GECCO 2003. LNCS, vol. 2724, pp. 2084–2095. Springer, Heidelberg (2003). https://doi.org/10.1007/3-540-45110-2_105

7. Johnson, E., Calise, A., Corban, J.E.: Reusable launch vehicle adaptive guidance and control using neural networks. In: AIAA Guidance, Navigation, and Control Conference and Exhibit (2001). https://doi.org/10.2514/6.2001-4381

8. Kamio, S., Mitsuhashi, H., Iba, H.: Integration of genetic programming and reinforcement learning for real robots. In: Cantú-Paz, E., et al. (eds.) GECCO 2003. LNCS, vol. 2723, pp. 470–482. Springer, Heidelberg (2003). https://doi.org/10.1007/3-540-45105-6_59

9. Koza, J., Keane, M., Yu, J., Bennett III, F., Mydlowec, W.: Automatic creation of human-competitive programs and controllers by means of genetic programming. Genet. Program Evolvable Mach. **1**(1/2), 121–164 (2000). https://doi.org/10.1023/A:1010076532029

10. Luke, S., Panait, L.: Fighting bloat with nonparametric parsimony pressure. In: Guervós, J.J.M., Adamidis, P., Beyer, H.-G., Schwefel, H.-P., Fernández-Villacañas, J.-L. (eds.) PPSN 2002. LNCS, vol. 2439, pp. 411–421. Springer, Heidelberg (2002). https://doi.org/10.1007/3-540-45712-7_40

11. Marchetti, F., Minisci, E., Riccardi, A.: Single-stage to orbit ascent trajectory optimisation with reliable evolutionary initial guess. Optim. Eng. (submitted to)

12. Marchetti, F., Minisci, E., Riccardi, A.: Towards intelligent control via genetic programming. In: 2020 International Joint Conference on Neural Networks (IJCNN) (2020)

13. Pescetelli, F., Minisci, E., Maddock, C., Taylor, I., Brown, R.E.: Ascent trajectory optimisation for a single-stage-to-orbit vehicle with hybrid propulsion. In: 18th AIAA/3AF International Space Planes and Hypersonic Systems and Technologies Conference 2012, pp. 1–18 (2012)

14. Rosca, J.P.: Entropy-driven adaptive representation. In: Proceedings of the Workshop on Genetic Programming: From Theory to Real-World Applications, pp. 23–32 (1995)

15. Salichon, M., Turner, K.: A neuro-evolutionary approach to Micro Aerial Vehicle control. In: Proceedings of the 12th Annual Genetic and Evolutionary Computation Conference, GECCO 2010, pp. 1123–1130 (2010). https://doi.org/10.1145/1830483.1830692

16. Saridis, G.N.: Toward the realization of intelligent controls. Proc. IEEE **67**(8), 1115–1133 (1979). https://doi.org/10.1109/PROC.1979.11407

17. Shir, O.M.: Niching in evolutionary algorithms. In: Rozenberg, G., Bäck, T., Kok, J.N. (eds.) Handbook of Natural Computing. Springer, Berlin Heidelberg (2012). https://doi.org/10.1007/978-3-540-92910-9_32
18. Wilson, C., Marchetti, F., Di Carlo, M., Riccardi, A., Minisci, E.: Classifying intelligence in machines : a taxonomy of intelligent control. Robotics 9(3), 64 (2020). https://doi.org/10.3390/robotics9030064

Extreme Learning Machine with Evolutionary Parameter Tuning Applied to Forecast the Daily Natural Flow at Cahora Bassa Dam, Mozambique

Alfeu D. Martinho[1,2] (ID), Celso B. M. Ribeiro[3] (ID), Yulia Gorodetskaya[2], Tales L. Fonseca[2] (ID), and Leonardo Goliatt[2(✉)] (ID)

[1] Púnguè-Tete University, Chimoio, Mozambique
[2] Computational Modeling Program, Federal University of Juiz de Fora, Juiz de Fora, Brazil
goliatt@gmail.com
[3] Civil Engineering Program, Federal University of Juiz de Fora, Juiz de Fora, Brazil

Abstract. This paper proposes a hybrid approach combining an Extreme Learning Machine and a Genetic Algorithm to predict the short-term streamflow at the Cahora Bassa dam, the largest hydroelectric power plant in southern Africa. To predict the streamflows seven days ahead, the model uses as input the past river flows, information from humidity, rainfall, and evaporation measures from the lake upstream of the dam. The choice of the Extreme Learning Machine's internal parameters, crucial for excellent model performance, is performed by a Genetic Algorithm. A set of five metrics was used to assess the performance of the hybrid approach. The computational experiments show the proposed approach outperforms other machine learning methods such as ElasticNet linear model, Support Vector Machines, and Gradient Boosting. However, the ELM prediction model overestimates higher flows. The approach arises as a practical tool to predict the streams which have the potential to help the dam operations balancing the needs of energy production and the safety of the population living downstream of the dam.

Keywords: Extreme learning machines · Genetic algorithms · Hydrology

1 Introduction

Located in the province of Tete, the Cahora Bassa dam is the fourth-largest dam in Africa, on the terminal section of the so-called Zambezi medium Mozambique. The reservoir is the 12th largest in the world and also the fifth in Africa, with a maximum capacity of $6300\,\mathrm{m}^3$ of water (after Aswan, Volta, and Kariba), has a maximum length of 250 km in length and 38 km of spacing between banks, occupying about $2700\,\mathrm{km}^2$ and having an average depth of 26 m. It is currently the

© Springer Nature Switzerland AG 2020
B. Filipič et al. (Eds.): BIOMA 2020, LNCS 12438, pp. 255–267, 2020.
https://doi.org/10.1007/978-3-030-63710-1_20

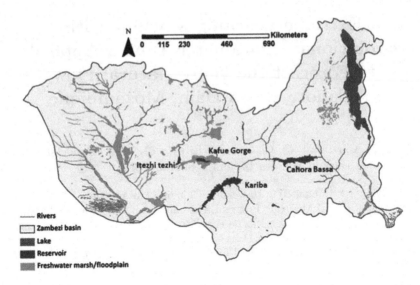

Fig. 1. Zambezi River basin, showing the location of the Cahora Bassa dam. Adapted from [16].

largest electricity producer in Mozambique, with over 2000 MW, which supplies Mozambique, South Africa, Zimbabwe, and Malawi.

In addition to energy production, it contributes to the development of the economy of the Zambezi River delta, downstream of it, by enabling activities such as agriculture, pastoralism, fishing, construction of access roads and, in reducing the risk of the occurrence of natural disasters, such as drought, floods. However, due to the maximization of energy production, by releasing stored water during the season drought, while preparing for low flows on dry season. As a result, the Zambezi's regulated flow has been drying out the wetlands, previously fed by the Zambezi floodwaters, ceasing to be multiple secondary channels and branches that regularly changed, becoming a single main channel. The water released by the dam erodes the banks and deepens the riverbed. The now dry floodplains have severe consequences for biodiversity. Floods have become unpredictable, making communities across the Zambezi much more vulnerable to their negative impacts. This paper presents a tool to help understand the dynamics of the Zambezi River in Cahora-Bassa, by forecasting the flow in the affluence to the dam. The Cahora Bassa lake receives contributions from the Luangwa River Sub-basin, Kafue River Sub-basin, Hunyani River Sub-basin, and direct tributaries to the reservoir and by the effluence generated by Kariba, the upstream dam, depending on its storage status. This forecast appears to be extremely important because it can help make decisions about dam operations, contributing to the construction of a policy of sustainable exploitation of the hydrographic basin, that is, the adoption of the ecological flow. Figure 1 shows the Zambezi River basin and the location of the Cahora Bassa dam.

Time series prediction models have been widely applied for the characterization of hydrological variables. Several methods developed in the literature are used to this task, ranging from hydrological and meteorological modeling, statistical approaches, and computational intelligence and machine learning models. As reported in the recent literature [1, 15, 20] the machine learning models deserve a particular highlight in their modeling and forecasting abilities, often obtaining better results.

A comparison of machine learning techniques for monthly river flow forecasting is reported in [13] and [21]. By comparing eight machine learning models for time series prediction, Ahmed et al. [2] have concluded that multilayer perceptron neural networks and Gaussian processes produced the most accurate estimations. Sun et al. [19] reported that Gaussian Process outperformed ARIMA-based methods in more than 400 river basins. Other computational intelligence approaches have also have shown to be accurate tools for water level and discharge forecasting with uncertainty, such as Fuzzy neural networks [3].

Despite the impressive results reported in the literature, machine learning approaches' proper performance depends on adjusting internal parameters [14], and their choice directly affects the performance of the models. For example, neural networks need the number of layers, the number of neurons, and the learning rate to be set. Gaussian processes need the choice of the kernel function and the associated parameters. This task can exhibit high complexity [6], and smart search techniques are an alternative to find the best possible set. To tackle these drawbacks, an alternative is to apply an optimization algorithm. This approach can be called hybrid. Hybrid strategies combine the capabilities of different methods to produce accurate predictions, covering physical modeling, concentrated and distributed conceptual models, methodologies combining both machine learning and stochastic models, and techniques of artificial intelligence and data mining.

This study aims to assess the abilities of the Extreme Learning Machine (ELM) model as a practical technique for predicting the natural flow of the Zambezi River to the Cahora-Bassa dam. The results show that ELM outperforms other machine learning methods producing accurate estimations. However, the technique should be applied with care when estimating extreme flow values. The ELM can be used to estimate natural flows helping to develop an alert system for the dam's operations. This paper is organized follows. Section 2 describes the study area and the historical data, the streamflow estimation model, and the proposed hybrid approach. The computational experiments and discussion are presented in Sect. 3. Finally, Sect. 4 draws the conclusion.

2   Materials and Methods

2.1   Study Area and Data

The data consist of a historical daily series of 5844 observations covering 15 years, referring to 2003 and 2018. The variables under analysis are: natural flow affluent to the Cahora Bassa dam (Q), rainfall (R), evaporation (E) and relative humidity (H). The database provided by the Water Resources and Environment Management Department of the Cahora Bassa Hydroelectric, the managing company of the Cahora Bassa dam. The observed streamflow data is partitioned into the model development (training) and model evaluation (testing) part, according to Fig. 2.

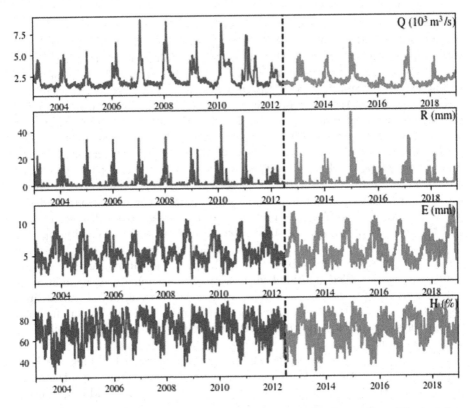

Fig. 2. Historical flow data of the Zambezi river at Cahora Bassa dam. The training set ranges from 2003-01-01 to 2012-06-30 and is shown in blue, while the test set ranges from 2012-07-01 to 2018-12-31 and appears in orange. (Color figure online)

2.2   Streamflow Estimation Model

To carry out the predictions, we selected periods with seven days in the historical flow series. The forecast model receives an input consisting of 28 values: 7 values of precipitation, 7 of evaporation, 7 humidity, and 7 values of flow. The model returns the corresponding estimated flow 7-days ahead. There are three forms of flow forecasting, with a few hours or days in advance, called short-term forecasts, medium-term or seasonal forecasts, and long-term forecasts, based on probabilities, trend analysis or climate change scenarios.

The estimated flow was considered as a function of finite sets of antecedent precipitation, evaporation and humidity and flow observations at the stations. The predictive model has the following form:

$$Q_{t+7} = F(\overbrace{R_t, \cdots, R_{t-6}}^{\text{rainfall}}, \underbrace{E_t, \cdots, E_{t-6}}_{\text{evaporation}}, \overbrace{H_t, \cdots, H_{t-6}}^{\text{humidity}}, \underbrace{Q_t, \cdots, Q_{t-6}}_{\text{streamflow}}) \quad (1)$$

where Q_{t+j} is the streamflow at day $t + j$, R_{t+j} is the precipitation (rainfall) at day $t + j$, E_{t+j} is the evaporation at day $t + j$, H_{t+j} is the humidity measured at day $t + j$, and F is an estimation function.

2.3   Extreme Learning Machine (ELM)

Extreme Learning Machine (ELM) [12] is a particular case of feedforward artificial neural network, where the vast majority is composed of only one hidden layer. Compared with the Artificial Neural Network (ANN), the Support Vector Machine (SVM), and other traditional prediction models, the ELM model retains the advantages of fast learning, good ability to generalize, and convenience in terms of modeling [7]. According to authors, these models are able to produce good generalization performance and learn thousands of times faster than networks trained using backpropagation. In literature, it also shows that these models can outperform support vector machines in both classification and regression applications.

In ELMs, there are three levels of randomness: (1) fully connected, hidden node parameters are randomly generated; (2) the connection between inputs to hidden nodes can be randomly generated, not all input nodes are connected to a particular hidden node; (3) a hidden node itself can be a subnetwork formed by several nodes resulting in learning local features.

The output function of ELM used in this paper is given by [18]

$$\hat{y}(\mathbf{x}) = \sum_{i=1}^{L} \beta_i G(\mathbf{w}_i, b_i, \mathbf{x}) \quad (2)$$

where $\hat{y}$ is the ELM prediction associated to the input vector $\mathbf{x}$, $\mathbf{w}_i$ is the weight vector of the ith hidden node, b_i are the biases of the neurons in the hidden layer, β_i are output weights, $G(\cdot)$ is the nonlinear activation function and L is the number of hidden nodes. The parameters $(\mathbf{w}, b)$ are randomly generated (normally distributed with zero mean and standard deviation equals to one), and weights β_i of the output layer are determined analytically. The activation functions $G(\mathbf{w}, b, \mathbf{x})$ with the hidden nodes weights $(\mathbf{w}, b)$ are shown in Table 1. The output weight vector $[\beta_1, ..., \beta_L]$ can be determined by minimizing [11]

$$\min_{\boldsymbol{\beta} \in \mathbb{R}^L} (\|\mathbf{H}\boldsymbol{\beta} - \mathbf{y}\| + C\|\boldsymbol{\beta}\|^2) \quad (3)$$

Table 1. Activation functions used in ELM. The hidden node parameters $(\mathbf{w}, b)$ are randomly generated using a normal distribution $N(0, 1)$.

#	Name	Activation function G
1	Identity	$G(\mathbf{w}, b, \mathbf{x}) = \|\mathbf{w} \cdot \mathbf{x} + b\|$
2	Sigmoid	$G(\mathbf{w}, b, \mathbf{x}) = \frac{1}{1 + exp(-\mathbf{w} \cdot \mathbf{x} + b)}$
3	Hyperbolic Tangent	$G(\mathbf{w}, b, \mathbf{x}) = \frac{1 - exp(\mathbf{w} \cdot \mathbf{x} + b)}{1 + exp(\mathbf{w} \cdot \mathbf{x} + b)}$
4	Gaussian	$G(\mathbf{w}, b, \mathbf{x}) = exp(-(\mathbf{w} \cdot \mathbf{x} + b)^2)$
5	Multiquadrics	$G(\mathbf{w}, b, \mathbf{x}) = \sqrt{\|\mathbf{w} - \mathbf{x}\|^2 + b^2}$
6	Inverse Multiquadrics	$G(\mathbf{w}, b, \mathbf{x}) = 1/(\|\mathbf{w} - \mathbf{x}\|^2 + b^2)^{1/2}$
7	Swish	$G(\mathbf{w}, b, \mathbf{x}) = \frac{\|\mathbf{w} \cdot \mathbf{x} + b\|}{1 + exp(-\mathbf{w} \cdot \mathbf{x} + b)}$
8	ReLU	$G(\mathbf{w}, b, \mathbf{x}) = \max_i (0, (\mathbf{w} \cdot \mathbf{x} + b))$

where $\mathbf{y}$ is the output data vector, $\mathbf{H}$ is the hidden layer output matrix

$$\mathbf{H} = \begin{bmatrix} G_1(\mathbf{w}_1, b_1, \mathbf{x}_1) & \cdots & G_L(\mathbf{w}_L, b_L, \mathbf{x}_1) \\ \vdots & \ddots & \vdots \\ G_1(\mathbf{w}_1, b_1, \mathbf{x}_N) & \cdots & G_L(\mathbf{w}_L, b_L, \mathbf{x}_N) \end{bmatrix} \text{ and } \mathbf{y} = \begin{bmatrix} y_1 \\ \vdots \\ y_N \end{bmatrix}$$

is the output data vector with N the number of data points. The optimal solution is given by

$$\beta = (\mathbf{H}^\mathbf{T}\mathbf{H})^{-1}\mathbf{H}^\mathbf{T}\mathbf{y} = \mathbf{H}^\dagger\mathbf{y}$$

where $\mathbf{H}^\dagger$ is the pseudoinverse of $\mathbf{H}$.

2.4 Parameter Tuning Guided by a Genetic Algorithm

We use in this work a Genetic Algorithm (GA) to find the internal parameters of the ELM neural network. In this scenario, each individual/candidate in the population represents an ELM neural network. There are practically four fundamental blocks for a genetic algorithm [10]: (i) Selection: the purpose of the selection is to choose the individuals who will serve as parents in the reproduction process. (ii) Crossover: this operator creates new individuals by mixing the characteristics of two parents. (iii) Mutation: this operator introduces diversity among the new individuals of the population. (iv) Reinsertion: elitism strategy is used to preserve part of the population that has superior performance. Hence, the best-known solutions found so-far in the search process were not lost. Using the these blocks we can describe GA with the following steps:

1. Create an initial population of random models (randomly generate a set of hyperparameters values);
2. Evaluate each individual (model) of the population and acquire their fitness value (performance metric of the model);
3. Select individuals for the recombination process;

4. Create a new population of new models (from a new set of internal parameters) generated through crossover and mutation on the selected individuals;
5. Combine the old population with the new one and keep only the best models (elitism strategy);
6. Repeat steps 2–5 until to satisfy the stopping criteria.

Table 2 shows the set of hyperparameters. Considering the ELM setup, a candidate solution $\theta = (\theta_1, \theta_2, \theta_3)$ represents the number of neurons in the hidden layers, the value of the parameter C in Eq. (3) and the activation function as shown in Table 1.

Table 2. Encoding of ELM candidate solutions. The column DV indicates the Decision Variable in the GA encoding.

DV	Description	Settings/Range
θ_1	No. neurons in the hidden layer, L	[1, 500]
θ_2	Regularization parameter C, Eq. (3)	[0.0001, 10000]
θ_3	Activation function G, Table 1	1: Identity; 4: Sigmoid; 3: Hyperbolic Tangent 4: Gaussian; 5: Multiquadric; 6: Inverse Multiquadric; 7: Swish; 8: ReLU;

3   Computational Experiments and Discussion

The internal parameters of each ELM model were set through the search performed by the Genetic Algorithm with a population size of 16 individuals evolving in 25 generations, crossover probability of 80%, and mutation rate of 10%. The fitness function is the RMSE calculated according to 3-fold cross-validation in the training set that ranges from 2003-01-01 to 2012-06-30. The training set appears in blue in Fig. 2. After the end of the evolutionary search, the best model's performance is calculated using the test set, a slice of the historical data ranging from 2012-07-01 to 2018-12-31 that appears in orange in Fig. 2. The lower and upper bounds θ_L and θ_U, are given respectively by $\theta_L = (1, 0.001, 1)$ and $\theta_U = (100, 10^4, 8)$. Tournament selection was used to select individuals for the recombination process, using five individuals in the tournament. The experiments were repeated 25 times with different random seeds.

To assess the ELM performance, we have implemented three other machine learning methods in the same computational framework: ElasticNet linear model (EN) [9], Support Vector Regression (SVR) [4], and Extreme Gradient Boosting (XGB) [5]. All models had their internal parameters optimized by the genetic algorithm using the same population size, crossover probabilities, mutation rates, and the number of generations. The encondig for EN models involves three parameters, $(\theta_1, \theta_2, \theta_3)$, where θ_1 is a penalty term, θ_2 is the ratio between L_1 and L_2 regularization, and θ_3 is a bolean variavle that allows only positive coefficients. The upper and lower bounds are $\theta_1 \in [10^{-6}, 2]$, $\theta_2 \in [0, 1]$, and $\theta_3 \in \{\text{True}, \text{False}\}$. The SVR model implements RBF (radial basis function) kernel and each individual encodes three SVR parameters in the form

$(\theta_1, \theta_2, \theta_3) = (\gamma, C, \varepsilon)$. The lower and upper bounds are $\boldsymbol{\theta}_L = (0, 0.1, 0.01)$ and $\boldsymbol{\theta}_U = (1, 10^4, 100)$. The candidate solutions for XGB models encodes four parameters $(\theta_1, \theta_2, \theta_3, \theta_2)$, where θ_1 is the learning rate, θ_2 controls the number of estimators of the ensemble model, θ_3 is the maximum depth of each estimator, and θ_4 is the regularization parameter. The lower and upper bounds are $\boldsymbol{\theta}_L = (10^{-6}, 10, 1, 0)$ and $\boldsymbol{\theta}_U = (1, 100, 20, 100)$. Table 3 presents the metrics used in this paper and their brief description.

Table 3. Performance metrics. R^2 is the coefficient of determination, RMSE is the Root Mean Squared Error, while MAPE is the Mean Absolute Percentage Error. NSE is the Nash-Sutcliffe efficiency for the estimation model [17], and KGE is the Kling-Gupta efficiency between simulated and observed values [8]. O_i represents the observed data and P_i the predicted values. $\overline{O}$ is the mean observed streams. r is the Pearson product-moment correlation coefficient and α is the ratio between the standard deviation of the predicted values and the standard deviation of the observed values. Finally, β is the ratio between the mean of the predicted values and the mean of the observed values.

Metric acronym	Expression
R^2	$\frac{\sum_{i=1}^{N}(O_i - P_i)^2}{\sum_{i=1}^{N}(O_i - \overline{O})^2}$
RMSE	$\frac{1}{N}\sqrt{\sum_{i=1}^{N}(O_i - P_i)^2}$
MAPE	$100 \times \frac{1}{N}\sum_{i=1}^{N}\frac{|O_{(i)} - P_{(i)}|}{|O_{(i)}|}$
NSE	$1 - \frac{\sum_{i=1}^{N}(O_i - P_i)^2}{\sum_{i=1}^{n}(O_i - \overline{O})^2}$
KGE	$1 - \sqrt{(r-1)^2 + (\alpha - 1)^2 + (\beta - 1)^2}$

Table 4 presents the descriptive statistics for the performance metrics. The results produced by the ELM model are compared with other models of machine learning, such as EN, SVR, XGB. From this table, we can observe ELM produced competitive results concerning all metrics. However, ELM presents better estimates showing lower standard deviations.

Table 4. Averaged metrics produced by ELM and comparison with other approaches. The standard deviations appear within parentheses. The first column shows the metric acronym. The second column summarizes ELM results, the second and third columns, the results for EN and SVR, while the last column presents the metrics for XGB. A total of 25 runs were performed.

Estimator	ELM	EN	SVR	XGB
R^2	**0.71** (0.004)	0.66 (0.073)	0.71 (0.062)	0.70 (0.005)
RMSE	**0.42** (0.003)	0.47 (0.060)	0.42 (0.041)	0.43 (0.003)
MAPE	**14.85** (0.182)	16.61 (2.438)	15.20 (2.457)	16.05 (0.234)
NSE	**0.72** (0.003)	0.60 (0.118)	0.68 (0.025)	0.68 (0.005)
KGE	**0.86** (0.001)	0.81 (0.055)	0.82 (0.020)	0.84 (0.003)

The results of the statistical tests for all metrics are displayed in Table 5. The null hypothesis is that the mean in each evaluation metric is equal for all models. As can be seen, we reject the null hypothesis for MAPE, NSE, RMSE, and KGE because their p-values were smaller than the significance level of 0.05. This means that these metrics can be used as a criterion to evaluate the performance of the models in the forecast 7-days ahead. All models produced similar results for R^2, however, with relatively low. Table 5 shows the results of multiple comparisons applying the Tukey test ($\alpha = 0.05$) to ELM pairs and other models for each metric. The null hypothesis is that the means in each pair of models are equal, which leads to a similar conclusion in Table 6.

Table 5. p-values of ANOVA test for each metric.

Metric	R^2	RMSE	MAPE	NSE	KGE
p-value	0.101	0.032	0.020	0.000	0.000

Table 6. Pairwise Tukey test. The null hypothesis is that the estimators' means are equal. The entries show the outcome for rejecting the null hypothesis.

Estimator 1	Estimator 2	R^2	RMSE	MAPE	NSE	KGE
ELM	EN	False	True	False	True	True
ELM	SVR	False	False	False	True	True
ELM	XGB	False	False	True	True	True

Figure 3 shows the best hydrograph according to RMSE for the 7-days ahead flow Q_{t+7} in 25 runs. A hydrograph is a graph of the flow in a stream over a period in a specific location. From this figure, we observe that ELM is capable of representing the characteristics in the flow series, such as the change in level in the critical periods with lower flows and higher flows. The simulated hydrograph showed a very close behavior with good adherence to the observed data. However, the ELM solution overestimates the peak flows.

The internal parameters of ELM models produced by the genetic search were collected for all runs, and their distributions are shown in Fig. 4. This figure shows the parameter distribution for activation function G, the number of neurons in the hidden layer L, and the regularization parameter C. From this figure, we observe from a total of eight activation functions shown in Table 1, only three were chosen in the final solutions: Multiquadric, Swish, and Sigmoid. As shown in Fig. 4, the Multiquadric activation function was selected in 22 out of 25 runs, while the Swish function appears in the final solutions in two runs and the Sigmoid in one run. The number of neurons (parameter L) in the hidden layer is around 450, ranging from 350 to 500 neurons. More than half the solutions were set with 425–475 neurons, as shown in the boxplot's interquartile.

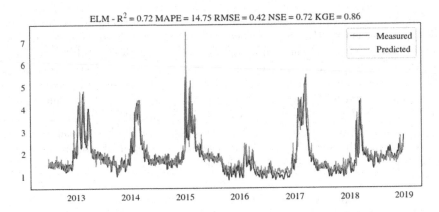

Fig. 3. Best solution according to RMSE for 7-day ahead streamflows.

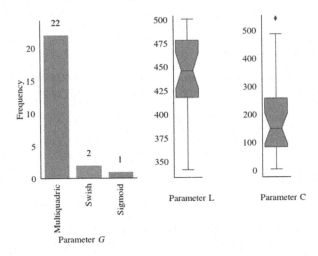

Fig. 4. Distribution of ELM parameters over 25 runs. The activation function G and the number of neurons L influence the solutions according to Eq. 2. The activation functions are described in Table 1. The regularization parameter C in Eq. 3 controls the smoothness.

The distribution of penalization shows the parameter C was set in a relatively wide range, but the boxplot shows more than 50% of the values lie in the interval [100–250].

Figure 5 displays the scatter plot of the solution with smallest RMSE over 25 runs. We observe that ELM produced solutions with a good agreement up to flows of $2500 \, \mathrm{m}^3/\mathrm{s}$, indicated by the dotted line. Furthermore, it can be seen that the quality of the solutions deteriorates as the flow value of 7-days ahead increases. One can observe that the estimation of extreme events or extreme flows is difficult to predict by ELM. We highlight that accurately identifying extreme flows are critical to the decision policy of the dam operations. Due to the river

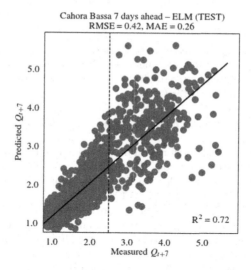

Fig. 5. Scatter plot of the solution with smallest RMSE over 25 runs.

bed's geographic characteristics downstream, the dam, the valley broadens, and the river develops a narrow floodplain [16]. As a result, extreme streamflows can abruptly change the river flow, which may cause floods and disasters. Accurate extreme streamflow predictions help safely control the river flow, allowing fit the demands for energy generation.

4 Conclusions

The present study shows the ability of the ELM model for the daily forecast of the natural flow to the Cahora Bassa dam. The results show that using a genetic algorithm to guide the selection of ELM parameters provides superior results in the flow forecast 7-days ahead. The ELM technique showed good potential to perform flow predictions; however, it seemed to overestimate peak flows. As observed in this study, ELM has been shown to obtain better results than EN, XGB, and SVR. Further studies include exploring other models, such as deep learning and online machine learning models to evaluate their forecasting capacity. The proposed ELM model can be useful for flow forecasting, which is most important to reservoir operation. It also helps to allocate the dam's waiting volume and optimize the operating rules, balancing the energy generation while ensuring the reservoir's ecological flows.

Acknowledgment. The authors acknowledge the Cahora Bassa Hydroelectric Company for the essential support during this work and the financial support from CNPq (429639/2016-3), FAPEMIG (APQ-00334/18), and CAPES - Finance Code 001.

References

1. Adnan, R.M., Liang, Z., Heddam, S., Zounemat-Kermani, M., Kisi, O., Li, B.: Least square support vector machine and multivariate adaptive regression splines for streamflow prediction in mountainous basin using hydro-meteorological data as inputs. J. Hydrol. **586**, 124371 (2020)

2. Ahmed, N.K., Atiya, A.F., Gayar, N.E., El-Shishiny, H.: An empirical comparison of machine learning models for time series forecasting. Econom. Rev. **29**(5–6), 594–621 (2010)

3. Alvisi, S., Franchini, M.: Fuzzy neural networks for water level and discharge forecasting with uncertainty. Environ. Model. Softw. **26**(4), 523–537 (2011)

4. Chang, C.C., Lin, C.J.: LIBSVM: a library for support vector machines. ACM Trans. Intell. Syst. Technol. **2**(3), 1–27 (2011)

5. Chen, T., Guestrin, C.: Xgboost. Proceedings of the 22nd ACM SIGKDD International Conference on Knowledge Discovery and Data Mining, August 2016

6. Claesen, M., Moor, B.D.: Hyperparameter search in machine learning. CoRR abs/1502.02127 (2015)

7. Guo, P., Cheng, W., Wang, Y.: Hybrid evolutionary algorithm with extreme machine learning fitness function evaluation for two-stage capacitated facility location problems. Expert Syst. Appl. **71**, 57–68 (2017)

8. Gupta, H.V., Kling, H., Yilmaz, K.K., Martinez, G.F.: Decomposition of the mean squared error and NSE performance criteria: implications for improving hydrological modelling. J. Hydrol. **377**(1), 80–91 (2009)

9. Hastie, T., Tibshirani, R., Friedman, J.: The Elements of Statistical Learning. SSS. Springer, New York (2009). https://doi.org/10.1007/978-0-387-84858-7

10. Holland, J.H.: Hidden Order: How Adaptation Builds Complexity. Helix books, Basic Books, New York (1995)

11. Huang, G., Huang, G.B., Song, S., You, K.: Trends in extreme learning machines: a review. Neural Netw. **61**(Supplement C), 32–48 (2015)

12. Huang, G.B., Zhu, Q.Y., Siew, C.K.: Extreme learning machine: a new learning scheme of feedforward neural networks. In: Proceedings of the IEEE International Joint Conference on Neural Networks, vol. 2, pp. 985–990. IEEE (2004)

13. Hussain, D., Khan, A.A.: Machine learning techniques for monthly river flow forecasting of Hunza River, Pakistan. Earth Sci. Inf. **13**(3), 939–949 (2020). https://doi.org/10.1007/s12145-020-00450-z

14. Kuhn, M., Johnson, K.: Applied Predictive Modeling. Springer, New York (2013). https://doi.org/10.1007/978-1-4614-6849-3

15. Li, J., Wang, Z., Lai, C., Zhang, Z.: Tree-ring-width based streamflow reconstruction based on the random forest algorithm for the source region of the Yangtze River, China. CATENA **183**, 104216 (2019)

16. McCartney, M., Beilfuss, R.D., Rebelo, L.-M.: Zambezi River Basin. In: Finlayson, C.M., Milton, G.R., Prentice, R.C., Davidson, N.C. (eds.) The Wetland Book, pp. 1217–1232. Springer, Dordrecht (2018). https://doi.org/10.1007/978-94-007-4001-3_91

17. Nash, J., Sutcliffe, J.: River flow forecasting through conceptual models part I - a discussion of principles. J. Hydrol. **10**(3), 282–290 (1970)

18. Saporetti, C.M., Duarte, G.R., Fonseca, T.L., da Fonseca, L.G., Pereira, E.: Extreme learning machine combined with a differential evolution algorithm for lithology identification. RITA **25**(4), 43–56 (2018)

19. Sun, A.Y., Wang, D., Xu, X.: Monthly streamflow forecasting using Gaussian process regression. J. Hydrol. **511**, 72–81 (2014)
20. Thakur, B., Kalra, A., Ahmad, S., Lamb, K.W., Lakshmi, V.: Bringing statistical learning machines together for hydro-climatological predictions - case study for Sacramento San Joaquin River Basin, California. J. Hydrol. Reg. Stud. **27**, 100651 (2020)
21. Wang, W.C., Chau, K.W., Cheng, C.T., Qiu, L.: A comparison of performance of several artificial intelligence methods for forecasting monthly discharge time series. J. Hydrol. **374**(3), 294–306 (2009)

A 3D Path Planning Algorithm Based on PSO for Autonomous UAVs Navigation

Alireza Mirshamsi[1] [ID], Simone Godio[2(✉)] [ID], Amin Nobakhti[3] [ID],
Stefano Primatesta[2] [ID], Fabio Dovis[3] [ID], and Giorgio Guglieri[2]

[1] Department of Electrical Engineering, Sharif University of Technology, Tehran, Iran
alireza.mirshamsi@ee.sharif.ir
[2] Department of Mechanical and Aerospace Engineering, Politecnico di Torino,
Turin, Italy
{simone.godio,stefano.primatesta,giorgio.guglieri}@polito.it
[3] Department of Electronics and Telecommunications, Politecnico di Torino,
Turin, Italy
nobakhti@sharif.ir, fabio.dovis@polito.it
https://www.en.sharif.edu, https://www.dimeas.polito.it,
https://www.det.polito.it

Abstract. In this paper, a new three-dimensional path planning approach with obstacle avoidance for UAVs is proposed. The aim is to provide a computationally-fast on-board sub-optimal solution for collision-free path planning in static environments. The optimal 3D path is an NP (non-deterministic polynomial-time) hard problem which may be solved numerically by global optimization algorithms such as the Particle Swarm Optimization (PSO). Application of PSO to the 3D path planning class of problems faces typical challenges such slow convergence rate. It is shown that the performance may be improved markedly by implementing a novel parallel approach and incorporation of new termination conditions. Moreover, the exploration and exploitation parameters are optimized to find a reasonably short, smooth, and safe path connecting the way-points. As an additional precaution to avoid collisions, obstacle dimensions are artificially slightly enlarged. To verify the robustness of the algorithm, several simulations are carried out by varying the number of obstacles, their volume and location in space. A certain number of simulations exploiting the random nature of PSO are performed to highlight the computational efficiency, and the robustness of this new approach.

Keywords: Particle swarm optimization (PSO) · 3D path planning algorithm · Unmanned aerial vehicle (UAV) · Autonomous navigation

1 Introduction and Related Works

The problem of path planning in the presence of obstacles is one of the cornerstones of autonomous UAVs navigation. In all those critical scenarios where it is

B. Filipič et al. (Eds.): BIOMA 2020, LNCS 12438, pp. 268–280, 2020.
https://doi.org/10.1007/978-3-030-63710-1_21

necessary to act quickly, such as earthquake-stricken areas, quarries, crevasses, or in others GPS denied/degraded environments, for UAVs the ability to process the path independently in a short time is critical. In [1], an interesting path planning solution is developed for urban environments based on MPC (Model Predictive Control) for a UAV rotary-wing fleet.

In 2007, a seminal contribution for real-time 2D path planning based on PSO in dynamic environments in the presence of circular obstacles was published [2]. PSO-based path planning algorithms were subsequently used in several studies such the one presented in [3] to solve path planning problems in complex 2D scenarios populated by a large number of articulated-shaped obstacles. In this work the PSO is used to optimize trajectories in terms of smoothing and path length. In [4] a path planning in 2D environments in limited survival time without obstacles is presented which aims to reduce the computational time associated with PSO. In subsequent years, further PSO-based approaches were developed, for 2D path planning with static or dynamic obstacles, in [2,5–9] PSO based path planning for multi-robot applications is considered by [5] in which both collision-avoidance with obstacles, and also with trajectories of other units is considered simultaneously.

One of the early studies on 3D path planning is presented in [6]. This work is built on an analogy between trajectories and fluid lines around a body. Subsequently, PSO-based algorithms are developed in [7] and [8] in order to improve upon the computational time and trajectory optimization point of view. Despite this, the 3rd dimension significantly increases the complexity of the algorithm and, for this reason the computational times are in the order of minutes or hours. As a consequence, only simplified environments are still considered.

Since algorithms of this nature (evolutionary algorithms) are useful to find the global minimum for a problem, the PSO is therefore effective to the search for trajectories of minimum length; and for this reason that it is adopted in the following discussion.

In this paper we propose an innovative approach to find a global sub-optimal solution of a 3D path planning problem with a significant reduction in computational time, even in the presence of several obstacles. This, enables full autonomous UAVs navigation in several previously unattainable possibilities. Simulation results demonstrate that the proposed strategy is able to compute a sub-optimal solution with a computational time lower than 1 s. The main feature of the proposed algorithm in parallel implementation of the 3D path planning problem.

The paper is organized as follow. In Sect. 2, the classic particle swarm optimization is presented with the novel modifications developed in this work. The definition of the objective function for the path planning problem and the parameters tuning are also presented in this section. In Sect. 3, results are presented for 4 different environments of increasing complexity. Several simulations are considered by varying the starting point and the target.

2   Problem Formulation

In this paper, the proposed PSO-based algorithm solves a path planning problem searching for the shortest path connecting a starting point to a target or sequence of targets. It is assumed that the precise offline map of the environment is available to the drone. Moreover, the drone is required to reach complete stop (zero-velocity) above each target, if there are more than one target to reach.

In this section, the standard PSO algorithm and the improvements proposed to have fast and reliable results for the problem of 3D path planning are presented. After the introduction of the objective function, the value of different parameters of the heuristic approach is presented. For each path, i.e. target i to target $i + 1$ we compute N_t points and a smooth and feasible flight path will be determined for the drone by considering spline interpolation between N_{Var} auxiliary points.

It is assumed that path planning is performed in a bounded space: the minimum and maximum of the positions in each direction in 3D space are determined based on the environment where the UAV flies. These are defined as Min_p and Max_p, where p could be x, y, or z. For stability of the algorithm, a boundary for the velocity of particles is needed: V_{min_p} and V_{max_p} are defined in Eq. 1.

$$V_{max_p} = \alpha(Max_p - Min_p)$$
$$V_{min_p} = -V_{max_p}, \tag{1}$$

where α is a tuning parameter.

2.1   Particle Swarm Optimization

The origin of this algorithm takes its cue from the study of the social behavior of a bird flock or a fish school by Berhart and Kennedy [9,10]. It solves optimization problems by introducing a population of candidate solutions, called particles, and iteratively trying to improve each of them in relation to an objective function. In this study, this function is represented by a combination of smoothness, shortness, and safety of the proposed flight path. For the ith particle of the swarm, the position and the velocity vector in the current and in the following time instant are defined as:

$$\begin{cases} V_i^{k+1} = wV_k^{\ k} + r_1c_1(\overrightarrow{Pb_i}^k - x_i^k) + r_2c_2(\overrightarrow{Gb_i}^k - x_i^k) \\ X_i^{k+1} = X_i^{\ k} + V_i^{\ k+1} \end{cases} \tag{2}$$

where the particle velocity is defined by the sum of the inertial contribution, the cognitive contribution and the global one with their respective speed values: V_i^k, $\overrightarrow{Pb_i}^k$ and $\overrightarrow{Gb_i}^k$. While, for the calculation of the position of the particle at instant $k + 1$ the pose at instant k and the velocity at instant $k + 1$ are added. What is more, w denotes the inertia weight, c_1 and c_2 are the personal and global learning constants respectively, r_1 and r_2 random values in $[0,1]$. Figure 1 shows a schematic of Eq. 2.

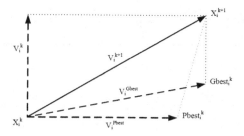

Fig. 1. PSO search mechanism in multidimensional search space, [11]

2.2 Improvement with Respect to Standard PSO Algorithm

Due to the slow convergence of the standard PSO algorithm for intensive problems such as 3D path planning, it is essential to tune and change the parameters of the standard algorithm to obtain satisfactory results. In this paper, minor changes in the standard algorithm itself are performed, and the parameters of PSO for the 3D path planning problem in an obstructed environment are appropriately tuned. Algorithm 1 shows the pseudocode of our PSO algorithm. Main features of our proposed algorithm versus the standard PSO algorithm is as follows:

1. Implementing parallel computing to find a sub-optimal path between different targets. In the standard PSO the best path between multiple targets is found by increasing the number of variables. However, this leads to costly computations and poor results. By proposing and successfully implementing a parallel form of path-planning we show that an efficient and accurate path can be found by multiple instances of parallel PSO with low number of variables and a low computational cost.
2. Parallel computing for each direction, i.e. x, y and, z, which leads to fast convergence in each direction with a low computational cost.
3. Control of the velocity of particles to remain within the permitted range. When these ranges aren't respected, to obtain reliable results, it is wise not only to saturate the magnitude of velocities, but also using velocity mirroring, which guarantee the particles to stay in the right path and to reach positions with lower cost in less time.
4. Considering 3 distinct stop conditions including, maximum number of iterations, obtaining reduced cost less than γ % in N_γ consecutive iterations, and, finding a path which its length is equal to K_L times minimum path length possible, where minimum path length possible is direct line between the starting point to destination point. Note that, γ, N_γ, and, K_L are tunable parameters, which will define in tuning section.

Algorithm 1: Proposed PSO algorithm for the problem of 3D path planning

---

%% initialization

Generate particle individuals with these structures; position, velocity, cost, bestPosition and bestCost;

Set positions of the particles randomly and velocities equal to zero and bestPosition equal to position;

Set costs of the particles by evaluating positions based on cost function and bestCost equal to cost;

Find global best position between these particles;

%% Main loop

Set IT = 0;

Set all(ActiveFlag) = true;

while *any(ActiveFlag) is true* **do**

> IT = IT + 1;
>
> **for** *i = 1 : numel(targets)* **do**
>
> > **if** *ActiveFlag(i) is true* **then**
> >
> > > **for** *j = 1 : numel(particles)* **do**
> > >
> > > > **for** *p = [x,y,z]* **do**
> > > >
> > > > > Update velocities based on equation 2, and apply velocity mirroring if velocity is out of range.
> > > > >
> > > > > Update positions based on equation 2, and check they be in the valid intervals.
> > > > >
> > > > > Evaluate the costs of each position.
> > > > >
> > > > > Update local best of each particle (bestPosition, bestCost) and global best position and cost.
> > > > >
> > > > **end**
> > > >
> > > **end**
> > >
> > > **if** *any stop conditions has been satisfied* **then**
> > >
> > > > Set ActiveFlag(i) = false;
> > > >
> > > **end**
> > >
> > **end**
> >
> **end**
>
end

2.3 Objective Function

The objective function consists of two parts, one for path length and one for obstacle avoidance. Equation 3 illustrates the objective function to be minimized in our problem.

$$Cost = R + \beta V, \tag{3}$$

where R is the total length of the path, V indicates a violation of path defined in Eq. 4, more than 0 when the path crosses an obstacle and, β is the coefficient of the penalty part.

$$V = \sum_{i=1}^{N_o} \prod_{p=x,y,z} \max\left(\frac{\sum_{j=1}^{N_t}(R_{p_i} - |p(t_j) - O_{p_i}|)}{N_t}, 0\right), \tag{4}$$

where N_o is the number of obstacles, R_{p_i}, and O_{p_i} are respectively dimension and center of ith obstacle corresponding to each direction, $x(t_j)$, $y(t_j)$, and $z(t_j)$ are the coordinates of the path at time t_j in each direction, and, N_t is the resolution of path over time. Note that, R_{p_i} is greater than actual dimension of obstacle corresponding to each direction, and $R_{p_i} = r_{p_i} + R_{Cons}$, where r_{p_i} $(p = x, y, z)$ are actual dimension of obstacle and R_{Cons} is a conservative margin which is related to dimensions of the drone itself.

2.4   Parameter Setting

To reach accurate and fast results, $\alpha = 0.1$, $\beta = 200$, $\gamma = 1\%$, $N_\gamma = 5$, $N_{Var} = 3$, $N_t = 100$, and, $K_L = 1.08$ are found by trail and error. For a small quad-copter, we consider $R_{Cons} = 0.4\ m$. The number of particles for this problem is 150 with maximum iterations of 50, i.e. the final solution should be reachable in less than or equal to 50 iterations.

For best performance, it is important to tune exploration and exploitation parameters, i.e. c_1 and c_2, correctly. Therefore, by simulating different conditions, we use the constriction coefficient introduced by Kennedy [12] based on Eq. 5 to tune c_1 and c_2.

$$\phi_1, \phi_2 > 0, \phi = \phi_1 + \phi_2 > 4$$

$$\chi = \frac{2}{\phi - 2 + \sqrt{\phi^2 - 4\phi}} \tag{5}$$

$$c_1 = \chi\phi_1$$

$$c_2 = \chi\phi_2$$

where the optimal solution is $\phi_1 = \phi_2 = 2.05$, so $\chi = 0.7298$ and $c_1 = c_2 = 1.4962$. Therefore, the exploration and exploitation coefficients have a balance and lead to fast and robust results for the problem of 3D path planning. Moreover, we consider inertia wight as $w = w_{damp}\chi$, where w_{damp} is variable by iterations and as $w_{damp} = 0.99^{it}$. This approach has a significant role in reducing the computational time for our problem.

For what concerns the reliability of the algorithm, the following stopping criteria are fixed:

- Cost below $\gamma\%$ in N_γ consecutive iterations, where γ and N_γ are 1 and 5 respectively. This condition means that a feasible solution is obtained as there is not a strong reduction in the cost during the last consecutive iterations.
- A path length equal to K_L (1.08) times the minimum path length possible is obtained. Where minimum path length possible is represented by the direct line between the starting point to destination point.
- Maximum number of PSO iterations always below 100 (to limit the computational time).

3   Results and Considerations

In order to evaluate the efficiency of the algorithm in terms of computational time and path length, 4 different environments are built with increasing complexity. In all these 4 maps a fixed rectangular base parallelepiped control volume (CV) containing several obstacles is considered (length $= 25$ m, width $= 11$ m, height $= 5$ m), which represents also the limit within the path can be elaborated by the algorithm. Figure 2 shows the testing environment with detailed the percentage of obstacles defined as V_{Obst}/V_{CV} %, with V_{Obst} the volume occupied by obstacles.

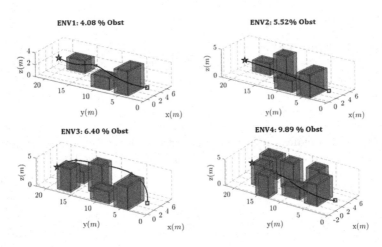

Fig. 2. MATLAB® simulated environments with their respective percentage of obstacles

3.1   Simulation in Different Environments

Due to the random nature of the PSO algorithm various runs with the same starting point ($[0; 0; 2]$ m) and destination point ($[6; 22; 1.0]$ m) are performed for each environment to test the robustness of the algorithm and its path length and computational time results in terms of variance and average value. In this case, 50 runs for each environment are performed. Simulations are performed in MATLAB ® (R2020a) in a PC of Windows 10 OS, Intel(R) Core(TM) i7-7700 CPU with 2.80 GHz and 16 GB RAM.

In Fig. 3, the results for the first environment are shown; the path length has a moderate oscillation between the maximum and minimum value of approximately $\simeq 1.3$ m. The computational time, except for the initial outlier due to the environment setting, is quite stable and oscillate around $\simeq 0.30$ s.

In Fig. 4, results for the second environment are shown. The path length average value is varies negligibly. Instead, its variance starts growing and the max gap between the maximum and minimum value of approximately increase up to $\simeq 2.3$ m. While, the computational time trend and the average is not varied considerably.

Figure 5 shows results for the 3rd environment where the percentage of obstacle increase up to 6.40 %. In the path length an important outlier manifests; while, the rest of the simulation results are stable and similar to the Fig. 4 results. In this case, the increased % of obstacles involves a rise in the computational time average, which increases to $\simeq 0.45$ s. Slight growth in the computational time variance can be noted too.

In the last environment a high degree of environment complexity is applied. Seven obstacles and 9.89% of obstruction make up the environment, as shown in Fig. 2. Figure 6 reports an increase in the variance of path length and computational time. Also, an increase in the computational time average is registered, which settles around the still limited value of $\simeq 0.85$ s.

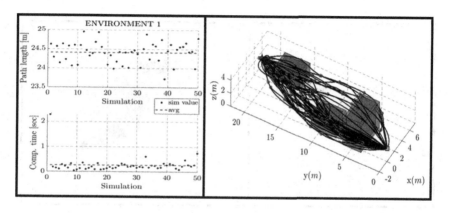

Fig. 3. Path length and computational time results for environment 1

To find the std of different parameters of the algorithm, 200 simulations for each environment were performed. The results are shown in Fig. 7. Simulations are performed in MATLAB ® (R2020a) in a PC of Windows 10 OS, Intel(R) Core(TM) i5-2400 CPU with 3.10 GHz and 16 GB RAM.

In this case, the total cost and the number of iterations are plotted also. As previously shown, it is notable that a consequence of increasing complexity of the environment is to raise the standard deviation of each magnitude. Another consequence is the increase of the gap between the maximum path length and the minimum one; this problem can be overcome thanks to the considerably short computational time that allows elaborating different solutions every second and selection of the best. The discrepancy notable in the average computational time compared to previous results shown in Fig. 3, 4, 5, and 6, is mainly due to the use of different PCs in the two cases, as specified.

To resume, in the simplest environment there is a reduced standard deviation with the presence of a reduced number of outliers. As the complexity of the

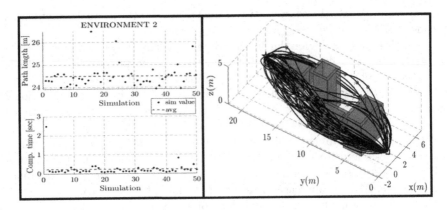

Fig. 4. Path length and computational time results for environment 2

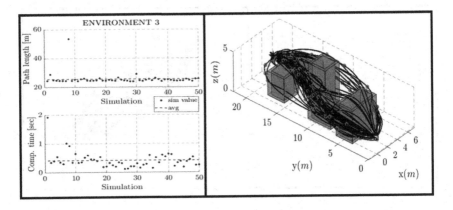

Fig. 5. Path length and computational time results for environment 3

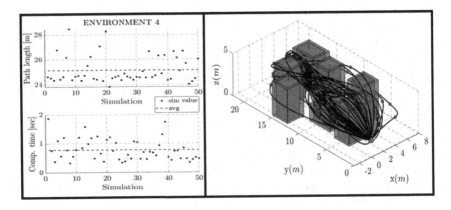

Fig. 6. Path length and computational time results for environment 4

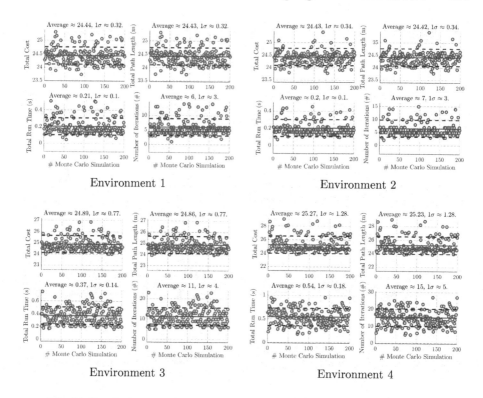

Fig. 7. Simulations results for the 4 different environments with 200 runs

environment increases, the standard deviation rises and the presence of outliers consequently decreases.

In Fig. 8, the results are plotted in terms of average values of path length and computational time. As expected, the path length and the computational time mean values increase with the complexity of the environment simulated. But, the positive result is the reduced value of the derivative of both curves.

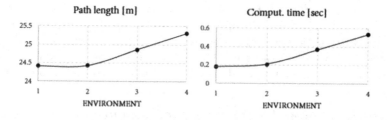

Fig. 8. Path length and computation time over more complex environment

3.2 Comparison with Standard PSO

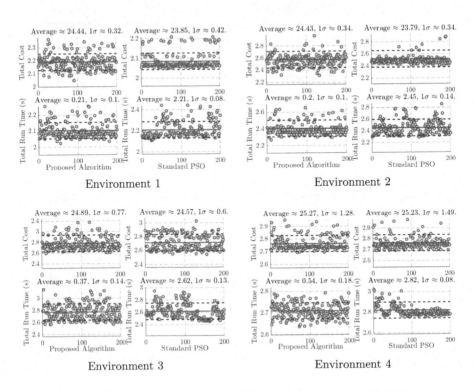

Fig. 9. Comparison results for the 4 different environments with 200 runs

To show the effectiveness of the proposed approach, a comparison for each environment with the standard PSO is performed. The differences between the proposed approach and standard PSO are 4 mentioned points in Sect. 2.2 and Eq. 5. In this comparisons, the standard PSO parameters are $c_1 = c_2 = 1.7$, and $w = 0.6$ based on [13]. Other common parameters are the same as proposed algorithm including the cost function in Eq. 3. Both algorithms are performed in MATLAB ® (R2020a) in a PC of Windows 10 OS, Intel(R) Core(TM) i5-2400 CPU with 3.10 GHz and 16 GB RAM.

As Fig. 9 shows the standard PSO has lower total cost (less than 3%), but the total run time of the proposed algorithm is almost $6 \sim 10$ times faster.

4 Conclusions and Further Developments

It is shown that even for the hardest scenario, the computational time always stays below one second with a stable sub-optimal path solution. This consistency in achieving stable fast sub-optimal path solution represents a marked improvement over previous algorithms such as [7] and [8]. In fact, as shown in Sect. 3, the computational time never exceeds 1 s, even in the most complex environment analyzed with a stable and reliable 3D path planning solution.

Moreover, since all the simulations run on MATLAB® for convenience; then the computational time can still be reduced by implementing the logic in an embedded platform with a lower level language code as C/C++ in on-board platforms. For further developments, other optimizations are in consideration to further reduce the calculation time and meet the real-time requirements without losing the quality of solution. Moreover, due to fast convergence of the proposed algorithm, it could be used for dynamic obstacles in real time. The final aim of this work is to provide the UAV with the ability of autonomous real-time path planning, for critical environments with a high percentage of obstacles also, which is one of those key aspects for autonomous flight in unknown GPS denied/degraded and critical environments in general.

References

1. Shim, D.H., Sastry, S.: A dynamic path generation method for a UAV swarm in the urban environment. In: AIAA Guidance, Navigation and Control Conference and Exhibit, p. 6836 (2008)
2. Hao, Y., Zu, W., Zhao, Y.: Real-time obstacle avoidance method based on polar coordination particle swarm optimization in dynamic environment. In: 2007 2nd IEEE Conference on Industrial Electronics and Applications, pp. 1612–1617. IEEE (2007)
3. Masehian, E., Sedighizadeh, D.: A multi-objective PSO-based algorithm for robot path planning. In: 2010 IEEE International Conference on Industrial Technology, pp. 465–470. IEEE (2010)
4. Dewang, H.S., Mohanty, P.K., Kundu, S.: A robust path planning for mobile robot using smart particle swarm optimization. Procedia Comput. Sci. **133**, 290–297 (2018)
5. Ayari, A., Bouamama, S.: A new multiple robot path planning algorithm: dynamic distributed particle swarm optimization. Robot. Biomimetics **4**(1), 8 (2017). https://doi.org/10.1186/s40638-017-0062-6
6. Yao, P., Wang, H., Su, Z.: UAV feasible path planning based on disturbed UID and trajectory propagation. Chin. J. Aeronautics **28**(4), 1163–1177 (2015)
7. Shao, Z., et al.: Path planning for multi-UAV formation rendezvous based on distributed cooperative particle swarm optimization. Appl. Sci. **9**(13), 2621 (2019)
8. Liu, Y., et al.: Collision free 4D path planning for multiple UAVs based on spatial refined voting mechanism and PSO approach. Chin. J. Aeronautics **32**(6), 1504–1519 (2019)
9. Kennedy, J., Eberhart, R.: Particle swarm optimization. In: Proceedings of ICNN 1995-International Conference on Neural Networks, vol. 4, pp. 1942–1948 (1995)
10. Eberhart, R., Kennedy, J.: A new optimizer using particle swarm theory. In: MHS 1995, Proceedings of the Sixth International Symposium on Micro Machine and Human Science, pp. 39–43. IEEE (1995)
11. Alam, M.N.: Particle swarm optimization: algorithm and its codes in MATLAB. ResearchGate **8**, 1–10 (2016)

12. Clerc, M., Kennedy, J.: The particle swarm-explosion, stability, and convergence in a multidimensional complex space. IEEE Trans. Evol. Comput. **6**(1), 58–73 (2002)
13. Zhang, W., Jin, Y., Li, X., Zhang, X.: A simple way for parameter selection of standard particle swarm optimization. In: Deng, H., Miao, D., Lei, J., Wang, F.L. (eds.) AICI 2011. LNCS (LNAI), vol. 7004, pp. 436–443. Springer, Heidelberg (2011). https://doi.org/10.1007/978-3-642-23896-3_54

Hybrid Variable Selection and Support Vector Regression for Gas Sensor Optimization

Margarita Rebolledo[1(✉)], Ruxandra Stoean[2,3], A. E. Eiben[4],
and Thomas Bartz-Beielstein[1]

[1] Institute for Data Science, Engineering, and Analytics, TH Köln, Köln, Germany
{margarita.rebolledo,thomas.bartz-beielstein}@th-koeln.de
[2] Romanian Institute of Science and Technology, Cluj-Napoca, Romania
[3] Grupo Ingeniería de Sistemas Integrados, E.T.S.I. Telecomunicación,
Universidad de Malaga, Malaga, Spain
ruxandra.stoean@rist.ro
[4] Department of Computer Science, Vrije Universiteit Amsterdam,
Amsterdam, Netherlands
a.e.eiben@vu.nl

Abstract. The improvement of combustion processes in industry, especially in the automotive branch, is of great importance to maintain the environmental permitted limits. Carbon monoxide concentration in the exhaust gases can give an insight into the efficiency of the combustion taking place and for this reason, it is important to have sensors that can measure it accurately. First results of a long term study with one of the leading sensor manufactures showed high performance using genetic programming. However, this expensive approach is difficult to apply in real-world settings. Therefore a hybrid optimization that combines support vector regression (SVR) with variable pre-selection is proposed. Three different methods for variable selection are compared for this application, a genetic algorithm, and two methods from Bayesian statistics: statistical equivalent signatures and projection predictive variable selection. Furthermore, a multi-objective approach using the same hybrid definition is implemented for the cases in which several sensors need to be considered simultaneously. Our results show that the hybrid model is an improvement compared to the previous study, while delivering good performance when dealing with a multivariate formulation. Genetic algorithms in combination with SVR lead to enhanced variation on the groups of selected variables.

Keywords: Support vector regression · Feature selection · Projection predictive · Statistical equivalent signatures

1 Introduction

The automotive industry is increasingly concerned with building high performance cars while also adhering to the normative set in place for environment

© Springer Nature Switzerland AG 2020
B. Filipič et al. (Eds.): BIOMA 2020, LNCS 12438, pp. 281–293, 2020.
https://doi.org/10.1007/978-3-030-63710-1_22

protection. Among other things, this requires a cutback on the emission levels of carbon monoxide. The efficiency increase of motor combustion processes plays an important role in the reduction of pollutant levels. The different concentrations of gases resulting from combustion allow to make an approximate analysis of said efficiency and thus a reliable in-situ sensing system is required.

In addition to the already existent oxygen sensor, a reliable carbon monoxide in-situ sensor is also needed. The sensor should have a high sensitivity for carbon monoxide and be able to vary its output according to the proportion of gases found in the exhaust gases. Furthermore the interpretability of the system describing these sensors needs to be maintained in order to keep a clear understanding of how each different gas affects the system output.

Under these conditions, an accurate and informative computational model can be constructed to examine the dependency of the sensor output to the complex interactions of the exhaust gases. Therefore, an important trait of a model would be the ability to reveal if there are such synergies between the attributes. Finally, the underneath workings of the combustion process should be better revealed by more than one sensor at a time, which would require a multivariate approach for an adequate modelling of the entire problem. The findings can then determine if the designed sensors are robust or need to be further enhanced by the engineers.

Rebolledo et al. [17] proved the efficiency of Genetic Programming (GP) when modelling single carbon monoxide gas sensors. However, the expensive GP implementation and its excessive time demanding approach made the method infeasible for the real world setting. Instead the Least Absolute Shrinkage and Selection Operator (LASSO) [19] model was favored given its interpretability and ability to identify the effect each variable had on the output.

The main goal of this paper is to put forward a hybrid model strategy to improve the modelling of single sensors and go one step further into the formulation and solution of the multi-objective case. This in order to handle the situation when there is more than one sensor required to be investigated. The well performing support vector regression (SVR) technique is combined with variable selection methods to accelerate the sensor optimization and at the same time to enable the understanding of parameter importance. Furthermore, a lower number of parameters will limit SVR high flexibility, reducing in this way its variance and avoiding overfitting [10].

Three different methods of variable selection are compared for this application: a genetic algorithm (GA) and two methods from Bayesian statistics, i.e. the statistically equivalent signature (SES) and projection predictive variable selection (Projpred). By this we want to answer two questions:

Q-1. Can these methods be applied as a feasible approach to single and multivariate sensor optimization scenarios yielding minimal mean square error (MSE)?

Q-2. Which method performs best among the ones tested?

The findings will help determine whether the designed sensors are robust to work in single and/or multiple arrays, while maintaining a clear presentation of the influence that the different gases have on the sensor reading.

The paper is structured in the subsequent manner. Section 2 presents the description of the problem and the available data set. Section 3 explains the setup of our experiments and the workings of the three tested hybrid algorithms. Section 4 presents the results obtained. Finally, Sect. 5 discusses results and presents answers to questions (Q-1) and (Q-2).

2   Problem Description

The efficiency of motor combustion processes can be indirectly measured by monitoring the concentrations of carbon monoxide and other harmful gases releases into the atmosphere. This paper focuses on the modelling and optimization of a sensor that is able to discern carbon monoxide concentration apart from other six exhaust gases. This is difficult because the sensor is exposed and influenced by these gases. Thus, the sensor output will represent the underneath process influenced by all the other gases and not directly the carbon monoxide concentration.

The optimization task can be given in a general formulation as two problems ranging from single to multi-objective. Given the data set $\{\mathbf{A}_i, \mathbf{B}_i\}$, $i = 1, 2, ..., m$, where each $\mathbf{A}_i = (A_i^1, A_i^2, ..., A_i^n)$ refers to the concentrations of the X_1, X_2, ..., X_n gases involved in the combustion process, with $A_i^j \in \mathbb{R}$, $j = 1, 2, ..., n$, and every $\mathbf{B}_i \in \mathbb{R}^p$ denotes the output of the p sensors Y_1, Y_2, ..., Y_p (i.e., a multivariate regression formulation), the two main objectives of the experiments can be named as:

1. *Find* the (combination of) predictors A_i^j that *minimizes* the MSE for each sensor measurement independently.
2. *Find* the (combination of) predictors A_i^j that *minimizes* the MSE for all sensor measurements $Y_1, Y_2, ..., Y_p$ simultaneously.

A first simple way to address the presence of several sensor is to appoint a naive approach where the fitness evaluation of an individual is a summation of several objective function, i.e. sum of SVR estimated MSE for each output. $f(c) = f_1(c) + f_2(c)... + f_p(c)$.

At this point the hybrid approaches GA-SVR, SES-SVR and Projpred-SVR can be appointed to solve both the single and the multi-objective task.

2.1   Data Description

The data set for this work was presented in [17] and is included on the R package SPOT [2] where it can be freely accessed for comparative studies.

During four years, the data was collected from an extensive real-world project in cooperation with one of the leading sensor manufacturers. The data was recorded from a series of experiments following a response surface design. This design constraints itself to the maximum and minimum expected concentration values of each gas under normal working conditions. Given the cost and time consumption required for the experiments, only a limited amount of samples could be measured.

The data contains $m = 140$ samples and every record is defined by seven attributes, X_1 to X_7, which represent the concentrations of each of the measured exhaust gases, here anonymized due to confidentiality reasons. Carbon monoxide is identified as X_1. Two sensor outputs, denominated $Y1$ and $Y2$, were recorded. The data is standardized, meaning that every sample had its mean subtracted and was then divided by the standard deviation. Following the nomenclature of the above defined optimization task, the variables m, n and p have the following particular values: $m = 140$, $n = 7$, $p = 2$.

3   Experiments

Following the standard procedure in machine learning described in detail in [7], the data is divided into training, test, and validation sets.

To give stability and statistical significance to the results, several experimental runs were performed by drawing different compositions for the three sets. 30 partitions are constructed by repeatedly selecting 80/25/35 samples correspondingly. The selection is done randomly.

The variable selection and model building will be evaluated in terms of MSE using the validation set. The best obtained result will be evaluated on the test set to acquire the final result.

All the executed experiments use the R package *e1071* [12] to implement the SVR. All the instances of SVR use the radial basis function (RBF) kernel, $\exp(-\gamma||x - x'||^2)$, with parameter $\gamma = 0.1$ indicating the spread of the kernel.

The exact implementation of the different hybrid methods differs according to their inner workings and their exact experimental settings are presented in more detail in the following sections.

3.1   GA-SVR

In this approach a genetic algorithm (GA) [5] selects the predictors X_i that influence the output for each available sensor and learns from the training data.

Evolutionary and swarm computation have been often successfully partnered with support vector machines for variable or parameter selection, as demonstrated by other application areas in industry, medicine and biology [8,9,14,18].

Since the current task is variable selection, a binary representation was chosen. An individual is a binary vector $c \in \{0,1\}^n$, where $c_n = 1$ signifies that the corresponding gas n influences the sensor signal and $c_n = 0$ that its effect on the sensor output is insignificant.

This approach is depicted by Algorithm 1. Here *no_of_repeats* corresponds each of the 30 train/validation/test sets partitions.

Evolution at each repeat follows the standard cycle of parent selection, variation, and survivor selection. The GA binary encoded individual c indicates the attributes that will be included in the modelling step. A SVR is trained on the obtained attribute collection and the MSE is computed on the validation data. The MSE value is returned as the current individual's fitness. At the end of each GA run, the best individual $best_l$, is retained. After the 30 trials are finished, the number of times a feature l was selected in the preserved best individuals is counted in $score_l$. Therefore, a ranking of the involved attributes is achieved. Additionally, the MSE of each of the preserved best individuals is computed on its respective test set. The final test MSE is obtained as the average of the results over these runs.

---

for $i = 1 : no\_of\_repeats$ **do**
    use train/validation/test set partition i ;
    initialization of population pop_{GA};
    evaluate pop_{GA} by calculating MSE;
    for $j = 1 : no\_of\_generations$ **do**
        parent selection in pop_{GA};
        variation in pop_{GA};
        obtain offspring population *off* ;
        evaluate *off* by calculating MSE;
        survival selection in pop_{GA};
    end
    store the best individual of pop_{GA} in $best_i$;
end
for $l = 1 : n$ **do**
    $score_l$ = sum of selected attributes in $(best)$;
end
rank variables according to $score$;

Algorithm 1: Hybrid GA-SVR algorithm. The algorithm accepts the different partitions of the data set and returns a score of most important variables.

The GA-SVR meta-heuristic can be easily extended to be able to simultaneously handle several sensors. The objective function will be the summation of each several objective function as stated on the problem definition. The problem can be therefore defined as a multi-objective discrete and combinatorial optimization problem [4], where every objective refers to the measurement of one sensor and needs to be minimized.

The GA was implemented using the R package *genalg* [22]. The GA population size is set to 20, with 50 generations. Bit flip mutation with a probability of 0.3 was used with elitist selection.

3.2   SES-SVR

Statistically equivalent signature (SES) [11] is a constraint-based feature selection algorithm with roots in causal analysis, where the optimal set of predictors consist in the Markov Blanket (MB) of the variable in the Bayesian Network (BN) representing the data distribution [21]. SES has already been proved to work on several high-dimensional gene-expression data sets including temporal data [20] and text mining applications [1].

Given a subset of variables, $\mathbf{W}$, an statistical independence test, $ind()$, is used to test the null hypothesis that a variable $\mathbf{X}$ is conditionally independent on the output $\mathbf{T}$ given $\mathbf{W}$, $ind(\mathbf{X}, \mathbf{T}|\mathbf{W})$. Variables that cannot be proven as independent, that is they show a connection (functional relation) to the output, are selected.

Once the variables with the most expected predictive power have been selected, a SVR model is built on the training set including only these variables. The group of variables with the smallest MSE in all validation sets is selected as the best. For the final test MSE, the SVR models are generated again on all 30 data partitions using the best variables and the average MSE on the test sets is computed. Algorithm 2 illustrates the steps for the SES-SVR approach.

---

for $i = 1 : no\_of\_repeats$ **do**
  use train/validation set partition i ;
  initialize variable selection algorithm ;
  Select variables with the configured criteria ;
  estimate MSE in validation set ;
end
store selected variables with best MSE in *best* ;
for $l = 1 : n$ **do**
  $score_l$ = sum of selected attributes in (*best*);
end
for $i = 1 : no\_of\_repeats$ **do**
  use test set partition i ;
  estimate MSE using *best* in test ;
end
rank variables according to *score* ;

Algorithm 2: General algorithm for SES-SVR and Projpred-SVR. The algorithm accepts the different partitions of the data set and returns a score of most important variables.

The multi-objective formulation needs only a new definition of the independence test used while selecting the variables. In this case the multivariate regression test is applied. The MSE of the best variables will be defined as the MSE sum of all the sensors outputs.

SES was implemented using the R package *MXM* [11]. Since both variables and outputs have continuous values, the Fisher test (*testIndFisher*) is computed for the single objective case and the multiple regression test (*testIndMVred*) for the multiobjective case. A maximum of four variables is used as the conditioning set and the threshold for the p-value is set at 0.05 because this is considered as a standard value.

3.3   Projpred-SVR

The projection predictive variable selection (Projpred) [16] is a Bayesian model selection method, in which the posterior information of a reference model that includes all possible variables (M_*) is projected onto candidate models ($M_\perp$) containing only a subset of the variables. The goal is to find a submodel $M_\perp$ whose predictive distribution is as close as possible to that of M_*. The Kullback-Leibler (KL) divergence is used to determine the divergence between both distributions.

The method works as follows: a Gaussian linear model is used to build the reference model M_* with input variables f_i as in Eq. 1.

$$f_i = \mathbf{W}^\top \mathbf{X}_i$$
$$y_i = f_i + \epsilon_i, \ \epsilon \sim N(0, \sigma^2) \tag{1}$$

To encourage sparsity an extra prior is added to the weights $\mathbf{W} = (w_1, ... w_n)$ to count for their relevance or irrelevance to the output. The Horseshoe prior [3] accomplishes this by introducing a global scale, τ, inferred by the data, and a local scale, λ, inferred by $\mathbf{W}$, as seen in Eq. 2, where t_v^+ refers to the half-Student-t prior with $v = 1$ degrees of freedom. Both scale parameters are unknown quantities and will be inferred during the Markov chain runs. The scale parameter λ will be high for inputs with high relevance and small for those with low or no relevance.

$$w_i | \lambda_i, \tau \sim N(0, \lambda_i \tau)$$
$$\lambda_i \sim t_v^+(0, 1) \tag{2}$$

After model fitting is finish, variable selection starts searching for important variables using L1-search, a LASSO related method in which a subspace to project the model is defined using L1 constraints on the parameters of the full model [13]. The variables that achieve the most similitude to the predictive distribution of the original model are selected.

The algorithm works following the same steps as illustrated in Algorithm 2. First the full Gaussian linear model is fitted using the horseshoe prior. To specify the prior beliefs about the number of relevant variables, the results from [17] are used. According to their findings four variables showed a higher influence on the model output. This information will be transmitted to the model through the prior definition. After the full model is fitted, the variable selection starts using L1-search. The chosen variables are the ones that most decrease the KL-divergence between the predictive distribution of the full model and the one of the candidate model. At the end of the runs the variables with minimum MSE on the validation set are chosen as the best. The SVR model uses only the best variables to give the final result on the test set. Moreover, the best variables are encoded as a binary vector to allow to calculate the ranking for each attribute.

The implementation of the described algorithm is implemented using the *projpred* R package [15]. The model fitting was done using the *rstanarm* package [6]. The definition of the Horseshoe prior uses a global scale parameter ≈ 0.149. Four Markov chains are run, each with 1000 iterations and leaving 500 iteration as burn-in.

4   Results

The constructed algorithms were applied to the gas sensor data described in Sect. 2. The experiments were first conducted for the single objective formulation using the output given by sensor Y_1 and subsequently by sensor Y_2. The results obtained on the test data are shown in Table 1. These correspond to the average MSE value across all 30 test set partitions. To enable comparison with previous results, the results obtained using LASSO in [17] are also presented as a baseline.

Table 1. MSE with standard deviation obtained for GA-SVM, SES-SVM and Projpred-SVM on the single-objective formulation experiments. As a baseline the results obtained in [17] using LASSO are also presented. Smaller values mean better performance.

	GA-SVM	SES-SVM	Projpred-L1	Baseline
Y1	0.3321 ± 0.0875	0.3367 ± 0.1062	0.3928 ± 0.1375	0.56
Y2	0.2827 ± 0.0633	0.2868 ± 0.0797	0.2880 ± 0.0721	0.27

The variable ranking given by all the three different methods coincide on clearly pointing parameters X_1 and X_4 as the ones with the strongest influence on outputs Y_1 and Y_2. Results start to diverge when observing the other parameters. While GA-SVR algorithm finds parameters X_3 and X_7 as the second most influential parameters this trend, although visible, is not as marked for SES-SVR or Projpred-SVR. Figure 1 shows the ranking differences between two of the algorithms. It is clear that the GA method includes more variation in variable selection.

The MSE results for the multi-objective formulation are given separately for the two sensors in Table 2.

It is interesting to observe that the performance of the compared methods is not greatly affected when changing between single and multi-objective formulations. It is again significantly improved when compared to the baseline in Table 1.

The parameter ranking for the multi-objective formulation of all three methods is shown in Fig. 2. The same most influential parameters are identified and the least important X_5 and X_6 are hardly considered. These two parameters

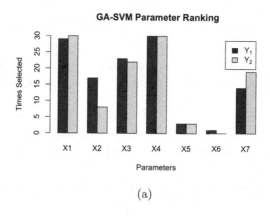

(a)

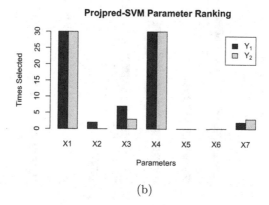

(b)

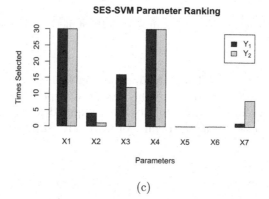

(c)

Fig. 1. Variable importance ranking for the (a) GA-SVR, (b) Projpred-SVR, and (c) SES-SVR. All three algorithms are in their single objective formulation for Y_1 and Y_2.

Table 2. MSE with standard deviation obtained for GA-SVM, SES-SVM and Projpred-SVM on the multi-objective formulation. Here smaller values mean better performance.

	GA-SVM	SES-SVM	Projpred-L1
Y1	0.3619 ± 0.0917	0.3460 ± 0.0882	0.3525 ± 0.0939
Y2	0.2993 ± 0.0641	0.3010 ± 0.0759	0.3022 ± 0.0721

are only selected by GA-SVR on a low number of occasions. It is interesting to note that the variable selection implemented by the GA maintained the same behavior in the single- and multi-objective case.

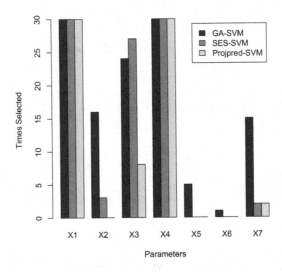

Fig. 2. Ranking of the variable importance of all three methods in the multi-objective formulation.

Lastly, it is of interest to know the difference in wall-clock time each of these methods need in order to complete the described experiments. Using a dual core 1.4 GHz Intel Core i5 processor the time required for the multi objective formulation was 10 min, 12 s and 15 min for GA-SVR, SES-SVR, and Projpred-SVR respectively.

5   Conclusions

The current data analysis considers seven gases resulting from a combustion process and two built-in sensors to measure the concentration of each gas as provided by an industrial testing station. The optimization problem required to find the minimal MSE while preserving the system interpretability.

Our proposed solution makes use of the well performing SVR to model the sensor output. To avoid overfitting and to maintain model interpretability only a subset on the input parameters is used when building the model. Three variable selection methods are tested in order to select the input subset: Projection predictive method, binary genetic algorithm, and statistical equivalent signatures. There three methods use different strategies when selecting the most important variables.

The experiments show there is clear improvement over the results presented in [17] and prove the hybrid approach has good performance for both the single- and multi-objective formulation of the gas sensors.

To answer the first question (Q-1), can these methods be applied as a feasible approach to single and multi-variate sensor optimization scenarios yielding minimal MSE?, single- and multi-objective solutions were tested. All three methods showed an increase in the performance when compared to the baseline in the single objective approach. This performance level was maintained when testing the methods on the multi objective scenario.

In the single-objective formulation the GA-SVR approach showed slightly better results than the other two competing methods. Even though LASSO was the preferred method in [17], the analog implementation used in Projpred did not show any solid advantage. In the multi-objective formulation all methods presented a performance comparable to that obtained on the single sensor approach. Here GA-SVR showed again a slightly better result.

Regarding the second question (Q-2), which method performs best among the ones tested?, the dynamics of the variable selection were observed across the experiments. As seen in the results all three approaches showed similar performances but there were two significant differences. On the one hand, GA-SVR shows more variation between the best variable groups while the other two methods find only a couple different best options and repeat them for several models. On the other hand, SES-SVR allows an implementation that is by far faster that the other two methods. Following these observations GA-SVR is our preferred method in scenarios where there is no time pressure. Here the variability on the best variable groups can be beneficial for data sets with complex input interactions.

References

1. Adamou, M., Antoniou, G., Greasidou, E., Lagani, V., Charonyktakis, P., Tsamardinos, I.: Mining free-text medical notes for suicide risk assessment. In: Proceedings of the 10th Hellenic Conference on Artificial Intelligence, SETN 2018, pp. 47:1–47:8. ACM, New York (2018). https://doi.org/10.1145/3200947.3201020, http://doi.acm.org/10.1145/3200947.3201020
2. Bartz-Beielstein, T., Lasarczyk, C., Preuss, M.: Sequential parameter optimization. In: Proceedings Congress on Evolutionary Computation 2005 (CEC 2005), Edinburgh, Scotland, p. 1553 (2005). http://www.spotseven.de/wp-content/papercite-data/pdf/blp05.pdf

3. Carvalho, C.M., Polson, N.G., Scott, J.G.: The horseshoe estimator for sparse signals. Biometrika **97**(2), 465–480 (2010). https://doi.org/10.1093/biomet/asq017

4. Ehrgott, M.: Multicriteria Optimization, 2nd edn. Springer, Heidelberg (2005). https://doi.org/10.1007/3-540-27659-9

5. Eiben, A.E., Smith, J.E.: Introduction to Evolutionary Computing. NCS. Springer, Heidelberg (2015). https://doi.org/10.1007/978-3-662-44874-8

6. Goodrich, B., Gabry, J., Ali, I., Brilleman, S.: rstanarm: Bayesian applied regression modeling via Stan (2018). http://mc-stan.org/. r package version 2.17.4

7. Hastie, T., Tibshirani, R., Friedman, J.: The Elements of Statistical Learning. SSS. Springer, New York (2009). https://doi.org/10.1007/978-0-387-84858-7

8. Hoang, T.T., Cho, M.Y., Alam, M.N., Vu, Q.T.: A novel differential particle swarm optimization for parameter selection of support vector machines for monitoring metal-oxide surge arrester conditions. Swarm Evol. Comput. **38**, 120–126 (2018). https://doi.org/10.1016/j.swevo.2017.07.006, http://www.sciencedirect.com/science/article/pii/S2210650217303942

9. Huang, H.L., Chang, F.L.: ESVM: evolutionary support vector machine for automatic feature selection and classification of microarray data. Biosystems **90**(2), 516–528 (2007). https://doi.org/10.1016/j.biosystems.2006.12.003, http://www.sciencedirect.com/science/article/pii/S0303264706002875

10. James, G., Witten, D., Hastie, T., Tibshirani, R.: An Introduction to Statistical Learning. STS, vol. 103. Springer, New York (2013). https://doi.org/10.1007/978-1-4614-7138-7

11. Lagani, V., Athineou, G., Farcomeni, A., Tsagris, M., Tsamardinos, I.: Feature selection with the R Package MXM: discovering statistically-equivalent feature subsets. arXiv e-prints arXiv:1611.03227, November 2016

12. Meyer, D., Dimitriadou, E., Hornik, K., Weingessel, A., Leisch, F.: e1071: Misc Functions of the Department of Statistics, Probability Theory Group (Formerly: E1071), TU Wien (2018). https://CRAN.R-project.org/package=e1071. r package version 1.7-0

13. Nott, D.J., Leng, C.: Bayesian projection approaches to variable selection in generalized linear models. Comput. Stat. Data Anal. **54**(12), 3227–3241 (2010). https://doi.org/10.1016/j.csda.2010.01.036

14. Perolini, A.: A fast approximated evolutionary approach to improve SVM accuracy. In: Bramer, M., Petridis, M., Hopgood, A. (eds.) Research and Development in Intelligent Systems XXVII SGAI 2010, pp. 193–206. Springer, London (2011). https://doi.org/10.1007/978-0-85729-130-1_14

15. Piironen, J., Paasiniemi, M., Vehtari, A.: projpred: Projection Predictive Feature Selection (2018). https://CRAN.R-project.org/package=projpred. r package version 1.1.0

16. Piironen, J., Vehtari, A.: Comparison of Bayesian predictive methods for model selection. Stat. Comput. **27**(3), 711–735 (2017). https://doi.org/10.1007/s11222-016-9649-y

17. Rebolledo Coy, M.A., Krey, S., Bartz-Beielstein, T., Flasch, O., Fischbach, A., Stork, J.: Modeling and optimization of a robust gas sensor. In: Papa, G., Mernik, M. (eds.) Bioinspired Optimization Methods and their Applications, pp. 267–278 (2016)

18. Stoean, C.: In search of the optimal set of indicators when classifying histopathological images. In: 18th International Symposium on Symbolic and Numeric Algorithms for Scientific Computing (SYNASC), pp. 449–455 (2016). https://doi.org/10.1109/SYNASC.2016.074

19. Tran, M.N., Nott, D.J., Leng, C.: The predictive lasso. Stat. Comput. **22**(5), 1069–1084 (2012). https://doi.org/10.1007/s11222-011-9279-3
20. Tsagris, M., Lagani, V., Tsamardinos, I.: Feature selection for high-dimensional temporal data. BMC Bioinform. **19**(1), 17 (2018). https://doi.org/10.1186/s12859-018-2023-7
21. Tsamardinos, I., Aliferis, C.: Towards principled feature selection: relevancy, filters and wrappers. In: Proceedings of the Ninth International Workshop on Artificial Intelligence and Statistics. Morgan Kaufmann Publishers (2003)
22. Willighagen, E., Ballings, M.: genalg: R Based Genetic Algorithm (2015). https://CRAN.R-project.org/package=genalg. r package version 0.2.0

Diversity Promoting Strategies in a Multi- and Many-Objective Evolutionary Algorithm for Molecular Optimization

Susanne Rosenthal[✉]

Department of Information Systems, RFH - University of Applied Sciences of Cologne, 50676 Cologne, Germany
susanne.rosenthal2@rfh-koeln.de

Abstract. Computer-aided drug design is an approach to effectively identify and analyse molecules for therapeutic and diagnostic interventions. Generally, libraries with a broad range of compounds revealing a high genetic diversity with an at most similar behavior in bioactivity have to be created. For this purpose, an evolutionary process for multi- and many-objective Molecular Optimization (MO) has been designed and improved during the past decade. Diversity plays a central role in Evolutionary Algorithms (EAs) to prevent premature convergence to suboptimal solutions and several methods to promote diversity on different levels of an EA have been proposed. The aspect of genetic diversity in MO is a further challenge that has to be controlled and promoted by different strategies on various stages of a problem-specific EA. This work presents an application-specific re-interpretation of different diversity aspects on various stages of an EA for MO. A sophisticated survival selection strategy combining a specific ranking method with application-specific diversity promoting technologies is introduced and benchmarked to the recently proposed many-objective evolutionary algorithm AnD on four molecular optimization problems with 3 up to 6 objectives.

Keywords: Genetic dissimilarity · Genotype and fitness diversity · Multi- and many-objective molecular optimization

1 Introduction

Drug discovery for therapeutical and diagnostic entities is a highly complex process and still costly, difficult and time-consuming. The aim of drug discovery is to identify candidate antibodies to disease-relevant targets that are complementary in shape and charge to these targets with which they interact and bind. This process is often a combination of computer techniques, bioinformatic approaches and laboratory experiments to simultaneously improve molecular properties like affinity, selectivity and metabolic stability [1].

For this purpose, a single-objective EA for MO has been evolved revealing exponential fitness improvement of candidate peptides within 10 iterations,

© Springer Nature Switzerland AG 2020
B. Filipič et al. (Eds.): BIOMA 2020, LNCS 12438, pp. 294–307, 2020.
https://doi.org/10.1007/978-3-030-63710-1_23

slowed down to linear fitness improvement afterwards [2]. A sophisticated version of this approach with similar properties for multi-objective MO, termed as COmponent-Specific Evolutionary Algorithm for Molecular Optimization (COSEA-MO), has been reported and benchmarked on a 3- and 4-dimensional physiochemical optimization problems in [3]. The components have been compared to several state-of-the-art components and a fine-tuning of the parameters, number of recombinations and population size, has been performed [3–5]. Furthermore, COSEA-MO has been enhanced for the application on multi- and many-objective MO problems by a winning-score based ranking method as survival selection [6] providing again exponential fitness improvement within 10 iterations. This enhanced version has been evolved under specific conditions:

- provides exponential convergence improvement within 10 iterations on multi- as well as many-objective molecular optimization problems,
- components are parameter-free in the sense that no parameters have to be chosen by the user which have a high impact on the performance,
- the algorithm does not make use of reference points, weight vectors or a division of the search space by hyperboxes, which also have a high impact on the performance and have to be chosen carefully by the user.

The genetic diversity with the meaning of genetic material among the candidate optimized peptides is an important feature and less work has been done so far to control this aspect of diversity in an evolutionary process, especially in the field of MO.

Generally, diversity is the second important aim in evolutionary optimization and is usually addressed in an evolutionary process to prevent premature convergence on suboptimal solutions. Therefore, several diversity strategies are included on different stages in an evolutionary process acting on the three levels genotype, phenotype and fitness with a different impact on the performance [7].

The contribution of this work is a application-specific re-interpretation of diversity promoting aspects in an evolutionary process for multi- and many-objective molecular optimization and an enhancement of this evolutionary process, COSEA-MO, to control diversity among the candidate optimized peptides by a sophisticated selection procedure to identify a significant number of highly qualified peptides with an at most wide range of genetic diversity among themselves. For these issues, the following questions are addressed in this work:

1. What does *diversity* mean in the field of MO?
2. How to address *diversity* on different stages of an evolutionary process?

A sophisticated selection strategy as a linear combination with the terms molecular quality, genetic diversity and dissimilarity is introduced. The molecular quality is measured by a winning-score technique [8]. Hamming distance and a dissimilarity measure based on the matrix of Sneath [9] is used to calculate the diversity of the genetic material. The performance of COSEA-MO with the new selection function is evaluated on four MO problems with 3 to 6 objectives and is compared the recently proposed many-objective evolutionary algorithm AnD (ANgle-based selection and shift-based Density estimation strategy)

[10] with the survival selection principle 'diversity-first-and-convergence-second'. AnD has the same simple framework structure as COSEA-MO, is also independent of problem-specific weight vectors and reference points and outperformed several state-of-the-art many-objective EAs on standard benchmark problems. AnD has been chosen for comparison as it is currently the only state-of-the-art algorithm that is compatible with the second and third condition mentioned above.

The outline of this work is as follows: Sect. 2 gives an overview of preliminary knowledge, re-interprets these general aspects of diversity in the application field of MO and describes related work. Section 3 introduces the proposed approach COSEA-MO with the new survival selection strategy and discusses the methods of diversity promotion on different stages of the algorithm. Section 4 presents the simulation onsets and the experimental results, which are discussed in Sect. 5.

2   Preliminary Knowledge and Related Work

Analyzing an evolutionary process regarding the term diversity, at least three levels are recognizable to promote diversity: genotype, phenotype and fitness. Genotype is the internal representation of an individual in an evolutionary process and is directly manipulated by the evolutionary operators. In the case that the genotype presentation cannot be directly evaluated by the fitness functions, a transformation into a phenotype representation is necessary. In this case, fitness distance measures are also effective measures for genotype and phenotype distance [7].

In the field of MO, individuals are usually represented as amino acids sequences and molecular functions - assuming that approximate molecular fitness functions for property prediction are available - directly work on this representation, therefore genotype and phenotype coincide. The fitness values are real numbers in the so-called chemical space. In [11], chemical space is defined as a N-dimensional Cartesian space in which molecules are mapped using chemoinformatic descriptors, which quantify physical, chemical and topological properties of molecules. The Euclidean distance is an intuitive distance measure to calculate the chemical space diversity based in the descriptor values of two molecules i and j:

$$D_{i,j} = \sqrt{\sum_{k=1}^{N}(d_{i,k} - d_{j,k})^2}$$

On genotype level, the common Hamming Distance is a straightforward metric to evaluate genetic diversity:

$$D_{i,j}^{ham} = \frac{XOR(i,j)}{N},$$

where i and j are two strings of length N, $XOR(i,j)$ is the number of positions that differ in two strings.

The locality principle states that small changes in genotype correspond to small changes in phenotype and result in small variations on fitness level. This principle is not an intrinsic character of the optimization problem, but of the genotype-phenotype-fitness-mapping. Generally, phenotype variation in multi-objective optimization causes more fitness variations because obtaining identical fitness values is less probable in higher-dimensional spaces [7].

This locality principle does not hold in molecular landscapes [12]. The reason for this is a further aspect according to the work of Sneath [9] that has to be considered: A correlation study is performed between changes of amino acids in the chemical structure of a molecule and its impact on the molecule bioactivity. The 20 canonical amino acids are considered in this work evaluating their single influence on the bioactivity of a molecule by a systematical substitution of one or more amino acids. The outcome of this work is a correlation matrix of the canonical amino acids quantifying their dissimilarity (D) or similarity (1-D) respectively to each other. The resemblance of the amino acids is obtained by comparing as many chemical properties as possible. The consequence from this work transferred to the field of MO is that diversity and dissimilarity are two complementary aspects on genotype level which have to be equally considered in MO: two peptides potentially have the same Hamming Distance value but highly differ in their dissimilarity values regarding the varying amino acids and therefore provide highly differing physiochemical fitness values.

Diversity in Evolutionary Algorithms (EAs) is usually quantified in three different ways: firstly, as a distance metric between individuals, secondly as an individual attribute reflecting how far an individual is positioned from the population (individual diversity). Thirdly, the population diversity is defined as the average individual diversity.[7]

It has to be noted that individual and population diversity in EAs usually refers to diversity on fitness level and transferred to MO, individual and population diversity is related to distances in chemical space.

In the related work [13], dissimilarity inspired by biodiversity measures has firstly been applied to address diversity in many-objective evolutionary optimization. A new diversity measure, which is an accumulation of dissimilarity in the population based on an adopted L_p-norm, enhances diversity maintenance in a many-objective evolutionary process. The diversity of a solution is determined by the sum of dissimilarity values to the remaining members of the population. Diversity performance of four popular multi-objective evolutionary algorithms has been improved on four standard benchmark problems with two to ten objectives.

In this work, COSEA-MO with the sophisticated selection strategy is compared to AnD (ANgle-based selection and shift-based Density estimation strategy) [10] in this work. To the best of the authors knowledge, AnD is currently the only available state-of-the-art algorithm that is compatible with the second and third condition mentioned in the introduction and provides a specific diversity promoting strategy within the selection. AnD selects promising individuals from the union of parent and child population for the next iteration with a diversity-first-and-convergence-second principle. In AnD, the well-known vector angle and shift-based density estimation in the selection process are combined. Angle-based selection is used to identify two individuals with minimal angle. This is by the idea that these individuals represent the search in the same direction and waste computational resources if both individuals survive. The individual with lower shift-based density estimation is deleted in order to ensure convergence. AnD has been compared to seven state-of-the-art MaOEA on a variety of benchmark problems with 5, 10 and 15 objectives and reveals highly competitive performance. AnD is chosen for experimental comparison in this work as it the same simple framework structure like COSEA-MO (Algorithm 1), provides optimized default parameters for the non-expert use and is independent of weight vectors or reference points, which usually have a strong impact on the performance and are usually unknown in real-world applications.

3   Proposed Approach

This section describes an enhanced version of COSEA-MO to promote high genetic diversity and to ensure exponential fitness improvement within 10 iterations at the same time. The framework of COSEA-MO is given in Algorithm 1. The algorithm starts with the random initialization of the start population P_0 of size N. The individuals represent peptides encoded as character strings consisting of 20 different characters symbolizing the 20 canonical amino acids. During the evolution process, an offspring generation Q_t of size N is generated by the variation operators recombination and mutation (*RandomMatingAndVariation*). Then, P_t and Q_t are combined to a population U_t of size $2N$. Finally, a survival selection strategy (*LinearSelection*) is performed to select N individuals of U_t for the next generation P_{t+1}. An overview of diversity-preserving methods on different stages of the evolutionary process is given and the components of COSEA-MO are introduced.

Algorithm 1: Framework of COSEA-MO

Input: Population P_t, population size N, number of optimal solutions m, total
          number of generations T
Output: Next generation P_{t+1}
1: Random initialization of P_0;
2: **while** $t < T$ **do**
  | $Q_t \leftarrow RandomMatingAndVariation(P_t)$;
  | $U_t \leftarrow P_t \cup Q_t$;
  | $P_{t+1} \leftarrow LinearSelection(U_t)$;
  | $t \leftarrow t + 1$;
end

3.1   Diversity Strategies on Different Stages of COSEA-MO

COSEA-MO uses diversity strategies on three stages, firstly in parent selection for recombination, secondly on the stage of variation by guiding the search process with a suitable balance of exploration and exploitation on the basis of deterministic dynamic operators and thirdly by a new sophisticated survival selection strategy: Firstly, three parents are randomly selected from the population P_t for variation. The specific number of parents is motived to ensure a higher genetic diversity of the genetic material in the offspring genotype compared to the common choice of two parents. Secondly, deterministic dynamic variation operators are used for a high explorative search in early generations and a exploitative search in later generations. A linear dynamic recombination operator and an adapted version of the deterministic dynamic mutation operator of Bäck and Schütz [14] are used to generate offspring. The variation rates are adapted dynamically by predefined decreasing functions with the iteration progress: the recombination operator varies the number of recombination points by a linearly decreasing function

$$x_R(t) = \frac{l}{4} - \frac{l/4}{T} \cdot t,$$

where l is the peptide length, T the total number of the generations and t the index of the current generation. The adapted mutation operator determines the mutation probabilities via

$$p_{BS} = (a + \frac{l-2}{T-1}t)^{-1}$$

with $a = 5$. The mutation rates of the traditional operator are reduced by a higher value for a.

Thirdly, a new selection strategy is used in COSEA-MO as survival selection. A fitness value is assigned to each peptide in U_t by a linear combination consisting of a term reflecting the peptide quality, a term for genetic diversity and one for genetic dissimilarity as well as similarity respectively. Peptide quality is measured by a winning-score (WS) value for each peptide relative to the remaining members of the population. The WS method describes the difference between the number of superior and inferior objectives between two individuals: let sup_{ij} be the number of objectives in a solution i that is superior to the corresponding objectives in a solution j while inf_{ij} is the number of objectives in i that is inferior to j. The WS-value of the i-th solution in a population of size N is given by [8]:

$$WS(i) = \sum_{j=1}^{N} w_{ij} \text{ with } w_{ij} = sup_{ij} - inf_{ij}$$

Obviously, it is $w_{ij} = -wji$ and $w_{ii} = 0$. This assignment ensures that solutions with high WS-values are close to the true Pareto front.

The genetic diversity is measured by the traditional Hamming Distance (HD) relative to a predefined reference peptide. The genetic dissimilarity (D) is calculated averaging the dissimilarity values of a peptide i to a predefined reference peptide r according to the dissimilarity matrix of Sneath

$$D(i) = \frac{1}{l} \sum_{j=1}^{l} D(i_j, r_j),$$

where i_j and r_j refers to the j−th amino acid position. Since the amino acids at each position of both peptides are compared, they have to be of the same length l. The values of WS, HD and D are scaled to are range of 0 to 1 ensuring an equal impact on the fitness value.

The selection procedure starts with assigning of a fitness value to each individual of U_t by the following linear combination:

$$F(i) = a \cdot WS(i) + b \cdot HD(i) + c \cdot D(i) + d \tag{1}$$

with the weights a, b, c and d (Table 1). The terms WS, HD and D have to be maximized: peptides with an average high number of superior objectives relative to other members of the population, a high genetic diversity of the material and a high average similarity in bioactivity $(1 - D(i))$ to a reference peptide at the same time are preferred. The peptides with the N-highest fitness values are selected for the next generation.

4   Experimental Studies

The performance of COSEA-MO with different selection configurations are compared to the recently published AnD on four differently dimensional MO problems and are evaluated according to the convergence behavior, diversity in chemical space and average dissimilarity. AnD has the same framework structure as COSEA-MO and the same variation operators are used for a fair comparison of the selection strategies. The different configurations of COSEA-MO are given by different selection function with various weights (Eq. 1). All experiments are implemented in the open source jMetal library 4.5. [15]. Each configuration is run 30 times on each MO problem with 10 iterations and a population size of 100.

Table 1. Applied linear selection functions in COSEA-MO

Abbr.	Weights	Selection by
V1	$a = c = 0.5, b = d = 0$	WS value and dissimilarity
V2	$a = 1, b = c = d = 0$	Only WS value
V3	$a = b = 0.5, c = d = 0$	WS value and Hamming Distance
V4	$a = b = d = 0.333, c = -0.333$	WS value, Hamming Distance and similarity

The individuals are 20-mer peptides composed of the 20 canonical amino acids. Short peptides of length 20 are of specific interest because of their favorable properties as drugs.

4.1   Physiochemical Optimization Problems

Four optimization problems (Table 2) with 3 up to 6 objective functions are applied predicting physiochemical peptide properties. The optimization problems comprise molecular properties like charge, solubility in aqueous solutions, molecule size, molecule stability and structure. The six physiochemical functions are generic in the sense that the physiochemical properties are determined by descriptor values of the amino acids in the molecule sequence and are provided by the open source BioJava library [16]. A description of the determination methods and a motivation for the physiochemical function selection is given in [6]: Needleman Wunsch Algorithm (NMW), Molecular Weight (MW), Average Hydrophilicity (Hydro), Instability Index (InstInd), Isoelectric Point (pI) and Aliphatic Index (aI). These six objective functions act comparatively to reflect the similarity of a particular peptide to a pre-defined reference peptide: $f(\text{CandidatePept.}) := |f(\text{CandidatePept.}) - f(\text{ReferencePept.})|$. Therefore, the four objective functions have to be minimized. Furthermore, the objective values are normalized by the theoretical maximal value of each objective.

Table 2. Physiochemical functions of the different optimization problems

Dimension	Abbr	Objective functions
3D	3D-MOP	NMW, MW, Hydro
4D	4D-MaOP	NMW, MW, Hydro, InstInd
5D	5D-MaOP	NMW, MW, Hydro, InstInd, pI
6D	6D-MaOP	NMW, MW, Hydro, InstInd, pI, aI

4.2   Performance Metrics

Three metrics are used to measure convergence, diversity and dissimilarity. These metrics are applied on 20% approximately optimal individuals in each iteration for all configurations. These optimal individuals are determined by WS values in all configurations. The Average Cuboid Volume (ACV) is used to measure the convergence behavior [17]. ACV calculates the averaged spanned space of each solution to an ideal reference point, which is usually known in real-world applications. The ACV indicator is given by

$$ACV = \frac{1}{n} \sum_{i=1}^{n} (\prod_{j=1}^{k} (x_{ij} - r_j)), \tag{2}$$

where n is the number of individuals that are evaluated, k the number of objectives and r_j the ideal point. The lower the ACV values, the better the convergence behavior since the MO problems have to be minimized. ACV as a simple statistical measure is preferred over traditional convergence metrics since it is independent of Pareto optimal solution sets which are usually unknown in real-world applications, of low computation cost, independent of the problem dimension and relative to the number of solutions allowing a comparison of differently sized solution sets.

A state-of-the-art statistical evaluation method is used to evaluate the diversity performance. The diversity is determined by the standard deviation of the solution set to the gravity point of this set. Therefore, this diversity measure refers to population diversity in chemical space.

The dissimilarity is determined as average dissimilarity of the 20% candidate peptides to a pre-defined reference peptide according to the dissimilarity matrix of Sneath. This measure is a diversity measure on genotype level and a problem-specific measure to evaluate diversity of the genetic material.

4.3   Experimental Results

The performance results of the COSEA-MO configurations V1 - V4 on 3D-MOP for the three indicators are depicted in Fig. 1, 3 and 5, the results of AnD for all test problems are depicted in Fig. 13, 14 and 15. The graphs present the average performance results for 10 iterations including the start population. The overall favorable performance is given by very low ACV results with high diversity and high average dissimilarity values. Generally, the ACV performance results of V1 to V4 are remarkably close especially in the last generations. The configurations V1 to V4 reveal outstanding convergence behavior within 10 iterations by significantly lower ACV values compared to AnD, that does not provide any convergence behavior at all but has the highest diversity values in terms of population diversity in chemical space. Best convergence behavior with the lowest scattering of the ACV results is achieved by V2, WS solely selection, followed by V3. But V2 has also the lowest diversity and dissimilarity results. V4 achieves good convergence results with the best diversity and average dissimilarity values and therefore provides best overall performance.

In 4D-MaOP (Fig. 2, 4, 6), V1 to V4 achieve again outstanding convergence behavior compared to AnD that does not reveal any convergence but has the highest diversity values. V4 provides very good performance results with very good convergence and diversity values as well as high average dissimilarity results. V2 provides again fast convergence in the first generations but with the lowest diversity and dissimilarity results. V1 achieves second best overall performance.

In 5D-MaOP (Fig. 7, 9, 11), V1 to V4 reveal again very good convergence results. Here, AnD also provide a slight convergence improvement, but far from the results of V1 to V4. Diversity values are once again the highest. Best convergence results are achieved by V2 with lowest diversity and dissimilarity results. Both, V1 and V4 provide very good convergency and diversity results. High average dissimilarity results are provided by V1 followed by V3 and V4.

Similar results are observable for 6D-MaOP (Fig. 8, 10, 12): outstanding convergence behavior is achieved by V1 to V4, AnD reveals slight convergence

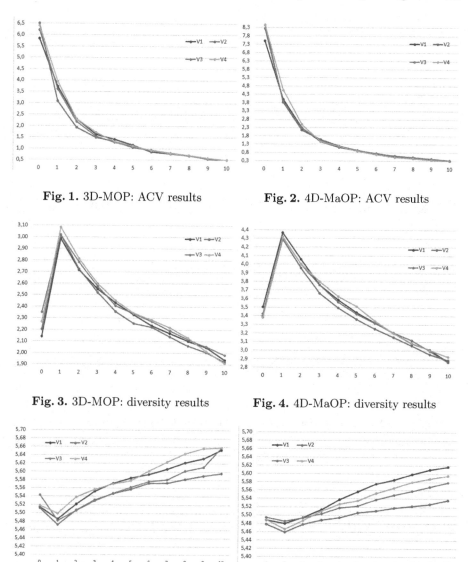

Fig. 1. 3D-MOP: ACV results

Fig. 2. 4D-MaOP: ACV results

Fig. 3. 3D-MOP: diversity results

Fig. 4. 4D-MaOP: diversity results

Fig. 5. 3D-MOP: dissimilarity results

Fig. 6. 4D-MaOP: dissimilarity results

improvement with the highest diversity values. Best convergence behavior is achieved by V4 followed by V1. V4 reveals constantly good diversity and acceptable dissimilarity results.

Summarizing, AnD does only provide slight convergence behavior on 5D- and 6D-MaOP with highest diversity in chemical space. This corresponds to the diversity-first-and-convergence-second principle. It has to be noted that this principle solely act in chemical space. Moreover, AnD seems to be a real

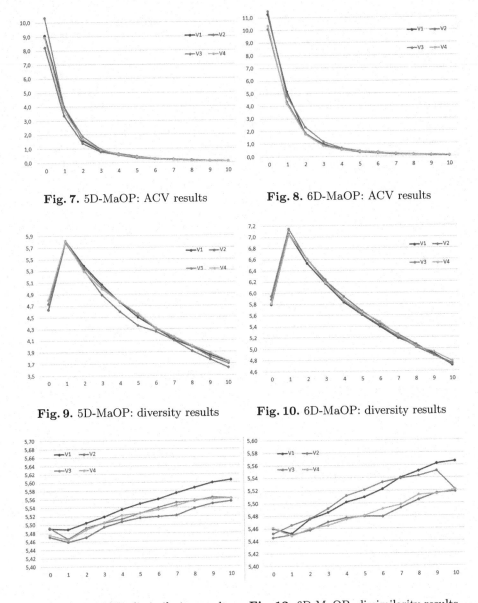

Fig. 7. 5D-MaOP: ACV results

Fig. 8. 6D-MaOP: ACV results

Fig. 9. 5D-MaOP: diversity results

Fig. 10. 6D-MaOP: diversity results

Fig. 11. 5D-MOP: dissimilarity results

Fig. 12. 6D-MaOP: dissimilarity results

many-objective EA, since no convergence behavior is observable on 3D-MOP and 4D-MaOP. In general, V2 provides the overall best convergence performance but poor diversity and average dissimilarity results caused by the solely WS selection technique. V1 generally provides good convergence, very good average dissimilarity and generally good diversity results, which is caused by equal WS and

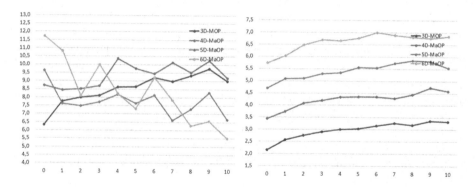

Fig. 13. AnD: ACV results   **Fig. 14.** AnD: diversity results

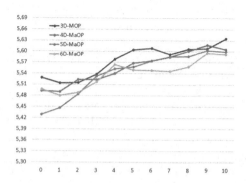

Fig. 15. AnD: dissimilarity results

dissimilarity based selection. V4 achieves good overall performances in all test cases. V4 selects individuals according to the highest WS values, high diversity in genetic material (HD) and high similarity on amino acid level. Since V3 also selects individuals based on WS values and according to high genetic diversity, HD empirically seems to be an important measure to promote diversity in MO. The configuration V4 is preferred as selection strategy due to the complementation of HD with the aspect of amino acid similarity within the selection strategy. The experimental results reveal the identification of highly qualified candidate molecules with a high diversity in genetic material and high average dissimilarity at the same time.

5   Discussion and Conclusion

The aim of MO is the identification of highly qualified candidate peptides according to the physiochemical objectives with a high diversity of the genetic material and comparable bioactivity. Diversity is addressed in EA on different levels with various methodologies and performance measures. In this work, the aspect of diversity is re-defined and re-interpreted on different stages of a proposed EA for MO. At this point, the issues raised in the introduction have to be focussed: The first issue addresses the re-definition of diversity in MO. Diversity has to be considered on genotype and fitness level and different techniques have to be applied to control and promote diversity on these levels. Two complementary aspects define diversity on gentoype level: firstly, the diversity of genetic material measured by the number of differing amino acids between two molecule sequences and secondly, diversity in terms of amino acid dissimilarity according to Sneath. Both aspects together have an impact on variations in fitness level. Diversity in fitness level is referred to diversity in chemical space and measurable by distance metrics.

Different diversity promoting methods have been included in COSEA-MO on three stages: in parent selection for recombination, in the variation operators and in survival selection. This work also presents a sophisticated selection strategy based on the diversity considerations in MO. Individuals for the next iteration are chosen by a linear combination as selection function with the terms molecular quality, genetic diversity and dissimilarity calculated by a WS method, HD and average dissimilarity of the amino acids relative to a predefined reference peptide. The performance has been compared to the diversity-first-convergence-second selection principle and AnD on four different dimensional MO problems, where diversity refers to diversity in chemical space. The four selection configurations of COSEA-MO clearly outperform AnD in terms of convergence in all test cases which emphasizes the clear and application-specific definition of the term diversity. AnD reveals a slight convergence behavior only in the two higher-dimensional test cases. Especially the COSEA-MO selection configurations with diversity promoting strategies on genotype level provide remarkble results in all test cases.

In future work, a deeper understanding of genotype diversity and amino acid dissimilarity in MO and its impact on molecular landscapes have to be analyzed to control and improve the search behavior in evolutionary strategies. Furthermore, different methodologies have been proposed for sequence alignment and a systematic comparison regarding diversity promoting in evolutionary search prozesses will be focussed.

References

1. Zhou, S.F., Zhong, W.: Drug design and discovery: principles and applications. Molecules **22**(2), 279 (2017)
2. Röckendorf, N., Borschbach, M.: Molecular evolution of peptide ligands with custom-tailored characteristics. PLOS Comput. Biol. **8**(12) (2012). https://doi.org/10.1371/journal.pcbi.1002800
3. Rosenthal, S., Borschbach, M.: Design perspectives of an evolutionary process for multi-objective molecular optimization. In: Trautmann, H., et al. (eds.) EMO 2017. LNCS, vol. 10173, pp. 529–544. Springer, Cham (2017). https://doi.org/10.1007/978-3-319-54157-0_36

4. Rosenthal, S., El-Sourani, N., Borschbach, M.: Impact of different recombination methods in a mutation-specific MOEA for a biochemical application. In: Vanneschi, L., Bush, W.S., Giacobini, M. (eds.) EvoBIO 2013. LNCS, vol. 7833, pp. 188–199. Springer, Heidelberg (2013). https://doi.org/10.1007/978-3-642-37189-9_17

5. Rosenthal, S., Borschbach, M.: Impact of population size, selection and multi-parent recombination within a customized NSGA-II for biochemical optimization. Int. J. Adv. Life Sci. IARIA **6**(3&4), 310–324 (2014)

6. Rosenthal, S., Borschbach, M.: A winning score-based evolutionary process for multi-and many-objective peptide optimization. IJCC **I**, 49–58 (2019)

7. Squillero, G., Tonda, A.: Divergence of character and premature convergence: a survey of methodologies for promoting diversity in evolutionary optimization. Inf. Sci. **329**, 782–799 (2015)

8. Maneeratana, K., Boonlong, K., Chaiyaratana, N.: Compressed-objective genetic algorithm. In: Runarsson, T.P., Beyer, H.-G., Burke, E., Merelo-Guervós, J.J., Whitley, L.D., Yao, X. (eds.) PPSN 2006. LNCS, vol. 4193, pp. 473–482. Springer, Heidelberg (2006). https://doi.org/10.1007/11844297_48

9. Sneath, P.: Relations between chemical structure and biological activity in peptides. J. Theor. Biol. **12**(2), 157–195 (1966)

10. Liu, Z.Z., Wang, Y., Huang, P.Q.: AnD: a many-objective evolutionary algorithm with angle-based selection and shift-based density estimation. Inf. Sci. **509**, 400–419 (2018)

11. Rupakheti, C., Virshup, A., Yang, W., Beratan, D.: Strategy to discover diverse optimal molecules in the small molecule universe. J. Chem. Inf. Model **55**(3), 529–537 (2015)

12. Emmerich, M., Lee, B., Render, A.: Analyzing molecular landscapes using random walks and information theory. Chem. Central J. **3**, P20 (2009). https://doi.org/10.1186/1752-153X-3-S1-P20

13. Wang, H., Jin, Y., Yao, X.: Diversity assessment in many-objective optimization. IEEE Trans. Cybern. **47**, 1510–1522 (2017)

14. Bäck, T., Schütz, M.: Intelligent mutation rate control in canonical genetic algorithms. In: Raś, Z.W., Michalewicz, M. (eds.) ISMIS 1996. LNCS, vol. 1079, pp. 158–167. Springer, Heidelberg (1996). https://doi.org/10.1007/3-540-61286-6_141

15. Nebro, A., Durillo, J.: jmetal: Metaheuristic Algorithms in Java (2019)

16. BioJava: CookBook, r. http://www.biojava.org/wiki/BioJava

17. Rosenthal, S., Borschbach, M.: Average cuboid volume as a convergence indicator and selection criterion for multi-objective biochemical optimization. In: Emmerich, M., Deutz, A., Schütze, O., Legrand, P., Tantar, E., Tantar, A.-A. (eds.) EVOLVE – A Bridge between Probability, Set Oriented Numerics and Evolutionary Computation VII. SCI, vol. 662, pp. 185–210. Springer, Cham (2017). https://doi.org/10.1007/978-3-319-49325-1_9

Constrained Multiobjective Optimization for the Design of Energy-Efficient Context Recognition Systems

Aljoša Vodopija[1,2]([✉]) [ID], Vito Janko[1,2] [ID], Mitja Luštrek[1,2] [ID],
and Bogdan Filipič[1,2] [ID]

[1] Jožef Stefan Institute, Jamova cesta 39, 1000 Ljubljana, Slovenia
{aljosa.vodopija,vito.janko,mitja.lustrek,bogdan.filipic}@ijs.si
[2] Jožef Stefan International Postgraduate School,
Jamova cesta 39, 1000 Ljubljana, Slovenia

Abstract. Context recognition (CR) systems infer the user's context, such as their physical activity, from sensor data obtained, for example, with smartphone sensors. Designing an energy-efficient CR system, however, is a complex optimization problem involving conflicting objectives and several constraints arising from real-world limitations and designers' preferences. To address this task, we propose a constrained multiobjective formulation of the CR design problem. Unlike most studies in this domain, we use a true multiobjective approach in solving it. Specifically, we apply a multiobjective evolutionary algorithm equipped with two different constraint handling techniques. Their performance is demonstrated in optimizing six CR systems of various complexity. The proposed problem formulation and the optimization results make it possible to better understand the CR systems operation and provide valuable information to the designers.

Keywords: Multiobjective optimization · Constraint handling · Context recognition · Energy efficiency

1 Introduction

Context recognition (CR) is a vague term encompassing a wide array of tasks where (usually wearable) sensors are used to detect something about the person wearing them. Possible applications range from counting steps, localization, detecting activities such as walking or running, to monitoring someone's physical and mental health.

CR is an already mature research area [13] and many applications using CR systems come pre-installed on average smartphones. However, a common problem that occurs when designing such systems is the energy consumption of the device that is collecting and processing the sensor data. It is easy to imagine that a smartphone application that uses all its sensors (e.g., GPS, Bluetooth,

B. Filipič et al. (Eds.): BIOMA 2020, LNCS 12438, pp. 308–320, 2020.
https://doi.org/10.1007/978-3-030-63710-1_24

Wi-Fi, accelerometer, etc.) can detect much about its user, but also quickly drains the phone's battery, making it useless in practice.

There are many ways of preserving the battery life of a CR system. One of the most effective ways is the choice of the right sensors for the task (as different sensors can be used for the same CR task) and duty-cycling them, e.g., periodically turning them on and off again. Energy savings can be further increased if the sensors used and the duty-cycle durations adapt to the current context. For example, one might want to use GPS when the user is driving, but accelerometer when walking.

The issue with creating such adaptive CR systems is that doing so requires either a lot of expert knowledge of the domain or manual experimentation. Thus, any process that could at least partially automate the task of searching for energy-efficient solutions would be greatly beneficial.

Janko et al. [8] were the first to show that this problem can be formulated as a multiobjective optimization problem (MOP) with the objectives being the accuracy and energy consumption of the CR system. Their work, however, lacked a thorough experimentation in solving the resulting MOP and did not consider constraints in its formulation. The constraints naturally arise from real-world limitations of some sensors and from additional desires from the system designers.

In this work we expand on both of these aspects by performing a more comprehensive experimental evaluation, and more importantly, adding real-world constraints to the proposed MOP. The resulting constrained MOP is solved using the well-known Nondominated Sorting Genetic Algorithm II (NSGA-II) [2]. Two constraint handling techniques (CHTs) are applied: the original constrained-domination principle (CDP) [2] and a more recent approach based on an ensemble (ENS) of multiple CHTs proposed in our previous work [12]. Their performance in solving the CR optimization problem is assessed on six progressively harder CR systems.

We first present two different datasets—Commodity12 and Opportunity—that represent two different CR problems (Sect. 2). In Sect. 3, we then elaborate on how to represent the semantics of these datasets as a MOP. Special consideration is given to the constraint formulation (Sect. 3.1), and for each dataset we prepare three different, progressively harder, sets of these constraints. In Sect. 4, we test the difficulty of the proposed CR optimization problems and evaluate the quality of the found energy-efficient solutions, and finally conclude in Sect. 5.

2   Datasets

In this section, we present two datasets from two CR problems. They both contain streams of sensor data, which are then split into windows and can be used to calculate features. These features are then fed into machine-learning classifiers whose goal is to classify each window into one of the predetermined contexts as accurately as possible and with as little sensor data as possible.

2.1   Commodity12

The aim of the Commodity12 project was to create a system that can be used by diabetics to monitor their activities and help them manage their lifestyle more easily. All details can be found in the previous work on the domain [1].

For data collection, a smartphone and a chest-worn heart-rate monitor were used to monitor ten participants. Each participant continuously collected data for two weeks and manually labeled the following contexts: *sleep, work, home, eating, transport, exercise, out* (out of house, but not in any of the previous contexts). The data was collected from ten sensors: accelerometer, barometer, light sensor, GPS location, a list of visible Wi-Fi networks, a description of location by the Foursquare web service, sound, time, heart rate and respiration rate. The first eight were measured with the smartphone, and the last two with the heart rate monitor connected to the smartphone via Bluetooth.

Random Forest was identified as the best-performing classifier and was therefore selected for the present work on this dataset. While the classification accuracy was reasonably high (between 73% and 88%, depending on the user), the energy consumption made the application impractical to use—and thus the need for energy optimization.

To use energy consumption as one of the optimization objectives, it needs to be estimated for each sensor combination (as the energy consumption of different sensors do not add up linearly). This was done empirically by attaching a multimeter device directly to the smartphone battery [8].

2.2   Opportunity

Opportunity [9] is a popular publicly available dataset designed to evaluate algorithms for detecting human activity. Data on four users were recorded while they were performing various tasks in an apartment.

There were 30 sensor clusters in this apartment, some on the user's body and some on the objects the user interacted with. The complete list of sensor locations is as follows: user's left knee, left and right upper arm, left and right forearm, user's hips, left and right shoe, left and right wrist, left and right hand, as well as a cup, salami, water bottle, cheese, bread, knife, sugar, plate, and drinking glass. Each cluster contained some of the following sensors: accelerometer, gyroscope and magnetometer.

The dataset provides various sets of labels, out of which we decided to test the case where the problem was to recognize which object the user is currently holding in their right hand. There were 18 classes: *bottle, bread, chair, cheese, cup, dishwasher, door, drawer, fridge, glass, knife, milk, plate, salami, spoon, sugar, switch, table, none*), each representing an object held, except for the *none* class that represented no object in hand. The class distribution was highly unbalanced with the *none* class having a representation of 57%.

The classification process was made relatively simple in order to conform to the introductory paper [10] of the dataset. The data from each sensor was divided into 500-ms non-overlapping windows on which we calculated the mean and standard deviation. The k-nearest neighbors classifier ($k = 3$) was then used for the classification.

This problem domain has an unusually high number of sensors (30 sensor clusters), which creates an enormous space for possible sensor subsets. Therefore we decided to use only some sensor subsets (not all, as with Commodity12) as the search-space for multiobjective optimization. These subsets were selected in the following way. We started with an empty set. Then we added the sensor cluster that increased the F-score the most to the set. This was repeated until no single sensor cluster could increase the F-score. Each resulting subset was added as a sensor setting (each subset had one more sensor than the previous one). The procedure was then repeated for each context, this time adding sensors only if it increased the F-score for recognizing this context. All generated subsets were added again as sensor settings. The justification for this greedy procedure is that most sensor subsets are redundantly large, both inflating the energy consumption and unnecessarily increasing the search space of different system configurations.

For the sake of simplicity (and since we did not have access to the details about the sensors) we assumed that all existing sensors had similar energy consumption. To model their combined consumption, we simply added up the individual energy consumptions.

3   Problem Formulation

Suppose the CR system can detect c different contexts. It can do so by using different settings—the setting being which sensors to use and with which duty-cycle schedules (sensors can work for a time periods, then sleep for s time periods, and repeat). Whenever a context is detected, the setting used changes to the one assigned for the current context (e.g., whenever *transport* is detected, the GPS gets turned on). This opens up the problem of finding the ideal assignment of each context to the one of the possible settings. Each such assignment will result in a different CR system that will generally have a different trade-off between its accuracy and its energy consumption. We can assume that both of these objectives can be accurately estimated using either a simulation or a mathematical model [6–8].

The problem can be naturally formulated as a multiobjective optimization problem with the accuracy of the system, f_1, and its energy consumption, f_2, being two conflicting objectives. A setting-to-context assignment can be represented with an integer (*decision*) *vector*,

$$x = (x_1, \ldots, x_D)^{\mathrm{T}} \in S \subset \mathbb{N}^D$$

where S denotes the *decision space* of dimension $D = 2c+1$. The first c entries of x dictate which sensor subset to use when the corresponding context is detected (possible sensors subsets are enumerated). Similarly, the second c entries dictate for how long the system sleeps in each duty cycle (no sensor is working). Finally, the last component indicates how long the sensors are active between the sleeping periods. It is of note that the length of a duty cycle is not fixed, therefore the lengths of the sleeping and active periods do not necessarily sum into a given total. Two duty cycles of different lengths may have different performance, even with the same ratio of active and sleeping periods.

The number of possible sensor subsets was roughly 200 for both datasets, while the lengths of both the sleeping and active periods were capped at 30. The ranges of these parameters were chosen to be semantically sensible and, in the case of no constraints, all parameter values have the potential to be part of a Pareto-optimal solution. The fitness of these integer vectors was calculated using the mathematical model from [7,8].

To make it possible to compare the performance of various CR systems, we consider normalized objective values. The values of f_1 are already normalized since they represent the achieved accuracy. On the other hand, the values of f_2 are normalized by the maximum possible energy consumption. This is obtained when all the sensors are used and they are never turned off.

3.1   Constraints

For both the Commodity12 and Opportunity datasets we derived three versions of constraints, each progressively harder than the previous one. The difficulty was increased either by adding additional constraints or by making the existing ones harder to satisfy. In the latter case we used the variable z to denote the value that was changing from one problem version to another. The used values of z for each problem setting are summarized in Table 1.

The first category of constraints is based on the precisions and recalls of specific contexts when the system is using a particular solution. In each dataset, we selected a subset of contexts (denoted as L) that represents contexts important for the real-life application of the system. In the Commodity12 problem the system has to give diabetic patients recommendations about their lifestyle, thus the most important contexts are: *eating*, *exercise* and *transport* (as it includes walking). In the Opportunity problem we wanted to detect the preparation of a sandwich, so the crucial contexts are: *bread*, *salami*, *plate*, *knife*, *fridge*, *drawer* and *none*.

For each of these contexts we wanted to ensure that their precision and recall do not significantly deviate from their maximum possible values (M_i). The maximum values are achieved when all the sensors are used and are never turned off (duty-cycled).

$$g_{1,i}(x) = \text{precision}(i,x) \geq z \cdot M_i, \quad i \in L \tag{1}$$

$$g_{2,i}(x) = \text{recall}(i,x) \geq z \cdot M_i, \quad i \in L \tag{2}$$

Here, $\text{recall}(x,i)$ is the recall of the i-th activity when the system is using solution x, and z is a fraction that varies from problem to problem.

For other contexts, we still wanted that they are "balanced" and that the system is not entirely omitting one in favor of the others. Thus, the next set of constraints ensures that the precisions and recalls of these contexts are in a certain range from each other.

$$g_3(x) = \max\{\text{precision}(i, x) \mid i \notin L\} - \min\{\text{precision}(i, x) \mid i \notin L\} \leq 0.25 \quad (3)$$

$$g_4(x) = \max\{\text{recall}(i, x) \mid i \notin L\} - \min\{\text{recall}(i, x) \mid i \notin L\} \leq 0.25 \quad (4)$$

In many domains it has been shown [5] that the accuracy of the system can be improved by "smoothing" the predictions, i.e., classifying a few consecutive data windows and then taking the most frequent prediction for that time period. To allow for this post-processing step, we try to enforce a longer active period if the accuracy of the system is below some threshold.

$$g_5(x) = \begin{cases} x_{2c+1} \geq 5, & 0.5 < f_1(x) < 0.75 \\ x_{2c+1} \geq 3, & f_1(x) \leq 0.5 \\ x_{2c+1} \geq 1, & \text{otherwise} \end{cases} \quad (5)$$

Our duty-cycle scheme assumes that sensors can be switched on and off in short intervals, and can do so without any additional energy cost. This is frequently not the case and it creates additional constraints on the system design. For example, if the GPS is active, the sleeping part of the duty cycle has to be longer to account for the extra time needed for turning the GPS on and off again. In Eq. (6) used for the Commodity12 problem, we used binary variables, x_i^s, that indicate if sensor s is active when using the sensor set x_i (g stands for GPS, b for sensors that use Bluetooth and w for Wi-Fi). For the Opportunity problem we used a similar scheme, but made different weights based on whether the sensor is on the body or in the environment.

$$g_{6,i}(x) = \begin{cases} x_{i+c} \geq 8 + z, & x_i^g \\ x_{i+c} \geq 5 + z, & \neg x_i^g \wedge x_i^b \\ x_{i+c} \geq 3 + z, & \neg x_i^g \wedge \neg x_i^b \wedge x_i^w \\ x_{i+c} \geq 0, & \text{otherwise} \end{cases} \quad i \in \{1, \ldots, c\} \quad (6)$$

The final constraint arises from the number of sensors being used by the system, as ideally we would like to use as few sensors as possible. Doing so in the case of Opportunity would mean reducing the cost of the hardware, while in Commodity12 it would reduce the number of different data types that system designers have to analyze. In the Opportunity problem we also want to limit the number of sensors worn by the user to increase the practicality of the system.

$$g_7(x) = |\bigcup_{i=1}^{c} \text{sens}(x_i)| \leq z \quad (7)$$

$$g_8(x) = |\bigcup_{i=1}^{c} \text{bsens}(x_i)| \leq z \quad (8)$$

Table 1. Values of z for each problem/constraint combination and the characteristics of the resulting test CR systems: the number of contexts c, dimension of the decision space D, and number of constraints N. If the parameter z is not used, the sign $+/-$ denotes whether the given constraint category is used ($+$) or not ($-$). In the case of OPP3 and constraints $g_{1,i}$ and $g_{2,i}$, all contexts have bounded precision and recall, not only the crucial ones.

System	$g_{1,i}$	$g_{2,i}$	g_3	g_4	g_5	$g_{6,i}$	g_7	g_8	c	D	N
COM1	0.8	0.8	$-$	$+$	$+$	-2	$-$	$-$	7	15	15
COM2	0.9	0.9	$-$	$+$	$+$	0	$-$	$-$	7	15	15
COM3	0.8	0.9	$+$	$+$	$+$	0	5	$-$	7	15	17
OPP1	0.7	0.7	$-$	$-$	$+$	-1	18	10	18	37	35
OPP2	0.8	0.8	$-$	$-$	$+$	-1	18	10	18	37	35
OPP3	0.9	0.9	$-$	$-$	$+$	0	18	10	18	37	57

Here, $\text{sens}(x_i)$ is the set of all sensors used by x_i, and $\text{bsens}(x_i)$ the set of all body-worn sensors used.

Throughout the paper we use COM as the abbreviation for Commodity12 test CR systems and OPP for Opportunity test CR systems. The characteristics of the test CR systems are summarized in Table 1. Additionally, we provide the feasibility ratio (the proportion of feasible solutions) of each optimization problem. The estimation is based on two samples of 10^6 solutions generated by random sampling and Latin hypercube sampling. The feasibility ratio for COM1 is approximately $5.3 \cdot 10^{-5}$ according to random sampling and $6.1 \cdot 10^{-5}$ according to Latin hypercube sampling. On the other hand, no feasible solutions can be found for other test CR systems regardless of the sampling method used. Therefore, their feasibility ratios are estimated to be less than 10^{-6}. Particularly hard constraints are g_3, g_7, and g_8 that are each satisfied in less than 1% of the sampled solutions.

4   Experiments and Results

Based on the multiobjective formulation of the CR optimization problem, the experimental evaluation aimed at finding sets of trade-off solutions in the form of Pareto front approximations. For this purpose we used the well-known NSGA-II multiobjective optimization algorithm equipped with CDP [2] and ENS [12].

The CDP technique is the most frequently used method to solve constrained MOPs in practice. It strictly favors feasible solutions over infeasible ones. While feasible solutions are ranked based on Pareto dominance, the infeasible solutions are ranked according to constraint violations.

The ENS method combines multiple CHTs into an ensemble-based method where solutions for a new generation are selected based on a weighted voting provided by various CHTs. This approach considers only CHTs which are applied in the replacement phase, i.e., survivor selection, of an evolutionary algorithm.

Table 2. Average cumulative hypervolume values obtained by both CHTs on the test CR systems.

System	CDP $[\mu \pm \sigma]$	ENS $[\mu \pm \sigma]$
COM1	1.0081 ± 0.0018	1.0215 ± 0.0028
COM2	0.9497 ± 0.0095	0.9517 ± 0.0111
COM3	0.8873 ± 0.0277	0.8905 ± 0.0269
OPP1	0.8011 ± 0.0054	0.8419 ± 0.0047
OPP2	0.7111 ± 0.0189	0.7614 ± 0.0127
OPP3	0.6131 ± 0.0199	0.6705 ± 0.0141

Each CHT in the ensemble is supposed to provide a quality measure combining individuals' objective values and constraint violations. These quality measures are normalized to allow for comparison of individuals' quality among various CHTs. The quality measure produced by the ensemble of CHTs is a weighted average of the corresponding quality measures.

In this work, four CHTs were considered for the ensemble: normalized overall constraint violation [11], CDP, dynamic penalty function [3], and multiple constraint ranking [4]. In contrast to the original work [12], we decided to change the nondominated sorting with the normalized overall constraint violation, since the proposed test CR systems are heavily constrained.

The experimental setup was defined in the following way. Both methods were run with populations of 200 solutions for 1000 generations. The crossover probability was set to 0.9 and the mutation probability to 0.1. These parameter values were selected based on the experimental results from [6,8]. Specifically, for ENS, uniform weights ($w_i = 1/4$ for $i \in \{1, 2, 3, 4\}$) were used, while the two parameters of the dynamic penalty function, C and α, were set to 0.5 and 2, respectively. On each test CR system, every CHT was run 31 times, each time with a new randomly initialized population.

Additionally, the implementation details and parameter settings concerning data preprocessing, feature extraction, Random Forest classifier learning, and calculation of energy consumption were defined as in [6].

The quality of the optimization algorithm runs was measured with the cumulative hypervolume of the Pareto front approximation found in each run. Given $f_1, f_2 \in [0, 1]$, the reference point for hypervolume calculations was set to $(-0.1, 1.1)^{\mathrm{T}}$.

The means of cumulative hypervolume values are shown in Table 2. As we can see, ENS obtains better cumulative hypervolume means than CDP on all test CR systems. However, the differences are negligible on both COM2 and COM3. Indeed, the independent Welch's t-test (the normality assumption was confirmed by the Shapiro-Wilk test, while the homoscedasticity was rejected by the Levene's test) shows statistically significant differences in algorithm performance for COM1, OPP1, OPP2 and OPP3 ($p < 0.05$), while there are no significant differences observed on COM2 and COM3 ($p \approx 0.24, 0.47$).

The results are even easier to interpret through visualization of the obtained Pareto front approximations. Figure 1 shows Pareto front approximations for the test CR systems resulting from typical runs. In more detail, all the runs corresponding to a given test CR system are sorted based on the obtained cumulative hypervolume, and the front obtained in the median run is shown in the figure. We can see that the fronts obtained by ENS are superior in both convergence and diversity. This is especially true on OPP test CR systems, where ENS obtains significantly better Pareto-optimal solutions than CDP. It is worth noting that the performance of CDP compared to ENS decreases with constraint complexity.

Interestingly, on COM2, a few solutions obtained by CDP dominate the solutions obtained by ENS (see Fig. 1, COM2, around $f_2 \approx 0.4$) although its front seems to be well converged. This observation suggests that ENS gets stuck in a sub-optimal region and reveals the problem's multimodal nature. Nevertheless, further investigation is needed to explain this phenomenon. Another interesting observation is the sharp knee appearing in the fronts for all COM test CR systems. Investigating the found solutions revealed that solutions on one side of the knee only use sensors for one time period in every duty cycle (and thus have low energy consumption), while the solutions on the other side have an increasingly longer active period. Finally, in all cases the energy consumption quickly drops (in exchange for a small accuracy loss), indicating that smaller sensor subsets can be almost as effective as all sensors.

Figure 2 shows the progress of the mean cumulative hypervolume during optimization for the test CR systems. The x-axis indicates the spent function evaluations and y-axis the corresponding cumulative hypervolume values. Although the performance of CDP and ENS are comparable on COM test CR systems, we can see that ENS is more efficient. On average ENS needs less function evaluations to converge than CDP, and this gap increases for more constrained CR systems. In addition, the graphs show that both CHTs converge on all test CR systems except on OPP3. For this reason, it is unlikely that an increase in the computational budget would drastically improve these results (except on OPP3).

Finally, since CR optimization is a design problem, the results with respect to efficiency (spent computational resources) are not of great importance. The most computationally expensive task is solution evaluation. A single solution evaluation takes around 0.016 s for COM test CR systems, and 0.217 s for OPP test CR systems. All the experiments were run on a 3.40 GHz Intel(R) Core(TM) i7-6700 CPU with 16 GB RAM.

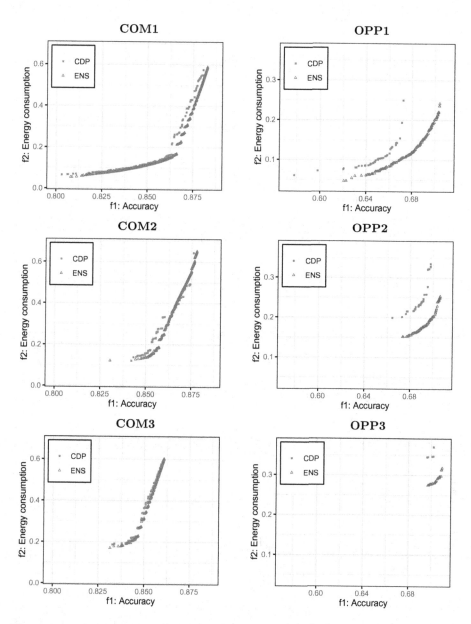

Fig. 1. Pareto front approximations for COM (left) and OPP (right) test CR systems.

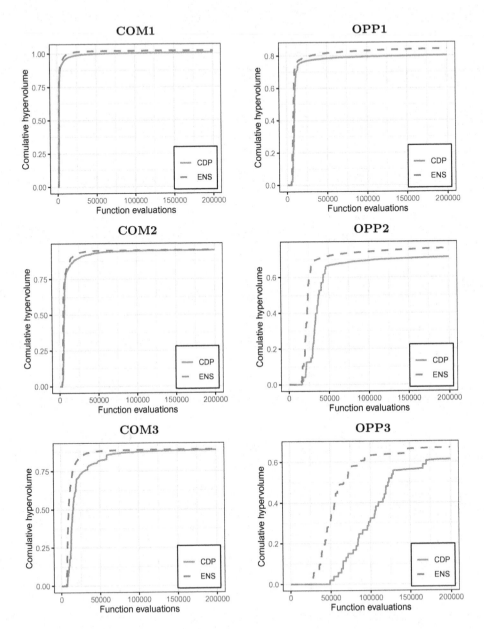

Fig. 2. Cumulative hypervolume progress for COM (left) and OPP (right) test CR systems.

5 Conclusions

In this paper, we expanded the work of Janko et al. [6] by proposing a constrained multiobjective optimization problem formulation for the design of energy-efficient CR systems. The proposed CR optimization problem takes into account the accuracy and overall energy consumption of the CR system and, at the same time, considers real-world limitations and designers' preferences. As opposed to most related work, the resulting optimization problem was solved using a true multiobjective optimizer capable of finding approximations of Pareto-optimal solutions. Specifically, the constraints were handled both by a classic technique frequently used in constrained multiobjective optimization, and our novel ensemble-based approach.

The experimental results on six progressively harder test CR systems show that the approach based on the ensemble paradigm performs better than the classic technique. The ensemble was superior on four test CR systems, while no differences in performance were observed on two easier CR systems. Additionally, an initial investigation of the produced Pareto front approximations reveals the multimodal nature of the CR optimization problem.

The found solutions were semantically meaningful as well as energy-efficient, especially in comparison to the base case where all the sensors were used. As an example, the "knee" solution for the COM1 test system represents a trade-off where, by sacrificing less than 2% of classification accuracy, the energy consumption is reduced by 82%.

In the future, we plan to investigate the CR optimization problem in more detail and assess the scalability of the applied optimization methodology. For the first task, we will examine the landscapes of the introduced optimization problem by investigating the produced solutions. For the second task, we will design new test CR systems, preferably using new datasets. Finally, the test CR systems will be made publicly available to the optimization community.

Acknowledgment. This work is part of a project that has received funding from the *European Union's Horizon 2020 research and innovation program* under Grant Agreement no. 692286. We also acknowledge financial support from the Slovenian Research Agency (young researcher program and research core funding no. P2-0209).

References

1. Cvetković, B., Janko, V., Romero, A.E., Kafalı, Ö., Stathis, K., Luštrek, M.: Activity recognition for diabetic patients using a smartphone. J. Med. Syst. **40**(12), 1–8 (2016). https://doi.org/10.1007/s10916-016-0598-y
2. Deb, K., Pratap, A., Agarwal, S., Meyarivan, T.: A fast and elitist multiobjective genetic algorithm: NSGA-II. IEEE Trans. Evol. Comput. **6**(2), 182–197 (2002). https://doi.org/10.1109/4235.996017
3. Eiben, A.E., Smith, J.E.: Introduction to Evolutionary Computing. NCS. Springer, Heidelberg (2015). https://doi.org/10.1007/978-3-662-44874-8

4. Garcia, R.d.P., de Lima, B.S.L.P., Lemonge, A.C.d.C., Jacob, B.P.: A rank-based constraint handling technique for engineering design optimization problems solved by genetic algorithms. Comput. Struct. **187**, 77–87 (2017). https://doi.org/10.1016/j.compstruc.2017.03.023

5. Gjoreski, M., et al.: Classical and deep learning methods for recognizing human activities and modes of transportation with smartphone sensors. Inf. Fusion **62**, 47–62 (2020). https://doi.org/10.1016/j.inffus.2020.04.004

6. Janko, V.: Adapting sensor settings for energy-efficient context recognition. Ph.D. thesis, Jožef Stefan International Postgraduate School (2020). https://www.researchgate.net/publication/343230379

7. Janko, V., Luštrek, M.: Choosing duty-cycle parameters for context recognition. In: 14th International Conference on Intelligent Environments, pp. 83–86. IEEE (2018). https://doi.org/10.1109/IE.2018.00020

8. Janko, V., Luštrek, M.: Using Markov chains and multi-objective optimization for energy-efficient context recognition. Sensors **18**(1), 80 (2018). https://doi.org/10.3390/s18010080

9. Roggen, D., et al.: Collecting complex activity datasets in highly rich networked sensor environments. In: Seventh International Conference on Networked Sensing Systems (INSS), pp. 233–240. IEEE (2010). https://doi.org/10.1109/INSS.2010.5573462

10. Sagha, H., et al.: Benchmarking classification techniques using the Opportunity human activity dataset. In: IEEE International Conference on Systems, Man, and Cybernetics, pp. 36–40. IEEE (2011). https://doi.org/10.1109/ICSMC.2011.6083628

11. Tanabe, R., Oyama, A.: A note on constrained multi-objective optimization benchmark problems. In: IEEE Congress on Evolutionary Computation (CEC), pp. 1127–1134. IEEE (2017). https://doi.org/10.1109/CEC.2017.7969433

12. Vodopija, A., Oyama, A., Filipič, B.: Ensemble-based constraint handling in multi-objective optimization. In: Proceedings of the Genetic and Evolutionary Computation Conference Companion (GECCO 2019), pp. 2072–2075. ACM (2019). https://doi.org/10.1145/3319619.3326909

13. Yürür, Ö., Liu, C.H., Sheng, Z., Leung, V.C., Moreno, W., Leung, K.K.: Context-awareness for mobile sensing: a survey and future directions. IEEE Commun. Surv. Tutor. **18**(1), 68–93 (2016). https://doi.org/10.1109/COMST.2014.2381246

Author Index

Printed in the United States
By Bookmasters